JUDAISM FROM CYRUS TO HADRIAN

VOLUME ONE

JUDAISM FROM CYRUS TO HADRIAN

VOLUME ONE:
THE PERSIAN AND GREEK PERIODS

Lester L. Grabbe

FORTRESS PRESS MINNEAPOLIS

JUDAISM FROM CYRUS TO HADRIAN
Volume One: The Persian and Greek Periods

Interior design by Publishers' WorkGroup
Cover design by Spangler Design Team
Cartography by Parrot Graphics

Library of Congress Cataloging-in-Publication Data

Grabbe, Lester L.
Judaism from Cyrus to Hadrian / Lester L. Grabbe.
p. cm.
Includes bibliographical references and index.
Contents: v. 1. The Persian and Greek periods—v. 2. The Roman period.
ISBN 0-8006-2620-6 (v. 1)—ISBN 0-8006-2621-4 (v. 2)
1. Jews—History—586 B.C.–70 A.D.—Sources. 2. Jews—History—586 B.C.–70 A.D.—Historiography. 3. Jews—History—168 B.C.–135 A.D.—Sources. 4. Jews—History—168 B.C.–135 A.D.—Historiography. 5. Judaism—History—Post-exilic period, 586 B.C.–210 A.D.—Sources. 6. Judaism—History—Post-exilic period, 586 B.C.–210 A.D.—Historiography. I. Title.
DS121.65.G68 1991
933—dc20 91-36738
CIP

The paper used in this publication meets the minimum requirements of American National Standard for Information Sciences—Permanence of Paper for Printed Library Materials, ANSI Z329.48-1984. ∞™

Manufactured in the U.S.A. AF 1-2620

96 95 94 93 92 1 2 3 4 5 6 7 8 9 10

To Elizabeth

اي واي بران دل كه درو سوزي نيست
سودازدهٔ مهر دلفروزي نيست
روزي كه تو بي عشق بسر خواهي برد
ضايع‌تر از آن روز ترا روزي نيست

SUMMARY OF CONTENTS: VOLUMES 1 AND 2

Abbreviations

Preface

1. Introduction
2. The Persian Period
3. The Jews and Hellenization
4. Alexander, the Diadochi, and the Ptolemies
5. Seleucid Rule, the Maccabean Revolt, and the Hasmonean Priest-Kings
6. The Roman Conquest and Herod the Great
7. Province, Kingdom, Province—and the War with Rome
8. Sects and Violence: Religious Pluralism from the Maccabees to Yavneh
9. Epilogue: To Bar Kokhba (70–135 C.E.)
10. The Jewish Theocracy from Cyrus to Hadrian

Chronology

Bibliography

Index

CONTENTS: VOLUME ONE

Abbreviations xvii

Preface xxv

1. Introduction 1

1.1 Major Original Sources 1
1.1.1 An Archeological Note 1
1.1.2 Collections of Literature 3
1.1.3 Josephus 4
1.1.3.1 Josephus's Life 5
1.1.3.2 Writings 6
1.1.3.3 Evaluation as a Historian 10
1.1.3.4 Aids and Tools for Utilizing Josephus 12
1.1.4 Rabbinic Literature 13
1.1.4.1 Introductions for Students 13
1.1.4.2 Methodology in the Use of Rabbinic Literature 14
1.2 A Socioeconomic Overview 16
1.2.1 Introduction and Bibliographical Guide 17
1.2.2 The Ancient Near East 20
1.2.3 Judah 23

2. The Persian Period 27

2.1 Bibliographical Guide 27
2.2 Sources 29
2.2.1 Old Testament 29
2.2.1.1 Books of Ezra and Nehemiah 30
2.2.1.2 The "Aramaic Source" and Alleged Persian Documents in Ezra 32

2.2.1.3 The Nehemiah Memorial 36
2.2.1.4 The Ezra Source 36
2.2.1.5 Miscellaneous Lists of Persons 38
2.2.1.6 Minor Prophets 42
2.2.1.7 Isaiah 56–66 46
2.2.1.8 Books of Chronicles 49
2.2.1.9 Esther, Ruth, Song of Songs 51
2.2.1.10 1 Esdras 53
2.2.1.11 Daniel 1–6 53
2.2.2 Aramaic Papyri and Inscriptions 53
2.2.3 Iranian and Mesopotamian Sources 56
2.2.3.1 The Babylonian Chronicles 57
2.2.3.2 The Cyrus Cylinder 57
2.2.3.3 The Behistun Inscription 58
2.2.3.4 The Elamite Texts from Persepolis 58
2.2.3.5 The Murašu Documents 58
2.2.3.6 Gadatas Inscription 59
2.2.3.7 Berossus 59
2.2.4 Egyptian Texts 60
2.2.5 Josephus 61
2.2.6 Greco-Roman Writers 64
2.2.6.1 Herodotus 64
2.2.6.2 Thucydides 64
2.2.6.3 Ctesias 65
2.2.6.4 Xenophon 65
2.2.6.5 Ephorus 66
2.2.6.6 Diodorus Siculus 66
2.2.6.7 Pompeius Trogus 67
2.2.6.8 Plutarch 67
2.2.7 Archeological Finds 67
2.2.7.1 Seals and Seal Impressions 68
2.2.7.2 Coins 70
2.2.7.3 Summary of Archeological Results 72
2.3 Major Historical Issues 73
2.3.1 Judah as a Theocracy 73
2.3.2 Sheshbazzar and the First Return 75
2.3.3 The Leadership of Zerubbabel and Joshua 77
2.3.4 Extent and Status of the Jewish State 79
2.3.5 Samaria and the Other Neighbors of Judah 83
2.3.5.1 General 83
2.3.5.2 Samaria 84

2.3.5.3 Phoenicia and the Coast 84
2.3.5.4 Arabia, including Edom, Gaza, and Transjordan 84
2.3.6 Date of the Return under Ezra 88
2.3.6.1 Ezra First 89
2.3.6.2 Thirty-seventh Year of Artaxerxes I 90
2.3.6.3 Seventh Year of Artaxerxes II 91
2.3.6.4 Analysis 92
2.3.7 Destruction of Jerusalem between Zerubbabel and Nehemiah? 93
2.3.8 The Mission of Ezra 94
2.3.8.1 Scholarly Hypotheses 95
2.3.8.2 Analysis 97
2.3.9 Judah and the Tennes Rebellion 99
2.3.10 Iranian Influence on the Jewish Religion? 100
2.3.11 The Rise of Sectarianism 103
2.3.11.1 General 103
2.3.11.2 Morton Smith 104
2.3.11.3 O. Plöger and P. Hanson 107
2.3.11.4 Analysis 111
2.3.12 The Thesis of Frank M. Cross 112
2.3.13 Economic, Social, Demographic Factors 114
2.3.13.1 The Persian Empire in General 115
2.3.13.2 The Province of Yehud 116
2.4 Synthesis 119
2.4.1 Overview 119
2.4.2 The Early Persian Period and the Initial Return 122
2.4.2.1 Cyrus the Great (539[559]–530 B.C.E.) 122
2.4.2.2 Cambyses (530–522 B.C.E.) 124
2.4.2.3 Darius I (522–486 B.C.E.) 124
2.4.2.4 First Return and Rebuilding of the Temple 126
2.4.3 From Zerubbabel to Nehemiah 129
2.4.3.1 Xerxes I (486–465 B.C.E.) 129
2.4.3.2 Artaxerxes I (465–424 B.C.E.) 130
2.4.3.3 Nehemiah's Mission 131
2.4.3.4 The Place of Ezra and His Activities 136
2.4.3.5 Darius II Ochus (424–404 B.C.E.) 138
2.4.3.6 Artaxerxes II Memnon (404–359 B.C.E.) 139
2.4.4 The Last Part of Persian Rule 140
2.4.4.1 Artaxerxes III Ochus (359–338 B.C.E.) 140
2.4.4.2 Arses (338–336 B.C.E.) 141

2.4.4.3 Darius III Codommanus (336–331 B.C.E.) 141
2.4.4.4 Events in Judah 141
2.4.5 Religious Developments 142

3. The Jews and Hellenization 147
3.1 Introduction and Bibliographical Guide 147
3.2 Major Studies 148
3.2.1 Martin Hengel 148
3.2.1.1 Hengel's Basic Thesis 148
3.2.1.2 Criticisms of Hengel 150
3.2.2 Victor Tcherikover 153
3.2.3 Saul Lieberman and H. A. Fischel 154
3.2.4 Morton Smith 155
3.3 Examination of Selected Examples 156
3.3.1 Language 156
3.3.2 Religion 158
3.3.3 Babylonia 159
3.3.4 Syria and Phoenicia 160
3.3.5 Pergamum 161
3.3.6 Art and Architecture 162
3.3.7 Resistance to Hellenization 163
3.4 Synthesis 164
3.4.1 Hellenization in General 164
3.4.2 Conclusions about the Jews and Hellenization 169

4. Alexander, the Diadochi, and the Ptolemies 171
4.1 Bibliographical Guide 171
4.2 Sources 172
4.2.1 Zenon Papyri 172
4.2.2 Hecateus of Abdera 173
4.2.3 Josephus 174
4.2.4 History of the Tobiads 174
4.2.5 Other Jewish Literature 175
4.2.5.1 Qohelet (Ecclesiastes) 175
4.2.5.2 Ben Sira (Ecclesiasticus) 176
4.2.5.3 Tobit 176
4.2.5.4 3 Maccabees 177
4.2.5.5 Judith 178
4.2.5.6 *Letter of (Pseudo-)Aristeas* 179
4.2.5.7 Ethiopic Enoch (*1 Enoch*) 180
4.2.5.8 Demetrius the Chronographer 181
4.2.5.9 The Jewish Alexander Legend 181

4.2.5.10 Daniel 11 183
4.2.6 Greek Historians 183
4.2.6.1 Alexander Historians 183
4.2.6.2 Diodorus Siculus 183
4.2.6.3 Polybius 184
4.2.6.4 Plutarch 184
4.2.6.5 Porphyry 184
4.2.7 Papyri, Inscriptions, Coins 184
4.2.7.1 Elephantine Papyrus (Cowley No. 81) 184
4.2.7.2 Khirbet el-Kom Ostraca 185
4.2.7.3 Decree of Ptolemy II 185
4.2.7.4 Other Inscriptions and Ostraca 187
4.2.7.5 Coins 187
4.2.8 Archeology 188
4.3 Historical Problems and Studies 189
4.3.1 Government and Administration 189
4.3.2 The Tobiad Family 192
4.3.3 The Rise of Apocalypticism 198
4.3.4 Translation of the Bible into Greek 200
4.3.5 Letter of Antiochus III to Zeuxis 201
4.3.6 Socioeconomic Questions 202
4.4 Synthesis 204
4.4.1 Overview 204
4.4.2 Alexander and His Conquests (336–323 B.C.E.) 205
4.4.3 The Diadochi (323–281 B.C.E.) 209
4.4.4 Ptolemaic Rule to 200 B.C.E. 212
4.4.5 Judea under the Ptolemies 215
4.4.6 Religious Developments 218

5. Seleucid Rule, the Maccabean Revolt, and the Hasmonean Priest-Kings 221
5.1 Bibliographical Guide 221
5.2 Sources 222
5.2.1 1 Maccabees 222
5.2.2 2 Maccabees 224
5.2.3 Daniel 225
5.2.4 Josephus 227
5.2.5 Nicolaus of Damascus 228
5.2.6 Qumran Scrolls 229
5.2.6.1 The Documents 231
5.2.6.2 The Archeology 232
5.2.6.3 Historical Data 233

5.2.7 *1 Enoch* 83–105 234
5.2.8 Book of Jubilees 234
5.2.9 *Third Sibylline Oracle* 235
5.2.10 Fragmentary Jewish Greek Writings 236
5.2.10.1 Demetrius the Chronographer 236
5.2.10.2 Eupolemus 237
5.2.10.3 Artapanus 237
5.2.10.4 Aristobulus 237
5.2.10.5 Ezekiel the Dramatist 238
5.2.11 *Testament of Moses* 238
5.2.12 Other Jewish Literature 239
5.2.13 Greek Historians 239
5.2.13.1 Strabo 239
5.2.13.2 Livy 240
5.2.13.3 Appian 240
5.2.13.4 Cassius Dio 240
5.2.14 Archeology, Inscriptions, and Coins 240
5.2.14.1 Decrees of Antiochus III 240
5.2.14.2 Jerusalem Inscription 241
5.2.14.3 Coins and Seals 242
5.2.14.4 Archeology 245
5.3 Historical Problems 246
5.3.1 Antiochus III's Decrees concerning the Jews 246
5.3.2 Causes of the Maccabean Revolt 247
5.3.2.1 Ancient Views 247
5.3.2.2 Antiochus's Character 248
5.3.2.3 Hellenization of Antiochus's Empire 248
5.3.2.4 Thesis of E. J. Bickerman 250
5.3.2.5 Thesis of V. A. Tcherikover 251
5.3.2.6 Thesis of J. A. Goldstein 252
5.2.3.7 Thesis of K. Bringmann 253
5.2.3.8 Socioeconomic Causes 255
5.2.3.9 Conclusions 255
5.3.3 Who Were the "Hellenizers"? 256
5.3.4 What Was the Cult in Jerusalem? 258
5.3.5 Documents in 1 and 2 Maccabees 259
5.3.6 Supposed Kinship with the Spartans 263
5.3.7 Chronology 264
5.3.8 The Temple at Leontopolis 266
5.3.9 Socioeconomic Matters 267
5.4 Synthesis 269
5.4.1 Overview 269

5.4.1.1 Sources 269
5.4.1.2 Seleucid and Roman History (200–63 B.C.E.) 270
5.4.1.3 Rise and Fall of the Jewish State 272
5.4.2 Antiochus III and the Seleucid Conquest 274
5.4.3 Hellenistic Reform and Religious Suppression 276
5.4.3.1 Antiochus IV (175–164 B.C.E.) 276
5.4.3.2 A New Constitution for Jerusalem 277
5.4.3.3 The Practice of Judaism Prohibited 281
5.4.4 The Maccabean Revolt to the Death of Judas 285
5.4.5 Jonathan Maccabee (161–143 B.C.E.) 293
5.4.6 Simon (143–135 B.C.E.) 297
5.4.7 John Hyrcanus (135–104 B.C.E.) 299
5.4.8 Aristobulus I (104–103 B.C.E.) 301
5.4.9 Alexander Janneus (103–76 B.C.E.) 302
5.4.10 Alexandra Salome (76–67 B.C.E.) 304
5.4.11 Aristobulus II and Hyrcanus II (67–63 B.C.E.) 306
5.4.12 Religious Developments 307

Index to Volumes One and Two **xxxiii**

List of Maps
Map 1 The Persian Empire at Its Greatest Extent 86
Map 2 The Persian Province of Judah 87
Map 3 Palestine under the Ptolemies and the Seleucids 194
Map 4 The Hellenistic World 195
Map 5 Herod's Kingdom 342
Map 6 The Kingdom of Agrippa I 415
Map 7 Palestine during the Bar Kokhba Revolt 582

ABBREVIATIONS

When used before an author's name or page number, an asterisk refers to items listed in the bibliography at the beginning of that particular chapter.

AASOR	Annual of the American Schools of Oriental Research
AAWG	*Abhandlungen der Akademie der Wissenschaften zu Göttingen*
AB	Anchor Bible
Adver. pagan.	Orosius, *Adversus paganos*
AfO	Archiv für Orientforschung
AGAJU	Arbeiten zur Geschichte des antiken Judentums und des Urchristentums
AHR	American Historical Review
AJA	*American Journal of Archaeology*
AJAH	*American Journal of Ancient History*
AJBA	*Australian Journal of Biblical Archaeology*
AJP	*American Journal of Philology*
AJS Review	*American Jewish Studies Review*
AJSL	*American Journal of Semitic Languages and Literature*
ALGHJ	Arbeiten zur Literatur und Geschichte des hellenistischen Judentums
AnBib	Analecta biblica
ANET	J. B. Pritchard (ed.), *Ancient Near Eastern Texts*
AnOr	Analecta orientalia
ANRW	*Aufstieg und Niedergang der römischen Welt*
AOAT	Alter Orient und Altes Testament
AOS	American Oriental Series
Appian	
Bell. Civ.	*Bella civilia*
Syr.	*Syriakē*

ASOR Sp. Vol.	American Schools of Oriental Research Special Volume
ASTI	*Annual of the Swedish Theological Institute*
Athen. Polit.	Aristotle, *Athenian Politeia*
ATR	*Anglican Theological Review*
AUSS	*Andrews University Seminary Studies*
b.	son of (Hebrew *ben*; Aramaic *bar*)
b. Avod. Zara	Babylonian Talmud, *Avoda Zara*
b. B. Batra	Babylonian Talmud, *Baba Batra*
b. Qid.	Babylonian Talmud, *Qiddušin*
b. Sanh.	Babylonian Talmud, *Sanhedrin*
b. Suk.	Babylonian Talmud, *Sukka*
b. Ta'an.	Babylonian Talmud, *Ta'anit*
b. Yeb.	Babylonian Talmud, *Yebamot*
b. Yoma	Babylonian Talmud, *Yoma* (= *Kippurim*)
BA	*Biblical Archaeologist*
BAR	*Biblical Archaeology Review*
BASOR	*Bulletin of the American Schools of Oriental Research*
B.C.E.	Before the Common Era (= B.C.)
Beh. Inscr.	*Behistun Inscription*
BETL	Bibliotheca ephemeridum theologicarum lovaniensium
Bib	*Biblica*
BibOr	Biblica et orientalia
BJRL	*Bulletin of the John Rylands University Library of Manchester*
BJS	Brown Judaic Studies
BO	*Bibliotheca orientalis*
BSOAS	*Bulletin of the School of Oriental and African Studies*
BTB	*Biblical Theology Bulletin*
BWANT	Beiträge zur Wissenschaft vom Alten und Neuen Testament
BZ	*Biblische Zeitschrift*
BZAW	Beihefte zur *ZAW*
CAH	*Cambridge Ancient History*
CBQ	*Catholic Biblical Quarterly*
CBQMS	Catholic Biblical Quarterly—Monograph Series
CCL	Corpus Christianorum, Series Latina
CCS	Cincinnati Classical Studies
CCWJCW	Cambridge Commentaries on Writings of the Jewish and Christian World 200 B.C. to A.D. 200
CD	*Damascus Document*

C.E.	Common Era (= A.D.)
CHCL	P. E. Easterling, et al. (eds.), *Cambridge History of Classical Literature* (1982–85)
CHI	*Cambridge History of Iran*
CHJ	W. D. Davies and L. Finkelstein (eds.), *Cambridge History of Judaism*
Collect.	Solinus, *Collectanea*
Com. in Dan.	Jerome, *Commentary on Daniel*
ConBNT	Coniectanea biblica, New Testament
ConBOT	Coniectanea biblica, Old Testament
CPJ	V. A. Tcherikover, et al., *Corpus papyrorum Judaicarum*
CRAIBL	*Comptes rendus de l'Académie des inscriptions et belles-lettres*
CRINT	Compendia rerum iudaicarum ad novum testamentum
CSCO	Corpus scriptorum christianorum orientalium
CSCT	Columbia Studies in Classical Texts
CSEL	Corpus scriptorum ecclesiasticorum latinorum
Dial. Trypho	Justin Martyr, *Dialogue with Trypho*
DJD	Discoveries in the Judaean Desert
EB	Etudes bibliques
Eccl. Rabba	*Ecclesiastes Rabbah*
ECL	Early Christian Literature
EI	Eretz-Israel
EJ	*Encyclopaedia Judaica*
Eng.	English text
Eusebius	
Chron.	*Chronicle*
Hist. eccl.	*Historia ecclesiastica*
Praep. evang.	*Praeparatio evangelica*
FRLANT	Forschungen zur Religion und Literatur des Alten und Neuen Testaments
FS	Festschrift
GCS	Griechischen christlichen Schriftsteller
Gen. Rab.	*Genesis Rabbah*
GLAJJ	M. Stern, *Greek and Latin Authors on Jews and Judaism*
GRBS	*Greek, Roman, and Byzantine Studies*
GTA	Göttinger theologische Arbeiten
Hadr.	*Hadrian* (in *Scriptores Historiae Augustae*)
HAR	*Hebrew Annual Review*
HAT	Handbuch zum Alten Testament
HdA	Handbuch der Archäologie

HdO	Handbuch der Orientalisk
Ḥev	Naḥal Ḥever texts
Ḥev Ep	Ḥever Epistles
Ḥev Ep gr	Ḥever Epistles (in Greek)
Hist. nat.	Pliny, *Naturalis historia*
HR	*History of Religions*
HSCP	*Harvard Studies in Classical Philology*
HSM	Harvard Semitic Monographs
HSS	Harvard Semitic Studies
HTR	*Harvard Theological Review*
HTS	Harvard Theological Studies
HUCA	*Hebrew Union College Annual*
ICC	International Critical Commentary
IDB	G. A. Buttrick (ed.), *Interpreter's Dictionary of the Bible*
IDBSup	Supplementary volume to *IDB*
IEJ	*Israel Exploration Journal*
INJ	*Israel Numismatic Journal*
Int	*Interpretation*
IOS	*Israel Oriental Society*
ITQ	*Irish Theological Quarterly*
JAAR	*Journal of the American Academy of Religion*
JANES	*Journal of the Ancient Near Eastern Society of Columbia University*
JAOS	*Journal of the American Oriental Society*
JBL	*Journal of Biblical Literature*
JCS	*Journal of Cuneiform Studies*
JEA	*Journal of Egyptian Archaeology*
JES	*Journal of Ecumenical Studies*
JHS	*Journal of Hellenic Studies*
JJS	*Journal of Jewish Studies*
JLBM	G.W.E. Nickelsburg, *Jewish Literature between the Bible and the Mishnah*
JNES	*Journal of Near Eastern Studies*
Josephus	
Ag. Ap.	*Against Apion*
Ant.	*Antiquities*
War	*War of the Jews*
JQR	*Jewish Quarterly Review*
JR	*Journal of Religion*
JRS	*Journal of Roman Studies*
JSHRZ	Jüdische Schriften aus hellenistisch-römischer Zeit

JSJ	*Journal for the Study of Judaism in the Persian, Hellenistic and Roman Period*
JSNT	*Journal for the Study of the New Testament*
JSOT	*Journal for the Study of the Old Testament*
JSOTSS	Journal for the Study of the Old Testament—Supplement Series
JSP	*Journal for the Study of the Pseudepigrapha*
JSPSS	Journal for the Study of the Pseudepigrapha—Supplementary Series
JSS	*Journal of Semitic Studies*
JTS	*Journal of Theological Studies*
JWSTP	M. E. Stone (ed.), *Jewish Writings of the Second Temple Period*
KAI	H. Donner and W. Röllig, *Kanaanäische und aramäische Inschriften*
KAT	Kommentar zum Alten Testament
LCL	Loeb Classical Library
Lives	Plutarch, *Parallel Lives*
LXX	Septuagint
m. Avot	Mishnah tractate *Avot*
m. Mig.	Mishnah tractate *Megilla*
m. Rosh ha-Shan.	Mishnah tractate *Rosh ha-Shana*
m. Shab.	Mishnah tractate *Shabbat*
m. Suk.	Mishnah tractate *Sukka*
m. Ta'an.	Mishnah tractate *Ta'anit*
Meg. Ta'an.	*Megillat Ta'anit*
MGWJ	*Monatsschrift für Geschichte und Wissenschaft des Judentums*
MSS	Manuscripts
MT	Masoretic Text
Mur.	Wadi Murabba'at texts
Nab. Chron.	*Nabonidus Chronicle*
NCB	New Century Bible
NEB	New English Bible
NHS	Nag Hammadi Studies
NIGTC	New International Greek Testament Commentary
NovT	*Novum Testamentum*
NovTSup	Novum Testamentum, Supplements
NTS	*New Testament Studies*
OCD	*Oxford Classical Dictionary*
OTL	Old Testament Library

OTP	J. H. Charlesworth (ed.), *The Old Testament Pseudepigrapha*
OTS	*Oudtestamentische Studien*
PAAJR	*Proceedings of the American Academy of Jewish Research*
PEQ	*Palestine Exploration Quarterly*
Philo	
Congr.	*De congressu eruditionis gratia*
Flaccum	*In Flaccum*
Gaium	*Legatio ad Gaium*
Hyp.	*Hypothetica*
Probus	*Quod omnis probus liber sit*
PSI	*Pubblicazioni della Società Italiana, Papiri Greci et Latini*
PVTG	Pseudepigrapha Veteris Testamenti graece
PW	Pauly-Wissowa, *Real-Encyclopädie der classischen Altertumswissenschaft*
PWSup	Supplement to *PW*
P. Zen.	Zenon papyri
Qumran Scrolls	
CD	*Damascus Document*
1QH	*Thanksgiving Hymns*
1QM	*War Scroll*
1QpHab	*Habbakuk Commentary*
1QS	*Community Rule* (*Manual of Discipline*)
1QSa	*Appendix A to 1QS* (*Rule of the Congregation*)
4QMMT	*Halakic Letter*
4QpNah	*Commentary on Nahum*
4QpPsa	*Commentary on Psalm 37*
11QMelch	*Melchizidek text*
11QT	*Temple Scroll*
RB	*Revue biblique*
REG	*Revue des études grecs*
REJ	*Revue des études juives*
RevQ	*Revue de Qumran*
RSR	*Religious Studies Review*
RSV	Revised Standard Version
SANE	Studies on the Ancient Near East
SAWH	*Sitzungsbericht der Akademie der Wissenschaften zu Heidelberg*
SBAW	*Sitzungsberichte der bayerischen Akademie der Wissenschaften*
SBLASP	SBL Abstracts and Seminar Papers

SBLBMI	SBL The Bible and Its Modern Interpreters
SBLDS	SBL Dissertation Series
SBLMS	SBL Monograph Series
SBLRBS	SBL Resources for Biblical Study
SBLSBS	SBL Sources for Biblical Study
SBLSCS	SBL Septuagint and Cognate Studies
SBLSP	SBL Seminar Papers
SBLTT	SBL Texts and Translations
SBT	Studies in Biblical Theology
SC	Sources chrétiennes
Schürer	E. Schürer, *The History of the Jewish People in the Age of Jesus Christ* (rev. G. Vermes, et al.)
SCI	*Scripta Classica Israelica*
SEG	*Supplementum epigraphicum Graecum*
SFSJH	South Florida Studies in Jewish History
SibOr	*Sibylline Oracle*
SJLA	Studies in Judaism in Late Antiquity
SNTSMS	Society for New Testament Studies Monograph Series
SPAW	Sitzungberichte der preussischen Akademie der Wissenschaften
SPB	Studia postbiblica
SPHS	Scholars Press, Hommage Series
SPSH	Scholars Press, Studies in the Humanities
SR	*Studies in Religion/Sciences religieuses*
SSAW	Sitzungsbericht der sachischen Akademie der Wissenschaften
STDJ	Studies on the Texts of the Desert of Judah
Suetonius	
Claud.	*Claudius*
Tib.	*Tiberius*
SUNT	Studien zur Umwelt des Neuen Testaments
SVTP	Studia in Veteris Testamenti pseudepigrapha
t. Hag.	Tosefta, *Hagiga*
t. Shab.	Tosefta, *Shabbat*
Tacitus	
Ann.	*Annals*
Hist.	*Histories*
TAPA	*Transactions of the American Philological Association*
TDNT	G. Kittel and G. Friedrich (eds.), *Theological Dictionary of the New Testament*
TLZ	*Theologische Literaturzeitung*
TSAJ	Texte und Studien zum antiken Judentum

TSSI	J.C.L. Gibson, *Textbook of Syrian Semitic Inscriptions*
TT	Texts and Translations
TU	Texte und Untersuchungen
TWAT	G. J. Botterweck and H. Ringgren (eds.), *Theologische Wörterbuch zum Alten Testament*
VigChr	*Vigiliae christianae*
VigChrSupp	VigChr, Supplements
VT	*Vetus Testamentum*
VTSup	Vetus Testamentum, Supplements
WBC	Word Bible Commentary
WHJP	*World History of the Jewish People*
WMANT	Wissenschaftliche Monographien zum Alten und Neuen Testament
WUNT	Wissenschaftliche Untersuchungen zum Neuen Testament
y. Ned.	Jerusalem Talmud, *Nedarim*
y. Sanh.	Jerusalem Talmud, *Sanhedrin*
y. Ta'an.	Jerusalem Talmud, *Ta'anit*
YCS	*Yale Classical Studies*
ZA	*Zeitschrift für Assyrologie*
ZAW	*Zeitschrift für die alttestamentliche Wissenschaft*
ZDMG	*Zeitschrift der deutschen morganländischen Gesellschaft*
ZDPV	*Zeitschrift des deutschen Palästina-Vereins*
ZNW	*Zeitschrift für die neutestamentliche Wissenschaft*
ZPE	*Zeitschrift für Papyrologie und Epigraphik*

PREFACE

This work has two basic purposes and is intended for two kinds of readers. It is a handbook for students studying the history and religion of the Judean state during the Second Temple period (539 B.C.E.–70 C.E.). (Although Diaspora Judaism is often referred to, I do not attempt a comprehensive treatment of that topic. Rather my focus is on the Jews and Judaism in the Land of Israel.)

It is also a two-volume reference for scholars, especially those who work in the period but are specialists in only one aspect of it or those who do research in a neighboring discipline (e.g., Old Testament, New Testament, Jewish literature) but want a handy reference.

There has been a noticeable gap in both student texts and scholarly handbooks that deal with this period. Histories of Israel there are aplenty, but they tend to concentrate on the pre-exilic period. Although most histories of Israel cover the Persian period, they are uncertain how much further to proceed. Several recent histories are commendable for recognizing that Israel as a state came to an end only in 70 C.E. and that the logical terminus is the Bar Kokhba revolt (135 C.E.). Some of these works, however, do not engage the most recent scholarship and tend to give only a survey, rather than the solid foundation students need for adequate understanding.

The scholar generally has available such specialist reference works and monographs as are noted in the section below on major secondary studies, but these are not designed for the student or even for quick reference by the scholar. Moreover, the progress of scholarship determines that such works can quickly become out-of-date in some respects. Finally, the major scholarly references cover only a part of the Second Temple period. Schürer begins with the Seleucid conquest, omitting the Persian and early Greek periods; Smallwood begins even later, with the conquest of Pompey in 63 B.C.E. Thus there is still a serious gap, which this work intends to fill.

In this work I have attempted to provide sufficient information to enable the student to gain a firm understanding of the sources and their interpretation. Important also is the aim of displaying different major interpretations of many topics. Students thereby can see the foundation on which historical interpretation rests and more easily begin the process of further investigation.

BASIC FORMAT OF EACH CHAPTER

With the exceptions of chapters 1, 3, 8, and 10 (whose contents necessitate a different framework), each chapter has an identical format:

1. Bibliographical guide. A short section at the beginning of each chapter discusses the major secondary studies important for that chapter. An asterisk (*) in a reference within the text reminds the reader to refer to the beginning of the chapter for a full citation of the work. All such works are also found in the bibliography at the end of Volume 2.
2. Primary sources. Historical knowledge is ultimately dependent on the primary sources, and students should be constantly taken back to the roots of knowledge, rather than offered prepackaged reconstructions. The sources are not only literary—indeed, in some cases literary sources are sadly lacking—but also archeological and artifactual. Such things as coins, inscriptions, art, and human remains can tell us a great deal, especially if literary histories can give them a context. See 1.1.1 for more on this.
3. Historical studies and issues. The third section of each chapter looks at individual points important for that particular period of time, especially those that need detailed or technical treatment. In addition, for any historical period or issue there are usually several opinions. The major positions currently taken, as well as the arguments for and against them, are noted. Global reconstructions, which attempt to interpret a major event or whole historical period, are summarized as well, sometimes at the risk of a certain amount of distortion. One subdivision of this section in each chapter concerns socioeconomic matters. See 1.2 for more on this.
4. Synthesis. The heart of each chapter (1) summarizes and ties together the data of the other sections (with cross-references), (2) brings in the necessary background history, and (3) gives my own interpretation and reconstruction. The section also forms a constant dialogue with the original sources and the opinions of other

scholars, so that the reader is still brought face-to-face with the foundations on which the interpretation rests.

Background history is given in lesser or greater detail, depending on its importance for Jewish history and how likely the student is to be familiar with it. For example, events in Judea between 63 and 31 B.C.E. are intimately connected with Roman history, and therefore a more detailed account of the Roman side is given. For Persian history, which is not very well known and may be quite important for reconstructing Jewish history, a somewhat detailed survey is also given.

The terms "Judah" and "Judea" as a reference to the nation and its territory are synonyms. I generally use "Judah" for the time before Alexander and "Judea" for the Greek and Roman periods.

CROSS-REFERENCES

Each chapter is organized in a numerical outline according to the decimal system; that is, each chapter, major section, and subsection is numbered and indicated by an arabic numeral preceded by a decimal (e.g., 2.1, 2.1.1). The first number is always the chapter number; the others represent subsections. Cross-references direct the reader to other relevant sections or a more detailed discussion of a particular topic.

BIBLIOGRAPHY

This book contains no notes. Instead, each division or subdivision is preceded by a bibliography relevant to the subject treated. All books and articles cited are also listed in the main bibliography at the end of Volume 2. Full bibliographical data are provided in the main bibliography. In the text itself these titles are referred to by author (or author and date, if more than one writing is listed in the section bibliography) and the appropriate page citation. Works used throughout this book are referred to by an abbreviation (sometimes the author's name); these volumes are also listed in the main bibliography. For the editions of original sources used, see 1.1.2–3.

No attempt has been made to provide an exhaustive bibliography. Three sorts of items are included in the sectional bibliography:

1. All items cited in the text.

2. Surveys, introductions, and other guides for the student and non-specialist. Sometimes, areas containing a considerable wealth of scholarship are touched on: for example, chapter 2, which overlaps with Old Testament studies. In such cases, at least one recent commentary or other introductory work is listed, so that the non-specialist can locate further discussion and bibliography.
3. Other current specialized studies, especially those that supplement and update the bibliographical listings in Schürer and other references.

MAJOR SECONDARY STUDIES

This book is meant to lead the student into the texts, secondary literature, and historical problems. However, some students may want to know of reliable yet briefer surveys.

For history, one can refer to H. Jagersma, *A History of Israel in the Old Testament Period* (1982), for the Persian period, and his *A History of Israel from Alexander the Great to Bar Kochba* (1985) for the Greek and Roman periods. Roughly equivalent in scope and quality are P. Schäfer, *Geschichte der Juden in der Antike* (1983), and C. Saulnier (with C. Perrot), *Histoire d'Israël,* Vol. 3: *De la conquête d'Alexandre à la destruction du temple* (1985). There are also chapters on the Persian, Greek, and Roman periods in *Israelite and Judaean History,* edited by J. Hayes and J. M. Miller (1977).

Some reference works are cited so frequently (e.g., Schürer) that they appear in the abbreviations list (pp. xvii–xxiv).

Several encyclopedic works are important, even if not yet finished. The *Encyclopaedia Judaica* (1971) covers all areas of Jewish history, literature, and culture. Many of its articles on the Second Temple period are of great value, especially when they summarize work otherwise available only in modern Hebrew. The *Interpreter's Dictionary of the Bible* (*IDB*) and its supplementary volume (*IDBSup*) have articles on many aspects of Jewish literature and history, as well as the expected entries on Old Testament subjects. The *Cambridge History of Judaism* (*CHJ*) has the potential of being a useful reference for all periods of Jewish history, but it is not complete and progress on it so far has been sporadic. The Compendia Rerum Iudaicarum ad Novum Testamentum (CRINT) is intended to be a full coverage of Jewish culture, literature, and history of the first century C.E. The first two volumes consist largely of contributions from Israeli scholars, some of them excellent, but the quality of others is uneven. The third volume, edited by M. E. Stone (*Jewish Writings of the Second*

Temple Period [*JWSTP*]), is more international in its list of writers and makes a significant contribution to the field. The volume on the Bible (*Mikra*) also has many good articles.

The *World History of the Jewish People*, apparently intended to cover all of Jewish history, is only partially complete. However, there are volumes on the Hellenistic period (including the Maccabean revolt and Hasmonean rule [4.1]), the Herodian period (6.1), and society and religion in the Second Temple period. Additional volumes are apparently available in Hebrew but have not yet appeared in English.

Another encyclopedic work, *Aufstieg und Niedergang der römischen Welt* (*ANRW*), attempts to cover all aspects of Roman history, literature, and culture. A number of the volumes in the second section (*Principat*) focus on Jewish matters.

The standard historical reference for the latter part of the Second Temple period (ca. 175 B.C.E. to 135 C.E.) has been the monumental work of Emil Schürer, *The History of the Jewish People in the Age of Jesus Christ* (Schürer), translated and revised by G. Vermes et al. (1973–87). It covers many aspects of Judaism in this period, including the history and literature, and should remain the standard detailed reference work for many years to come. However, in the last fifteen years scholarship has rendered parts of the new Schürer out-of-date. Moreover, initial editorial uncertainty as to how far to revise Schürer's text resulted in notes that sometimes contradict the text! Although this is less of a problem in the later volumes, even there the revision did not always take account of new methodological developments, especially as they affect the use of rabbinic literature (see 1.1.4). For example, Schürer's discussion of the synagogue was allowed to remain substantially unaltered, even though it indiscriminately mixed data from a wide geographical area and a period of time covering many centuries.

E. M. Smallwood's *The Jews under Roman Rule* (1976) covers the period from the Roman conquest of Judah in 63 B.C.E. to the reign of the emperor Diocletian (284–305 C.E.). Thus there is considerable overlap between it and Schürer, and despite a good deal of repetition, the two works complement each other. As well as benefiting from volume 1 of the new Schürer, Smallwood covers particular episodes of the history in more detail. The 1981 reprint contains some minor corrections and some bibliographic updating in the notes. A recent volume surveying the present state of scholarly study on early Judaism is *Early Judaism and Its Modern Interpreters*, edited by R. A. Kraft and G.W.E. Nickelsburg (1986).

A number of the encyclopedic works listed above give information on Jewish literature. In addition to *JWSTP* and Schürer (vol. 3), a useful one-volume critical introduction is G.W.E. Nickelsburg's *Jewish Literature between the Bible and the Mishnah* (*JLBM*). Nickelsburg treats in chronological order all the major extrabiblical literature during the Persian, Greek, and Roman periods and includes an accompanying historical framework. Indeed, one could say that my two volumes are a companion to Nickelsburg's, in that his gives some history while concentrating on the literature, whereas I give the history but must treat the literature as one of the main sources for the history. The main omission in Nickelsburg's book is a discussion of Josephus and Philo of Alexandria. An annotated bibliography on many of these writings appears in J. H. Charlesworth, *The Pseudepigrapha and Modern Research* (1981). For editions of Jewish and other literature used in the present work, see 1.1.2–3.

The list of books and articles on Second Temple Judaism is not endless—it only seems that way. A book of this sort is often rightly used as a checklist of relevant literature on a particular question. No doubt I have overlooked important studies and should be criticized for doing so. In many cases, I have been aware of items of potential value but have not been able to find them or have judged that other items had priority. Cataloguing North American publications has been a bigger problem than might, at first, be realized (for example, some books have been difficult to acquire). This has produced a dilemma: Should I include publications that I have not been able to consult? My final decision was to list only those that I had actually seen. To do so creates an anomaly in a few cases, because I knew of works that should have been consulted and included but have been unobtainable. Even so, I was finding references to and acquiring relevant studies right up to submitting the manuscript (e.g., J. Maier's *Zwischen den Testamenten*, which came too late to use).

Whatever the merits and deficiencies of this book, the former are greater and the latter fewer because of generous help. A number of people were kind enough to read and comment on parts of the manuscript at some stage in its writing: P. R. Ackroyd (chap. 2), P. R. Davies (chaps. 5, 8), Martin Goodman (chaps. 3–9), Jacob Neusner (chap. 8), J. L. North (chap. 8), Wendy Sproston (chap. 8), R. N. Whybray (chap. 2), and H.G.M. Williamson (chap. 2). Elizabeth H. Wood read parts of the manuscript from the point of view of that most important of readers, the nonspecialist. My colleagues J. L. North and Wendy Sproston also answered some questions on New Testament matters. John Rogerson invited me to present chapter 2 to a meeting of the Sheffield postgraduate seminar. P. R. Davies gave me permission to cite some articles from a volume he is editing. D.J.A. Clines provided a copy of a forthcoming article. Jacob Neusner recommended publication of the book to Fortress Press. My sincere thanks to them all for their expenditure of time and effort (very considerable in some cases) on my behalf. However, this expression of gratitude does not imply their agreement with all—or even any—of what I have said.

The British Academy provided partial travel funding to read papers relevant to my research at the Society of Biblical Literature International Meetings in Copenhagen and Vienna. The Lee and Lou Kuhn Foundation awarded a grant toward research expenses, for which I thank its director, Robert L. Kuhn, as well as the foundation.

LESTER L. GRABBE
University of Hull, England

1 INTRODUCTION

Grabbe, L. L. "The Jewish Theocracy from Cyrus to Titus: A Programmatic Essay." *JSOT* 37 (1987) 117–24.

1.1 MAJOR ORIGINAL SOURCES

Most of the original sources referred to cover only a fairly brief span of time and are thus relevant to only one or two chapters of this work. In these cases the sources are discussed in the chapter in question. Some groups of literature, however, have been collected into standard editions or translations that will be used throughout this volume. These are discussed in 1.1.2. We need first, however, to note a major source of information, the nonliterary or archeological data, which are discussed in 1.1.1. Two other bodies of literature also need a thorough discussion: one because it is constantly used, the other because it is not. The historian Josephus is one of our major resources for the entire period under discussion. Although many of the chapters discuss his data and his value for the period in question, a general introduction to Josephus's work is given below in 1.1.3. A second body of literature often cited in histories of Judaism is rabbinic literature. However, I will seldom refer to rabbinic literature (except in chap. 8), and then only with great caution; the reason for this is given in 1.1.4.

1.1.1 An Archeological Note

Arav, R. *Hellenistic Palestine* (1989).
Avigad, N. *Discovering Jerusalem* (1984).
Avi-Yonah, M., and E. Stern, eds. *Encyclopedia of Archaeological Excavations in the Holy Land* (1975–78).
Isaac, B., and I. Roll. *Roman Roads in Judaea* (1982).

Kanael, B. "Ancient Jewish Coins and Their Historical Importance." *BA* 26 (1963) 38–62.
———. "Altjüdische Münzen." *Jahrbuch für Numismatik und Geldgeschichte* 17 (1967) 159–298.
Kuhnen, H.-P. *Palästina in griechisch-römischer Zeit* (1990).
Levine, L. I. "Archaeological Discoveries from the Greco-Roman Era." *Recent Archaeology in the Land of Israel* (1981) 75–88.
Meshorer, Y. *Jewish Coins of the Second Temple Period* (1967).
———. *Ancient Jewish Coinage.* Vol. 1: *Persian Period through Hasmonaeans;* Vol. 2: *Herod the Great through Bar Kokhba* (1982).
Meyers, E. M., and A. T. Kraabel. "Archaeology, Iconography, and Nonliterary Written Remains." *Early Judaism and Its Modern Interpreters* (1986) 175–210.
Segal, A. "Archaeological Research in Israel: 1960–1985." *BTB* 16 (1986) 73–77.
Shiloh, Y. *Excavations at the City of David* (1984).
Stern, E. *Material Culture of the Land of the Bible in the Persian Period 538–332 B.C.* (1982).
Urman, D. *The Golan* (1985).
Vogel, E. K. "Bibliography of Holy Land Sites: Part I." *HUCA* 42 (1971) 1–96.
———. "Bibliography of Holy Land Sites: Part II." *HUCA* 52 (1981) 1–92.
———. "Bibliography of Holy Land Sites: Part III, 1981–1987." *HUCA* 58 (1987) 1–63.
Weippert, H. *Palästina in vorhellenistischer Zeit* (1988).
Wilkinson, J. "The Streets of Jerusalem." *Levant* 7 (1975) 118–36.
Yadin, Y., ed. *Jerusalem Revealed* (1975).

The increase in the number of archeological publications and the amount of data in recent years is welcome. Nevertheless, until recently there have been few attempts to synthesize the great amount of scattered data about the Second Temple period. For the Persian period we can draw on Stern, supplemented by the briefer treatment in Weippert (682–728). For the Hellenistic and Roman periods we now have the welcome new studies by Arav (337–31 B.C.E.) and Kuhnen (the time of Alexander to 640 C.E.). In addition to Kuhnen and Arav, Avi-Yonah/Stern, Vogel (1971; 1981; 1987), and Segal are useful summaries and guides for individual excavations. Probably the most studied site is Jerusalem, for which there are a number of publications (Avigad; Shiloh; Wilkinson; Yadin), although the excavations continue. Journals that regularly publish or report on archeological work include the *Biblical Archaeologist, Biblical Archaeology Review, Bulletin of the American Schools of Oriental Research, Israel Exploration Journal, Levant, Palestine Exploration Quarterly, Revue biblique,* and *Zeitschrift des deutschen Palästina-Vereins*. Furthermore, many biblical and Near Eastern journals have occasional articles on or related to archeology.

An important but often overlooked subject is coins. The recent study by Meshorer (1982; see also 1967) not only catalogues almost all the coins currently known but summarizes much of the discussion. There is, however, considerable debate on specific points, and individual chapter bibliographies should be consulted for interpretations that disagree with Meshorer. Thus Kanael's older articles still have value, his 1967 article being largely an annotated bibliography of previous studies.

1.1.2 Collections of Literature

Greek and Roman literature will be cited throughout, sometimes for direct information on Judea but more often for general information on the background history and culture. Most of the major Greco-Roman writers are available in the Loeb Classical Library (Cambridge: Harvard University Press; London: Heinemann). Unless otherwise indicated, quotations from Greek or Roman writings are from LCL. M. Stern's three-volume *Greek and Latin Authors on Jews and Judaism* (*GLAJJ*) contains a collection of all direct references to Jews in classical literature, together with translation and commentary. A useful collection of Greek and Latin inscriptions is found in the series edited by R. K. Sherk, Translated Documents of Greece and Rome, two volumes of which are S. M. Burstein, *The Hellenistic Age from the Battle of Ipsus to the Death of Kleopatra VII* (1985), and R. K. Sherk, *Rome and the Greek East to the Death of Augustus* (1984). Other single-volume works include M. M. Austen, *The Hellenistic World from Alexander to the Roman Conquest* (1981), R. S. Bagnall and P. Derow, *Greek Historical Documents: The Hellenistic Period* (1981), and D. C. Braund, *Augustus to Nero* (1985). An important older collection is C. B. Welles, *Royal Correspondence in the Hellenistic Period* (1934).

Several collections of Jewish literature have recently appeared. Josephus is available in a reliable translation with useful notes in LCL, as is Philo of Alexandria. For the Qumran Scrolls, the translation of Geza Vermes (*The Dead Sea Scrolls in English*) is used (5.2.6). The so-called Apocrypha is found in many Bible translations, including the RSV, NEB, and the *Jerusalem Bible*; it can also be found with commentary in R. H. Charles (ed.), *Apocrypha and Pseudepigrapha of the Old Testament* (1913), which, despite its age, is still a useful collection that also contains some of the major Pseudepigrapha. There are also more recent and complete editions of the Pseudepigrapha, in more reliable translations with up-to-date introductions, although none of these contains a real commentary, as Charles does. The most extensive is J. H. Charlesworth (ed.), *Old Testament Pseudepigrapha* (*OTP*). Briefer in the number of writings included, as well as in length of introduction, is H.F.D. Sparks (ed.), *The Apocryphal Old Testament* (1984). Paradoxically, despite the title, the Apocrypha is not included; nor is the important *Apocalypse of Ezra* (*4 Ezra*), but otherwise Sparks serves as a useful supplement—and in some cases, a correction—to *OTP*.

Unless otherwise indicated, citations from the Hebrew Bible are taken from the recent Jewish Publication Society translation. Quotations from the Apocrypha and the New Testament usually follow the RSV.

1.1.3 Josephus

Attridge, H. W. "Josephus and His Works." *JWSTP* (1984) 185–232.
Bilde, P. *Flavius Josephus between Jerusalem and Rome* (1988).
Cohen, S.J.D. *Josephus in Galilee and Rome* (1979).
Feldman, L. H. *Josephus and Modern Scholarship (1937–1980)* (1984).
Feldman, L. H., and G. Hata, eds. *Josephus, Judaism, and Christianity* (1987).
———. *Josephus, the Bible, and History* (1989).
Grabbe, L. L. "Josephus." *Dictionary of Biblical Interpretation* (1990) 365–68.
Moehring, H. R. "The *Acta pro Judaeis* in the *Antiquities* of Flavius Josephus." *Christianity, Judaism and Other Greco-Roman Cults* (1975) 3.124–58.
———. Review of Cohen, *Josephus in Galilee and Rome*. *JJS* 31 (1980) 240–42.
———. "Joseph ben Matthia and Flavius Josephus: The Jewish Prophet and Roman Historian." *ANRW* 2 (1984) 21.2.864–944.
Rajak, T. *Josephus: The Historian and His Society* (1983).
Rengstorf, K. H. *A Complete Concordance to Flavius Josephus* (1973–83).
Schreckenberg, H. *Bibliography zu Flavius Josephus* (1968).
———. *Bibliography zu Flavius Josephus: Supplementband mit Gesamtregister* (1979).
Schwartz, S. *Josephus and Judaean Politics* (1990).
Thackeray, H. St. J., et al. *Josephus* (1926–65).
Villalba i Varneda, P. *The Historical Method of Flavius Josephus* (1986).

One of the most useful but frustrating sources for Jewish history is the historian Flavius Josephus. If it were not for his writings, our knowledge of Jewish history—especially in the Greek and Roman periods—would be drastically reduced. So much that we know of persons and events central to Jewish history comes from Josephus and is available from no other source. Even when other sources refer to the person or event in question, it is still usually Josephus who tells us the most. This makes his writings invaluable for much of the history of the Jews over the half-millennium from about 400 B.C.E. to almost 100 C.E.

Nevertheless, Josephus is not necessarily a simple source to use. One of the most fundamental mistakes made by students of this period is to take Josephus's account at face value and repeat it in light paraphrase. To do so ignores the gaps, the biases, the poor quality of some of his authorities, and the fact that his accounts frequently cannot be checked. One of the main reasons Josephus is so valuable is that his works are extant. If we had the writings of other contemporary Jewish writers (e.g., Justus of Tiberias), we might find that Josephus's accounts are decidedly inferior. At least we would have the matter described from another point of view and would thus have a means of evaluating and overcoming some of the prejudices of any one version. Even the best source sees things from a particular point of view and needs to be qualified and filled out by other sources. How much more is this the case with Josephus, who is not always a good source.

1.1.3.1 Josephus's Life

Josephus was born about 37 C.E. (*Life* 1 §5), of a priestly family. From the first, however, his statements about his own life are often exaggerated and sometimes unbelievable. For example, he claims that he progressed so rapidly in the traditional Jewish learning that by the age of fourteen even chief priests and leading men were consulting him about the law (*Life* 2 §9), a statement exceeded in its incredibility only by its frequent quotation by modern scholars without comment, as if to take it at face value. Even Jesus is alleged only to have astounded the priests with his wisdom, not to have been consulted by them (Luke 2:41-47). By Josephus's own account, he tried out the "three sects" (Pharisees, Sadducees, and Essenes) and "passed through" (*diēlthon*) each. Then he spent three years with an ascetic in the desert. After this, at the age of nineteen, he says he decided to become a Pharisee. This chronology does not add up. How could he at sixteen have actually "passed through" the courses of the Pharisees, Sadducees, and Essenes, then spent three years in the desert, and yet be only nineteen? The first level of entering the Essenes alone took an entire year. Furthermore, in his actual writings (outside of another passage or two in the *Life*) Josephus nowhere makes an issue of his being a Pharisee, although he does claim knowledge because of being a priest.

The next event in his life was his trip to Rome in 63 C.E., at the age of twenty-six, to help bring about the release of priests who had been sent by the governor Felix to be tried before Nero. Like the Christian writer Paul, he claims to have been shipwrecked and to have swum all night before being picked up. In Rome he was introduced to Nero's consort Poppea and received gifts from her, although he does not say if he obtained the object of his mission, the freedom of the priests.

He claims that during the disturbances leading up to the war with Rome, he repeatedly attempted to convince the belligerents that it was madness to fight Rome, even to the point of taking refuge in the temple lest he be arrested. Then he joined others in going along with the rebels because he could not stop them, even while secretly hoping that the revolution would be quickly put down. When Cestius was defeated, however, he accepted a rather strange commission: "They dispatched me . . . to induce the disaffected to lay down their arms and to impress upon them the desirability of reserving these for the picked men of the nation" (*Life* 7 §29). Not only is this difficult to understand in itself but also it contradicts *War* 2.20.3–4 §§562–68, which states that he was chosen as a military governor to oversee the preparations for war in Galilee.

His months in Galilee were largely spent in conflict with other Jewish leaders and towns such as Tiberias and Sepphoris, who wanted to avoid siding with the rebels. As soon as Vespasian arrived, Josephus took his stand in Jotapata, one of the first cities to fall to the Romans, although only after a lengthy siege. Josephus himself was captured, but his account of the circumstances generally sounds suspect. However, he claims to have prophesied to Vespasian that the latter would become emperor. Something like that must have taken place, not only because *War* was dedicated to Titus, who was alleged to have witnessed the prophecy, but also because of Vespasian's subsequent treatment of Josephus.

When Vespasian was declared emperor in 69, Josephus was released from his bonds and rewarded by Vespasian. He then accompanied Titus on the final siege of Jerusalem in 70, during which he acted as an interpreter and attempted to persuade the defenders of the city to surrender. After the fall of the city he was taken to Rome by Titus, adopted into the Flavian family, made a Roman citizen, and given a lifetime pension. The rest of his life was evidently spent in Rome and was mainly devoted to his writings. The last dated event in his life is the appearance of the *Antiquities* in 93–94 C.E., when he was fifty-five, although *Against Apion* seems to have been written after this (*Ag. Ap.* 1.1 §1).

1.1.3.2 Writings

Petersen, H. "Real and Alleged Literary Projects of Josephus." *AJP* 79 (1958) 259–74.

Schwartz, S. "The Composition and Publication of Josephus's 'Bellum Judaicum' Book 7." *HTR* 79 (1986) 373–86.

Although Josephus refers to a number of literary works or projects in his writings, only four have come down to us. It is questionable whether any others were actually completed, apart from perhaps an earlier version of the *War*. More likely, the references to other works represent planned writings, rather than actual, completed writings.

1.1.3.2.1 The *War of the Jews* (*Bellum Judaicum*) was Josephus's first writing, produced basically during the 70s and presented to Titus and Vespasian (*Life* 65 §§361–63; *Ag. Ap.* 1.9 §50). The fact that Vespasian was still alive would put its completion before 79 C.E.; however, it was Titus who authorized publication, suggesting a date around 79–81. Perhaps Vespasian was only shown earlier portions or drafts. There is also evidence that the last book of the work (Book 7) was not part of the original but was added later, under Domitian (81–96 C.E. [Cohen: 87–89]), although this might represent only a revision (Schwartz). Josephus undoubtedly had a number of reasons for writing the *War*, and it would be simplistic to assume that everything in it was subordinated to one or two aims. Nevertheless, several dominant themes suggest the major aims of the *War*, even if there may have been others.

1. Rome is too strong militarily to be defeated. This should have been clear to the rebels before the war and should deter any would-be rebels afterward. Such passages as Agrippa's speech (2.16.4 §§345–401) and the excursus on the Roman army (3.5.1–8 §§70–109) illustrate this.
2. On the Roman side, the revolt was caused by a few incompetent, greedy administrators, especially the governors sent after the death of Agrippa I. The Roman leadership was forced into the war and did not undertake it willingly.
3. On the Jewish side, most of the people, especially the chief priests and leading citizens, were against the war. A few hotheaded individuals inflamed the rabble and forced the moderates to participate against their will.
4. Glorification of Vespasian's family, especially Titus.

Josephus tells us that he wrote a version of the *War* in Aramaic, which was circulated in Mesopotamia (presumably among the Jews), apparently with the aim of making sure they were not tempted to revolt as well (1.Pref.1 §3). Because none of this has survived, there is no way to check his claim; however, it seems doubtful that such a work would have been as extensive as the present work in Greek. It is also clear that, contrary to what Josephus implies, the surviving Greek writing is an original composition and not a translation from Semitic.

The bulk of the *War* is devoted to the events immediately preceding the war, the war itself, and the mop-up operations afterward (including the taking of the fortress at Masada). After a few preliminaries, the narrative begins with the reign of Antiochus IV and the Maccabean revolt. Book 1 moves rapidly forward, ending with the death of Herod in 4 B.C.E. Book 2 covers the events of the first century to the defeat of Cestius and the preparations for war in Judea and Galilee. Book 3 begins with the appointment of Vespasian to take charge of the war (winter 66/67) and goes to September 67, including the siege of Jotapata and the capture of Josephus. Book 4 completes the capture of Galilee, the investment of Jerusalem, the events in Rome after the death of Nero (November 68), and the declaration of Vespasian as emperor. The siege and fall of Jerusalem under Titus are described in Books 5 and 6. Book 7 details the subsequent events, especially the siege of Masada and the fortress's capture in 73 or 74 C.E.

1.1.3.2.2 The *Antiquities of the Jews* (*Antiquitates Judaicae*), which appeared around 94 C.E., had a rather different purpose from the *War.* It is very much an apology for the Jews. Although Josephus probably had a number of reasons for writing it, his overriding aim was to present Jewish history, religion, and people in a manner that would be understood and admired by educated Greeks and Romans. He wanted to show that Jewish religious customs, rather than peculiar and misanthropic, were actually sensible and rational, and conformed with the highest ideals of Greco-Roman thought. He also noted that the Jews had an ancient history that preceded not only the Greeks' and Romans' but even the Egyptians' and Babylonians'. Indeed, Abraham, one of the ancestors of the Jews, taught the Egyptians astrology and mathematics (*Ant.* 1.8.2 §§166–68), and he and other Jewish figures were the very model of the Hellenistic sage or hero (as shown by Feldman in a number of articles). Another point of emphasis in Josephus's later books is the extent to which Greek leaders such as Alexander and Roman emperors such as Julius Caesar and Augustus admired the Jews and conferred benefits on them.

Books 1 through 10 of *Antiquities* are essentially a paraphrase of the Old Testament narrative books, naturally omitting much of the prophetic, wisdom, and psalmic writings. These books, however, represent much more than just a summary of history as presented by the Old Testament. Occasionally, extrabiblical traditions are included, which give an extra boost to the importance of biblical figures such as Abraham and Moses. Embarrassing events are sometimes omitted, for example, the episode of the golden calf. Above all, everything is interpreted in a way that would be understandable—and present a positive image—to one educated in Greek literature and values. Although Josephus's textual source is not always clear, at times he obviously used a version of the LXX. There is little or no evidence that he worked from the original Hebrew text.

Once he had finished with the biblical material, Josephus seems to have been at a loss for good sources for a lengthy period of time. The Old Testament literature extends as far as the Persian period, and Josephus filled out his account of the Persian period with the Greek books of 1 Esdras and Esther. Concerning the next two centuries and more, he seems to have had very little information, filling up the space with a few bits and pieces of valuable material but largely with dubious, legendary works. Only when he reached the second century and was able to draw on 1 Maccabees does he seem to have had a reliable, connected source again. This means that most of his account of the Persian period, the conquest of Alexander, and the Ptolemaic rule of Palestine is of little value.

For the period after about 175 B.C.E., however, Josephus was able to draw on 1 Maccabees. After that, he had the histories of Nicolaus of Damascus and Strabo as far as the death of Herod. The early part of the first century C.E. is another gap, with little recorded for the period from 6 to 26 C.E. After this he used a variety of sources, including Roman ones, some of more value than others, but in many instances we have no idea of his sources. He finally ended this work on the eve of the revolt with the governorship of Florus. Thus there is some overlap between *War* and *Antiquities*, and the narratives can profitably be compared (see the individual chapters below).

1.1.3.2.3 The *Life* (*Vita*) was issued as an appendix to the *Antiquities*, probably about 94/95 C.E. (Cohen: 170–80). The occasion was the appearance of a history of the Jewish war by a rival, Justus of Tiberias. Unfortunately, most of what we know of Justus comes from Josephus's attack on him, ruling out any detailed knowledge of what Justus said, but it seems that Justus disagreed with Josephus's account and perhaps even accused him of personal misdeeds. The *Life* is Josephus's defense of his actions, mainly those in Galilee from the time of his appointment as military governor (ca. November 66) to the arrival of Vespasian's army in May 67. Also included is an attack on Justus. Again, although Josephus may have had several purposes, it seems to me that the attack of Justus was uppermost in his mind when writing (contra Bilde: 110–13). Because most of the *Life* parallels a section of Book 2 of the *War*, a comparison of the two is very interesting and shows how the narrative changes, depending on Josephus's purpose (see further at 7.4.11.4).

1.1.3.2.4 Josephus's final work seems to have been *Against Apion* (*Contra Apionem*). Apion was a Greek citizen of Alexandria and, apparently, one of the delegation that appeared before Claudius to accuse the Jews in 41 C.E. He was the author of an anti-Semitic tract that made a variety of allegations about Jewish history and religion. *Against Apion* is Josephus's reply. It represents the first in a long line of such defenses in Judeo-Christian tradition (cf., e.g., Origen, *Contra Celsum*). Although many of Josephus's statements about the history and antiquity of the Jews cannot be taken at face value, the work is especially valuable for its quotations from Greek and Oriental writers who are otherwise lost to us (e.g., Manetho and Berossus). It also shows in detail the sorts of slanders leveled at the Jews in some of the anti-Semitic literature of the time.

1.1.3.3 Evaluation as a Historian

The problem with Josephus has been well stated by the late Horst Moehring:

> The writings of Flavius Josephus have at times achieved semi-canonical status, but there exists no orthodox line of interpretation, at least apart from . . . the unscrupulousness with which everybody exploits his writings for whatever purpose may at the moment be in mind. Josephus has truly been all things to all men. . . . there certainly is a great amount of pseudo-history present: the use of Josephus for contemporary apologetic purposes without regard for the intentions of his writings. (1975: 124)

Most specialists on Josephus would agree that the Jewish historian's works have often been misused and cited without actually being read. This does not mean that there is a consistent approach to his work, even among those who have become Josephus experts. The variations in approach to Josephus can best be illustrated by looking at the recent monograph by Shaye Cohen and its evaluation by Moehring and Tessa Rajak. Cohen's study is, in general, a look at the *Life* and the parallel section in the *War,* in an attempt to put the historian's life and method of writing in historical perspective. In his review of Cohen, Moehring seemed to doubt any possibility of historical reconstruction on the basis of Josephus:

> It has become fashionable in some circles, for patriotic or ecclesiastical reasons, to return to the naive view that historians of the Graeco-Roman age can be made to yield information that would allow us to reconstruct the "historical facts" of Hellenistic Judaism or the early church. Cohen seems to believe that it is actually possible to separate "fact" from "fiction." He fails to realize that every single sentence of

> Josephus is determined and coloured by his aims and tendencies. The raw historical data that can be isolated are usually without much interest. (1980: 241)

Rajak's review (1981) takes a quite different approach, arguing that Cohen is too skeptical of Josephus and that "Cohen despairs too readily of Josephus' story. . . . Cohen is hard on Josephus. Some of his just criticisms are taken too far" (252).

These represent three rather different positions taken by students of Josephus. Although specialists would accept the insight of even some of Moehring's most stringent comments, I think many of them in their actual work would tend to take a position more similar to that of Cohen—a cautious and critical use of Josephus's historical data to arrive at some sort of reasonable synthesis. Rajak's would seem a rather credulous approach, best exemplified in a statement made when trying to reconstruct Josephus's lineage: "While there are some features which are improbable, there are none which are impossible and, as long as what Josephus tells us is *possible*, we have no right to correct it" (16). This is a strange statement for a historian to make, because historical reconstruction is generally undertaken on the basis of what is probable, not what is possible. Although Rajak is not completely clear as to how her sweeping statement is to be taken—and perhaps it is meant to apply only to this very specific example—hers nevertheless is symbolic of a credulous approach, which reviewers have not been slow to point out. In contrast, in her detailed work Rajak can be quite critical of Josephus (e.g., 83, 89, 151), suggesting that some of her blanket statements should not be taken at face value.

Indeed, the sweeping, summary statement is perhaps the bane of Josephus scholarship. Josephus is—or is not—reliable. He is—or is not—a good historian. He is—or is not—this, that, and the other thing. Frequently, however, no such evaluation is possible, because the evaluation depends on which part of his work one has in mind. Josephus is perhaps typical of the Hellenistic historian—better than some and worse than others. Nevertheless, the dominant conclusion is that each section of his history must be examined on its own merits. Some sections will show him up extremely positively, whereas others would make historians hide their heads in shame. Therefore, to use Josephus effectively and critically, several general considerations should be kept in mind.

1. Parallel accounts should be compared and their differences carefully evaluated. It is not enough simply to synthesize them or to take the one that suits the immediate purpose. On the con-

trary, Josephus's aims and biases in each case must be carefully examined.

2. Josephus's underlying sources must always be considered. Although in many cases there is no way of knowing what these are, this is not always so. Even when not precisely known, the source's characteristics may indicate its credibility.
3. The general characteristics of ancient historiography must be taken into account. For example, it was common practice for historians to invent speeches for their characters, and it would be foolish to assume that a speech represents what was actually or even approximately said on a particular occasion.
4. Special care should be taken with passages clearly intended for apologetic purposes or which lend themselves to this use. In *Antiquities* and *Against Apion* Josephus is out to present the Jews in as favorable a light as possible, not only using—and misusing—a variety of older works but also molding his narrative according to the expectations of a Hellenistic audience. Thus, Jewish patriarchs become culture heroes, founders of civilizations, and examples of Hellenistic sages; Jewish laws are rationalized according to Greco-Roman sensibilities, and Jewish religion and custom are made the envy of the civilized world.
5. All other relevant historical and literary sources must be utilized: Roman historians, the Qumran writings, other early Jewish literature, rabbinic literature, archeology, and epigraphy. This may seem to be common sense, yet it is surprising how often Josephus is cited as a proof text for some point without considering the other sources available.

These are some of the general points that should be kept in mind; however, each particular section of Josephus has its own problems, uses, and tradition of scholarly interpretation. I examine these in more detail in the individual chapters for the periods in question.

1.1.3.4 Aids and Tools for Utilizing Josephus

Students of early Jewish history are well supplied with the scholarly tools for making use of Josephus's works. The LCL has not only the excellent translation and useful textual edition produced by Thackeray and his successors (Ralph Marcus, Allen Wikgren, Louis Feldman) but also many valuable notes and appendixes. The last volume also has one of the best indexes of any ancient work. The massive concordance to the Greek text has been completed under Rengstorf's editorship and forms an essential resource.

The secondary literature on Josephus is endless. The best of the shorter introductions to Josephus scholarship is the article by Attridge (see also Grabbe). Bilde provides a more detailed overview, which is especially valuable for its survey of current scholarship. Schreckenberg produced a chronological listing of publications since 1470, with symbols to indicate the subjects treated by the individual studies. Feldman has now come out with an annotated bibliography that not only summarizes much scholarship but also provides his own judgment on the merits of various studies (although one often finds occasion to disagree with Feldman's evaluation). The volumes edited by him and Hata give a useful critical overview of Josephus and many aspects of his writings. For other editions of the Greek text, as well as translations into English and many other modern languages, see the relevant chapters in Schreckenberg and Feldman.

1.1.4 Rabbinic Literature

1.1.4.1 Introductions for Students

Bowker, J. *The Targums and Rabbinic Literature* (1969).
Mielziner, M. *Introduction to the Talmud* (1968).
Neusner, J. *Invitation to the Talmud* (1973).
———. *Invitation to Midrash* (1989).
Strack, H. L. *Introduction to the Talmud and Midrash* (1931).
Strack, H. L., and G. Stemberger. *Introduction to the Talmud and Midrash* (1991).
Townsend, J. T. "Rabbinic Sources." *The Study of Judaism* (1972) 35–80.

Rabbinic literature comprises a vast body of writings, ranging from the Mishnah (completed ca. 200 C.E.) to medieval collections made a thousand years later. No attempt is made here to give an introduction to the literature as such. Those who would like to know about various rabbinic writings, their content, authorship, and dating should consult the standard reference works. The best introduction to date is Strack/Stemberger (see also Bowker and Townsend). Mielziner also gives an introduction to the talmudic literature (but not the midrashic) and discusses aspects of rabbinic hermeneutics. Neusner (1973) provides a hands-on approach by taking the student through the same passage in the Mishnah, Tosefta, and the two Talmuds, showing how the tradition and interpretative process develop. A similar textual approach is used in his 1989 volume on the Midrash.

1.1.4.2 Methodology in the Use of Rabbinic Literature

Neusner, J. *Development of a Legend* (1970).
———. *The Rabbinic Traditions about the Pharisees before 70* (1971).
———. *From Politics to Piety* (1973).
———. "The Formation of Rabbinic Judaism: Yavneh (Jamnia) from A.D. 70 to 100." *ANRW* 2 (1979) 19.2.3–42.
———. *Judaism: The Evidence of the Mishnah* (1981).
Saldarini, A. "'Form Criticism' of Rabbinic Literature." *JBL* 96 (1977) 257–74.
———. "Reconstructions of Rabbinic Judaism." *Early Judaism and Its Modern Interpreters* (1986) 437–77.

The traditio-historical study of rabbinic literature is still in its infancy. As little as two decades ago, some of the major methodological questions about the use of rabbinic literature for historical purposes had not been asked. Since that time there has been no less than a revolution in the subject, thanks primarily to Jacob Neusner. Since Neusner's pioneering study of Yohanan ben Zakkai in 1970, an enormous amount of work has been done on the methodological questions and a good foundation has been laid for traditio-historical matters. Even if the next generation finds much to critique and rethink, the value of what Neusner has done cannot be underestimated. He asked the right questions, pointed the way toward answers, laid the foundation on which to build, and singlehandedly changed the orientation of the entire field. No one attempting to use rabbinic literature for historical purposes can afford to ignore what has happened in the "Neusnerian revolution."

The basic problem tackled by Neusner was that rabbinic scholarship was essentially still at the pre-critical stage, somewhat as biblical study was two centuries ago. Much valuable work had been done on language, text, traditional commentary, and the like, but rabbinic literature was used in a fundamentalist fashion for historical study, as if writings of the Amoraic period (about 200–500 C.E.) could be used to find out what was happening during the Hasmonean period or even earlier. There was no concept of historical development, of the religious bias of the tradents (those who pass down the tradition), and of the fact that the rabbis were not generally interested in historical matters. It was assumed that the late talmudic literature could be cited to prove arguments about the Second Temple period many centuries earlier. Biblical scholars had long recognized that prooftexting was not a correct procedure, but rabbinic studies had received little benefit from the insights gained from biblical scholarship.

Not surprisingly, there has been considerable resistance to Neusner's work. Traditional scholars have found it difficult to understand what he is doing, just as biblical criticism was misunderstood two hundred years ago (and is still misunderstood in some conservative quarters). In addition, Neusner's methods have developed rapidly, which means that it is often difficult for the rabbinic scholar—not to mention the non-specialist—to keep up. Nevertheless, over the past two decades great progress has been made in the field, especially in North American scholarship but also among the younger generation in Germany and Great Britain. One may disagree with Neusner, but the debate can only be carried out on the foundation he has laid and according to the agenda he has set. Those who still choose to ignore his scholarship only damage their own credibility.

The critical study has shown that rabbinic literature has its own unique problems, which require new ways of applying the methodologies developed for other literatures. Most rabbinic writings represent a conglomeration of material from widely differing periods of time. For example, a rabbi of the fifth century C.E. might be cited next to one of the first century, as if they were contemporaries carrying on a debate. To the believing Jew this was no problem, because religious study did not require any attention to historical development. To the historian, however, it is important to distinguish between sayings from different periods and different sources. The fact that Hillel (an older contemporary of Jesus), for instance, is alleged in the Babylonian Talmud to have said something for which we have no information in earlier sources should raise questions for historical study. How can one be sure that this saying is accurate? Was it preserved by oral tradition and recorded only many centuries later, as some will argue? Or is it really only a late invention—a pious fraud—that may have religious value but tells us nothing about the historical Hillel?

Form criticism, which has been so useful in understanding the development of tradition in biblical literature, has not produced the hoped-for results in rabbinic study, although it has made a contribution (see Saldarini 1977; Saldarini 1986). Although often labeled "form critical," Neusner's method is actually different from the form criticism traditionally practiced by biblical scholars. Because of the special nature of rabbinic literature, he has had to develop new methods and new approaches; those that seemed promising at an earlier stage have in some cases become problematic or in need of alteration. Thus despite the extremely rapid progress made in the past two decades, the present efforts can still be considered pioneering. For this reason, my use of rabbinic literature will, for the most part, be extremely sparse and skeptical of anything before the first century C.E. In contrast, in certain areas (e.g., the development of the Pharisees) rabbinic literature can provide some useful information if used carefully. As will become clear, I am heavily dependent for this information on the work of Neusner, his students, and other scholars who apply historical-critical methods.

Because of Neusner's vast output, as well as the work of others following in his footsteps, it is impossible to give a complete bibliography here. Some of the more important summaries, especially as they relate to the Second Temple period, are listed above. Individual studies are listed at appropriate points in the subsequent chapters; see especially 8.1 and 9.4.6.

1.2 A SOCIOECONOMIC OVERVIEW

Archer, L. J. *Her Price Is beyond Rubies* (1990).

Atkinson, K.T.M. "A Hellenistic Land-Conveyance: The Estate of Mnesimachus in the Plain of Sardis." *Historia* 21 (1972) 45–74.

Ben-David, A. *Talmudische Ökonomie* (1974).

Briant, P. *Rois, tributs et paysans* (1982).

Broshi, M. "La population de l'ancienne Jérusalem." *RB* 82 (1975) 5–14.

———. "Estimating the Population of Ancient Jerusalem." *BAR* 4, no. 3 (June 1978) 10–15.

Broughton, T.R.S. "Roman Asia Minor." *An Economic Survey of Ancient Rome* (1938) 4.499–916.

Byatt, A. "Josephus and Population Numbers in First-Century Palestine." *PEQ* 105 (1973) 51–60.

Carlo, Z. "Patterns of Mobility among Ancient Near Eastern Craftsmen." *JNES* 42 (1983) 245–64.

Dalman, G. *Arbeit und Sitte in Palästina* (1928–42).

Dandamaev, M. A. *Slavery in Babylonia* (1984).

Dandamaev, M. A., and V. G. Lukonin. *The Culture and Social Institutions of Ancient Iran* (1989).

Davies, J. K. "Cultural, Social and Economic Features of the Hellenistic World." *CAH*[2] (1984) 7.1.257–320.

Diakonov, I. M., ed. *Ancient Mesopotamia* (1969).

Dunn, S. P. *The Fall and Rise of the Asiatic Mode of Production* (1982).

Finley, M. I. *The Ancient Economy* (1985).

Frank, T., ed. *An Economic Survey of Ancient Rome* (1933–40).

Freyne, S. *Galilee from Alexander the Great to Hadrian* (1980).

Garnsey, P., ed. *Non-slave Labour in the Greco-Roman World* (1980).

Garnsey, P., and R. Saller. *The Roman Empire: Economy, Society, and Culture* (1987).

Garnsey, P., and C. R. Whittaker, eds. *Trade and Famine in Classical Antiquity* (1983).

Garnsey, P., et al., eds. *Trade in the Ancient Economy* (1983).

Hamel, G. *Poverty and Charity in Roman Palestine* (1990).

Harper, G. M. "Village Administration in the Roman Province of Syria." *YCS* 1 (1928) 105–68.

Heichelheim, F. M. "Roman Syria." *An Economic Survey of Ancient Rome* (1938) 4.121–257.
Henry, K. H. "Land Tenure in the Old Testament." *PEQ* 86 (1954) 5–15.
Hopkins, K. "Taxes and Trade in the Roman Empire (200 B.C.–A.D. 400)." *JRS* 70 (1980) 101–25.
Horsley, R. A. *Jesus and the Spiral of Violence* (1987).
Kippenberg, H. G. *Religion und Klassenbildung im antiken Judäa* (1982).
Krader, L. *The Asiatic Mode of Production* (1975).
Krauss, S. *Talmudische Archäologie* (1910–11).
Kreissig, H. *Die sozialökonomische Situation in Juda zur Achämenidenzeit* (1973).
———. "Landed Property in the 'Hellenistic Orient.'" *Eirene* 15 (1977a) 5–26.
———. "Tempelland, Katoiken, Hierodulen im Seleukidenreich." *Klio* 59 (1977b) 375–80.
———. *Wirtschaft und Gesellschaft im Seleukidenreich* (1978).
Mayer, G. *Die jüdische Frau in der hellenistisch-römischen Antiken* (1987).
Momigliano, A. "M. I. Rostovtzeff." *Studies in Historiography* (1966) 91–104.
O'Leary, B. *The Asiatic Mode of Production* (1989).
Reinhold, M. "Historian of the Classic World: A Critique of Rostovtzeff." *Science and Society* 10 (1946) 361–91.
Rostovtzeff, M. *The Social and Economic History of the Roman Empire* (1926).
———. *The Social and Economic History of the Hellenistic World* (1941).
Ste. Croix, G.E.M. de. *The Class Struggle in the Ancient Greek World* (1981).
Svencickaja, I. S. "Some Problems of Agrarian Relations in the Province of Asia." *Eirene* 15 (1977) 27–54.
Welwei, K. W. "Abhängige Landbevölkerungen auf <<Tempelterritorien>> im hellenistischen Kleinasien und Syrien." *Ancient Society* 10 (1979) 97–118.
Whittaker, C. R. "Rural Labour in Three Roman Provinces." *Non-slave Labour in the Greco-Roman World* (1980) 73–99.
Will, E. "Pour une 'Anthropologie coloniale' du Monde hellénistique." *The Craft of the Ancient Historian* (1985) 273–301.
Will, E., et al. *Le monde grec et l'Orient* (1975) 2.495–565.

1.2.1 Introduction and Bibliographical Guide

Most chapters have a socioeconomic section, which will discuss the situation in Judah and any relevant background for that period. The overview here is presupposed in the discussions in individual chapters.

The socioeconomic history of the ancient Near East is a sufficiently new inquiry that literature exists only in scattered form; there is no good synthetic history for the area on which to draw, although there have been some studies of individual periods or regions. A further problem is that any study must cut across a number of individual specialties. For example, the well-known monograph by Finley is restricted to the Greco-Roman sources. A number of the studies by Orientalists focus on earlier times, although sometimes their information has value for the Persian and Greek periods as well (e.g., Diakonov). For the Persian period, the study by Dandamaev/Lukonin gives a good basic overview. A variety of studies cover the Hellenistic period. Davies gives a useful survey with extensive bibliography (see also Will, et al.). Still fundamental is Rostovtzeff (1941), which is less dominated by his theory of capitalism than is his earlier work on the Roman Empire (1926; for an evaluation of his work overall, see Momigliano and Reinhold). Kreissig (1978), writing from a Marxist perspective, has been heavily criticized but has relevant material if used carefully; see also Briant. Garnsey/Saller gives a helpful survey for the Roman Empire. Still very useful despite its age is the multivolume work edited by Frank. Even though it concentrates on the Roman Empire, it often cites inscriptions and other sources from earlier periods and even discusses them for background.

A number of individual studies are available on Judah, although they are usually for the Roman or later periods. An important problem concerns the value of information in the talmudic and later sources. However, because these usually reflect the life and customs contemporary with the writers and because there had often been a strong continuity of day-to-day life from earlier centuries, it seems legitimate to draw on information from the later sources—if done with care—in a way not justified when it comes to political history (cf. Hamel: 4–6). Therefore, Dalman's massive study, which derived information even from the customs of Palestinian Arabs in the early twentieth century, still has considerable value if used critically, as does Krauss. More recent works include Ben-David and Hamel.

In recent years historians in many disciplines have given increasing attention to cultural, social, and economic factors and to the lives of ordinary men and women. These not only constitute an aspect of history in their own right but also are important factors in historical change (some would say the primary factors in historical change). This volume concentrates on political and religious developments, partly because these are still likely to be the main concerns of the book's readership and partly because so much still needs to be done in the socioeconomic area. Nevertheless, I attempt to discuss and take account of socioeconomic matters to a greater extent than has occurred before. Some might argue that these should be the dominant concern, but there are difficulties with attempting a socioeconomic history of Judah at this stage of scholarly study. As several scholars have pointed out (Finley: 17–34; Garnsey; Hopkins; Garnsey/Whittaker), there are formidable obstacles to extracting economic and sociological data from the sources. The sort of information available in ancient sources does not lend itself to statistical analysis, and there is a constant danger of ignoring the limits of the extant data. We usually know very little even when there appears to be abundant detail. Many interpretations are often possible, and much depends on one's starting point and interests or prejudices. For example, it is often asserted how much the people hated Herod the Great and how hard he made life for the Jews; yet the available data can and, in some cases, probably should be synthesized in a completely different light (6.3.7; 6.4.9.5). There are reasons to think that the average Jew in Palestine was better off in the later part of Herod's reign than before or after. Moreover, the question of people's like or dislike of a person is extremely difficult to quantify.

Much is often built on assumptions about the tax burden on the average person. One comes across statements in literature on the Old Testament, New Testament, or Judaism about how difficult things were because of the crushing taxes. This was no doubt true for some and may well have been true for many, but it is hard to estimate. We do not actually know in most cases what taxes were paid, what percentage of income they made up, whether they were in coin or kind, and how much they impinged on day-to-day living. No one welcomes taxes, and most people complain about them at some time or other, but to what extent taxes actually make people's lives a misery is not easy to quantify. What we would call abject poverty seems to have been widely accepted in antiquity, and circumstances other than poverty or wealth may have been a more important factor in discontent or acquiescence (cf. Hamel: 94–101).

Demography is another area in which it is difficult to obtain reliable statistics (Davies: 264–69). One of the few apparently credible pieces of information is the population of Egypt, known from several sources and possibly based on actual census information. Nevertheless, most such numbers, whether population figures (cf. Broshi 1975, 1978 v. Byatt) or the size of armies (cf. 5.4.4), are very unreliable. In a striking example, Finley notes how even so careful a historian as Thucydides gives a figure for the number of escaped slaves when he could have had no properly recorded count (24). Any statistical data extracted from literary sources are generally suspect.

Therefore, despite recent studies of merit, it is doubtful whether an economic history of Judea could be written from the data currently known. This is not a problem peculiar to Jewish history; it extends to much of antiquity. Because of the same absence of data, it is not usually possible to say much about the average man in antiquity, much less the average woman (cf. Mayer; Archer). Individuals named in the sources are usually the wealthy or the powerful, most frequently men but sometimes women. We have a few striking accounts about queens and a few other highly placed women, but the occasional find about an ordinary person, such as the archive of the first-century Jewish woman Babatha (9.2.4.2), is as rare as it is precious.

The general comments that follow provide a context and overview for the discussion in the individual chapters.

1.2.2 The Ancient Near East

The economy of this period was agrarian, whether one has in mind the Achaemenid or the Roman empire. Trade played an important role in each period, but it was always secondary to farming. Despite some technological developments through the centuries, work on the land changed little in the Near East (and in much of the Mediterranean world) over several millennia. Farming methods were primitive and labor-intensive, yielding only a small surplus on average. The vast majority of the population was employed in agrarian activities, and most wealth derived from the land. Those who were well-off (a small minority) almost always derived their wealth from land holdings. Even those few who made their fortune from mercantile activities usually invested it in land rather than reinvesting in trade (Garnsey/Saller: 44–45). This is naturally a simplified picture, but the overall truth of it must be kept in mind in any socio-economic discussion. Most people lived at a subsistence level and would be considered by modern standards to live in grinding poverty. Whether men or women, we know little about them. There was no middle class to speak of, only the vast numbers of the poor and the tiny few of the rich. The difference in wealth between the upper class and the masses was enormous, whatever differences there were between individuals within each class.

The economy of the Greco-Roman world has often been contrasted with that of the ancient Near East. It is regularly affirmed that the economies of both ancient Greece and ancient Rome were slave-based, meaning that slave labor was the prime productive force in all areas of the economy, whether farming, building, shipping, or mining. The Athenian or Italian smallholder might work alongside his slaves, but it was still normal to have them. In contrast to this, in most of the ancient Near East (whether in the Persian, the Hellenistic, or the Roman period), the basis of production was allegedly that of the "free" peasant, who farmed land, whether privately owned or not, by means of his own labor and that of his family. The peasant was free only in relative terms, because he was bound to the soil by tradition and by the requirements of taxation and corvée labor, but he was not a slave to be sold or disposed of according to the whim of a master.

This type of economy is often referred to as the "Asiatic mode of production." In this system the basis of production was the village and its inhabitants, who engaged chiefly in subsistence farming (Krader: 286–96; O'Leary: 16–18). What little commodity trade existed was, by and large, for immediate local consumption, without significant division of labor; that is, each village had crafts workers who made certain essential products, but they were generally individual workers producing for local needs, not for distant export. Production may (although not necessarily) have made considerable use of irrigation systems ("hydraulic technology"). The small agricultural surplus was extracted by the ruling class (more or less the state officialdom) through taxes and forced labor on behalf of the state. The ruling class usually centered on an absolute monarch, who ruled with the help of the nobility (often referred to as "Oriental despotism"). The concepts of both capital investment and private property were only weakly developed. Land was usually worked on a family and community level, rather than privately. Indeed, in theory the land belonged to the king, but regardless of who was thought to own the land, the villagers had no choice about the payment of taxes and other dues such as corvée labor. There was no large merchant class.

This concept of production originated with Marx and Engels and has been debated especially in Marxist circles often dominated by ideological or political concerns (cf. Dunn). It is not my purpose to enter this debate as such, except as it relates to our immediate concern. Whether or not they use the actual term, however, many scholars have accepted a concept along the lines of the Asiatic mode of production. Although the recent critique of O'Leary is fundamental, his own conclusions are a bit unclear, partly because his ultimate aim is to evaluate the viability of the thesis of historical materialism. The specific empirical test he applies is that of Indian history, and he concludes that the Asiatic mode of production does not stand up in that case. Nevertheless, he seems to allow that it may be valid for other areas:

> Relatively centralized and autonomous pre-industrial state structures, capable of considerable fiscal exploitation of administratively subordinated urban settlements and corporate agrarian village communities, were features in some pre-industrial socio-political landscapes. (234; see 331)

Few historians have written on the economic and social history of Persia, but two who have argue on the basis of the Asiatic mode of production (Briant; Kreissig in various publications). The perplexities involved are indicated by O'Leary's actual defense of Briant and Kreissig against the attack of another Marxist historian, G. de Ste. Croix (O'Leary: 231–33; de Ste. Croix: 29, 155–56, 544 n.15). His criticisms of de Ste. Croix suggest that he might accept something not too different from the Asiatic mode of production for portions of the ancient Near East in the Persian and Hellenistic periods.

However, broad agreement with the thesis of an Asiatic mode of production does not require that it be embraced dogmatically or in all its detail. The situation was complex in both the Greco-Roman world and the East. A fundamental point is that the economies of Greece and Rome were not actually slave-based. Although both made considerable use of slaves, this was mainly in the domestic realm and in specialized forms of labor. The backbone of the economy, however, was still the free farmer or worker. There were *latifundia* (large, slave-worked estates) in both the Hellenistic and Roman worlds, but despite the attention given to these, they were not the major producers (Finley: 70–71, 179; Whittaker: 77–79).

In both the eastern and the western parts of the Mediterranean world, agrarian laborers ran the spectrum from chattel-slaves to free peasants. Slavery was characteristic of the Babylonian area, several other cultural centers of Persia, and perhaps many of the Greek areas of Asia Minor (Dandamaev/Lukonin: 152–77; cf. de Ste. Croix: 155–56). Nevertheless, even here the economy was not primarily slave-based: slave labor did not play the leading role in these economies and slaves were not widely used in agricultural work on large estates, whether of landowners or the king (Dandamaev: 649–52, 660–61). Furthermore, although some crafts workers were slaves (e.g., weavers), most were free individuals but usually palace dependents, thus comparable to serfs in the agrarian area (Carlo).

In most areas dependent labor was the norm; such workers were commonly referred to as *laoi* ("peoples"), although other terms were used, not always with a clear delineation (Whittaker: 83–86; Briant: 114–16). The main conclusion to be drawn is that a great variety of such dependent labor was in existence (Kreissig 1977a; Briant: 95–135; Davies: 300–301; Whittaker: 83–84). Part of the reason for the variety was the different types of estates; for example, those on temple estates may have had a different status from those on royal land (Welwei; Kreissig 1977b). However, the legal question was often less important than the reality (Davies: 296–97; Hamel: 152): land held in long-term tenancy often came into de facto ownership (especially with cleruchy land), whereas those legally free were often tied to the soil by custom, debt, and other factors (Whittaker: 84–89).

Throughout this period the ancient Near East was more or less dominated by what in modern terms would be called "colonial powers." Still, relatively little seems to have been done so far in drawing on modern sociological studies of colonialism, although Will indicates how fruitful such studies could be (see also Horsley). A colonial power has two main interests: taxes and military service. Although it would probably be wrong to claim that the dominant power had no concern for the welfare of those ruled, their well-being was not a high priority. Therefore, there was not a great impetus to invest in the subordinate peoples and nations of the empire. They were treated simply as milk cows, producers of wealth for the ruling power. Reasonable relations had to be maintained with the local administration, which was often made up of the native elite. Particular institutions, such as cities and temples, were frequently honored (e.g., Athens), and there were also building projects such as cities, harbors, aqueducts, and roads. Nevertheless, the colonial power usually benefited most, if not solely, from these projects.

Still, the picture is not clear-cut. The entire Roman economy was underdeveloped (Garnsey/Saller: 43–44, 41–52), and even more were the economies of the Persian and Hellenistic kingdoms. The importance of major investment was evidently not realized at the time. If the Roman government did not invest in the provinces and client states, neither did it invest in Italy and Rome. The administration found it convenient to provide certain public works in Rome itself, as well as to supply a corn dole and public spectacles to keep the masses from rioting, but this seems to have been the extent of public economic planning (Garnsey/Saller: 56).

1.2.3 Judah

The ultimate issue for our purposes is the situation prevailing in Judah. This is dealt with in the individual chapters, but some brief general comments can be made here. The situation in Judah was similar to that elsewhere in the ancient Near East under Persian, Greek, and Roman rule. The country was a small, subordinate state most of the time, paying its required tribute but otherwise carrying on at a fairly mediocre level economically and culturally. It was not a wealthy country. Its economy was heavily agrarian; Jerusalem was the only real urban area. There were major cities in the region, which participated strongly in the economic and cultural advantages of the ruling empire (especially the Greek foundations after Alexander), but few if any Jews lived in these. Only with the "Hellenistic reform" were attempts made to benefit from the advantages of the dominant culture in a systematic way.

The subject of land ownership is interesting. The Israelite tradition was that land was a heritage to be passed down from father to son and not to be alienated from the family, except perhaps temporarily (Lev 25:13-28). This theological theory seems not to have worked always in practice, because we know of "king's land" (1 Sam 8:14; Freyne: 156–59; 7.3.10), the sale of property (cf. 9.2.4.2), ownership by priests (4.4.5), and the like, which were not envisaged by Old Testament law (Henry). Nevertheless, it seems that at least at the beginning of the Second Temple period, most Jews in the Land of Israel worked their own soil (with the help only of their families) for essentially a subsistence living (cf. Freyne: 165–66). This conclusion arises from the lists in Ezra and Nehemiah that show the people settled on ancestral property (2.2.1.5.1). By contrast, we are left largely in the dark about what happened to those who had continued to live in Judah during the exile and had taken over land vacated by those in captivity. Furthermore, even at an early stage some Judeans were having difficulties and perhaps losing their property (Nehemiah 5; 2.3.13.2).

It is often asserted that with time the wealthy accumulated property, especially by making loans and then depriving of their land the poor who defaulted. The result is said to have been the concentration of land in the large estates of these wealthy people. No doubt there is some truth in this, because the desire of those with wealth was usually to acquire land. If problems had already arisen in the early Persian period, it is not difficult to imagine a gradual alienation of the land from its traditional ownership. This charge of land alienation, however, is often made for a wide range of times and regions, yet not necessarily with clear evidence (cf. the example of Italy in Garnsey/Saller: 58–63). Wealth could be lost as well as gained. Long-term tenancy does not seem to have been too different in practice from actual ownership of the land (Hamel: 158–60). The general picture of the peasantry is that it remained the same over many centuries. There may have been a time in which alienation of the land from the peasants was an acute problem in Judah, but this is difficult to quantify. If such a thing happened, it was probably in the decades preceding the 66–70 revolt (7.3.10). In the final analysis, however, there are insufficient data to come to more than the most tentative conclusions.

An associated issue concerns population numbers. It is not infrequently stated that problems were caused because the Jewish population had increased to such an extent that there was not enough land (cf. Freyne: 196–97). Estimating populations is extremely difficult, however, and is often based on dubious data and interpretations (e.g., Byatt). More recent studies have generally seen a lower population figure than the one to two million (or more) often cited (Broshi 1975, 1978; Hamel: 137–40). We really do not know whether land was scarce compared to population size.

As a result of various conquests, many Jews became slaves. The selling of free persons as slaves seems to have been a problem during Ptolemaic rule (4.2.7.3; 5.2.14.1). There was also the sale of a defeated city during some of the revolts (e.g., 2 Macc 5:14). When Judea came under Roman rule, many Jews were sold as slaves in Rome itself after several incidents (7.3.4). Because of general Roman policy and practice, however, their descendants were often freed after a generation or so and contributed to the vigorous growth of the Diaspora. Furthermore, Jews were also slaveowners. The Old Testament allows Jews to work off a debt by temporary enslavement—or, perhaps more accurately, by bond servitude—to other Jews. There are also indications that some Jews possessed (gentile?) slaves, although we do not have much data on this (Ben Sira 33:24–31).

These comments apply generally to Jewish history. There were some periods that saw considerable change, especially the rise of the Hasmonean state, the initial period of Roman rule, and the reign of Herod the Great. The implications of these are discussed in individual chapters.

2 THE PERSIAN PERIOD

2.1 BIBLIOGRAPHICAL GUIDE

Ackroyd, P. R. *Exile and Restoration* (1968).
———. *I and II Chronicles, Ezra, Nehemiah* (1973).
———. "Historical Problems of the Early Achaemenian Period." *Orient* 20 (1984) 1–15.
———. "Problems in the Handling of Biblical and Related Sources in the Achaemenid Period." *Achaemenid History* (1988) 3.33–54.
Batten, L. W. *A Critical and Exegetical Commentary on Ezra and Nehemiah* (1913).
Blenkinsopp, J. *Ezra-Nehemiah* (1989).
Boyce, M. *A History of Zoroastrianism* (1975–).
CAH[2]. Vol. 4: *Persia, Greece and the Western Mediterranean c. 525 to 479 B.C.* (1988).
CHI. Vol. 2: *The Median and Achaemenian Periods* (1985).
CHJ. Vol. 1: *The Persian Period* (1984).
Clines, D.J.A. *Ezra, Nehemiah, Esther* (1984).
Cook, J. M. *The Persian Empire* (1983).
Cowley, A. *Aramaic Papyri of the Fifth Century B.C.* (1923).
Dandamaev, M. A. *Persien unter den ersten Achämeniden (6. Jahrhundert v. Chr.)* (1976).
———. *A Political History of the Achaemenid Empire* (1989).
Dandamaev, M. A., and V. G. Lukonin. *The Culture and Social Institutions of Ancient Iran* (1989).
Eskenazi, T. C. *In an Age of Prose: A Literary Approach to Ezra-Nehemiah* (1988a).
———. "The Structure of Ezra-Nehemiah and the Integrity of the Book." *JBL* 107 (1988b) 641–56.
Frye, R. N. *History of Ancient Iran* (1984).
Galling, K. *Studien zur Geschichte Israels im persischen Zeitalter* (1964).
Grabbe, L. L. Review of *Persia and the Bible*, by E. M. Yamauchi. *JSJ* (1991).
Gunneweg, A.H.J. "Zur Interpretation der Bücher Esra-Nehemiah: Zugleich ein Beitrag zur Methode der Exegese." *VTSup* 32 (1981) 146–61.

———. *Esra* (1985).
———. *Nehemiah* (1987).
Hornblower, S. *The Greek World 479–323 B.C.* (1983).
In der Smitten, W. T. *Esra: Quellen, Überlieferung und Geschichte* (1973).
Kellermann, U. *Nehemia: Quellen, Überlieferung und Geschichte* (1967).
Kuhrt, A., and H. Sancisi-Weerdenburg, eds. *Achaemenid History.* Vol. 3: *Method and Theory* (1988).
Lebram, L.C.H. "Die Traditionsgeschichte der Ezragestalt und die Frage nach dem historischen Esra." *Achaemenid History* (1987) 1.103–38.
Meyer, E. *Die Entstehung des Judenthums* (1896).
Mowinckel, S. *Studien zu dem Buche Ezra-Nehemiah.* Vol. 1 (1964); Vol. 2 (1964); Vol. 3 (1965).
Noth, M. *The Chronicler's History* (1987).
Olmstead, A. T. *History of the Persian Empire* (1948).
Rudolph, W. *Ezra und Nehemia* (1949).
Sancisi-Weerdenburg, H., ed. *Achaemenid History.* Vol. 1: *Sources, Structures and Synthesis* (1987).
Sancisi-Weerdenburg, H., and A. Kuhrt, eds. *Achaemenid History.* Vol. 2: *The Greek Sources* (1987).
Stern, E. *Material Culture of the Land of the Bible in the Persian Period 538–332 B.C.* (1982).
Torrey, C. C. *The Composition and Historical Value of Ezra-Nehemiah* (1896).
———. *Ezra Studies* (1910).
Widengren, G. "The Persian Period." *Israelite and Judaean History* (1977) 489–538.
Williamson, H.G.M. *Ezra, Nehemiah* (1985).
———. *Ezra and Nehemiah* (1987).
Yamauchi, E. M. *Persia and the Bible* (1990).

Because much of the current discussion about the history of Judah centers on the books of Ezra and Nehemiah, recent major commentaries are included here (Ackroyd; Blenkinsopp; Clines; Gunneweg; Williamson), as well as some of the important older ones (Batten; Rudolph). On the literary structure and composition of the books, see Eshkenazi (1988a; 1988b). There are also a number of specialized monographs, studies, and collections (Ackroyd 1968; Galling; In der Smitten; Kellermann; Lebram; Meyer; Mowinckel; Torrey). Some of these encompass several areas and are frequently cited in this chapter. Yamauchi contains much useful information, although he takes a fundamentalist view of the biblical literature (see Grabbe).

Background history is also quite important for the Persian period, especially because Persian history in general is often as problematic as the specific history of Judah. The volume in *CAH* is very useful, with extensive bibliography. Unfortunately, the first volume of *CHJ* is rather disappointing. Although it has some very good articles, there seems not to have been much editorial control, so that articles are not always well integrated with one another. More importantly, most of them were a decade old when the volume appeared and were thus already well out-of-date in some areas. A useful overview is given by Widengren. On Persian history of this time, the older work of Olmstead is perhaps still the most extensive; however, it needs correcting in light of more recent studies (Cook; Dandamaev; Frye). Social, economic, and cultural issues are treated by Dandamaev/Lukonin. Hornblower gives a good survey of Greek history. The standard history of Zoroastrianism is by Boyce.

2.2 SOURCES

2.2.1 Old Testament

Childs, B. S. *Introduction to the Old Testament as Scripture* (1979).
Clines, D.J.A. *Job 1–20* (1989).
Eissfeldt, O. *The Old Testament: An Introduction* (1965).
Fohrer, G. *Introduction to the Old Testament* (1968).
Hurvitz, A. "Dating the Priestly Source in Light of the Historical Study of Biblical Hebrew: A Century after Wellhausen." *ZAW* 100 *Supplement* (1988) 88–100.
Knight, D. A., and G. M. Tucker, eds. *The Hebrew Bible and Its Modern Interpreters* (1985).
Pope, M. *Job* (1973).
Soggin, J. A. *Introduction to the Old Testament* (1989).
Whybray, R. N. *The Making of the Pentateuch* (1987).

A good deal of the Old Testament potentially dates from the Persian period, in either its composition or its editing. The problem is determining what of the vast amount of possible material belongs to this time. It is the task of the historian not to pass judgment on the many debates by biblical scholars but to make use of what can reasonably be used for historical purposes, recognizing that future study may reduce or add to the pool of sources. Thus, for example, many scholars would date the "Priestly source" (P) to the Persian period for its editing and even its composition. The problems for the historian are that (1) not a few scholars today would reject a P document as such (Whybray: 108–11; Knight/Tucker: 285–86), and (2) some of those who accept it are now arguing that it is a pre-exilic composition (e.g., Hurvitz). Another example is Job, which some have used to cast light on socioeconomic conditions in the Persian period (2.3.13). Although many would date the composition of the work to post-exilic times, others argue that the major part of the poetic section is pre-exilic, even if the present form of the book might be later (cf. Pope: XXXII–XL). As for the prophetic corpus, many passages of the pre-exilic prophets are thought to be post-exilic additions. Most of these represent small blocks of material, and the questions of editing and dating may still be controversial. Therefore, it has not been thought useful for the most part to depend on this material. The decision of which sources to use is necessarily subjective; nevertheless, my choice of what to include would command a good deal of agreement, even if what is left out might be more controversial.

For further information on the individual writings, the student should consult critical introductions (e.g., Childs; Soggin; Fohrer), the recent volume edited by Knight/Tucker, and encyclopedic works such as *IDB* and *EJ*.

2.2.1.1 Books of Ezra and Nehemiah

Japhet, S. "Sheshbazzar and Zerubbabel—Against the Background of the Historical and Religious Tendencies of Ezra-Nehemiah." *ZAW* 94 (1982) 66–98; 95 (1983) 218–30.

McConville, J. G. "Ezra-Nehemiah and the Fulfilment of Prophecy." *VT* 36 (1986) 205–24.

Mallau, H. H. "The Redaction of Ezra 4–6: A Plea for a Theology of Scribes." *Perspectives in Religious Studies* 15 (1988) 67–80.

Williamson, H.G.M. "The Composition of Ezra i–vi." *JTS* 34 (1983) 1–30.

Note: The commentaries and some monographs are listed in 2.1, above.

The books of Ezra and Nehemiah are important sources for the history of the Jewish people in the Persian period. A large part of each book is in narrative form, and there is the prima facie impression of considerable history. A closer examination shows that matters are much more complicated. The books themselves are a composite, drawing on several sources with different degrees of trustworthiness. Of prime interest is the "Nehemiah Memorial" (2.2.1.3), but other sources include the books of Haggai and Zechariah (2.2.1.6.1) and various lists that are quoted at length in several places in the books. More controversial are the "Aramaic source" and alleged Persian documents in Ezra 1–7 (2.2.1.2) and the "Ezra source" in Ezra 7–10 and Nehemiah 8 (2.2.1.4).

These and other problems mean that the different sections of the books are not of equal value for the historian. For example, Ezra 1–6 gives a narrative which professes to tell us a good deal about the history of Jerusalem during the initial return and rebuilding of the temple, between about 539 and 515. Some of the documents quoted actually speak of a later period, however, and much of the entire narrative is suspect. For example, Williamson has argued that the author of these chapters had only the books of Haggai and Zechariah, the list of Nehemiah 7, and some Persian documents—the rest of the narrative being the composition of the later editor. If so, much of the narrative has no independent value for trying to write the history of the early Persian period.

Therefore, it is widely agreed that the narrative sections of Ezra and Nehemiah are the product of a later age, although they attempt to put into context a variety of earlier material and documents. Until recently the scholarly consensus was that the framework of the two books was the responsibility of "the Chronicler," who also composed the books of 1 and 2 Chronicles. This consensus has now been challenged and can no longer be accepted as a basis from which to work without further justification (2.2.1.8). The question is how much later the narrative sections, primarily Ezra 1–6 but also sections of Nehemiah 8–12 (and Ezra 7–10, in the opinion of some [2.2.1.4]), were written, and how reliable is the picture drawn in them.

According to Japhet, the apparent historical account of events in the narrative sections is illusory. Not only did the author(s) write long after the events occurred, but they also had particular objectives that resulted in a rather tendentious account. Her major points include:

1. The narrative sections (as opposed to source material such as the Nehemiah Memorial and Haggai-Zechariah) give no titles to the major protagonists. Such figures as Sheshbazzar, Zerubbabel, and Nehemiah are not called "governor" in the editorial material, even though we know from the source material and the prophecies of Zechariah and Haggai that this title was applied to them. Even Joshua is not called "high priest" in the narrative sections.
2. The editor has "democratized" the account; that is, there is a de-emphasis on individual leaders and a particular stress placed on the activities of groups (such as "the elders of Judah") or the whole community ("with all the people," "the Jews," "with his brethren").
3. The inferred aim of the editor is that all good gifts come eventually from the Persian administration and that desires for independence and a native king are misplaced. In other words, the author sees the way of the future in close cooperation with the Persian authorities and in doing nothing to challenge their rule or antagonize them.
4. Although emphasis is placed on the communal work of the people, there is a tendency to pair those leaders named in the text (Zerubbabel and Joshua; Ezra and Nehemiah). This could help explain why Sheshbazzar has tended to drop out of the narrative, because he does not easily fit this grouping.

5. The tendency of the text is made clearer when contrasted with later versions of the tradition in 1 Esdras and Josephus. These later accounts incline toward the glorification of individuals, especially Zerubbabel (who becomes the restorer par excellence of Judah).

It is generally agreed that this editor was working long after the time of Zerubbabel, although precise dating remains controversial. Japhet sees no reason to place him later than the first quarter of the fourth century (1982: 89 n.55). Although Williamson argues that the final editor could not have worked earlier than the Hellenistic period, he assumes that the high priests given in Nehemiah 12 extend as far as the time of Alexander (*1985: xxxv–xxxvi). Those who see the final editor as the Chronicler must take into account the books of Chronicles in trying to date Ezra and Nehemiah. Most scholars would agree that the editor had little information other than the actual documents and sources quoted in his account (cf. *Williamson 1985: xxiii–xxiv). If so, the details of events are deductions or inventions and mislead rather than help. Most also agree that the narrative in Ezra 3–6 is very confused in its present form. Documents from the time of Xerxes and Artaxerxes are quoted in reference to the situation in the early years of Darius I, long before their time (Ezra 4:4-24). It is difficult to see this as just a literary convention on the part of the author, who actually knew the correct order of Achaemenid kings (*Williamson 1985: 56–59; *Blenkinsopp: 105–6), because the later documents are cited as the cause of the cessation of the building.

2.2.1.2 The "Aramaic Source" and Alleged Persian Documents in Ezra

Blenkinsopp, J. "The Sage, the Scribe, and Scribalism in the Chronicler's Work." *The Sage in Israel and the Ancient Near East* (1990) 307–15.
Bickerman, E. J. "The Edict of Cyrus in Ezra 1." *Studies in Jewish and Christian History* (1976) 1.72–108.
Galling, K. "Die Proclamation des Kyros in Esra 1." *Studien* (1964) 61–77.
Grabbe, L. L. "Reconstructing History from the Book of Ezra." *Studies in the Second Temple: The Persian Period* (1991) 98–107.
Gunneweg, A.H.J. "Die aramäische und die hebräische Erzählung über die nachexilische Restauration—ein Vergleich." *ZAW* 94 (1982) 299–302.
Hensley, L. V. *The Official Persian Documents in the Book of Ezra* (1977).
Hout, M. van den. "Studies in Early Greek Letter-Writing." *Mnemosyne*. Series 4, vol. 2 (1949) 19–41, 138–53, esp. 144–52.
In der Smitten, W. T. "Historische Probleme zum Kyrosedikt und zum Jerusalemer Tempelbau von 515." *Persica* 6 (1972–74) 167–78.
Mallau, H. H. "The Redaction of Ezra 4–6: A Plea for a Theology of Scribes." *Perspectives in Religious Studies* 15 (1988) 67–80.

Schaeder, H. H. *Iranische Beiträge*. Vol. 1 (1930).
Vaux, R. de. "The Decrees of Cyrus and Darius on the Rebuilding of the Temple." *Bible and the Ancient Near East* (1971) 63–96.

A number of documents are quoted in Ezra, either partially or at length. All purport to be either the records of official decrees by the Persian king or letters written by Persian government officials. Most are in Aramaic (Ezra 4:11-16, 17-22; 5:7-17; 6:3-5, 6-12; 7:12-26), although one is in Hebrew (Ezra 1:2-4). It should be noted, however, that all the Aramaic documents but one (Ezra 7:12-26) are set in an Aramaic narrative. This is why many scholars have postulated that the author used an Aramaic source which already contained the documents (*Torrey 1896: 14; *Rudolph: xxiii, 47–48; *Clines: 8; *Gunneweg 1985: 85–86). Others have argued that the author had the actual documents and himself composed the surrounding narrative in Aramaic (*Williamson 1985: xxiii–xxiv). In either case, the value of the material ultimately owes a great deal to how one evaluates the documents themselves.

After an extensive debate in the first part of the twentieth century, the general consensus—at least in English-speaking scholarship—has been that the Aramaic documents are genuine and can be used as reliable contemporary records, even if their context in Ezra may in some cases be suspect. This agreement is primarily due to the work of Meyer (*8–71) and Schaeder. The arguments for genuineness note that:

1. The letters and decrees match similar literary types found among both the various Persian royal inscriptions and the abundance of Aramaic papyri that have survived from the Persian period.
2. The language of the quotations in Ezra is filled with Persian loanwords, as also preserved in legal and royal documents now known.
3. The somewhat later orthography can be explained as updating by scribes during copying to match the changed orthography of later times (Schaeder).
4. The Jewish expressions (e.g., "Yahweh the god of Israel") could be present because the decree in question is a reply to a petition from the Jews. In a few known cases the reply to the petition included its characteristic language (e.g., Cowley no. 32; the Xanthos trilingual inscription [2.2.2]). These expressions may also be the result of advice from Jewish bureaucrats who had a hand in a document's composition.
5. A number of the expressions once thought to be characteristically Jewish are now known to have been common in the ancient Near East, in some cases being traditional bureaucratic language: "god of

the heavens," "the god which is in such and such a place" (Jerusalem, in this case), "city which is in such and such a province" ("Jerusalem which is in Judah"), "may his god be with him."

Another scholarly tradition, however, has disputed the genuineness of the documents (*Torrey 1896; *Torrey 1910; *Gunneweg 1985; *Lebram). Even those who accept some of the documents have not accepted all or have thought that genuine documents were touched up by Jewish scribes (cf. *Batten: 307–8; *Blenkinsopp: 119–23, 126–28, 146–47; Blenkinsopp 1990: 312–14). Several problems can be cited (cf. *Lebram: 103–25; *Gunneweg 1985: 85–111; Mallau: 67–69):

1. The parallels found in Persian period documents lie often only in generalities, and there may be problems with the particulars (e.g., the absence of the dating formula in Ezra 5:6-17). Note also that we possess only a few documents from the Persian period with which to compare (Elephantine papyri, Xanthos inscription, Gadatas inscription), and not all of these are universally accepted as genuine. For example, we have only one royal letter or decree generally admitted as genuine (van den Hout: 34–35, 141–44), and this is only in Greek translation (Thucydides 1.128–29). The various letters in Herodotus are doubted (van den Hout: 25–33), as is the Gadatas inscription (2.2.3.6).
2. Some of the linguistic criteria from the Persian period also appear in much later writings (such as Daniel) and thus while allowing for genuineness do not prove it (e.g., genuine Iranian borrowings in the Aramaic of Ezra, such as the word *"dat"* ["law"] or "God of heaven," are also found in Daniel).
3. Some of the documents contain a good deal of Jewish theology, as is universally admitted (e.g., Ezra 6:6-12; 7:12-26). Meyer dealt with this by alleging that Jewish scribes helped compose the documents. Unfortunately, this is a circular argument and practically impossible to falsify. Further, it does not explain the unlikely sums of money and goods found in 6:9 and 7:22.
4. Even if the documents are original but reworked by Jewish scribes, this may not help us, because even minor editings can often change the basic meaning of a document (cf. 7.3.7; Grabbe).

Even more controversial than the Aramaic documents is the Hebrew decree of Cyrus allowing the return of the Jews to Jerusalem (Ezra 1:2-4). Some scholars follow Bickerman in accepting the basic decree as genuine, even if in its present form it has been somewhat revised, for some of the reasons mentioned above but also for the following reasons:

1. The decree of Ezra 6:3-5 was an official transcript for the Persian archives, whereas Ezra 1:2-4 represents an oral decree (cf. the messenger formula in v 2). Official documents were in Aramaic, but oral decrees were usually in the local language.
2. Although the benevolence of the Persian rule to its subject peoples has probably been exaggerated (cf. 2.2.3.2), efforts were made at the beginning of Cyrus's reign to repatriate the gods that had been brought to Babylon (*Nab. Chron.* iii.21 [2.2.3.1]). The equivalent of this for the Jews, who had no images, would be the temple vessels, which are part of the decree here. It would be strange if permission were given to return the temple vessels and to rebuild the temple, yet not for individuals from among the exiles to return.
3. The decree has been interpreted in its present context, which is partially incorrect, especially as concerns two aspects of it: first, it has been made into a universal decree, whereas most likely it was a very local one, of interest only to the Jewish community; second, the response was not a mass emigration from Babylon but a succession of small groups returning over a period of time. The editor has also put his theological stamp on the material by the way in which he has written the surrounding material.

However, a number of the points noted at the beginning of this section need to be taken into account. The fact of the return is not evidence that the decree in question here is genuine. A similar decree in Aramaic is found in Ezra 6:3-5. Even if this decree is genuine, it differs somewhat from that in Ezra 1. Moreover, few scholars have followed Bickerman (103–4) in his attempt to defend even the reference to prophetic fulfillment in v 1 (e.g., Williamson [*1985: 9–10] thinks it is the contribution of the editor). This is parallel to the editor's reference to gifts from "their neighbors" (i.e., Gentiles) in v 6, which is probably an attempt to evoke the events of the exodus (*Williamson 1985: 16). For these and other reasons, the decree has been rejected by many as an invention of the narrator (e.g., Galling; *Blenkinsopp: 74–76), even in the wake of Bickerman's arguments.

In sum, the genuineness and reliability of the alleged Persian documents in Ezra cannot be taken for granted, as so often has been done. The only recent detailed examination is still unpublished (Hensley). The time seems ripe to put aside Meyer and Schaeder and reopen the subject with a thorough study. Until that is done, the documents will remain problematic as sources.

2.2.1.3 The Nehemiah Memorial

Ackroyd, P. R. *The Age of the Chronicler* (1970).
Clines, D.J.A. "The Nehemiah Memoir: The Perils of Autobiography." *What Does Eve Do to Help?* (1990) 124–64.
*Kellermann.

There is general agreement that a significant portion of the book of Nehemiah is an account written by Nehemiah himself; it is usual to find this source in 1:1—7:72a (Eng. 1:1—7:73a); 11:1-2; and 12:31-43. Nehemiah 13:4-31 is also often assigned to the Nehemiah Memorial, or "Memoir," although this is disputed by Ackroyd, who thinks that it is an imitation of Nehemiah's style by a later editor (28, 41). Recognizing that we have Nehemiah's own words available to us does not, however, mean that his account can always be taken at face value (cf. Clines). The intensity and immediacy of his account are offset by its highly partisan approach. He gives us his side of the story, which is far from the only side.

One problem with using the Nehemiah Memorial is not knowing exactly why it was written. Although it is possible that it was a report to the Persian authorities, its style seems out-of-keeping with a factual report; it strikes the reader as more Nehemiah's defense of his record. Perhaps he had to defend his actions to the Persians against accusations made by his opponents. By contrast, his writing has in recent times been compared with the memorial inscriptions that Mesopotamian rulers addressed to the god(s) and deposited in the foundations of temples or public buildings (Ackroyd: 28–30). Although such inscriptions might still have been written with an eye to public consumption (because a public copy was not infrequently circulated), that they were primarily addressed to the god(s) meant that some attempt was made to be objective, at least as far as the author understood the term. In other words, the writer was not usually engaging in wholesale invention, however partisan his account was from another perspective. After looking at several recent alternatives, Williamson suggests that it originated as a report to the Persian authorities but was subsequently revised in the light of later events, so that it now represents a mixture of genres (*1985: xxiv–xxviii).

2.2.1.4 The Ezra Source

*In der Smitten.
*Lebram.

Mowinckel, S. "'Ich' und 'Er' in der Ezrageschichte." *Verbannung und Heimkehr* (1961) 211–33.

As with the Nehemiah Memorial, portions of Ezra 7–10 are in the first person. This has led to the hypothesis of an Ezra memoir for part or all of this section. However, whereas there is general agreement about the Nehemiah Memorial, the idea of an Ezra memoir is quite controversial and is rejected by a number of scholars (*Noth: 62–66; *Gunneweg 1985: 141; *Kellermann: 56–69; *In der Smitten: 63–66). As Noth expresses it, "there is nothing in Ezra 7–10 which Chr. [the Chronicler] himself could not have deduced from the sources which he used (Ezra 7.12-26; 8.1-14 and the Nehemiah Memoir) or have added on his own account" (*64). This opinion argues that the Ezra material is a "midrash" (interpretative expansion) on 7:12-19 (which some take as basically reliable), the list in 8:1-14, and the Nehemiah Memorial. There are reasons for rejecting such a source:

1. Much of the language of this narrative resembles that of the Chronicler (whose existence is presupposed [cf. 2.2.1.8]).
2. There are remarkable parallels with the Nehemiah Memorial, suggesting that the author attempted to show that Ezra not only accomplished the same things but did so to an even greater degree.
3. There are no details that suggest the use of an "Ezra source"; rather, such things as the chronological data belong to the editor's own calculations or invention (cf. *Noth: 64).

By contrast, the most recent English-language commentaries accept that there is an Ezra substratum to this section, even though there may have been a good deal of editorial reworking (*Clines: 6–8; *Williamson 1985: xxviii–xxxii; *Blenkinsopp: 44). Williamson argues that tensions within Ezra 7:1-10 show that an earlier account has been rewritten (*1985: 89–90). Otherwise, the defense of this thesis is generally limited to answering objections to it.

Whether one accepts or rejects the idea of an Ezra memoir seems ultimately to depend on one's subjective impression of the material: Does it, like the Nehemiah Memorial, seem to have the marks of a personal account? This interpretation is exemplified in a comment by Meyer. With regard to the prayer of Ezra in 7:27-28, he notes, "No one can consider this cry from the very bottom of the heart as a fabrication!" (*63: "Diesen aus tiefstem Herzen kommenden Ausruf wird niemand für eine Fälschung halten"). One expects to find no consensus on many points of academic study, but for reconstructing the history of Persian Judah, a great deal depends on whether or not an Ezra source exists. It seems an unfortunate state of scholarship when so much seems to hang on the a priori tendency of the individual scholar.

2.2.1.5 Miscellaneous Lists of Persons

Allrik, H. L. "The Lists of Zerubbabel (Nehemiah 7 and Ezra 2) and the Hebrew Numeral Notation." *BASOR* 136 (Dec. 1954) 21–27.

Clines, D.J.A. "Nehemiah 10 as an Example of Early Jewish Biblical Exegesis." *JSOT* 21 (1981) 111–17.

Galling, K. "Die Liste der aus dem Exil Heimgekehrten." *Studien* (1964) 89–108 = revision of "The 'Gola-List' according to Ezra 2//Nehemiah 7." *JBL* 70 (1951) 149–58.

Johnson, M. D. *The Purpose of the Biblical Genealogies* (1988) 37–76.

Kellermann, U. "Die Listen in Nehemia 11: Eine Dokumentation aus den letzten Jahren des Reiches Juda?" *ZDPV* 82 (1966) 209–27.

2.2.1.5.1 Ezra 2//Nehemiah 7 present two lists that are almost identical, although there is some difference in detail. They both purport to be a list of the returnees under Zerubbabel (Ezra 2:1-2; Neh 7:6-7). Several questions present themselves about this list. First, which is prior, Ezra 2 or Nehemiah 7? Or did both draw on a common source? A number of recent scholars conclude that Nehemiah 7 is the original and was copied in Ezra 2 (*Rudolph: 13; *Clines: 44–45; *Williamson 1985: 29–30). Among the reasons are (1) the reference to the seventh month in Neh 7:72 (Eng. 7:73) fits with 8:1, whereas its presence in the parallel passage of Ezra (3:1) is meaningless; (2) Ezra 2:68-69 seems to be an expansion of Neh 7:69 (Eng. 7:70); and (3) Ezra 2:68 contains a plus over against Neh 7:70 (Eng. 7:71), with the language of the extra material agreeing in style with that elsewhere in Ezra 1–6.

Blenkinsopp, however, has taken a converse position, arguing that (1) Ezra 3 also talks about the seventh month; (2) such things as the characteristic terminology and the temple endowment of the passage fit the Ezra context better; (3) the awkward syntax of Neh 7:69 (Eng. 7:70) suggests adaptation to a new context; and (4) month numbers instead of names are typical of Ezra (*43–44). Gunneweg argues that the list is not original at either place but was inserted at both points by the Chronicler to show the parallelism of the events (*1985: 54–56).

Second, is the list a straightforward, unified record of those who came from Babylon? The answer is that the list seems to be made up of diverse material (*Clines: 44; *Williamson 1985: 28; cf. *Blenkinsopp: 83): (1) the list of laymen (Ezra 2:3-35//Neh 7:8-42) is actually two lists, one according to family (Ezra 2:3-20//Neh 7:8-24) and one according to place of residence (Ezra 2:21-35//Neh 7:25-38); (2) the residence list is further divided according to "sons of" (*bĕnê*: Ezra 2:21, 24-26, 29-35//Neh 7:25, 34-42) and "men of" (*'anšê*: Ezra 2:22-23, 27-28//Neh 7:26-33); and (3) the heading (Ezra 2:1//Neh 7:6) speaks only of those who came up from Babylon, but the last few verses (Ezra 2:68-70//Neh 7:69-71) include a list of gifts for the building of the temple.

Third, from what period does the census material derive? There are indications that it does not record a single, mass return at the time of Cyrus's supposed decree (*Clines: 43–44; *Williamson 1985: 30–31; *Gunneweg 1985: 57, 65–66): (1) Ezra 2 shows no clear connection with chapter 1, ignoring Sheshbazzar but mentioning Zerubbabel and Joshua; (2) some of the list is by place of residence, which would be possible only after the people had time to settle down in the land; (3) the number of returnees (Ezra 2:64//Neh 7:66) is rather large compared with those who were exiled (2 Kings 24:14; Jer 52:28-30); (4) the Persian name Bigvai (Ezra 2:2//Neh 7:7) is not a likely name for a Jew only a year after the Persian conquest; and (5) the composite nature of the list suggests more than one time of origin. Albright argued that it actually represented the time of Nehemiah (see also *Blenkinsopp: 83), but Williamson thinks it belonged to the very early Persian period (*1985: 31): (1) the family of Hakkoz was initially excluded from the priesthood (Ezra 2:61//Neh 7:63) but had been reinstated by the time of Ezra (Ezra 8:33; cf. Neh 3:4, 21; 1 Chron 24:10); (2) the list indicates registration of those without genealogical record by Babylonian place of residence; (3) the use of the gold drachma (Ezra 2:69//Neh 7:69-71 [Eng. 7:70-72]) was probably prior to the introduction of the gold daric about 515 B.C.E., because gold coinage was reserved to the official Persian government after this; and (4) the population distribution is not from the time of Nehemiah.

We may conclude that the parallel lists of Ezra 2 and Nehemiah 7 are a record of immigrants and settlers, perhaps of several different groups, over a considerable period of time, not a single, mass return in the early years of Cyrus. As for its purpose, the suggestions range from Galling's (*106–8)—that it was needed when Tattenai was seeking advice about letting the Jews continue with building the temple (Ezra 5:3-4, 10)—to an official tax register or census list. With so many uncertainties, several possibilities must be recognized.

2.2.1.5.2 Nehemiah 10:2-28 (Eng. 10:1-27) is presented as the list of those who signed the pledge to keep the law. Many have accepted that it is indeed based on an actual document from the temple archives (*Rudolph: 173–74; cf. *Clines: 200; *Williamson 1985: 328). Although this may be the case, the original document is not found here. For one thing, the list of names comes first, whereas it was normal procedure to end any such declaration with the names. Rudolph has also noted that v 1 is naturally continued by vv 29-30 (*173); nevertheless, he believes it is a genuine list of those who signed the agreement, although placed in its present context by the editor. Mowinckel, in contrast, argues that the list was a fabrication (1964: 1.135–45), a view developed further by Williamson (*1985: 328–31; cf. *Blenkinsopp: 310–13). Reasons for this conclusion include (1) some of the names, although presented as personal names, are actually family names; (2) it is questionable that extended families had their own seals; and (3) the names seem to be copied from lists elsewhere in Ezra-Nehemiah, especially Nehemiah 3.

Williamson suggests that the list was compiled by the editor with a theological view in mind, "to demonstrate the united and wholehearted support of all the people for what was proposed" (*330). Most accept that this list was not a part of Nehemiah's memorial. The problem encountered in Nehemiah is found in chapter 13; if the pledge and signatures here are not a fabrication, they would have to be placed later than the events of this chapter (*Clines: 199–200). Even if it is a fabrication, it has value as an indication of how various priestly and other leading families developed, as well as their relationships with one another (*Gunneweg 1987: 132–34).

2.2.1.5.3 Nehemiah 11 claims to be a list of those who came to settle in Jerusalem in the time of Nehemiah (v 1). That it is a composite, however, is indicated by vv 25-36, which give the various villages and settlements outside Jerusalem. In addition, the LXX text is shorter. As far as the list's authenticity is concerned, it is perhaps significant that the names do not appear to come from elsewhere in Ezra-Nehemiah; in contrast, there are important parallels with 1 Chronicles 9, which is alleged to be a list of those who first returned from exile. Kellermann has argued that Nehemiah 11 represents a pre-exilic list of some sort, partly because of specific points in common with the settlement lists in Joshua. Supporting this argument is the fact that villages are included that were outside the area of Judah in the time of Nehemiah, whereas towns mentioned elsewhere in his book are not in this list; however, 11:25-30 might have been later combined with 11:1-24 or could be an idealized list based on Joshua (*Blenkinsopp: 329–30). Whether or not any of these possibilities is correct, it is difficult to take this as a reliable list of settlements in the time of Nehemiah. (For other suggestions of its dating, see *Clines: 220; *Williamson 1985: 350.)

2.2.1.5.4 Nehemiah 12:1-26 is an important list of priests and Levites but is clearly a composite. The list of Levites in vv 23-26 is dated both to the time of Johanan (v 23) and to the time of Joiakim (v 26). The priestly families of vv 1-7 not only parallel those in vv 12-21 but also are different from the four families given in Ezra 2:36-39 (//Neh 7:39-42), suggesting that the list of vv 1-7 cannot refer to the time of Zerubbabel as the heading states (v 1). The formulation of vv 6-7 and vv 19-21 (the "and" in the middle of the list of names) suggests a later addition to an original list. This leads to the conclusion that Neh 12:1-26 was an original (archival?) list of priests (vv 12-18) and Levites (vv 23a, 24-25), perhaps from the time of Joiakim (v 12); this was updated by the addition of the names in vv 19-21, whereas the list in vv 1-9 was artificially created from those of vv 12-25 (*Williamson 1985: 361).

Of greatest interest is the list of high priests in vv 10-11 and 22. The priests of v 22 parallel those in the last part of vv 10-11, except for Jonathan (v 11) instead of Johanan (v 22). This has led to the common explanation that the lists are the same, except that Jonathan is a scribal error for Johanan. Such a simple explanation is to be doubted, however, for two reasons (cf. *Mowinckel 1964: 1.158–62; *Williamson 1985: 363; *Blenkinsopp: 339): (1) the list in vv 10-11 begins with Joshua, who returned from exile with Zerubbabel, yet his grandson Eliashib was high priest about eighty years later in Nehemiah's day (3:1), suggesting that the list is not complete; and (2) in v 23 Johanan is said to be son of Eliashib, not of Joiada (as Jonathan is in v 11). This brings up the question of whether the list is meant to extend to the end of the Persian period, a conclusion of some who interpret "Darius the Persian" (v 22) as Darius III, the Persian king defeated by Alexander. However, this is not at all certain, and others take the reference as Darius II or even Darius I (*Williamson 1985: 364–65). Those who assume that these verses constitute a list of high priests to the time of Alexander note that Josephus (*Ant.* 11.7.2 §302) gave the high priest in the time of Alexander as Jadduas, whom they interpret to be the same as Jaddua. It is uncertain, however, that Josephus had any knowledge of the line of high priests beyond that given in these very verses, and even if he did, there is reason not to be confident of his assignment of historical dates to them (see 2.2.5 and 2.3.12). Therefore, one cannot be certain how late in the Persian period this list is meant to extend; a necessary correlation is that one cannot date the addition of these lists to Neh 12:1-26 (contra *Williamson 1985: 361, who asserts that they were added no earlier than the Hellenistic period).

2.2.1.6 Minor Prophets

*Ackroyd 1968: 153–217, 230–31.
Ahlström, G. W. *Joel and the Temple Cult in Jerusalem* (1971).
Blenkinsopp, J. *A History of Prophecy in Israel* (1984).
Burrows, M. "The Literary Category of the Book of Jonah." *Translating and Understanding the Old Testament* (1970) 80–107.
Clements, R. E. "The Purpose of the Book of Jonah." *VTSup* 28 (1975) 16–28.
Coggins, R. J. *Haggai, Zechariah, Malachi* (1987).
Glazier-McDonald, B. *Malachi: The Divine Messenger* (1987).
Hill, A. E. "Dating the Book of Malachi: A Linguistic Reexamination." *The Word of the Lord Shall Go Forth* (1983) 77–89.
Holbert, J. C. " 'Deliverance Belongs to Yahweh!': Satire in the Book of Jonah." *JSOT* 21 (1981) 59–81.
Koch, K. "Haggais unreines Volk." *ZAW* 79 (1967) 52–66.
———. *The Prophets.* Vol. 2: *The Babylonian and Persian Periods* (1983).
Landes, G. M. "Linguistic Criteria and the Date of the Book of Jonah." *EI* 16 (1982) 147*–70*.
Mason, R. "The Purpose of the 'Editorial Framework' of the Book of Haggai." *VT* 27 (1977) 415–21.
———. "The Prophets of the Restoration." *Israel's Prophetic Tradition* (1982) 137–54.
May, H. G. " 'This People' and 'This Nation' in Haggai." *VT* 18 (1968) 190–97.
Meyers, C. L., and E. M. Meyers. *Haggai, Zechariah 1–8* (1987).
Mitchell, H. G., et al. *Haggai, Zechariah, Malachi, Jonah* (1912).
Petersen, D. L. *Haggai and Zechariah 1–8* (1984).
Porten, B. "Baalshamem and the Date of the Book of Jonah." *De la Tôrah au Messie* (1981) 237–44.
Redditt, P. L. "The Book of Joel and Peripheral Prophecy." *CBQ* 48 (1986) 225–40.
———. "Israel's Shepherds: Hope and Pessimism in Zechariah 9–14." *CBQ* 51 (1989) 632–42.
Smith, R. L. *Micah-Malachi* (1984).
Wolff, H. W. *Hosea and Joel* (1977).
———. *Obadiah and Jonah* (1986).
———. *Haggai* (1988).
Woude, A. S. van der. "Malachi's Struggle for a Pure Community: Reflections on Malachi 2:10-16." *Tradition and Re-interpretation in Jewish and Early Christian Literature* (1986) 65–71.

A number of the Minor Prophets belong in part or whole to the Persian period. They are treated together here simply for convenience, because they are often found together in commentaries and other secondary literature. Only bibliography important for the discussion is included here; for an introduction to and further discussion of the books in question, see the Old Testament introductions, the commentaries, and Blenkinsopp, *A History of Prophecy*. Further bibliography on Haggai and Zechariah is at 2.3.3.

2.2.1.6.1 The books of Zechariah and Haggai are especially important, because the prophecies or visions proper (as opposed to the editorial framework [Mason 1977]) seem, by and large, contemporary with the events they discuss. Haggai is dated over only a short period of time and seems to be free from major editing. Zechariah 1–8 has a more complicated tradition-history, but the visions cover a period of only a few years at most. This has led the Meyerses to argue for the radical thesis that "Haggai-Zechariah 1–8 is a single compendious work, published in anticipation of the auspicious event of the temple's rededication" in 515 B.C.E. (xlvii). If so, this would make these books the most valuable of contemporary sources. The two main arguments for their thesis are (1) a literary unity for the combined work is shown by a sophisticated internal structure based on parallelism, and (2) within this structure the chronological indications demonstrate an acute concern for the completion of the temple, yet there is no reference to the rededication itself. Although both arguments have merit and must be considered in detail by reviewers, they do not seem decisive. The silence of Haggai and Zechariah 1–8 about the completion of the temple is indeed puzzling and could be the result of completion of the books before the temple, but there could be other reasons for the silence, and the dates in the framework may have a function other than leading up to rededication. If the rededication was as important as suggested, then why was an appendix not devoted to it once it took place? More importantly, the only date for the completion of the temple is that given in Ezra 6:15. Many argue that the editor of Ezra 1–6 had little in the way of sources (2.2.1.1). We do not know his source for this datum and cannot be assured that it is accurate. Indeed, there are good reasons to think the temple took much longer to complete (2.4.2.4). No doubt with time there will be considerable discussion of the Meyerses' proposal.

Zechariah 1–8 is composed of eight visions plus several other oracles, dated by the editorial framework as covering two years from the eighth month of Darius's second year (1:1) to the ninth month of his fourth year (7:1), or 520–518 B.C.E. The basic emphasis of these chapters is on the rebuilding of the temple and the establishment of a godly community in Jerusalem. This requires not just the human effort of physical building but also a cosmic reordering to remove both the causes and the effects of the exile. Several visions emphasize that the time of punishment is over and that of restoration imminent: the horses (1:7-17; 6:1-8), the horns and smiths (2:1-4 [Eng. 1:18-21]), and the man with the measuring line (2:5-17 [Eng. 2:1-13]). Other visions picture the removal of Israel's guilt: accusation against Joshua (3:1-5), the flying scroll (5:1-4), and the flying ephah (5:5-11). The vision of the lampstand and olive trees, with its accompanying oracle, explicitly says that Zerubbabel would complete the temple by God's power (4:1-10). Chapter 8 ends the section with a prophecy of prosperity and idyllic existence in Jerusalem, because God's presence is again there. Passages such as chapters 3–4 and 6:9-15 are important for their statements about the leadership of the new community (see 2.3.2).

Zechariah 9–14 is generally treated separately from Zechariah 1–8. Chapters 9–14 are much more difficult to date. The idea that they were originally pre-exilic oracles has now generally been given up (R. L. Smith: 242–49; Coggins: 63). It is even questionable that the widely accepted division into Deutero-Zechariah (chaps. 9–11) and Trito-Zechariah (chaps. 12–14) is valid. There is, however, widespread agreement that chapters 9–14 include a diversity of material with different origins and dating (cf. the recent redactional study in Redditt 1989). A dating of much or even all the material in the Persian period would be accepted by most scholars, but there is not likely to be any consensus for greater precision. Important aspects of this part of Zechariah are its eschatological message and apocalyptic qualities.

Haggai has only two short chapters, both of which are devoted to a series of prophetic exhortations to get on with rebuilding the temple and promises of the blessings that would follow as a result. The dates given cover only a few short weeks, from the first day of the sixth month (1:1) to the twenty-fourth day of the ninth month (2:10, 20), all in the second year of Darius (520 B.C.E.). The reality of the contemporary situation is baldly described in 1:6: "you have sowed much and brought in little; you eat without being satisfied; . . . and he who earns anything earns it for a leaky purse." It was often argued in the past that "this people and nation" considered unclean (2:14) was the Samaritans, who wanted to participate in the building of the temple. This is now generally rejected. It is also not possible to make a distinction between those returned from Babylon and those who had remained in the land (Koch 1967; May; Wolff 1988: 40, 73, 78–79). Haggai considered all the people unclean but also called on all to participate in the building of the temple. Although Haggai's message is simpler and more straightforward than Zechariah's, it involves more than just the reestablishment of the temple cult. As well as their part in the role implied for Zerubbabel in 2:20-23 (2.3.2), eschatological overtones permeate the book (cf. Mason 1982: 142–45).

2.2.1.6.2 Malachi is also difficult to date. Beyond the fact that the temple seems to have been rebuilt, there is no consensus for a specific time within the Persian period, despite attempts to be more precise (cf. Glazier-McDonald: 14–18; Hill). For example, the reference to Edom (1:2-5) is not only imprecise but may be symbolic, standing for any enemies or opponents. Although there are a number of parallels in Malachi's message to the reforms of Nehemiah (J.M.P. Smith [in Mitchell, et al.]: 7–8), the exact relationship between the two is still uncertain. Malachi's value is primarily for the religious and social issues which were important to the community at the time. Its major aim seems to be that of assuring the community of God's continuing love and concern for them. Because many Jews seemed to be looking in vain for evidence of that love, however, an explanation of why the promises were not being fulfilled was needed (1:2-5; 2:17; 3:13-18). The reason given is lack of obedience and reverence on the part of the community. The criticisms focus especially on proper cultic observance, with the priests themselves being strongly taken to task along with the people (1:6—2:9; 3:6-12). Lest it be thought that Malachi attacks the priesthood as such, however, it can be argued that he was part of the priestly establishment (Mason 1982: 149–50). The book also deals with social concerns, such as proper husband-wife relations (2:14-16; but cf. van der Woude). As with Haggai and Zechariah, eschatology is an important interest in 3:23-24 (Eng. 4:5-6), although this passage is often dated later than the main part of the book. As Mason observes, Malachi "holds together concern for the cultic needs of the present theocratic community and lively eschatological hope for the future" (1982: 151).

2.2.1.6.3 Many would date the entirety of the book of Joel to the Persian period. Although Wolff argues that the book is a literary unity (1977: 6–8), Childs concludes that this unity is achieved redactionally (1979: 389–92). Redditt argues for a single author (235–37), but one whose writing covers a period of time and reflects the changing status of his group (see further at 2.3.11.1). Although some would still place the first two chapters or even the whole of the book in the pre-exilic period, the majority date at least chapters 1–2 to the Persian period. More controversial are chapters 3–4, which many assign also to the Persian period but others put after Alexander's conquests (primarily because of 4:4-8 [Eng. 3:4-8]). A substantial number of scholars put the composition of the whole between the first return and Ezra-Nehemiah (Ahlström: 111–29; Redditt: 233–35). Two important aspects of the book are its emphasis on eschatology and the cult. In common with Zechariah 9–14 (or at least 12–14), Joel concentrates on the "Day of Yahweh" and supernatural intervention of God to exalt Israel, punish its enemies, and bring about a new order. Yet the cult is still vital and required for the salvation of the nation.

2.2.1.6.4 There is general agreement, because of the language and vague historical background of the book, that the author of Jonah is not the prophet contemporary with Jeroboam II (2 Kings 14:23-27). No internal indications require a dating later than the Persian period, but neither is the Greek period excluded (cf. Wolff 1986: 76–78). The book is almost certainly no later than 200 B.C.E. because of the reference to it in Ben Sira 49:10. Despite some attempts to date the book in the pre-Persian period (cf. Landes; Porten), the Persian period is still the most popular choice for scholars. With perhaps the exception of Jonah's prayer (2:3-10 [Eng. 2:2-9]), the book seems to be a unity. More problematic is its purpose, with two proposals important for concerns of the historian: (1) the problem of prophecy, and (2) the place of Gentiles within God's plan of salvation. The theme of the failure of prophecy is not new (assuming the book belongs to the Persian period) but is already addressed in such passages as Ezekiel 33 and Jeremiah 18. By contrast, the focus may not be on the failure of prophecy so much as on prophetic hypocrisy and narrow-mindedness (cf. Holbert: 75).

Related to the prophetic question is that of universalism. Although some deny this as a theme of the book (e.g., Clements), one of Jonah's messages still seems to be that non-Israelites can have access to the God of Israel. A similar idea is found in writings which probably also date to the same general period of time (Isaiah 56 and, perhaps, the book of Ruth and Mal 1:11); these indicate a tendency in some circles toward universalism of worship and salvation. This does not mean that Gentiles would be accepted just as they are, because conversion to Yahwism is presupposed, but it goes against the narrow genealogical and exclusivist view of some circles. Exactly how this universalist tendency is to be related to the views of Ezra-Nehemiah—whether as direct opposition (Burrows: 104–5) or as simply another view during this time—is not so clear (see 2.4.5 for a discussion).

2.2.1.7 Isaiah 56–66

Blenkinsopp, J. *A History of Prophecy in Israel* (1984) 242–51.
Koch, K. *The Prophets*. Vol. 2: *The Babylonian and Persian Periods* (1983).
Pauritsch, K. *Die neue Gemeinde* (1971).
Vaux, R. de. "The Cults of Adonis and Osiris: A Comparative Study." *The Bible and the Ancient Near East* (1971) 210–37.
Vermeylen, J. *Du prophète Isaïe à l'apocalyptique* (1977) 2.1–517.

Westermann, C. *Isaiah 40–66* (1969).
Whybray, R. N. *Isaiah 40–66* (1975).

The exact origin and unity of the material in Third Isaiah has been widely debated, with no clear consensus on the details. On one important point, however, there has been useful agreement: most of these chapters probably originate in the early part of the Persian period. Considering the problems involved, so minimal an agreement as this is both surprising and significant, which makes the use of this part of Isaiah to illustrate the early period following the return less controversial. In contrast, little can be related to specific historical events, and many problems of interpretation exist. Isaiah 56–66 may be most helpful in matters of cult, society, and ideology.

The themes and concerns of Trito-Isaiah are often similar to those of Isaiah 40–55. The historical setting is clearly different, however, because the perspective is from Judah and Jerusalem, rather than from Babylon. The return of the exiles envisaged by Deutero-Isaiah has now taken place, yet the high expectations of the earlier prophet have not been fulfilled as prophesied. Much of Isaiah 56–66 can be seen as an attempt to adapt and explain the message of Deutero-Isaiah in the light of the new realities. Following are several themes and events which emerge:

The return has been accomplished and the temple rebuilt (60:7, 13; 62:9), yet life is hard, crop failure frequent, and the returnees evidently are having a difficult time making a living (60:17; 62:8-9). Several passages suggest a universalist view, rare if not unknown in pre-exilic times (especially 56:3-7). The idea that non-Israelites could hope for salvation and God's blessings as long as they were obedient to God's law is relatively new to Yahwism.

When it comes to the individual prophecies of Trito-Isaiah, there is a wide variety of dating and suggested setting. Westermann (296–308) argued that 60–62 formed a core to the collection, although the same prophet was also responsible for 57:14-20; 65:16b-25; 66:6-16; and, probably, 58. Inserted into this collection of utterances by the original prophet were the exilic community laments of 59 and 63–64. Added to this original prophetic collection were some passages that reflected a split in the community, composed principally of 56:9—57:13; 59:2-8; 65:1-16a; plus a few other verses. Third and fourth strands seeking to interpret the collection further are made up mainly of isolated verses here and there. Except for the laments of 59 and 63–64, which are exilic (and strands three and four, which cannot be reliably dated), most of the Trito-Isaiah collection would be dated to the early post-exilic period.

Whybray is less optimistic about finding a core in 60–62 (229–30), but he would accept that most of the collection probably arose in the early Persian period, although a later date before the time of Nehemiah cannot be excluded with certainty. The exceptions are the laments of 63:7—64:12 (exilic) and particular, scattered verses (including 66:6, 15-23), which in some cases could be several centuries later. Koch agrees with Westermann on a core of 60–62 but sees little reason not to assign the same authorship to 56–59 and 65:16—66:14 (153). Therefore, except for the older laments in 63:7—64:12, he would give much of the collection to Trito-Isaiah himself at the beginning of the Persian period. In sum, despite much disagreement over details, there is a large consensus that most of the collection (except 63:7—64:12) should be put in the early post-exilic period.

A number of passages in Trito-Isaiah have been discussed as reflecting divisions within the religious community. It is even alleged that these passages are an attack on the functioning cult and priesthood of the Jerusalem temple. Isaiah 57:3-13 is difficult to date; some make it pre-exilic (Westermann: 321–25), but even if it is post-exilic, the type of worship here is reminiscent of that ascribed (rightly or wrongly) to the Canaanite cults of pre-exilic times (Whybray: 202). Isaiah 59:1-21 is a scathing attack, but its target is vague, likely the whole community rather than a particular group within it (Whybray: 221). The charges outlined have sometimes been taken seriously as reflecting the actual situation at the time, but to do so is to ignore the habits of preachers. It is difficult to believe that this is anything more than stylized invective or that the community was suddenly more wicked than at other times and places.

Koch (153) thinks that Isa 60:1-22 shows opposition to rebuilding the temple and is therefore to be dated before 520 B.C.E. Others are skeptical of an actual historical context and see the passage as eschatological (Westermann: 357). Whether or not 60:1-22 reflects the existence of the temple is debatable (Whybray: 229–30; cf. Pauritsch: 123). Isaiah 65:1-16 is difficult to date, depending on how one interprets the polemic. Many have seen some sort of syncretistic cult, perhaps even a Hellenistic one (Pauritsch: 172–73; cf. de Vaux). Although a religiously divided community is envisaged (Whybray: 266–68), there is no clear identity of those being criticized. Isaiah 66:1-6, more than any other passage, has been taken as a criticism of the current priesthood and temple. Is it condemning all forms of temple worship (Pauritsch: 198–202)? Is it directed against the view that God wants a temple built now, as in Hag 2:19 (Westermann: 412–13)? Is it an attack on the current priesthood for being corrupt (i.e., not seeing things the way the writer of the passage does: Blenkinsopp: 249–50; Hanson [2.3.11.3])? Or is it a type of pagan cult that existed among the Jews? If it constitutes criticism of the temple cult and priesthood as institutions, it would be unusual in the Old Testament literature. The vagueness of the description does not allow an easy determination of the question. For a further discussion of the question of sectarianism in Third Isaiah, see 2.3.11.

2.2.1.8 Books of Chronicles

Ackroyd, P. R. "Chronicles-Ezra-Nehemiah: The Concept of Unity." *ZAW* 100 *Supplement* (1988) 189–201.
Braun, R. L. "Solomonic Apologetic in Chronicles." *JBL* 92 (1973) 503–16.
———. "Chronicles, Ezra, and Nehemiah: Theology and Literary History." *VTSup* 30 (1979) 52–64.
———. *1 Chronicles* (1986).
Cazelles, H. Review of *Israel in the Books of Chronicles,* by H.G.M. Williamson. *VT* 29 (1979) 375–80.
Cross, F. M. "A Reconstruction of the Judean Restoration." *JBL* 94 (1975) 4–18.
Japhet, S. "Supposed Common Authorship of Chronicles and Ezra-Nehemiah Investigated Anew." *VT* 18 (1968) 330–71.
———. "Chronicles, Book of." *JE* (1971) 5.517–34.
———. *The Ideology of the Book of Chronicles and Its Place in Biblical Thought* (1989).
Johnson, M. D. *The Purpose of the Biblical Genealogies* (1988).
McKenzie, S. L. *The Chronicler's Use of the Deuteronomistic History* (1985).
Talshir, D. "A Reinvestigation of the Linguistic Relationship between Chronicles and Ezra-Nehemiah." *VT* 38 (1988) 165–93.
Throntveit, M. A. "Linguistic Analysis and the Question of Authorship in Chronicles, Ezra and Nehemiah." *VT* 32 (1982) 201–16.
Willi, T. *Die Chronik als Auslegung* (1972).
Williamson, H.G.M. *Israel in the Books of Chronicles* (1977a).
———. "Eschatology in Chronicles." *Tyndale Bulletin* 28 (1977b) 115–54.
———. *1 and 2 Chronicles* (1982).

In the last two decades a great deal of scholarly interest has centered on the books of Chronicles, ranging from textual criticism to theology. Only a fraction of that bibliography can be given here; for further reference, see Japhet (1971; 1989), Williamson (1982), and Braun (1986).

Much of Chronicles is a version of Samuel-Kings. Although the estimation for the date of its composition has sometimes placed it in the Hellenistic period (e.g., Noth: 69–73), recent studies tend to favor the later Achaemenid period (Japhet 1971: 533–34; Williamson 1977a: 83–86). All agree that there has been some later editing, but the question of various "editions" of the Chronicler's work has been hotly disputed, especially the view that a large part of Chronicles can be placed as early as 520 B.C.E. (e.g., Cross: 11–14, opposed by Williamson 1977b; see also below). There is also the question of whether the genealogies of 1 Chronicles 1–9 are an integral part of the composition; Williamson (1977b: 121–22; 1982: 40–92) and Johnson (55) argue that they are, against Cross (13–14) and a number of earlier scholars. Thus, there is general agreement that the books date from the Persian period and potentially tell us something about the community at that time.

The problem with utilizing Chronicles for historical purposes, however, is that the bulk of the material is a version of Israel's history under the monarchy, parallel to Samuel-Kings. Access to post-exilic history can sometimes be achieved in an indirect way: the genealogies seem to provide clues to the structure of the post-exilic community (2.2.1.5), whereas references to the cult probably reflect the situation in the Second Temple period, rather than the First Temple period (2.4.5). Another area of theological reflection by the editor of 1 and 2 Chronicles involves the question of Israel's identity. Recent study suggests that "Israel" to him includes the northern tribes, so that the sustained anti-Samaritan polemic identified by earlier scholarship must be abandoned (Braun 1973: 515–16; Williamson 1977a: 136–40; Japhet: 325–34; Willi: 190–93).

"The Chronicler" has long been considered the author not only of 1 and 2 Chronicles but also of Ezra and Nehemiah. This consensus was first significantly attacked by Japhet (1968); Williamson (1977a) has now built on her work and developed further arguments against the general view. Their major points are:

1. The linguistic usage of the books of Chronicles is sufficiently different from Ezra-Nehemiah to rule out common authorship, even though both works are good representatives of late biblical Hebrew.
2. The argument that 1 Esdras represents a portion of the original work of the Chronicler does not stand up.
3. The ideology of Chronicles differs from that of Ezra-Nehemiah on significant points of interest to the post-exilic community.

The debate on the subject continues. Certainly, the assumption of a common author/editor of Chronicles and Ezra-Nehemiah can no longer be taken for granted and must be justified. Nevertheless, a number of specialists still hold to the idea of a "Chronicler" who also compiled Ezra-Nehemiah (cf. Cazelles; *Clines: 9–10; *Blenkinsopp: 47–54). Ackroyd recently discussed the difficulties of determining the answer, although he has indicated his leanings toward common authorship in other publications. The only point of Williamson's argument with which McKenzie takes serious exception is that regarding 1 Esdras, although McKenzie's own approach is dominated by Cross's thesis of a redactional solution to the problem.

On the linguistic side, Throntveit has challenged the arguments of Japhet and Williamson, although he ultimately questions whether language can decide the question of common authorship (215; see also Ackroyd: 194–95). Talshir, however, argues that linguistic study cannot support a division between Chronicles and Ezra-Nehemiah, although he admits that it does not prove unity. In contrast, Braun (1979) supports the theological differences between Chronicles and Ezra-Nehemiah. The issue is not likely to be settled in the near future. The important point for historical purposes is that one cannot automatically assume common authorship but must now argue for the position taken.

2.2.1.9 Esther, Ruth, Song of Songs

Berg, S. B. *The Book of Esther: Motifs, Themes and Structure* (1979).
Brenner, A. *The Song of Songs* (1989).
Campbell, E. F. *Ruth* (1975).
*Clines.
———. *The Esther Scroll* (1984).
———. "In Quest of the Historical Mordecai." *VT* 41 (1991) 129–36.
Fox, M. *The Song of Songs and the Ancient Egyptian Love Songs* (1985).
Humphries, W. L. "A Life-style for Diaspora: A Study of the Tales of Esther and Daniel." *JBL* 92 (1973) 211–23.
Moore, C. A. *Esther* (1971).
———. *Daniel, Esther and Jeremiah: The Additions* (1977).
———. "Esther Revisited Again: A Further Examination of Certain Esther Studies of the Past Ten Years." *HAR* 7 (1983) 169–86.
———. "Esther Revisited: An Examination of Esther Studies over the Past Decade." *Biblical and Related Studies Presented to Samuel Iwry* (1985) 163–72.
Murphy, R. *The Song of Songs* (1990).
Pope, M. *Songs of Songs* (1977).
Sasson, J. M. *Ruth* (1989).
Wright, J. S. "The Historicity of the Book of Esther." *New Perspectives on the Old Testament* (1970) 37–47.

2.2.1.9.1 It would generally be agreed today that the book of Esther is a product of the Persian period, although a recent study finds some Hellenistic influences on the present form of the story (Berg: 169–73; cf. *Clines: 272), with the story itself existing in more than one version and having a long history (Clines 1984). The early dating of the book does not mean, however, that it is a work of history; rather, the term "historical novel," so often applied, still seems to be relevant. That is, the book contains genuine historical remembrances and knowledge of some customs and practices during the Persian rule of the East. It has even been suggested that the author was a native of Susa, because he seems to know the city so well. Nevertheless, the story it purports to tell about a Jewish adviser to the king and his niece who became queen consort is clearly ahistorical (despite the efforts of apologists such as Wright), as are such details as a Queen Vashti (cf. Moore 1971: xxxiv–liii; Berg: 1–30; *Clines: 256–61). The story represents a genre sometimes known as the *Diasporanovelle*. That is, its value for Jewish history may be summarized as a story that represents Jewish aspirations in the Diaspora: it was possible for Jews to become high officials at court. The story of Esther not only suggests that it could happen but also provides a model of how those fortunate enough to reach such a high level should conduct themselves vis-à-vis their Judaism (Humphries).

2.2.1.9.2 The book of Ruth has been variously dated over a huge span of time by recent scholars, all the way from the age of the judges to the Hellenistic period (see the survey in Sasson: 240–52), although a substantial number of scholars would still date the book in its present form to the Achaemenid period (Fohrer: 251–52; Soggin). One theme of the book lies in the favorable picture it gives of a non-Israelite, even to the extent of making her a close ancestor of David. This is not the only message, as recent commentators have pointed out, and it would be a mistake to place too much weight on it when the date is so uncertain. Nevertheless, if the book arose in the Persian period, it would go along with other passages at about the same time that have universalistic tendencies—or give such a message to a reader of that time, even if the book is earlier.

2.2.1.9.3 The Song of Songs or Song of Solomon probably grew over a long period of time, some of it undoubtedly going back well into preexilic times. However, much of the material and the present form of the book are probably products of the Persian or perhaps even the early Greek period (Brenner: 57–61). Although the form of the book is such that it tells us little of actual events, perhaps its most significant aspect is that it was considered of sufficient interest to become a part of the Hebrew canon. The argument that this was only because it had been allegorized is possible but hardly provable (one cannot rely on late rabbinic literature, such as the Targum to the book or the *Shir ha-Shirim Rabbah*). It is possible that the celebration of human love was welcomed in some circles without need for submerging this in theological sublimation.

2.2.1.10 1 Esdras

Cross, F. M. "A Reconstruction of the Judean Restoration." *JBL* 94 (1975) 4–18.
Eskenazi, T. C. "The Chronicler and the Composition of 1 Esdras." *CBQ* 48 (1986) 39–61.
JWSTP: 131–35, 157–60.
Pohlmann, K.-F. *Studien zum dritten Esra* (1970).
Schürer: 3.708–18.
Williamson, H.G.M. *Israel in the Books of Chronicles* (1977).

This writing, which consists of 2 Chron 35:1—36:21, Ezra, Neh 7:72 (Eng. 7:73)—8:12, is known only in a Greek version, although it has often been assumed that there was a Hebrew original. Many scholars have claimed that 1 Esdras represents the original form of Ezra-Nehemiah, of which the MT (and later Greek version) is a later stage (cf. most recently Pohlmann; also Cross). This argument has often been used to defend the idea that "the Chronicler" is author/editor of both Chronicles and Ezra-Nehemiah. An equally impressive number of scholars, however, have taken the stance that 1 Esdras was produced by combining the then-current texts of 2 Chronicles, Ezra, and Nehemiah but leaving out all the material relating to Nehemiah which would make 1 Esdras irrelevant to the question of common authorship (see recently Williamson: 12–36; Eskenazi).

2.2.1.11 Daniel 1–6

Although some of the material in these chapters may have originated in the Persian period, the present form is most likely from a later time. See further at 5.2.3.

2.2.2 Aramaic Papyri and Inscriptions

Bowman, R. A. *Aramaic Ritual Texts from Persepolis* (1970).
Bresciana, E., and M. Kamil. "Le lettere aramaiche di Hermopoli." *Atti della Accademia Nazionale dei Lincei.* Series 8, vol. 12 (1965–66) 358–428.
*Cowley, A.
Cross, F. M. "Papyri of the Fourth Century B.C. from Dâliyeh." *New Directions in Biblical Archaeology* (1969) 201–11.
———. "Samaria Papyrus 1: An Aramaic Slave Conveyance of 335 B.C.E. Found in the Wâdī ed-Dâliyeh." *EI* 18 (1985) 7*–17*.
———. "A Report on the Samaria Papyri." *VTSup* 40 (1988) 17–26.
Driver, G. R. *Aramaic Documents of the Fifth Century B.C.* (1957).

Dupont-Sommer, A., et al. "La stèle trilingue récemment découverte au Létôon de Xanthos." *CRAIBL* (1974) 82–93, 115–25, 132–49.
Greenfield, J. C., and B. Porten. *The Bisitun Inscription of Darius the Great* (1982).
Grelot, P. "Etudes sur le 'Papyrus Pascal' d'Eléphantine." *VT* 4 (1954) 349–84.
———. *Documents araméens d'Egypt* (1972).
———. "Sur le 'Papyrus Pascal' d'Eléphantine." *Mélanges bibliques et orientaux en l'honneur de M. Henri Cazelles* (1981) 163–72.
Koopmans, J. J. *Aramäische Chrestomathie* (1962) ##20–52.
Kraeling, E. G. *The Brooklyn Museum Aramaic Papyri* (1953).
Lapp, P. W., and N. L. Lapp, eds. *Discoveries in the Wadi ed-Dâliyeh* (1974).
Metzger, H., et al. *La stèle trilingue du Létôon* (1979).
Naveh, J., and S. Shaked. "Ritual Texts or Treasury Documents?" *Orientalia* 42 (1973) 445–57.
Porten, B. *Archives from Elephantine: The Life of an Ancient Jewish Military Colony* (1968).
———. "Aramaic Papyri and Parchments: A New Look." *BA* 42 (1979) 74–104.
Porten, B., with J. C. Greenfield. *Jews of Elephantine and Arameans of Syene (Fifth Century B.C.E.)* (1976).
Porten, B., and J. C. Greenfield. "Hermopolis Letter 6." *IOS* 4 (1974) 14–30.
Porten, B., and A. Yardeni. *Textbook of Aramaic Documents from Ancient Egypt: 1 Letters* (1986).
Segal, J. B. *Aramaic Texts from North Saqqâra* (1983).

The Aramaic documents from various places are an important source for details of both Persian history and the life and history of specific Jewish communities. Especially important are those from the Jewish colony at Elephantine in Egypt (Cowley; Kraeling; Grelot 1972; selections in *TSSI* 2: nos. 23–37; now newly edited in Porten/Yardeni). The papyri generally represent legal and business documents of the community; however, they also contain certain letters and decrees that form an important witness to Jewish history and religion, for example, the letters to Jerusalem and Samaria about the rebuilding of the local temple (Cowley: nos. 30–32). Porten (1968) has provided an important systematization and interpretation of the data within the documents.

One of the most interesting and curious of the Elephantine papyri is the so-called Passover Papyrus (Cowley no. 21). This is often seen as an example of an order by the Persian government to regulate a local cult or religion; however, it is not at all clear that this is the case (Porten: 130–33). Although the text is not completely preserved, it seems likely that it is an official response by the administration to a request from the Jewish community for approval of its normal Passover celebrations. Several ostraca indicate that Passover was a regular observance (Porten 1968: 131). It would not be surprising if the annual celebration of the Passover caused offense to some of the local Egyptians, who would have attempted to hinder it. The Passover Papyrus, then, is likely an official permit to the Jews for their worship. All older reconstructions of the text must now be corrected in light of Porten's recent study of the papyrus (1979: 90–92; followed by Grelot 1981; Porten/Yardeni: 54–55).

Regarding other finds in Egypt, the collections published by Bresciana/Kamil and Driver seem to be the products of non-Jews. The Hermopolis papyri basically represent a family archive of letters, written but apparently never delivered (Bresciana, supplemented by Porten/Greenfield 1974). The Arsham archive is especially important because it consists of administrative documents (Driver). Most of the Aramaic writings come from Egypt, but there have been important finds elsewhere. Bowman's collection comes from inscriptions on mortars, pestles, and the like found at Persepolis. They are short and repetitive and were understood by the editor to identify the objects as having been used at a particular Zoroastrian *haoma* ceremony. Reviews have generally rejected this interpretation, however, identifying the inscriptions as treasury records, although there is still uncertainty as to their exact purpose (Naveh/Shaked; Greenfield in *CHI*: 2.705). The chief interest is the presence of personal names and dates and, especially, that they represent the Mesopotamian usage of Aramaic. The recent trilingual from Lycia is not only of linguistic interest but also gives a brief glimpse into Persian history (Metzger, et al.). Its subject is a local cultic foundation in the first year of Artaxerxes III (or possibly Arses: *Dandamaev 1989: 304). The Aramaic section of *KAI* (nos. 201–76) has a number of texts from the Persian period.

The finds from the Wadi Daliyeh near the Jordan seem to be the remains of refugees who fled from Alexander's soldiers (Lapp/Lapp; Cross 1969). While Alexander was in Egypt, the local people rose up and burned the Greek governor alive. As punishment, the city was razed, the inhabitants slaughtered or enslaved, and the site resettled with Macedonians (Quintus Curtius 4.8–10). The refugees took various documents with them, which were among the remains excavated. These have often been mentioned and even drawn on, but little has actually been published so far. Until recently, only a few lines from bullae had been quoted in the literature (Cross 1969). Now two full documents have been published (Cross 1985; Cross 1988). Apparently, these represent the most complete papyri, suggesting that the total amount of usable text will be disappointingly small.

2.2.3 Iranian and Mesopotamian Sources

Kent, R. G. *Old Persian* (1953).
Kervran, M., et al. "Une statue de Darius découverte à Suse." *Journal asiatique* 260 (1972) 235–66.
Kuhrt, A. "Survey of Written Sources Available for the History of Babylonia under the Later Achaemenids (Concentrating on the Period from Artaxerxes II to Darius III)." *Achaemenid History* (1987) 1.147–57.
———. "Babylonia from Cyrus to Xerxes." *CAH*² (1988) 4.112–38.
Landsberger, B., and T. Bauer. "Zu neuveröffentlichten Geschichtsquellen der Zeit von Asarhaddon bis Nabonid." *ZA* 37 (1927) 61–98.
Mayrhofer, M. *Supplement zur Sammlung der altpersischen Inschriften* (1978).
Oppenheim, A. L. "The Babylonian Evidence of Achaemenian Rule in Mesopotamia." *CHI* (1985) 2.529–87.
Perrot, J., and D. Ladiray. "La porte de Darius à Suse." *Cahiers de la délégation archéologique française en Iran* 4 (1974) 43–56.
Roaf, M. "The Subject Peoples on the Base of the Statue of Darius." *Cahiers de la délégation archéologique française en Iran* 4 (1974) 73–160.
San Nicolò, M. *Beitrage zu einer Prosopographie neubabylonischer Beamten der Zivil- und Tempelverwaltung* (1941).
Smith, S. *Babylonian Historical Texts Relating to the Capture and Downfall of Babylon* (1924).
Stronach, D. "La statue de Darius le Grand découverte à Suse." *Cahiers de la délégation archéologique française en Iran* 4 (1974) 61–72.
Vallat, F. "Les textes cunéiformes de la statue de Darius." *Cahiers de la délégation archéologique française en Iran* 4 (1974a) 161–70.
———. "L'inscription trilingue de Xerxès à la porte de Darius." *Cahiers de la délégation archéologique française en Iran* 4 (1974b) 171–80.
Weissbach, F. H. *Die Keilinschriften der Achameniden* (1911).

Most of the documents discussed here are either in Babylonian or Persian cuneiform or depend on records in these scripts as their ultimate source (e.g., Berossus), although the languages in the documents vary from Babylonian to Old Persian to Elamite. Because these sources often represent official Persian inscriptions or documents, it seems best, regardless of the language or medium, to consider them together. The known inscriptions in Old Persian have almost all been translated and made available in convenient editions (especially Kent: 107–63). To this may be added the recent discovery of a statue and gate of Darius, with their multilingual inscriptions in Old Persian, Elamite, Babylonian, and Egyptian (Kervran, et al.; Perrot/Ladiray; Roaf; Stronach; Vallat 1974a, 1974b).

Two major finds of documents in Elamite from Persepolis have also been published in editions, with a variety of studies (see 2.2.3.4). By contrast, the neo-Babylonian and later periods have not been of the same interest to Assyriologists as earlier periods. The result is that many of the Babylonian documents have not been published or are available only in autograph copies and thus are not easily accessible to the nonspecialist. This is unfortunate because the Babylonian documents are the most abundant source of data for the Persian period. A useful overview of what Babylonian material is available, along with the major published editions and collections, is given by Oppenheim. See also Kuhrt (1987; 1988), especially the bibliographies.

2.2.3.1 The Babylonian Chronicles

ANET: 305–7.
Grayson, A. K. *Assyrian and Babylonian Chronicles* (1975).

A variety of chronicle sources that have come to light over the years have been edited into one convenient edition by Grayson. The one important for the Persian period is the *Nabonidus Chronicle* (Chronicle 7), which describes the rise of Cyrus, the fall of Babylon, and the events immediately following. One should also note an undated fragment from the Achaemenid period (Chronicle 8) and a fragment of the chronicle of Artaxerxes III (Chronicle 9).

2.2.3.2 The Cyrus Cylinder

ANET: 315–16.
Berger, P.-R. "Der Kyros-Zylinder mit dem Zusatzfragment BIN II Nr. 32 und die akkadischen Personennamen im Danielbuch." *ZA* 64 (1975) 192–234.
Cameron, G. G. "Ancient Persia." *The Idea of History in the Ancient Near East* (1955) 77–97.
Eilers, W. "Le texte cunéiforme du cylindre de Cyrus." *Commémoration Cyrus* (1974) 2.25–34.
Kuhrt, A. "The Cyrus Cylinder and Achaemenid Imperial Policy." *JSOT* 25 (1983) 83–97.

The Cyrus Cylinder is an inscription set up early in Cyrus's reign. It has been of interest because it seems to indicate a policy of generosity and respect toward other religions within his empire and to serve as an illustration of the decree that allowed the Jews to return and rebuild the temple. That is, it has usually been understood from the Cyrus Cylinder that the policy was not a unique decision on behalf of the Jews but rather one example of a general religious policy. This view has now been challenged in part by Kuhrt, who argues that sufficient attention has not been paid to the propagandistic and stereotypical nature of the inscription (see also Cameron: 81–86). The Chaldean rulers had allowed religious freedom, and the Persians were no more liberal in this than their predecessors. The basic but incomplete text of the inscription has long been available in Weissbach's edition; now, however, Berger has been able to restore much of the missing conclusion from another fragment.

2.2.3.3 The Behistun Inscription

Greenfield, J. C., and B. Porten. *The Bisitun Inscription of Darius the Great: Aramaic Version* (1982).

Kent: 116–35.

Voigtlander, E. N. von. *The Bisitun Inscription of Darius the Great: Babylonian Version* (1978).

This is the longest and best known of the Persian inscriptions, as well as the most important for historical data. It describes Darius's rise to power and the events in the first few years of his reign. Although there is no doubt that the Behistun Inscription is a useful historical source, debate has been heated as to how far Darius's own account of his coup can be trusted. Some historians have followed his account more or less faithfully, whereas others have argued that it hides a great deal and is really only propaganda to cover a rather sordid taking of the throne. For a further discussion of some of these questions, see 2.4.2.3. The text of the inscription with translation is conveniently available in Kent (116–35); see also Greenfield/Porten and von Voigtlander.

2.2.3.4 The Elamite Texts from Persepolis

Cameron, G. G. *Persepolis Treasury Tablets* (1948).

———. "New Tablets from the Persepolis Treasury." *JNES* 24 (1965) 167–92.

Hallock, R. T. *Persepolis Fortification Tablets* (1969).

———. "The Evidence of the Persepolis Tablets." *CHI* (1985) 2.588–609.

Two finds of tablets in Persepolis give some insight into the economic workings of the Persian Empire. Hallock's article in *CHI* gives a useful summary of the content and value of these tablets for Persian history in general.

2.2.3.5 The Murašu Documents

Bickerman, E. J. "The Generation of Ezra and Nehemiah." *Studies in Jewish and Christian History* (1986) 3.299–326.

Cardascia, G. *Les archives des Murašû* (1951).
Coogan, M. D. *West Semitic Personal Names in the Murašû Documents* (1976).

This group of texts is a personal archive from a family business firm in Nippur ca. 455–403 B.C.E. It has been of special interest to Old Testament scholars because, judging by their names, several individuals prominent in the firm were evidently Jews. The definitive study, with a complete listing of sources and many of the texts in transliteration and translation, is Cardascia. Coogan looks at the problem of the names and attempts to determine their ethnicity, as does Bickerman in his more recent article.

2.2.3.6 Gadatas Inscription

Boffo, L. "La lettera di Dario I [*sic*] a Gadata: I privilegi del tempio di Apollo a Magnesia sul Meandro." *Bulletino dell' Istituto di Diritto Romano, "Vittorio Scialojo"* 81 (1978) 267–303.
Brandstein, W., and M. Mayrhofer. *Handbuch des Altpersischen* (1964) 91–98.
Cousin, G., and G. Deschamps. "Lettre de Darius, fils d'Hystaspes." *Bulletin de correspondence hellénique* 13 (1889) 529–42.
Hansen, O. "The Purported Letter of Darius to Gadatas." *Rheinisches Museum* 129 (1986) 95–96.
Hout, M. van den. "Studies in Early Greek Letter-Writing." *Mnemosyne*. Series 4, vol. 2 (1949) 19–41, 138–53, esp. 144–52.
Meiggs, R., and D. Lewis. *A Selection of Greek Historical Inscriptions to the End of the Fifth Century B.C.* (1969) 20–22 (no. 12).
Wiesehöfer, J. "Zur Frage der Echtheit des Dareios-Briefes an Gadatas." *Reinisches Museum* 130 (1987) 396–98.

An inscription in Greek from Asia Minor tells of a decree of Darius II concerning the official Gadatas, whom Darius rebukes for imposing a tax on the gardens of Apollo and otherwise neglecting his duty. This inscription is often cited in commentaries and monographs for comparison with the documents in the book of Ezra (2.2.1.2). However, the inscription itself does not date from the fourth century but is a much later copy from the second century C.E. The authenticity of the inscription itself is the subject of debate; some Orientalists and classicists accept it as genuine (e.g., Brandstein/Mayrhofer; Meiggs/Todd; Wiesehöfer) but others reject it as a fake (van den Hout; Hansen). This makes problematic the use of this inscription for comparative purposes.

2.2.3.7 Berossus

Burstein, S. M. *The Babyloniaca of Berossus* (1978).
Jacoby, F. *Die Fragmente der griechischen Historiker* (1926–58).

Kuhrt, A. "Berossus' *Babyloniaka* and Seleucid Rule in Babylonia." *Hellenism in the East* (1987) 32–56.
Schnabel, P. *Berossos und die babylonische-hellenistische Literatur* (1923).

Writing in Greek in the early Seleucid period, perhaps about 290 B.C.E., the Babylonian priest Berossus seems to have had cuneiform sources available to him. Where he can be checked, he shows a good knowledge of native Babylonian literature. The major problem is that his work is known only from fragmentary quotations in such later writers as Josephus and Eusebius. For the Persian period, one quotation has survived that describes the conquest of Cyrus (Josephus, *Ag. Ap.* 1.20 §§145–53). The major study, with a collection of the fragments, is still Schnabel, although a more recent edition of the fragments is found in Jacoby (III C, no. 680). Burstein gives an English translation and an Assyriological commentary. Kuhrt discusses the contents, purpose, and historical context of the work.

2.2.4 Egyptian Texts

Blenkinsopp, J. "The Mission of Udjahorresnet and Those of Ezra and Nehemiah." *JBL* 106 (1987) 409–21.
Hughes, G. R. "The So-called Pherendates Correspondence." *Grammata Demotika: Festschrift für Erich Lüddeckens zum 15. Juni 1983* (1984) 75–86.
Johnson, J. H. "The Demotic Chronicle as an Historical Source." *Enchoria* 4 (1974) 1–17.
———. "Is the Demotic Chronicle an Anti-Greek Tract?" *Grammata Demotika: Festschrift für Erich Lüddeckens zum 15. Juni 1983* (1984) 107–24.
Lichtheim, M. *Ancient Egyptian Literature.* Vol. 3: *The Late Period* (1980).
Lloyd, A. B. "The Inscription of Udjahorresnet: A Collaborator's Testament." *JEA* 68 (1982) 166–80.
Otto, E. *Die biographischen Inschriften der ägyptischen Spätzeit* (1954).
Posener, G. *La première domination perse en Egypte* (1936).
Spiegelberg, W. *Die sogenannte demotische Chronik des Pap. 215 der Bibliothèque Nationale zu Paris; nebst den auf der Rückseite des Papyrus stehenden Texten* (1914).
———. "Drei demotische Schreiben aus der Korrespondenz des Pherendates, des Satrapen Darius' I., mit den Chnum-Priestern von Elephantine." SPAW, phil.-hist. Klasse (1928) 604–22.

Most of the Egyptian inscriptions from the Persian period are transcribed, translated, and studied by Posener, whose work is still the basic collection of Egyptian material for this period. The statue of Darius recently found at Susa also has a hieroglyphic text, among other inscriptions; on this text, see 2.2.3. Of considerable interest is the inscription of

Udjahorresnet, the Egyptian admiral who went over to the Persians, which describes his activities. It has often been drawn on to illustrate the activities of Ezra and Nehemiah (see further at 2.3.8). The Pherendates correspondence gives us an insight into the relationship between the Persian government and the temples and priesthood of Egypt (Spiegelberg 1928; Hughes). Also, the later Demotic Chronicle, with its accompanying texts, is an important document, even if its interpretation is not always easy (Spiegelberg 1914; Johnson 1974; Johnson 1984).

2.2.5 Josephus

Cross, F. M. "A Reconstruction of the Judean Restoration." *JBL* 94 (1975) 4–18.

Grabbe, L. L. "Josephus and the Reconstruction of the Judean Restoration." *JBL* 106 (1987) 231–46.

———. "Who Was the Bagoses of Josephus (*Ant.* 11.7.1 §§297–301)?" *Transeuphratène* 5 (1991) 49–55.

Williamson, H.G.M. "The Historical Value of Josephus' *Jewish Antiquities* XI. 297–301." *JTS* 28 (1977) 49–66.

Josephus's discussion of the Persian period takes up most of *Ant.* 11 (except for the last part, which is occupied with the conquest of Alexander). His knowledge of the Persian period seems to have been minimal. For a portion of the two centuries of Achaemenid rule, he had the Bible as a source and clearly used it, primarily in its Greek form. For instance, he made use of 1 Esdras and the Greek version of Esther. If he knew the book of Ezra in its MT form, he gives no indication in the *Antiquities*. The exact source of his information on Nehemiah is difficult to identify. He may have known the present book of Nehemiah, but this is not at all certain, because other versions of the Nehemiah tradition were extant (cf. Grabbe 1987), and he does not discuss Nehemiah until he finishes with the life and death of Ezra. His discussion of Nehemiah does not follow the text of the book of Nehemiah, although this could simply be a case of adaptation of material, and he also includes data not in the Hebrew Nehemiah or its extant Greek translation. Therefore, it may be that he had a form of the Nehemiah tradition rather different from that available to us in the MT and LXX Nehemiah (cf. 2 Macc. 1:18-36).

Josephus's use of the biblical material is, for the most part, fairly straightforward, following an entire biblical book to its end before going on to another, rather than integrating the data. The one exception to this, however, results in added confusion. Josephus was aware of the order of at least the first few Persian kings: Cyrus, Cambyses, Darius I, Xerxes, and Artaxerxes I, and may have been aware that there was more than one Artaxerxes (see the textual tradition of *Ant.* 11.7.1 §297; cf. Grabbe 1987). He makes use of this partial knowledge by attempting to associate particular biblical books with these kings, but the result is a hodgepodge in which a certain disarray in the biblical text (e.g., the documents in Ezra 4) causes Josephus to rearrange the text further according to his incorrect understanding of Persian history.

Josephus's knowledge of the Persian period outside the biblical material is extremely limited. Apart from knowing the order of the first Persian kings, he gives only one additional tradition, which may have a historical basis but which is otherwise unconfirmed (Williamson; cf. Grabbe 1987; Grabbe 1991). This is found in *Ant.* 11.7.1 §§297–301: Eliashib, the high priest, was succeeded by Jaddua, who was succeeded by Johanan. Johanan's brother Joshua (Jesus) attempted to obtain the high priesthood with the help of Bagohi (Bagoses), an official (*stratēgos*) of "the other" (*tou allou*) Artaxerxes. The two brothers quarreled in the temple, and Johanan killed Joshua. As a result of this, Bagohi not only defiled the temple by going into it but also punished the Jews as a whole for seven years, evidently by an extra impost or tribute.

It is undoubtedly correct that Josephus is simply reporting some tradition received in oral or written form (Williamson). That he has a source does not prove its accuracy, but the story has nothing in it to cause prima facie rejection. On the positive side, the names Johanan and Bagohi are those known from biblical or other sources, and the story of a murder in the temple is not likely to be simply a Jewish invention. But even if the basic account is considered sound, the difficulties are by no means solved. When did this high priest Johanan live and who was this Bagoses? Some recent researchers have connected him with Bagoas (note the slight difference in spelling from the name in Josephus), the general of Artaxerxes III (2.4.4.1), which would mean that Johanan was not the high priest of Ezra 10:6 but a later figure not otherwise attested to in the extant sources (Williamson: 56–60; Cross: 5). This would put the episode well into the middle of the fourth century B.C.E., because Bagoas first appears as Artaxerxes' general in the invasion of Egypt in about 343 B.C.E. Although this is certainly possible, there are strong arguments for retaining the more traditional identification with the high priest Johanan known from Ezra, placing him somewhere about 400 B.C.E. (Grabbe 1991):

1. Two of the Elephantine papyri from the year 407 B.C.E. (Cowley nos. 30–31) speak of the high priest Johanan. If Ezra's mission is dated to 398, this would probably be the same individual as the Johanan of Ezra 10:6.

2. The same papyri show that the Persian governor (*pḥt*) at the time was called Bagohi (*bgwhy*).
3. Josephus refers to his Bagoses as "general" (*stratēgos*), which is also a term applied by the Greek writers to the Bagoas under Artaxerxes III. This is the main reason that many choose this as the background of Josephus's episode (e.g., Williamson: 58). This is not a very strong argument, however, because Josephus often uses the term *stratēgos* for civil as well as military leaders, a prime example being the biblical Joseph, who was hardly a great general (*Ant*. 2.6.8 §§140, 155). Furthermore, one cannot rule out the possibility that Josephus himself has deduced the connection with Artaxerxes III's Bagoas because it was the only figure he was aware of from Greek sources.
4. Although the names Johanan and Bagohi were not uncommon for this period of Jewish history, it seems better to seek a background in firmly attested figures than to postulate individuals otherwise unknown. Although the Bagohi of Artaxerxes III is well known, we have no indication that he ever had anything to do with Judah; but the Bagohi of the late fifth century was clearly governor of the province. Similarly, no other high priest named Johanan is known (cf. 2.2.7.2), even though it would not be unusual if one were to find another of this name in the period. A background for the story of about 400 B.C.E. poses no difficulties and fits several of the known historical data; there is no need to postulate any other, even though certainty is impossible.

Apart from this tradition, probably based on traditions that had come down to Josephus and possibly with a historical basis, Josephus seems almost totally ignorant of the Persian period in Palestine. When his biblical material ran out, he skipped over almost a century and went to the time of Alexander. One must keep his ignorance in mind when trying to evaluate the small amount of additional material he does provide (Grabbe 1987; see also 2.3.12). In sum, for the Persian period Josephus had the following information and sources or probable sources, but, as should be clear, he had only a small amount of independent information, which is confined to *Ant*. 11.7.1 §§297–301:

Ant.	11.1.1–5.5 §§1–158	1 Esdras
	11.5.6–8 §§159–83	A Nehemiah tradition
	11.6.1–13 §§184–296	Greek Esther
	11.7.1 §§297–301	(Oral?) tradition
	11.7.2 §§302–3	Variant of Neh 13:28?

2.2.6 Greco-Roman Writers

Brown, T. S. *The Greek Historians* (1973).
Drews, R. *The Greek Accounts of Eastern History* (1973).
Kuhrt, A. "Assyrian and Babylonian Traditions in Classical Authors: A Critical Synthesis." *Mesopotamien und seine Nachbarn* (1982) 539–53.
Lesky, A. H. *A History of Greek Literature* (1966).

No direct mention of Judah during this time seems to exist in the surviving classical sources. Nevertheless, until the rediscovery in the nineteenth century of primary sources from the ancient Near East, the Greek accounts formed the basis for the reconstruction of Persian history. Despite methodological problems, in some cases these sources can still provide useful information and are an important supplement to the Near Eastern records. Because the Greek histories are of most use for general information on the Persian period in the eastern Mediterranean, only a brief survey is given here. For the use of this material along with other sources for reconstructing Persian history, see 2.3. Only some of the more important and directly relevant references are given in the bibliographies here. For further information and references, see Brown, Drews, *CHCL*, Lesky, and *OCD*.

2.2.6.1 Herodotus

Balcer, J. M. *Herodotus and Bisitun* (1987).
Fehling, D. *Herodotus and His "Sources"* (1989).
Reinhardt, K. "Herodots Persergeschichten: Östliches und Westliches im Übergang von Sage zu Geschichte." *Herodot* (1962) 320–69.

Modern study has found that Herodotus is one of our most important sources of information about the reigns of Cyrus, Cambyses, Darius, and Xerxes. The reason for this is his close access to certain Persian traditions of that time. This does not mean that these traditions are not themselves sometimes the product of distortion, misinformation, or deliberate propaganda, but this can also be the case with the native records. Where he can be checked, Herodotus often shows an accurate knowledge of Persian tradition, suggesting that his account can be used with some confidence, along with contemporary Persian inscriptions.

2.2.6.2 Thucydides

Gomme, A. W., et al. *A Historical Commentary on Thucydides* (1956).
Lewis, D. M. *Sparta and Persia* (1977).

As a writer of his own contemporary history during the Peloponnesian wars, Thucydides is generally acknowledged as having reached the pinnacle of the historian's craft. Although his interest is in events in Greece, he constantly refers to dealings with the Persians who were actively involved behind the scenes in the fight between Athens and Sparta. Therefore, a good deal can be pieced together about Persian history for the years covered by his history (ca. 431–411 B.C.E.).

2.2.6.3 Ctesias

Bigwood, J. M. "Ctesias' Account of the Revolt of Inarus." *Phoenix* 30 (1976) 1–25.

———. "Ctesias as Historian of the Persian Wars." *Phoenix* 32 (1978) 19–41.

Jacoby, J. "Ktesias." *Griechische Historiker* (1956) 311–32.

König, F. W. *Die Persika des Ktesias von Knidos* (1972).

Momigliano, A. "Tradizione e invenzione in Ctesia." *Quarto contributo alla storia degli studi classici e del Mondo Antico* (1969) 181–212.

Most of the extant and lost *Persika* written by Greek writers over the centuries were heavily dependent on Ctesias, not Herodotus. This is unfortunate because Ctesias is generally acknowledged to be an unreliable source. As a physician to Artaxerxes II, he spent many years at the Persian court. But even though he claims to have consulted Persian records "on leather," much of his history is anecdotal material about court intrigues and scandals among the eunuchs of the harem. Scholars continue to use him to supplement Herodotus, but this must be done with a good deal of caution. The most recent studies have continued to be negative concerning his reliability (Drews 1973; Bigwood 1976; Bigwood 1978). König's work gives a good assembly of the fragments, with a German translation, but his treatment otherwise is generally considered too credulous.

2.2.6.4 Xenophon

Breitenbach, W. "Xenophon." *PW* (1967) 9A2.1709–18.

Due, B. *The Cyropaedia: Xenophon's Aims and Methods* (1989).

Hirsch, S. W. *The Friendship of the Barbarians: Xenophon and the Persian Empire* (1985).

A participant in a Greek mercenary army in Persia ca. 400 B.C.E., Xenophon can be a valuable source for contemporary Persian history. Because he was in Cyrus's army, this is especially true for the fight of Cyrus the Younger against Artaxerxes II. Xenophon's *Anabasis* is a dramatic account of the escape of this small group of Greek soldiers through the Persian Empire to the Black Sea and freedom, after the defeat of Cyrus. The *Hellenica*, his Greek history which continues Thucydides' account, also contains occasional references to the Persians, which can be as trustworthy as his data about Greek history.

Xenophon's *Cyropaedia* or life of Cyrus is potentially the most interesting but also the most controversial document. Scholars accept that there are historical data of genuine value in the work, but there is also much creative interpretation, distortion, and fabrication. The problem is to sort out what is reliable from what is not (cf. Breitenbach). Most scholars feel that this cannot be done with any confidence and are reluctant to give credence to the *Cyropaedia* where it cannot be independently confirmed. Hirsch evaluates the *Cyropaedia* more positively but in the final analysis admits the difficulties of sorting fact from fiction. What Hirsch does demonstrate is that Xenophon's knowledge of the Persians of his own time was quite good. Therefore, even when his knowledge of their history is shaky, Xenophon is still important as a source of information about Persian customs, society, and government (cf. also Due).

2.2.6.5 Ephorus

Andrewes, A. "Diodorus and Ephoros: One Source of Misunderstanding." *The Craft of the Ancient Historian* (1985) 189–97.
Barber, G. L. *The Historian Ephorus* (1935).

The universal history of Ephorus (ca. 405–330 B.C.E.) has perished as an independent work but seems to be the main source for Diodorus's books 11–16 (2.2.6.6). Although not a particularly critical historian, he sometimes used sources now lost and is a main source for the history of the Persian Empire in its last fifty to seventy-five years.

2.2.6.6 Diodorus Siculus

Bigwood, J. M. "Diodorus and Ctesias." *Phoenix* 34 (1980) 195–207.
Drews, R. "Diodorus and His Sources." *AJP* 83 (1963) 383–92.
Schwartz, E. "Diodoros." *Griechische Geschichtschreiber* (1957) 35–97.

Diodorus (first century B.C.E.) wrote a universal history in forty books, some of which are preserved only in fragments. He was not a critical historian but primarily a compiler, although he probably supplemented and rewrote his sources more extensively than some scholars have allowed (Bigwood). This means that his work varies according to the quality of those whom he copied. For the Persian period his main sources were Ctesias and Ephorus. Recent study has tended to evaluate Diodorus more positively than in the past (Drews; Bigwood).

2.2.6.7 Pompeius Trogus

Seel, O., ed. *M. Iuniani Iustini Epitoma Historiarum Philippicarum Pompei Trogi* (1985).

———. *Pompei Trogi Fragmenta* (1956).

Watson, J. S. *Justin, Cornelius Nepo, and Eutropius Literally Translated, with Notes and a General Index* (1872).

In the Augustan age Trogus wrote in Greek a universal history, the *Historiae Philippicae*, in forty-four books. Unfortunately, apart from a few fragments, the original work is lost. The Greek work was summarized in the Latin epitome of Justin around the third century C.E., and survives. The epitome is not normally very detailed and shows considerable confusion in particular areas; nevertheless, it has some useful information to supplement other historians of the period.

2.2.6.8 Plutarch

A priest of Delphi for several decades of his life and devoted to his hometown of Chaeronea in Boetia, Plutarch (ca. 50–120 C.E.) found time to write numerous volumes. The *Moralia* contains essays on a diversity of topics, some of them of considerable interest on the topic of religion in antiquity. Of more direct value for political history are his *Parallel Lives* of noble Greeks and Romans. The quality of his sources for these varies, and his concern is usually more moralistic than historical. Nevertheless, in some cases he provides valuable information on certain individuals. For the Persian period, see his life of Artaxerxes II.

2.2.7 Archeological Finds

*Stern.

———. "The Archeology of Persian Palestine." *CHJ* (1984) 1.88–114.

Weippert, H. *Palästina in vorhellenistischer Zeit* (1988) 682–728.

Useful summaries of the archeological finds and their interpretation are provided by Stern. Unfortunately, the article (Stern 1984) was written in 1973 and is thus actually less up-to-date than the English edition of his book (*1982). There are no major differences between the two, however, and the article serves as a convenient overview. Stern can now be supplemented by the survey in Weippert.

2.2.7.1 Seals and Seal Impressions

Avigad, N. "New Light on the MṢH Seal Impressions." *IEJ* 8 (1958) 113–19.
———. *Bullae and Seals from a Post-exilic Judean Archive* (1976).
Colella, P. "Les abréviations ט et ☧ (XP)." *RB* 80 (1973) 547–58.
Cross, F. M. "Judean Stamps." *EI* 9 (1969) 20–27.
Delavault, B., and A. Lemaire. "La tablette ourgaritique RS 16.127 et l'abréviation 'T' en Nord-Ouest Sémitique." *Semitica* 25 (1975) 31–41.
Goldwasser, O., and J. Naveh. "The Origin of the Tet-Symbol." *IEJ* 26 (1976) 13–19.
Lipinski, E. "<<Cellériers>> de la province de Juda." *Transeuphratène* 1 (1989) 107–9.
Meyers, E. M. "The Shelomith Seal and the Judean Restoration: Some Additional Considerations." *EI* 18 (1985) *33–*38.

The inscribed seals are some of the most important archeological finds of this period. Stern devotes a chapter to the seals and seal impressions found to date in Palestine, whether inscribed or not (*196–214). Avigad (1976) is devoted to one of the largest groups of seals and impressions. Of particular importance are the "Yehud stamps," those that bear the name "Judah" (*yhd, yhwd*), including some stamped on jars and jar handles. Many of these have nothing but the name on them, except for perhaps a motif of some sort, but their distribution is of potential significance for determining the boundaries of the Persian province of Judah, because it is now generally agreed that Yehud is the name of the province and that the stamps are official marks of the administration for various purposes.

There are several sorts of Yehud stamps. One group has the name "Yehud" plus the letter *tet* (Goldwasser/Naveh; Delavault/Lemaire; Colela). The meaning of the *tet* is still uncertain, although the recent suggestion that it means a measure of volume is finding increasing acceptance (*Stern: 206). Within this group are stamps and impressions with letters in the Aramaic script and others in Hebrew script. There is now general agreement that those with Hebrew script belong not to the Persian period but to the Hellenistic period, perhaps the third or second centuries B.C.E. The agreement that those with Aramaic script belong to the Persian period has not prevented wide differences of dating within this two-century span. Avigad put them in the early part of the Persian rule, the late sixth and early fifth centuries (1976: 32). This differs from the majority of scholars who agree on a century later, the late fifth and early fourth centuries (*Stern: 206), although Avigad's early dating has been accepted in a recent article (Meyers: *33–*34).

A good deal of controversy has surrounded seals with the word now read as *hpḥw'* or *hpḥh*, which usually occurs in conjunction with Yehud and often with a personal name. Such stamps were originally found only on jars or jar handles. A number of scholars read *hpḥh* (or *hpḥw'*) as "the governor"; Cross, however, took the word as *hpḥr*, "the potter," and the accompanying name as the name of the potter (24–26). The same word has now turned up on seals (and even on coins [2.2.7.2; cf. *Stern: 225]), confirming the view that it means "governor" (or the like) rather than "potter" (*Stern: 204–6). A group of these seals in the name of "Shelomith, handmaid of Elnathan the governor" adds additional support. The exact connotation of "handmaid" (*'mt*) is not clear but is probably the female equivalent of "servant" (*'ebed*), which in contexts such as this means an official of the king (Avigad 1976: 11–13). In this interpretation, which is widely accepted, Shelomith was a woman with considerable authority in the administration, perhaps in charge of the official archives of tax receipts and the like. She may also have been the concubine or wife of the governor, although this is less certain. Meyers has recently argued that Shelomith was the daughter of Zerubbabel (1 Chron 3:19) and that Elnathan married her to unite with the Davidic family, which would be advantageous for his office of governor. According to the dominant view, then, several individuals named on the seals can be added to the list of governors of Judah during the Persian period: Elnathan, Yeho'ezer, and Ahzi. Now, however, Lipinsky has added a cautionary note, arguing that the reading on the seals should be *pḥw'* and that it means "cellarer, one in charge of stores," not governor. If he is correct, this significantly reduces the list of known governors of Judah. Even if his proposal is rejected, there is still a major question as to whether the governors on the seals should be placed in the late sixth/early fifth centuries or after the time of Nehemiah.

Another group of seals is referred to as the *môṣāh* seals, from the word that appears on them (*mwṣh, mṣh*; see Avigad 1958), which seems to be the name of the village Mosah. It is less certain exactly for what the village was significant, although it may be that the name was stamped on jars of tax-free wine from the governor's estate at Mosah. Similar stamps have been found at Gibeon in a stratum that suggests a date early in the Persian period (*Stern: 207–9). Some of these stamps are on jar handles identical to those from Gibeon, dating from the neo-Babylonian period. This confirms both the early dating and the identification of the jars with produce from the estate of the governor. (Cf. Neh 3:7, which mentions the governor's estate in Gibeon.)

For the seals found among the Samaritan papyri from Wadi Daliyeh, see Cross, listed at 2.2.2 and 2.3.12.

2.2.7.2 Coins

Barag, D. P. "Some Notes on a Silver Coin of Johanan the High Priest." *BA* 48 (1985) 166–68.

———. "A Silver Coin of Yohanan the High Priest and the Coinage of Judea in the Fourth Century B.C." *Israel Numismatic Journal* 9 (1986–87) 4–21.

Bivar, A.D.H. "Achaemenid Coins, Weights and Measures." *CHI* (1985) 2.610–39.

Davis, N., and C. M. Kraay. *The Hellenistic Kingdoms: Portrait Coins and History* (1973).

Jeselsohn, D. "A New Coin Type with Hebrew Inscription." *IEJ* 24 (1974) 77–78.

Kanael, B. "Ancient Jewish Coins and Their Historical Importance." *BA* 26 (1963) 38–62.

Kindler, A. "Silver Coins Bearing the Name of Judea from the Early Hellenistic Period." *IEJ* 24 (1974) 73–76.

Meshorer, Y. *Ancient Jewish Coinage*. Vol. 1: *Persian Period through Hasmonaeans* (1982).

Mildenberg, L. "Yehud: A Preliminary Study of the Provincial Coinage of Judaea." *Greek Numismatics and Archaeology* (1979) 183–96.

———. "*Yehūd* Münzen." *Palästina in vorhellenistischer Zeit* (1988) 721–28.

Rappaport, U. "Gaza and Ascalon in the Persian and Hellenistic Periods in Relation to Their Coins." *IEJ* 20 (1970) 75–80.

———. "The First Judean Coinage." *JJS* 32 (1981) 1–17.

———. "Numismatics." *CHJ* (1984) 1.25–59.

Sellers, O. R. "Coins of the 1960 Excavation at Shechem." *BA* 25 (1962) 87–95.

Spaer, A. "Jaddua the High Priest?" *Israel Numismatic Journal* 9 (1986–87) 1–3.

The best overview of coinage in the Persian period is Meshorer (cf. Mildenberg 1979; Mildenberg 1988; *Stern 215–28; Stern 1984: 109–12; Rappaport 1984). The coins from both the Persian and Ptolemaic periods are treated here because they are not easily separated. The use of coins as a medium of exchange began in Greece, but the practice of minting coins had been adopted by the Persians by the time of Darius in about 515, when the golden "daric" first appeared (Bivar: 617, 621). Early coins are rare, and the finds suggest that the use of coins became common only during the last part of the fifth century. Greek and Phoenician coins (and recently one Persian coin [*Stern: 277 n.49]) have all been found in Palestine, but the most frequent and important type is that referred to as "Philisto-Arabian" or "Philisto-Egyptian," which seems to be local coinage. All local coins were silver or bronze, because the Persians retained the monopoly on minting in gold. The coins found in Palestine have been chiefly of silver, suggesting that bronze minting was not widespread there.

The Philisto-Arabian coinage is characterized by a great variety of types and few duplicates. This is explained by the suggestion that the local Persian governors had the authority to mint, which was normally done by using the seals of the various treasury officials. Because these officials were frequently replaced and the seals of the outgoing officials were substituted for those of the new officeholders, the coinage was also frequently being changed. A special subgroup of the Philisto-Arabian coinage includes those on which appears the name "Yehud" (*yhd*), the Aramaic form of "Judah." Characteristic of the Philisto-Arabian coins, a variety of types exist, although most tend to imitate the Attic drachma. These Yehud coins too appear to be minted for local usage. Although most coins have not come from documented excavations, Jerusalem is the site of three of four coins whose provenance is known; the other site is Beth-Zur. This geographical restriction, together with their general uniformity, suggests they all come from one mint in Jerusalem. There seems to be no consensus on precise datings (cf. Mildenberg 1979 with Meshorer: 1.13–18). Meshorer thinks those minted under Persian authority were all Yehud but that this usage also survived into the Ptolemaic period. Although Mildenberg dated those with the name *Yehudah* (*yhdh*) to the Persian period as well, Meshorer thinks they are the latest of the Ptolemaic mintings.

Three coins of the Yehud type from two separate sites have the inscription "the governor Hezekiah" (*hpḥh yḥzqyh*), which seems to give another name to the incomplete list of Persian governors over Judah (the name appears to be Jewish). This individual has been widely identified with the high priest Hezekiah (Ezekias), who was an acquaintance of Ptolemy I (Josephus, *Ag. Ap.* 1.22 §§187–89). Even if this is so, it does not mean that the coin is from the Hellenistic period, because Hezekiah may well have been a Persian governor; there is also the possibility that one or more high priests were governors before Alexander's conquest. Rappaport (1981) argues against this identification, however, noting that it is not certain that Ezekias was high priest (*archiereus* could also mean merely a "chief priest") and that the name was not necessarily uncommon (cf. Meshorer: 1.33). A coin similar to the Hezekiah coins has recently had its inscription read as "Johanan the priest" (*ywḥnn hkwhn*) and dated no earlier than the mid-fourth century (Barag 1985; Barag 1986–87). If this is correct, it could help confirm the hypothesis that there was a high priest Johanan other than the one named in the Elephantine papyri (ca. 408 B.C.E.). It is not certain, however, that this individual was a high priest, rather than a Persian official who happened to be of a priestly family (Mildenberg 1988: 724–25). Spaer has also identified a "Jaddua" (*ydw'*) on a coin which he dates to the first half of the fourth century B.C.E. To connect it with a high priest Juddua, though, is no more than speculation.

One Yehud coin differs from the rest (Meshorer no. 1: 1.21–28) in weight (about ten times heavier), in script (Aramaic rather than Hebrew), and in motif (an image of a deity). This coin was first published in the early 1800s and has occasioned a great deal of speculation. According to one view, it is a picture of Yahweh, the God of Israel (partly because the name "Yehud" was misread as "Yahweh"). Meshorer suggests it was an issue of the governor Bagohi (1.27–28). It might even be an issue of a Persian authority higher than the governor of Judah, perhaps the satrap of Syro-Palestine. The other Yehud coins, while having no obvious divine images, still exhibit human and animal figures, thereby showing no concern with the later taboo against images of any sort, which became an important concern to Judaism. A deity would be a different matter, though. Perhaps more puzzling is whom the inscription is supposed to represent.

Coins from the Greek kingdoms are widely known (Davis/Kraay), and some Ptolemaic coins have been found in Palestine (Sellers). As noted, some of the Yehud coins may be from the Greek period, as well as those with the inscription "Judah" (*yhdh*) in paleo-Hebrew script (cf. Kindler; Jeselsohn; Rappaport 1981). The coins probably date from no earlier than 305, when Ptolemy I took the title "king" and began to mint. Because they bear his portrait, they have been associated with his reign (Mildenberg). Meshorer disagrees with this, pointing out that Ptolemy I was not on good terms with the Jews and would not have given them permission to coin (1.18–20). He thinks all the Jewish coin issues under the Ptolemies are from the reign of Ptolemy II. This may be true, but it seems to me that we know too little to say exactly what Ptolemy I's relations were with the Jews. They may have changed for the better or the worse with time, and it is far from inconceivable that he granted permission to issue coins at some point.

2.2.7.3 Summary of Archeological Results

The details of the material remains from Persian Palestine are too many to catalogue here but are readily available (*Stern; Weippert). Only some of the more important conclusions will be summarized at this point, although their contribution to the actual historical context will be discussed largely in 2.4.

The archeological remains divide the region into two main areas: the Judean hill country (plus Samaria) and Transjordan on the one hand and Galilee and the coastal plain on the other hand (*Stern: 236). The cultural influences on the former were mainly from the East and Egypt, whereas those on the latter derived to a large extent from the West, especially from the Greek area. This Greek influence was pervasive in parts of the area long before the Hellenistic period (3.3.4). Much of it seems to have been mediated by the Phoenicians, although Greek mercenaries and others may have helped. Persian influence is minimal, except in those areas directly related to the Persian administration: taxes (and other economic issues), military, and various levels of government (*Stern: 236–37). This geographical division may also to some extent be paralleled by the tombs (*Stern: 68–92, 230–31). The "transitional" tombs date from the sixth century and probably come from the local population. "Shaft" tombs, common in Phoenicia and the West, have contents that match the East/West division of the region. They can be interpreted as being generally Phoenician burials, most of them also being situated near settlements that were principally Phoenician. "Cist" tombs, a type common throughout the East, are thought to be those of soldiers from Persian garrisons. No tombs have been found that are certainly Jewish or Samaritan.

The destruction layers of various towns show that the Persian period was not necessarily stable (*Stern: 253–55; Stern 1984: 114). Some sites (e.g., Hazor) were occupied only during part of this time; two phases of occupation are found in cities such as Akko, Jaffa, Gezer, Lachish, and En-Gedi, whereas three or more have been found at Ashdod and some other coastal cities. Around the year 480 B.C.E. the areas of Benjamin and the southern part of Samaria show widespread destruction, although it has been difficult to relate this to a particular event known from history. A century later, about 380 B.C.E., another phase of destruction is indicated for parts of the Shephelah and the Negev. This may be related to the efforts of Egypt to free itself from Persian rule. Toward the end of Persian rule, disaster struck a number of places in the Palestinian area. Some of these are probably related to the conquests of Alexander (Samaria, Gaza, Megiddo, Akko), but others are probably to be attributed to the wars of the Diadochi (Tel Sippor) or even to events in the final years of Persian rule (e.g., the revolt of Sidon in 349 B.C.E.; but see 2.3.9).

2.3 MAJOR HISTORICAL ISSUES

2.3.1 Judah as a Theocracy

Blenkinsopp, J. "Temple and Society in Achemenid Judah." *Studies in the Second Temple* (1991) 22–53.

Broughton, T.R.S. "Roman Asia Minor." *An Economic Survey of Ancient Rome* (1938) 4.499–916.

———. "New Evidence on Temple-Estates in Asia Minor." *Studies in Roman Economic and Social History in Honor of Allan Chester Johnson* (1951) 236–50.

Laperrousaz, E.-M. "Le régime théocratique juif a-t-il commencé a l'époque perse, ou seulement à l'époque hellénistique?" *Semitica* 32 (1982) 93–96.

Rostovtzeff, M. [M. Rostowzew]. *Studien zur Geschichte des römischen Kolonates* (1910).

The term "theocracy" (literally, "rule by God") means government by the priesthood or clerical rule. Josephus seems to have coined the word when he stated that in setting up the nation, Moses "gave to his constitution the form of what—if a forced expression be permitted—may be termed a 'theocracy,' placing all sovereignty and authority in the hands of God" (*Ag. Ap.* 2.16 §165).

In the period of the First Temple, Israel and Judah were monarchies. Although there was a high priest, the major civil and even cultic official was the king. Throughout most of the period of the Second Temple, however, the high priest took on an increasingly prominent role. Judah during most of that time could be best characterized as a theocracy. That is, even when it was under foreign domination, as it usually was, the high priest was the main figure of government within Judah itself. He was also the representative of the nation to the foreign overlord. The high priest was advised by a council (*gerousia*, *boulē*, or *sunedrion* [Sanhedrin]), which was composed in part of priests, although members of the aristocracy and perhaps some others also seem to have been part of it (cf. 4.3.1; 7.3.2.3). The period of Hasmonean rule (chap. 5) was quintessentially theocratic, because the high priest was not only the chief civil authority but even took over the title of king.

There are some complications to this picture. First, under Herod there was a native king who had taken away most of the power of the high priest and Sanhedrin (6.3.4). Although some of this power was restored when Judea became a Roman province, the situation could not have been as before. Under Agrippa I the nation was again under a king (7.4.6); although he seems to have respected the priestly hierarchy more than his grandfather had, its actual powers were still limited almost entirely to the temple sphere. If we return to a concept from the time of Persian rule, then Judah could be said to be under a "dyarchy" of Persian governor and high priest. The concept of dyarchy arose during the early period of the return, when the governor appointed by the Persians was the Jewish leader Zerubbabel. Although there is no clear evidence that he was ever declared king, both Haggai and Zechariah give him an elevated status with royal overtones (2.3.3). To what extent the concept of dyarchy persisted after this time is not clear.

Although it has been proposed that all the governors of Judah appointed by the Achaemenid court were Jewish, this is not certain. Several of those known were Jewish (2.3.4), but we cannot be certain of all those recorded, much less those about whom nothing has survived. It may be, however, that dyarchy was the form basic administration took during much of the two centuries of Persian rule. If so, one could argue that theocracy as such did not really come about until the Hellenistic period (Laperrousaz); however, it is always possible that the high priest was himself appointed governor on some occasions (cf. 2.2.7.2). Furthermore, one could still see the governor as in the position of the overseer of the ruling government, even if himself Jewish, with the high priest still the representative from the Jewish side, so that even under Achaemenid rule the term "theocracy" is not an inaccurate description.

Judah was basically organized as a temple state, of which there seem to have been several in the ancient Near East (Rostovtzeff: 269–78; Broughton 1938: 641–46; Broughton 1951; Blenkinsopp). Our knowledge of other such entities is documented mainly from the Greek period, but the indication is that they were only continuing a constitution already in operation during the Persian period. Judah's main difference from other temple states lies in the area of land ownership: there is no clear evidence of temple estates in Judah, whereas these were a common feature of most temple states.

For the significance and ideology of the temple, see 8.3.3. For Weinberg's thesis about the *Bürger–Tempel–Gemeinde* and further bibliography, see 2.3.13.2.

2.3.2 Sheshbazzar and the First Return

Dion, P. E. "ששבצר and ססנורי." *ZAW* 95 (1983) 111–12.
Berger, P.-R. "Zu den Namen ששבצר und שנאצר (Esr $1_{8.11}$ $5_{14.16}$ bzw. I Chr 3_{18})." *ZAW* 83 (1971) 98–100.
Gelston, A. "The Foundations of the Second Temple." *VT* 16 (1966) 232–35.
Japhet, S. "Sheshbazzar and Zerubbabel—Against the Background of the Historical and Religious Tendencies of Ezra-Nehemiah." *ZAW* 94 (1982) 66–98; 95 (1983) 218–29.
Lust, J. "The Identification of Zerubbabel with Sheshbassar." *Ephemerides Theologicae Lovanienses* 63 (1987) 90–95.

One of the most enigmatic figures in the early Persian period is Sheshbazzar. He is mentioned as a "prince" (*nāśî'*) of Judah in Ezra 1:8 but then disappears from the narrative as any sort of participant in subsequent events. In one of the Aramaic documents, however, he is given an important role: "King Cyrus released them [the temple vessels from Jerusalem] from the temple in Babylon to be given to the one called Sheshbazzar whom he had appointed governor. . . . That same Sheshbazzar then came and laid the foundations for the House of God in Jerusalem" (Ezra 5:14-16). This conforms with the statement in Ezra 1:8-11 that Sheshbazzar was given the vessels, made an inventory of them, and brought them back to Jerusalem, but the later passage includes the important additional information that Sheshbazzar was a governor (*peḥāh*) and that he was responsible for actually laying the foundations of the temple (cf. Gelston on the connotation of this phrase; see also 2.4.2.4).

The questions are: Who was this Sheshbazzar? Why is he not further mentioned in the narrative portion of Ezra? What did he do? What is the meaning of the title *nāśî'*? It has been proposed that he is identical with Shenazzar, the son of Jeconiah who is mentioned in 1 Chron 3:18. This now seems unlikely (Berger; Dion), even though we know of other instances in which Jews apparently of the royal line were appointed as governor (e.g., Zerubbabel). More important is why such an important figure disappears from the account in Ezra. Is it that his role was basically forgotten and the editor had no further information on him (cf. Japhet 1982: 96)? In the present form of the narrative, Sheshbazzar does not fit easily, because the work of restoration is ascribed to Joshua and Zerubbabel; indeed, the editor seems to intend that he be identified with Zerubbabel (Lust). Did the editor have a tradition that he did not quite know what to do with? His pairing of leaders, specifically Zerubbabel and Joshua, may indicate that Sheshbazzar did not fit the pattern and thus was slighted (Japhet 1982: 94). If so, it may be that Sheshbazzar's status and role were suppressed for theological reasons of the editor. Another reason might be that Sheshbazzar's mission failed to complete one of its intended tasks; that is, the temple was begun but did not progress beyond the foundations.

A lot depends on how positively one evaluates the data in the Aramaic document (2.2.1.2), on the one hand, and in the narrative section of Ezra, on the other. For example, Japhet has suggested that the puzzling title "prince of Judah" is simply another way of saying "governor of the province of Judah" (1982: 96–98). Do we know, however, that this is a correct piece of information, which simply has to be interpreted? Or is it only a contribution of the editor, which should be explained theologically rather than historically?

2.3.3 The Leadership of Zerubbabel and Joshua

Ackroyd, P. R. "Two Old Testament Historical Problems of the Early Persian Period." *JNES* 17 (1958) 13–27.
Barker, M. "The Two Figures in Zechariah." *Heythrop Journal* 18 (1977) 38–46.
Beyse, K.-M. *Serubbabel und die Königserwartungen der Propheten Haggai und Sacharja* (1972).
Borger, R. "An Additional Remark on P. R. Ackroyd, *JNES*, XVII, 23–27." *JNES* 18 (1959) 74.
Halpern, B. "Ritual Background of Zechariah's Temple Song." *CBQ* 40 (1978) 167–90.
Harrelson, W. "The Trial of the High Priest Joshua: Zechariah 3." *EI* 16 (1982) 116*–24*.
Olmstead, A. T. "Tattenai, Governor of 'Across the River.'" *JNES* 3 (1944) 46.
Sauer, G. "Serubbabel in der Sicht Haggais und Sacharjas." *Das ferne und nahe Wort* (1967) 199–207.
Seybold, K. "Die Königserwartung bei den Propheten Haggai und Sacharja." *Judaica* 28 (1972) 69–78.
Waterman, L. "The Camouflaged Purge of Three Messianic Conspirators." *JNES* 13 (1954) 73–78.

Note: This section also uses the bibliography at 2.2.1.6.

The basic impression in Ezra is that Zerubbabel and Joshua (or Jeshua) the high priest returned to the land directly after the decree of Cyrus (Ezra 1:1—2:2), whereas in the very next year the temple was begun with the laying of the foundations (Ezra 3). This picture does not square with other information in the Old Testament (e.g., the activities of Sheshbazzar or the picture in Haggai and Zechariah), however, and it is probable that Zerubbabel and Joshua were part of a later migration to Palestine. Their group may not have come until the end of Cambyses' reign, in the mid- or late 520s.

One of the main issues in relation to Zerubbabel and Joshua is that of the leadership of the Jewish community in Jerusalem. A number of passages in Zechariah and Haggai concern this issue, indicating two main views: (1) that there was to be one leader, Zerubbabel, with the high priest definitely subordinate to him, or (2) that the leadership consisted of a dyarchy, in which Zerubbabel and Joshua governed jointly as civil and religious leader, respectively. Both views can be justified by various passages within the book, suggesting that different authors and editors had different points of view in the history of the tradition. For example, Petersen has noted that the visions of Zechariah seem to give a prominent place to the high priest, whereas the oracles focus on a royal figure (122).

Haggai gives the most straightforward message, especially in 2:20-23 where Zerubbabel is labeled "the signet ring" (*hôtām*). That this signifies royal authority is indicated by Jer 22:24-30, to which it alludes, as well as the use of traditional coronation language (cf. Psalms 2; 110). Haggai, however, is more subtle here than some allow, because his reference to kingship is implicit rather than explicit—it does not say, "Crown Zerubbabel!"—and no timetable is suggested as to when Zerubbabel might assume this authority (cf. Petersen: 105–6). Indeed, some have even argued that the lack of messianic language here takes the focus away from Zerubbabel directly (Wolff: 106–7; Meyers: 70), although most see a focus on Zerubbabel as a Davidide (Blenkinsopp 1984: 233; Beyse: 56–57).

Zechariah is more complicated, speaking on the subject in several passages. In Zechariah 3 the emphasis is on Joshua, who is purified and crowned with the sign of his priesthood. (Some have thought this purification suggests some lapse on Joshua's part [e.g., Blenkinsopp 1984: 238], but this has also been strongly denied [*Ackroyd 1968: 184; Petersen: 194–96].) Verse 8, however, refers to "my servant the Branch" who is to come, which most take as an insertion and interpret in the light of 6:12 as a reference to Zerubbabel. If the "Branch" is Zerubbabel (although perhaps it is Joshua [Coggins: 46]), this indicates an editorial attempt to divert attention from Joshua to Zerubbabel. The vision of the olive trees in chapter 4 originally alluded to coequal individuals, Joshua and Zerubbabel (4:1-6a; 10b-14). Into this have been inserted oracles, which focus on Zerubbabel as the builder of the temple, with royal overtones (4:6b-10a; cf. Halperin: 168–81; Petersen: 121).

Zechariah 6:9-15 has presented a problem to many interpreters (on the tradition history, see Beyse: 78–84, 89–91). One of the difficulties is whether the Hebrew "crowns" in v 11 is a mistake for "crown." Many advocate emending the text to the singular; however, a number of recent commentators have argued that the plural should be retained, because two individuals are being crowned (Petersen: 275; Meyers: 349–50; cf. Coggins: 46–47). The tendency has been to assume that an original oracle favoring Zerubbabel has been toned down by including Joshua at a later time, when Zerubbabel was no longer there (e.g., Mitchell, et al.: 185–86; Blenkinsopp: 238). Petersen, however, has argued that it is the reverse (277–78): an original oracle that applied equally to Joshua and Zerubbabel has been tilted in favor of Zerubbabel by the insertion of an oracle in which Zerubbabel is the sole recipient (vv 12-13). Ackroyd has also noted that an editing out of Zerubbabel is unlikely (*1968: 196; cf. Beyse: 99). In either case, one sees two tendencies, one which focuses on Zerubbabel as the dominant individual, and one which envisages a dyarchical form of governance.

A further question concerns the possibility that Zerubbabel had messianic pretensions (Waterman). The basic reasons for arguing this are (1) he was of the Davidic line, (2) such is suggested by Hag 2:20-23 and perhaps Zech 6:9-15, and (3) Zerubbabel disappears abruptly during the rebuilding of the temple and is not referred to at the dedication ceremony on its completion in Ezra 6:14-22. This view has been strongly opposed by Ackroyd, who points out (1) Zerubbabel was appointed by the Persians, who would not have been ignorant of his Davidic origins; (2) even after investigation, Darius was willing to confirm the decree of Cyrus and the activities of the Jews in rebuilding the temple; and (3) there was no further disruption of the building (1958; *1968: 164–66). Whatever the views of Haggai and perhaps Zechariah about Zerubbabel, we have no indication that he aspired to royal status or accepted their acclaim at face value. There is also an underlying eschatological focus in the books (even at Hag 2:20-23), which inevitably takes the emphasis off the immediate presence of a royal figure, even if one is ultimately envisaged. Perhaps this is due to the editor rather than the original prophet, but it is a moot point. There is also the question of how trustworthy the narrative in Ezra 6 is: Can we really be sure that the temple was completed in 515 B.C.E.? If so, can we be sure that Zerubbabel was not there? After all, the books of Haggai and Zechariah say nothing about the completion of the temple.

2.3.4 Extent and Status of the Jewish State

Ackroyd, P. R. "Archaeology, Politics and Religion: The Persian Period." *Iliff Review* 39 (1982) 5–24, 51.

Aharoni, Y. *The Land of the Bible: A Historical Geography* (1979).

Alt, A. "Die Rolle Samarias bei der Entstehung des Judentums." *Kleine Schriften zur Geschichte des Volkes Israel* (1953) 2.316–37.

Avi-Yonah, M. *The Holy Land from the Persian to the Arab Conquests* (1966).

Demsky, A. "*Pelekh* in Nehemiah 3." *IEJ* 33 (1983) 242–44.

Lemaire, A. "Populations et territoires de Palestine à l'époque perse." *Transeuphratène* 3 (1990) 31–74.

McEvenue, S. E. "The Political Structure in Judah from Cyrus to Nehemiah." *CBQ* 43 (1981) 353–64.

Smith, M. *Palestinian Parties and Politics That Shaped the Old Testament* (1971).

Stern, M. "The Province of Yehud: The Vision and the Reality." *The Jerusalem Cathedra* 1 (1981) 9–21.

Williamson, H.G.M. "The Governors of Judah under the Persians." *Tyndale Bulletin* 39 (1988) 59–82.

It is generally agreed that the basic divisions of Palestine remained the same throughout the latter part of Assyrian rule and through the Babylonian and Persian periods. When the kingdom of Judah was conquered by the Babylonians, it was initially ruled by a governor appointed by Nebuchadnezzar (Jer 40:5). After his assassination, however, the story breaks off, and the status of Judah after this time is unclear (Jer 41:2). With the coming of Persian rule and the return of Jews to rebuild the temple, it seems evident that Judah became an independent province, if it had not been one all along (see below on the question of independence).

Basic information about the status of Judah is not available until the time of Nehemiah. That the borders of Judah remained generally the same from his time to that of the Hasmoneans, however, suggests that the borders had been the same from the beginning of the Persian period (Avi-Yonah: 13–19). The northern and western borders were essentially those that existed under the kingdom of Judah, taking in the old area of Benjamin to the north and Azekah to the west (Lod probably being outside Judah's territory). The eastern border would have been the Jordan. Southward, much of the Negev area had been taken over by the Edomites (2.3.5.4; 6.3.6), and Judah extended now only as far south as Beth-Zur. The country thus was roughly in the shape of rectangle, about twenty-five by thirty miles or close to eight hundred square miles. Judging mainly from Nehemiah 3 (which lists the builders of the wall), it has been suggested that there were six districts, each divided into two subdistricts (Avi-Yonah: 19–23; cf. *Stern: 247–49; Aharoni: 418):

1. Jerusalem, with perhaps Ramath-Rahel as a subcenter.
2. Keilah, including the southwestern part of the province. The subcenter is uncertain but may have been at Adullam.
3. Mizpah, the northern district, with the subcapital at Gibeon.
4. Beth-haccerem, the western district, with Zanoah perhaps as the subcapital.
5. Beth-Zur, the southernmost district, Tekoah probably being the secondary capital.
6. Jericho, the eastern district, with the secondary center apparently at Senaah.

This detailed reconstruction has now been challenged by Demsky. The reconstruction depended on understanding the word *pelek* (Neh 3:9, 12, 14-18) as "district." Demsky's analysis indicates, rather, that the word means "corvée labor"; in other words, an individual such as Malchijah (Neh 3:14) should be designated "foreman over the work gang from Beth-haccerem" rather than "ruler over the district of Beth-haccerem." Therefore, the picture given by Avi-Yonah and others must be received with caution.

Following the hints of earlier scholars, Alt developed the hypothesis that Judah was included in the province of Samaria during the neo-Babylonian and Persian periods. This theory was followed by others (e.g., *Galling: 92 n.3) and has had a good deal of influence (see also *Stern: 213). It was attacked by Smith (193–201), however, and his arguments were accepted by Widengren (*509–11). Most recently, a detailed defense of the theory has been advanced by McEvenue, who recognizes that "the form of political authority in Judah from 597 to 445 B.C. remains obscure" but states that Alt's theory "remains the only proposal supported by probable arguments" (364). One can summarize Alt's hypothesis as follows (including the further developments of it by McEvenue):

1. With the fall of Samaria, a ruling upper class was imported to replace the Israelite upper class, which was deported to Assyria. This upper class maintained its independence, even from the surrounding Israelite lower classes, well into Persian times.
2. When Judah fell there was no importation of population to replace the Jews taken captive to Babylon. Instead, Judah was ruled as a part of the province of Samaria.
3. At the time of the building of the temple in Jerusalem in Ezra 4, members of the Samarian upper class came with the governor of Ebir-nari to investigate as a part of their ruling function, which continued under the Persians. No governor of Judah is mentioned at this time, showing that Tattenai did not regard Zerubbabel as governor. Further, why did not the Jews appeal directly to Darius, rather than simply citing a decree of Cyrus?
4. Although such figures as Sheshbazzar and Zerubbabel are referred to as *peḥāh*, this term has a very broad meaning. Alt assumes that they were only special commissioners with a specific duty, rather than regular governors. McEvenue argues that only in Aramaic does the term mean the ruler of a province or satrapy; in Hebrew it means the head of an extended family.
5. The term *mĕdînāh* also meant "extended family" in pre-exilic times and keeps this meaning in Ezra-Nehemiah. It does not mean "province" in these books, as is normally believed.
6. Only with the arrival of Nehemiah does Judah become a separate province with its own governor. The reaction of Sanballat and his companions is sufficient to show that they envisage a new situation that encroaches on their powers, rather than simply the appointment of a new governor of an independent province. Furthermore,

Nehemiah's building of the walls is to make Jerusalem into a provincial capital; earlier attempts to rebuild the walls were not allowed for the reason that it was not such a capital.

Because McEvenue wrote after Smith's attack on Alt (although hardly giving a detailed summary of Smith's case), the following points against Alt and McEvenue are only in part those advanced by Smith (cf. *Williamson 1985: 242–44; Williamson 1988):

1. That the imported population was a ruling upper class is stated but nowhere demonstrated (McEvenue only repeats Alt's assertions without argument). More likely, as Smith notes, the imported population was brought there after their own rebellion against the Assyrians.
2. McEvenue's arguments about the meaning of *mĕdînāh* and *peḥāh* seem to be only hair-splitting, which ignores the broader philological usage. Granted that both terms can be used in a variety of senses, his attempts to confine their usage in Ezra and Nehemiah to a "pre-exilic" and a "Hebrew" usage are unconvincing. For example, he admits that the book of Esther is Hebrew evidence for the use of both *mĕdînāh* and *peḥāh* in a sense contrary to his theory. He ignores linguistic argument, however, by stating that Esther is much influenced by Persian usage. Indeed, the usage in Ezra-Nehemiah may also be influenced by Persian usage. Although the two terms may not in every case refer to entities that we think of as "governor [of a province]" and "province," they usually do so. To establish his thesis, McEvenue must show that their usage in Ezra-Nehemiah and Haggai does not mean this; he does not do so.
3. McEvenue states that Zerubbabel received his authority directly from Darius. This seems unlikely. Rather, Zerubbabel probably came to Palestine before Darius assumed the throne. In the confusion which followed Darius's accession, Zerubbabel (on the advice of Zechariah and Haggai?) resumed (or began) work on the temple. It is hardly surprising that Tattenai investigated, and, indeed, there was no authority for this building. Governor or no governor, the sub-satrap of Ebir-nari had the right to approve or forbid the continuation of the work. Zerubbabel is, in fact, not mentioned and may not have been on the scene. Even if he was, however, he had no right to appeal to Darius over his superior, who was Tattenai.
4. McEvenue's attempts to prove that Neh 5:15 does not refer to actual governors of Judah are not very convincing. It is still a strong argument that Nehemiah would not be in a very powerful position if he

was comparing himself to satraps (rather than governors directly over Judah) or to governors of neighboring areas.

These points do not of themselves prove that there were governors before Nehemiah. Disproving the arguments of Alt and McEvenue does not thereby automatically establish the contrary hypothesis. One might think that coins and seals would settle the question, but their dating is still very controversial (2.2.7.1; 2.2.7.2). Ackroyd has recently approached the problem from another point of view, asking about the broader context in which one must place the subject: What was the basis of the opposition from Samaria? Why did the Elephantine community appeal to both Samaria and Jerusalem? Why does there seem to be a change of coinage and seal motifs about the middle of the fifth century (1982: 13–17)?

Nevertheless, when the balance of the arguments is considered, it seems likely that there were some governors over Judah before Nehemiah. Whether there were such governors continuously or only episodically is impossible to say (Smith [196–97] himself allows that for a period of several decades there was a union of Judah and Samaria). That Sheshbazzar, Zerubbabel, and probably several other individuals were governors of the province of Judah before Nehemiah seems, however, the best explanation in light of the present data.

On the question of Weinberg's thesis of a *Bürger–Tempel–Gemeinde*, see 2.3.13.2.

2.3.5 Samaria and the Other Neighbors of Judah

2.3.5.1 General

Avi-Yonah, M. *The Holy Land from the Persian to the Arab Conquests* (1966).
Forrer, E. *Die Provinzeinteilung des assyrischen Reiches* (1920).
*Galling: 185–210.
Leuze, O. *Die Satrapieneinteilung in Syrien und im Zweistromlande von 520–320* (1935).
Rainey, A. "The Satrapy 'Beyond the River.'" *AJBA* 1 (1969) 51–78.

As already noted (2.3.4), Palestine during Persian rule evidently continued to maintain the same basic governmental divisions as it had under Assyrian and Babylonian rule. When it conquered northern Israel, Assyria divided the former kingdom into three administrative districts: Megiddo, Dor, and Samaria (Forrer). After the conquest of Judah by the neo-

Babylonian Empire, it also evidently became another province (see 2.3.4). With the division of the Persian Empire into satrapies, Palestine fell into the satrapy of "Babylon and Ebir-nari"; Ebir-nari ("Beyond the River [Euphrates]"), which later became a satrapy in its own right and even later still was known as Coele-Syria, included all the land on the west side of the Euphrates as far as Egypt.

Descriptions of the Syrian area are found in Herodotus (3.91) and especially in the Greek writer pseudo-Skylax from the latter part of the fourth century (*Galling; Avi-Yonah: 28–31). Putting together archeological and historical data yields a basic picture as follows (*Stern: 237–45).

2.3.5.2 Samaria

A discussion of Samaritan literature, history, and religion, with bibliography, is given at 8.2.10. For the Sanballat of the book of Nehemiah, see 2.4.3.3. On the question of whether Judah was originally administered from Samaria in the Persian period, see 2.3.4.

2.3.5.3 Phoenicia and the Coast

Of the old Assyrian provinces, Megiddo took up most of Galilee, whereas Dor took in the Shephelah. At least some of this territory was administered by Phoenician cities under the Persians. The cities of Achzib, Acco, and Shiqmona were under Tyrian rule, as was Crocodilopolis farther south. Under Sidon were Dor, Adaros, and probably Jaffa. Whether Galilee as such was under Phoenician rule is uncertain, although the material remains suggest that it was settled mainly by a Phoenician population. The same applies to the old province of Ashdod, including such cities as Yavneh and Ashkelon: although it was possibly organized as a province, the coastal cities were more likely under Phoenician dominion, at least part of the time.

2.3.5.4 Arabia, including Edom, Gaza, and Transjordan

Bartlett, J. R. *Edom and the Edomites* (1989).

Dumbrell, W. J. "The Tell El-Maskhuta Bowls and the 'Kingdom' of Qedar in the Persian Period." *BASOR* 203 (Oct. 1971) 33–44.

Eph'al, I. *The Ancient Arabs* (1982).

Kasher, A. *Jews, Idumaeans, and Ancient Arabs* (1988).

Lemaire, A. "Un nouveau roi arabe de Qedar dans l'inscription de l'autel à encens de Lakish." *RB* 81 (1974) 63–72.

Naveh, J. "The Aramaic Ostraca from Tel Beer-sheba (Seasons 1971–1976)." *Tel Aviv* 6 (1979) 182–98.
Rabinowitz, I. "Aramaic Inscriptions of the Fifth Century B.C.E. from a North-Arab Shrine in Egypt." *JNES* 15 (1956) 1–9.
Rainey, A. F. "The Satrapy 'Beyond the River.' " *AJBA* 1 (1969) 51–78.

The Edomites especially, but also certain of the Arab tribes, are mentioned in the Old Testament. The Edomites moved from their traditional lands southeast of the Dead Sea into southern Judah during the sixth century (but possibly beginning as early as the seventh), most likely because of pressure from nomadic Arabic tribes, particularly the Qedarites. This area became their new home, known as Idumea from the Greek name for the country. Personal names indicate that a few remained in the old area and gradually assimilated to the Nabateans (Kasher: 2). Some Old Testament passages show a negative attitude toward Edom (e.g., the book of Obadiah), and it has often been thought that the Edomites participated in the destruction of Jerusalem in 587/586. However, "Edom" is symbolic in particular passages, and the arguments for Edomite atrocities in the fall of Jerusalem are not solidly founded (Bartlett: 151–57).

It is not entirely clear that "Arabia" was an organized satrapy under the Persians; it may have been only a more or less independent area of unruly tribes, which often gave "gifts" to the Persians (Herodotus 3.97). Arab tribesmen helped Cambyses in his invasion of Egypt and were rewarded for this (Herodotus 3.4–9), but there are indications that at other times they were not so friendly (Rainey: 65).

Several inscriptions mention a "king of Qedar" (Rabinowitz; Dumbrell; Lemaire). The distribution suggests that he had authority of some sort over a large area in southern Palestine and Transjordan and even as far as lower Egypt. The name "Geshem" appears for the king himself in one inscription, and also for the father of Qaynu, another king (Rabinowitz; *TSSI*: 2.122–23 [text no. 25]). This Geshem has been widely identified as the opponent of Nehemiah (Neh 2:19; 6:1-2, 6). This is a reasonable hypothesis but cannot be proved from the data presently available (Eph'al: 210–14; Bartlett: 170–71). The exact status of particular older areas at this time is unclear. Was there a separate province of Idumea? If so, there is no contemporary reference to it—no reference to the Edomites as Judah's southern neighbor. Perhaps this area south of Judah had come under Arab rule, but this seems doubtful, even though Qedarites had evidently settled there (Bartlett: 168–72). The same problem occurs with Gaza and perhaps also the old areas of Ammon and Moab, as there is no contemporary reference to them during the Persian period (Eph'al: 197). In the same context as Geshem the Arab, however, we hear of

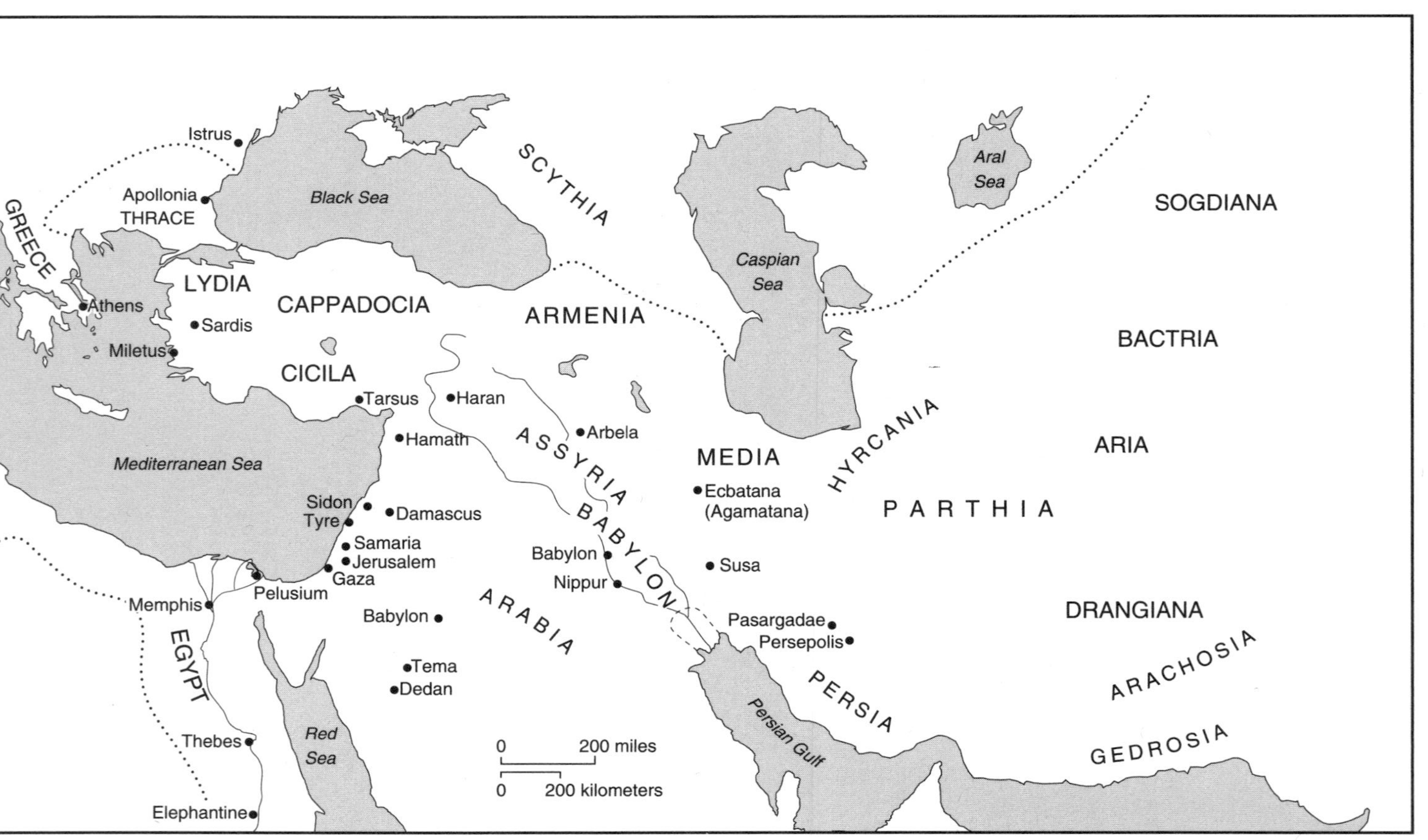

Map 1. The Persian Empire at Its Greatest Extent

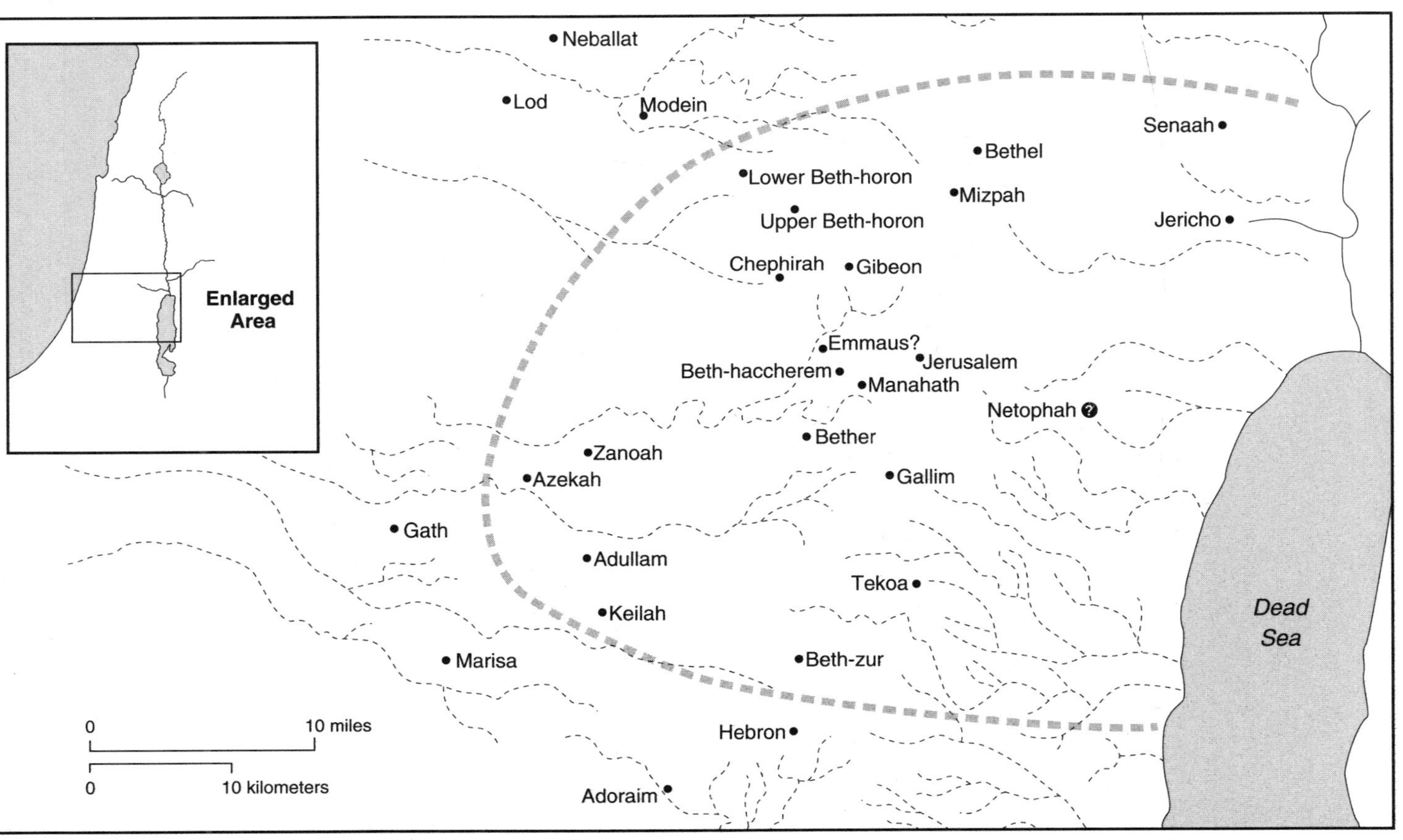

Map 2. The Persian Province of Judah

Tobiah "the Ammonite servant," who may have been governor of a province of Ammon (Neh 2:10, 19; 6:1; see further at 4.3.2).

2.3.6 Date of the Return under Ezra

Ackroyd, P. R. *Israel under Babylon and Persia* (1970) 191–96.
Bright, J. *A History of Israel* (1980).
Emerton, J. A. "Did Ezra Go to Jerusalem in 428 B.C.?" *JTS* 17 (1966) 1–19.
Porter, J. R. "Son or Grandson (Ezra X. 6)?" *JTS* 17 (1966) 54–67.
Rowley, H. H. "The Chronological Order of Ezra and Nehemiah." *The Servant of the Lord and Other Essays* (1965) 135–68.
Saley, R. J. "The Date of Nehemiah Reconsidered." *Biblical and Near Eastern Studies* (1978) 151–65.

The most certain date in Ezra and Nehemiah is the time of Nehemiah's coming to Jerusalem (twentieth year of Artaxerxes), which has been set by consensus to the year 445 B.C.E. Even this widespread view can be considered only as a matter of considerable probability, however, rather than as assured fact. Saley recently attempted to undermine this conclusion and establish the twentieth year of Artaxerxes II (ca. 484) as an equally valid alternative. His arguments may be summarized as follows: (1) Josephus gives a trustworthy account of a number of events, such as the founding of the Samaritan temple, a Sanballat III at the time of Alexander, and the marriage of this Sanballat's daughter to the son of the Jerusalem high priest; (2) the Bagoses of Josephus is the general of Artaxerxes III (2.4.8), rather than the governor of the Elephantine papyri; and (3) there were a number of high priests of the same name because of papponymy, so that the names attested to in historical records may not be the same as those in the book of Nehemiah.

Although a number of Saley's arguments are parallel to those of Cross (2.3.12), none in fact depends on Cross's reconstruction of the high priestly line. Nevertheless, the criticisms that have been leveled at Cross almost all apply with equal validity to Saley's arguments (2.2.5; 2.3.12): (1) except for one episode, Josephus does not have clear extrabiblical evidence for the Persian period; (2) although the Bagoses of Josephus may be the general of Artaxerxes III, a better argument can, in my opinion, be made that he is the governor known from the Aramaic papyri; and (3) although papponymy may have occurred among the high priests of the Persian period, such has not been demonstrated; any hypothesis that depends on this sort of argument is only supporting one hypothesis with another, rather than with actual data. Because we know that there was a high priest named Johanan in the late fifth century, it is a more reasonable reconstruction to connect his grandfather, Eliashib, with the figure of Neh 3:1 than to hypothesize another figure by the same name in the time of Artaxerxes II. Therefore, even though Saley is quite correct that the traditional dating is not firm, it is probably as firm as any conclusion one can draw about Judah in the Persian period.

Nehemiah is said to have come to Palestine in the twentieth year of Artaxerxes, returned to Babylon in the thirty-second year, and come back again to Palestine some time after this (Neh 2:1; 13:6-7). Assuming that Artaxerxes I is meant, the specified dates would be 445 and 433 B.C.E., respectively. According to the order of events in the book of Ezra, the priest and scribe Ezra came some years before Nehemiah, in the seventh year of Artaxerxes or 458 B.C.E. This traditional dating came under attack with the rise of critical scholarship and was once generally rejected by scholars. Now, however, there is an increasing trend to accept the traditional dating, although many who do so make no attempt to argue the question in detail. In contrast, most of those who treat the subject at length recognize that many of the arguments for each point of view are not decisive and that the best one can offer is a balance of probability.

2.3.6.1 Ezra First

Although a number of those who accept the traditional dating have given little or no argument, several have given detailed reasons for putting Ezra first (*Clines: 16–24; *Williamson 1985: xxxix–xliv; *Blenkinsopp: 139–44). The arguments advanced are as follows:

1. The "Ezra Memoir" gives no hint that Ezra's mission took more than a year. Once this is accepted, many of the objections to the traditional dating disappear.
2. More weight should be given to the biblical order than has often been done, although different reasons are given for this. Clines argues that if the Chronicler wrote in the fourth century, it seems strange that the correct order of Ezra and Nehemiah would have been forgotten. Williamson, who does not accept the Chronicler as the author of Ezra-Nehemiah, thinks that Ezra 1–6 was added in the latest editing of the book, whereas the combining of the material in Ezra 7–9 and the Nehemiah Memorial was done at an earlier stage. This indicates that the narrative putting Ezra first was finalized not all that long after the events it discusses (*1985: xliii).
3. That neither reformer mentions the other is not surprising, because they worked independently with individual purposes. Nehemiah's

concern with mixed marriages seems to relate only to a local matter, however, suggesting that the overall question had already been resolved by Ezra. Furthermore, Williamson argues that Ezra's method of interpretation in Ezra 9:1-2 is used by Nehemiah in Neh 13:25 (*1985: xliii).

4. The pledge of Nehemiah 10 is based on a broad sweep of pentateuchal law and on the hermeneutic found in Ezra 9. This would seem to make prior Ezra's mission to bring God's law to Judah.
5. Ezra received widespread support for his decrees, whereas Nehemiah's activities were divisive. It seems more likely that Ezra would have come first, or he would have been opposed from the start because of Nehemiah's measures.
6. If Nehemiah came first with the powers of a governor, it seems strange that Ezra would have followed, with much less support, to complete what Nehemiah had not been able to accomplish.
7. The reference to "Ezra the scribe" in Neh 12:36 is likely to be original (*Williamson 1985: xliv, 371–72; contra *Clines: 232).
8. Ezra 4:12 most likely refers to the mission of Ezra in 458.
9. The "Passover Papyrus" (Cowley: no. 21) seems to indicate the imposition of pentateuchal law on a rather remote corner of the Persian Empire by 419 B.C.E., which would fit best a dating of Ezra before 398 B.C.E. Bright concurs with this conclusion (399; cf. *Clines: 22), but Emerton (8–9) and Williamson (*1985: xli–xlii) are justified in noting that the interpretation of the Passover letter is too uncertain to carry much weight. It would be a mistake to assume that no festivals were known or celebrated until Ezra came with the law. The most likely understanding of the letter is that it was the Persian response to a request (made in the face of Egyptian opposition) and gave permission to keep the Passover (see further at 2.2.2). Therefore, it seems doubtful that the Passover Papyrus demands the prior circumstance of Ezra's mission, and the letter is probably irrelevant to the question one way or the other.

2.3.6.2 Thirty-Seventh Year of Artaxerxes I

Another interpretation has been especially defended by Bright (400–401). It states that in Ezra 7:7-8, the reading "seventh year" (*šĕnat-šeba'*) of Artaxerxes should read the "thirty-seventh year" (*šĕnat šĕlōšîm wĕšeba'*). Bright readily admits that this is a conjectural emendation, because there is no textual support for it of any kind, although the succession of three initial *š*'s would explain how such a reading could have been corrupted.

The heart of the issue is not the emendation, however, but the reasons for proposing it: it is thought that such an emendation would best explain specific assumptions that Bright and others believe are important to maintain:

1. The tradition of an overlap between the ministries of Ezra and Nehemiah should be accepted, but contrary to the biblical account, Ezra would have come in the time of Nehemiah's second term of office, rather than some years before him.
2. A number of the objections to the traditional order do not apply here, because Nehemiah is still assumed to have come first.
3. The Chronicler wrote no later than about 400 B.C.E., because no event or genealogy goes beyond this date. If so, it seems unlikely that he was unaware of the basic sequence of events only a few decades earlier. The Chronicler's work did not originally contain the Nehemiah Memorial and therefore did not actually date Ezra before Nehemiah; however, the tradition that their missions overlapped should be given considerable weight.
4. The Hattush of Ezra 8:2 would have been too old to have come in 398 (allowing twenty-seven and one-half years for a generation) and probably too young in 458, but just the right age to be a "head of the father's house" in 428.
5. The Passover Papyrus (see 2.3.6.1).

Although Bright continued to defend this dating in the latest edition of his *History*, it is generally considered that his position has been fairly decisively refuted by Emerton (cf. *Widengren: 505; *Williamson 1985: xl–xli). The emendation is purely conjectural for the sake of the theory. Trying to reckon chronology from a genealogy by imputing particular average generation lengths is a very haphazard business. Considering the recent arguments, the assumption that the Chronicler's work encompassed Ezra-Nehemiah can no longer be taken as self-evident, whereas the dating of even Chronicles to 400 B.C.E. cannot be accepted without considerable argument (see 2.2.1.8).

2.3.6.3 Seventh Year of Artaxerxes II

The view that has generally held until recently contends that Ezra came in the seventh year of Artaxerxes II, that is, 398 B.C.E. The reasons for arguing this are (Rowley; *Widengren: 504–5; Emerton: 16–19; Ackroyd 1970: 191–96):

1. The careers of Ezra and Nehemiah are actually recounted separately, apart from a few verses which are probably editorial: the inclusion of Nehemiah in Neh 8:9 is not found in 1 Esdras 9:49, whereas Ezra's name seems secondary in Neh 12:36. Furthermore, the same problems of mixed marriages and keeping God's law are addressed by both Ezra and Nehemiah. Although it seems strange that Nehemiah would have had to address the same problems only a decade or so after Ezra—indeed, while he was still in Jerusalem—it would not be strange if a general relapse had taken place in the three and one-half decades from about 432 to 398.
2. The wall of Jerusalem was not built until Nehemiah's governorship, yet Ezra 9:9 indicates a wall was there when Ezra arrived. The problem is determining whether Ezra 9:9 is only a metaphorical reference or one to an actual wall. The word "wall" (*gādēr*) here is normally used of a wall around a vineyard, rather than a city wall, which may be an argument for its metaphorical usage (*Williamson 1985: 136–37). It could be taken literally, however, so that a wall for "Judah and Jerusalem" would certainly imply one around Jerusalem (*Widengren: 504). Further, one should note that *gādēr* is used in Mic 7:11 to mean a city wall.
3. The high priest in the time of Nehemiah was Eliashib, but in the time of Ezra it was Johanan, son of Eliashib (Ezra 10:6, although according to Neh 12:11, the term "son" should probably be interpreted in the sense of "grandson").

2.3.6.4 Analysis

When the arguments and counterarguments are considered, there is a fundamental difference of approach between those who maintain that Ezra was first and those who put Nehemiah first. Those who support the traditional sequence see the biblical order as fundamental and accept it as long as it cannot be clearly contradicted. They argue that because no decisive evidence has been found against that order, it should be accepted. The others start with a different premise, namely, that there is no reason to give credence to the biblical order, because there is too much uncertainty about the growth of the tradition. Therefore, the dating is determined by considering various arguments pro and con. Although it is accepted that none of these may be decisive, there is still the matter of a cumulative effect. Thus one's ultimate position is heavily determined by how much weight is given to the biblical picture, and evaluation of other arguments will be greatly influenced by this starting point.

There is another factor, not touched on thus far. Those who argue for one of the three dates just discussed generally assume a high degree of historicity for the Ezra tradition. As discussed elsewhere (2.2.1.1; 2.2.1.2; 2.2.1.4), this cannot necessarily be taken for granted. At this stage of study it seems there are more basic questions to be answered: Did Ezra exist? What do we know about him? What was his mission? How historical are the sources? Only when these have been answered more satisfactorily will it be possible to debate the date of his coming (if he did come!) with any degree of usefulness.

2.3.7 Destruction of Jerusalem between Zerubbabel and Nehemiah?

Morgenstern, J. "Jerusalem—485 B.C." *HUCA* 27 (1956) 101–79; 28 (1957) 15–47; 31 (1960) 1–29.

———. "Further Light from the Book of Isaiah upon the Catastrophe of 485 B.C." *HUCA* 37 (1966) 1–28.

Smith, M. *Palestinian Parties and Politics That Shaped the Old Testament* (1971).

When Nehemiah received word of Jerusalem in 445 B.C.E. (Neh 1:1-4), he was shocked to find the city in a terrible state. The question arises as to why the city was in such a condition. Had Jerusalem remained with a broken-down wall and burnt gates since the time of Nebuchadnezzar? That is possible, but the context suggests that the people of the city were also in a rather bad way, a situation somewhat incongruous with the rebuilding of the temple in the time of Zerubbabel. Although it is possible that the rebuilding of the city had not progressed beyond the work done on the temple, this seems peculiar, especially when one considers that almost seventy-five years had supposedly passed since the temple was completed. The passage in Nehemiah therefore raises the possibility that some disaster had overtaken Jerusalem during those intervening decades, which are largely unrecorded.

A variety of proposals have been advanced. Beginning with the situation mentioned in Nehemiah 1, Morgenstern argued that a previously unknown catastrophe struck Jerusalem in 485, as the result of a revolt against Persian rule at the beginning of Xerxes' reign. Much of Morgenstern's argument depends on the specific dating of some rather unspecific Old Testament passages, a tendentious reinterpretation of their contexts, and often, a major rewriting (he calls it "reconstruction") of the text. It is, therefore, not very surprising that he has gained no converts to his point of view. Smith (123–25) has argued that Ezra's mission was a failure and connects it with the charges in the correspondence of Ezra 4:7-22. That is, Ezra went beyond his brief and began work on the city walls, a project stopped by the Persian authorities. He suspects, however, that some other event, such as a raid from the Arab tribes to the south, took place shortly before Nehemiah received the news, rather than that the entire catastrophe occurred during the time of Ezra (127–28).

It would not be surprising if there was a revolt (or what was interpreted by the Persians as a revolt) in Judah during the long decades between 515 and 445. There were often revolts on the fringes of the empire when a new king took the throne, such as at the beginning of the reigns of both Xerxes and Artaxerxes I (2.4.3.1; 2.4.3.2). Indeed, there are indications in the archeological record that suggest a widespread period of destruction around 480 (2.2.7.3), but the specific context cannot be determined from the physical remains alone. Ezra 4:6 mentions correspondence in the reign of Xerxes, indicating certain charges against the Jews; however, the specific situation is not described. More revealing is the document of Ezra 4:12, which does specifically mention the rebuilding of the city in such a way as to suggest the strengthening of its defenses. This was in the reign of Artaxerxes, usually taken to be Artaxerxes I, although the report seems to have been misplaced to the time of Zerubbabel. This imprecision makes it possible that Smith's interpretation is correct, although one must assume the traditional dating for Ezra and also accept his speculation that Ezra went beyond his Persian commission in order to adopt his interpretation. For the latter we have no evidence, even if it is not unthinkable. In contrast, a destruction around 448 would coincide with the alleged revolt of the western satrap Megabyzus (2.4.3.2) and might have little or nothing to do with the internal affairs of Judah. Finally, there remains the question of the authenticity of the documents quoted (2.2.1.2).

2.3.8 The Mission of Ezra

Ackroyd, P. R. "God and People in the Chronicler's Presentation of Ezra." *Bibliotheca Ephemeridum Theologicarum Lovaniensium* 41 (1976) 145–62.

Blenkinsopp, J. "The Mission of Udjahorresnet and Those of Ezra and Nehemiah." *JBL* 106 (1987) 409–21.

———. "The Sage, the Scribe, and Scribalism in the Chronicler's Work." *The Sage in Israel and the Ancient Near East* (1990) 307–15.

Cazelles, H. "La mission d'Esdras." *VT* 4 (1954) 113–40.

Grabbe, L. L. "What Was Ezra's Mission?" *Studies in the Second Temple: The Persian Period*. Vol. 2 (forthcoming).

Houtman, C. "Ezra and the Law: Observations on the Supposed Relation between Ezra and the Pentateuch." *OTS* 21 (1981) 91–115.
Koch, K. "Ezra and the Origins of Judaism." *JSS* 19 (1974) 173–97.
Margalith, O. "The Political Role of Ezra as Persian Governor." *ZAW* 98 (1986) 110–12.
Schaeder, H. H. *Esra der Schreiber* (1930).
Rendtorff, R. "Esra und das >>Gesetz<<" *ZAW* 96 (1984) 165–84.

2.3.8.1 Scholarly Hypotheses

The question of Ezra's mission depends on one's evaluation of the Artaxerxes rescript (Ezra 7:12-26) and the Ezra source. If these are not reliable, then much of the discussion about Ezra's actions and intent is beside the point. If these can chiefly be trusted, however, then the specific purpose of his mission is theoretically accessible. Even then it is still not immediately apparent when compared with, for example, Zerubbabel or Nehemiah, who came as governors. The missions of Sheshbazzar and Zerubbabel had cultic aims, as well as those of civil administration. In contrast to these, nowhere is it suggested that Ezra was sent as governor, although Ezra 7:25-26 implies some sort of authoritative office, and the temple had been built long before his time, so it was not as if he came to revive the cult or Israelite religion. Nevertheless, even though he was not high priest, he seems to act as if having this authority. Therefore, the puzzle remains, and a number of possible solutions have arisen over the years, some of which follow.

Darius I's regulation of Egyptian cultic and civil law has often been pointed to, with the suggestion that Ezra had the same task. Blenkinsopp has recently developed this further, with specific attention to the Egyptian admiral Udjahorresnet, who went over to the Persians and became an important administrator in the new puppet regime (1987). Cambyses initially sent Udjahorresnet to reestablish the "House of Life," which seems to have been a priestly institute for medical and cultic education. Later Darius ordered the codification of the Egyptian laws. As Blenkinsopp notes,

> The inscription therefore speaks of two phases in the career of Udjahorresnet after he had thrown in his lot with the Persian conquerors: the restoration of the cult in the dynastic sanctuary under Cambyses; the reorganization of the institutions of scribalism and religious learning as part of Darius's new order . . . (413)

Schaeder argued that by the term "scribe" the writer has two things in mind (39–59). First was the normal meaning of the term in Persian administration. In this usage it refers to one trained in the skills of reading and writing, primarily in the use of Aramaic as a written language and in the translation to Aramaic of the local, oral language and vice versa. It would also refer to the office of "secretary" in the bureaucratic sense. Thus Ezra not only held an administrative office but also was trained in the traditional literary skills of the scribe. Second, Ezra was thought of by the author of Ezra-Nehemiah in the later Jewish category of one learned in the Jewish law and tradition, a usage which in later centuries is associated with the terms "scribe" or "rabbi." As an analogy, Schaeder draws on the office of the Jewish exilarch of later Sassanian times. This figure of the Persian court was essentially the commissioner for Jewish affairs and thus combined both religious and administrative functions.

Schaeder's treatment has been widely quoted in subsequent scholarship on Ezra, but a number of criticisms have been advanced over the years (*Blenkinsopp: 137–38; Blenkinsopp 1990: 312–14; *Mowinckel: 3.121–24; *Galling: 166–67). Like several other critics, Koch has also rejected the comparison with the Sassanian exilarch and later rabbinic usage, arguing that the title must have meaning in the linguistic and political context of the Persian Empire of Ezra's own time (183). Koch admittedly has no alternative suggestion for the meaning of the term "scribe," but he goes on to delineate Ezra's role by means of several proposals (184–95, 196):

1. Ezra's function was not to establish Judah as a theocracy or to enforce divine law as the law of the land. On the contrary, he still saw it as religious law, with the function of making a distinction between profane and sacred.
2. He came to "all the people" of God, that is, to renew the twelve tribes of Israel. This included the Samaritans as remnants of the original northern Israel.
3. He saw his journey as a second exodus, taking inspiration from exilic prophets such as Deutero-Isaiah.
4. His mission was only pre-eschatological, to initiate a process that would have eschatological fulfillment only in time. In this he did not differ from such other leaders as Sheshbazzar, Zerubbabel, and Nehemiah.

Koch's thesis, although often cited, has received little discussion. It cuts across the usual interpretation of Ezra in a significant way, especially in denying the aim of Ezra to set up a Jewish religious state based on God's law. This seems to go against the Persian decree in Ezra 7. It is usually argued that Ezra's mission failed; at least, the account breaks off at the end of Ezra 10 without indicating that he had fulfilled his mission. If Koch is on the correct line, then the whole assessment of Ezra's mission and its success or failure must be differently approached.

These theories of Ezra's mission have assumed the basic reliability of the Ezra material. Others have rejected this and thus see the mission as mostly or completely the invention of the Chronicler and nothing to do with Jewish history in the Persian period (although it would naturally be of value for Jewish history at the time of the Chronicler). As discussed in 2.2.1.4, several scholars (e.g., Torrey; Gunneweg; Lebram) have seen little historical in the alleged mission of Ezra, whereas others, such as Noth and those following him (e.g., Kellerman; In der Smitten), have been almost as pessimistic.

2.3.8.2 Analysis

When we look at the primary data and the various suggestions made by scholars, several points arise (for a more detailed discussion, see Grabbe).

1. It was clearly Persian policy to allow and sometimes even to encourage the activities of local cults. This is shown by the inscription of Udjahorresnet, the decree of Darius I about Egyptian law, the Xanthos trilingual, and the Elephantine papyri, among others. On the whole, though, cults were tightly controlled and taxed like other revenue-producing entities.

2. The essential question comes down to whether the policy just noted under point 1 is sufficient to justify a thesis about Ezra. Some of the parallels do not fit well, especially in the details. For example, the Udjahorresnet inscription is formally closer to the Nehemiah Memorial than to Ezra 7–10 (Blenkinsopp: 417). Darius was acclaimed pharaoh of Egypt and would have considered it worth his while to be acknowledged as lawgiver of the country. Is it likely that the Persian king would have been so keenly interested in regulating the laws of a small province? Besides, the alleged law reform of Ezra was under not Darius but a later king (Artaxerxes I? II?).

3. A further question is how concerned the Persian government would have been about a local cult in Judah. It is not a question of whether they might have issued some sort of decree but rather of the extent of involvement that the Ezra material suggests. The overwhelming authority given to Ezra does not fit well with the restricted nature of some of the Persian decrees (e.g., the Xanthos inscription; Cowley nos. 30–32). The enormous sums alleged to have been given as gifts for the temple (Ezra 7:16; 8:25-27: 100 talents of gold, 650 talents of silver, various vessels—more than twenty-five metric tons) or appropriated from the treasury for the

running of the cult (Ezra 7:22: 100 talents of silver plus various commodities) appear unlikely, if not plainly absurd.

4. The theological interpretation of the Ezra material is also a problem which cannot be resolved simply by suggesting that Ezra or Jewish scribes drafted the decree, which Artaxerxes only signed: in addition to the impossible sums of money, the enormous authority given to Ezra and the almost superstitious concern for the Jerusalem cult by a loyal Zoroastrian make such an occurrence improbable. Such sweeping statements do not occur with regard to Zerubbabel or Nehemiah.

5. It is logical that a border region such as Judah would be strengthened, as is often pointed out. If this was the intent of the Persian government, however, then why send a religious leader (especially when he seems to have caused internal divisions, rather than keeping the area quiet)? Why not a military leader?

6. The Persian governor of the region, whose job it was to maintain the security of the area, seems to be completely ignored. Only Neh 8:9 mentions the governor (*tiršātā'*), and this is usually thought to be an editorial addition to connect Ezra with Nehemiah.

7. The "law of God in Ezra's hand" is a puzzle. Although there is still discussion about its precise nature, recent research has retreated from considering this a completely new law (such as the newly written Pentateuch, which Meyer argued for). It is now clear that a functioning cult and priesthood, with a variety of traditional laws and practices that in many cases dated to pre-exilic times, was in place. What precisely was Ezra supposed to be teaching the community, which already had the official traditional teachers and religious leaders among the priests? Rendtorff has recently argued that the law (*dāt*) mentioned in the decree (7:14) is not the same as the law (*tôrāh*) found elsewhere in the narrative (e.g., Neh 8:1). The connotation of *dāt* was that of justice, whereas *tôrāh* referred to a particular written collection of Jewish religious traditions. The two have become combined in Ezra 7:6, in which "scribe" (*sôfēr*, a function of *dāt*) has become associated with *tôrāh*. Houtman has wondered whether the law book of Ezra-Nehemiah has anything to do with the extant Pentateuch.

We can only conclude that the mission of Ezra has yet to be explained. Unlike the missions of Zerubbabel and Nehemiah, which seem straightforward enough, the various suggestions about the purpose of Ezra's Jerusalem excursion have left too many loose ends to create a consensus. The key to the problem may well lie in the nature of the Ezra material and tradition (2.2.1.4). Until this is better clarified, Ezra's mission—if it occurred—must also remain obscure.

2.3.9 Judah and the Tennes Rebellion

Barag, D. "The Effects of the Tennes Rebellion on Palestine." *BASOR* 183 (Oct. 1966) 6–12.

Note: For further information on some of the Christian chronicles cited here, see 9.2.2.

Since the appearance of Barag's article, it has been common to assume that Judah was involved in the revolt of Phoenician cities in the time of Tennes (ca. 350 B.C.E.). The arguments he advances are threefold.

1. A rebellion of Cyprus and Phoenicia is recorded about 350 in the work of the Greek historians.
2. Some late accounts seem to indicate that Judah was caught up in this revolt: (1) Eusebius (*Chron*. on the 105th Olympiad [Helm: 121]); (2) Orosius (*Adver. pagan*. 3.7.6), who basically agrees with Eusebius; (3) Syncellus (1.486.10–14); and (4) Solinus (*Collect*. 35.4 = *GLAJJ*: 2.418–22).
3. The archeology of the period indicates layers of destruction at various sites in Palestine for the mid-fourth century.

Barag's thesis has now been attacked by Widengren, who points out the following (*501–2):

1. Diodorus, the main source for the Tennes rebellion, says nothing about the participation of the Jews.
2. The trustworthiness of Eusebius's tradition is called into question by his misdating of Artaxerxes' reign by forty years.
3. Josephus is silent on such a rebellion, suggesting he was either ignorant of it or, inexplicably, suppressed reports of it.
4. Josephus's reference to Bagoses, during whose time the temple was defiled, is best identified with the governor known from the Elephantine papyri (2.2.5).
5. Hecateus of Abdera's statement about deportation of the Jews by Persians is probably a confusion with the Babylonian captivity, because Persians were often identified with the Babylonians in the Greek period.
6. Although some Jews may indeed have been settled in Hyrcania by the Persians during the fourth century, there are a number of possible reasons for this settlement other than their participation in a rebellion.

7. Most of the destroyed archeological sites lie outside Judah proper, with the exception of Jericho. There is no evidence to associate the various destructions with a particular date. According to Stern, the destructions of Palestinian sites are to be associated with a variety of campaigns and revolts over about 150 years during the fifth and fourth centuries (*253–55). Furthermore, it is not possible to distinguish between pottery of 345 B.C.E. and that from some decades later at the time of Alexander; that is, some of the destruction layers which Barag associates with the Sidonian revolt may in fact have been caused by the Greek conquest.

2.3.10 Iranian Influence on the Jewish Religion?

Bailey, H. H. *Zoroastrian Problems in the Ninth-Century Books* (1943).
Barr, J. "The Question of Religious Influence: The Case of Zoroastrianism, Judaism, and Christianity." *JAAR* 53 (1985) 201–35.
*Boyce.
———. *Zoroastrians* (1979).
———, ed. *Textual Sources for the Study of Zoroastrianism* (1984).
———. "On the Antiquity of Zoroastrian Apocalyptic." *BSOAS* 47 (1984) 57–75.
———. *Zoroastrianism: A Shadowy but Powerful Presence in the Judaeo-Christian World* (1987).
Collins, J. J. "Persian Apocalypses." *Semeia* 14 (1979) 207–17.
Day, P. L. *An Adversary in Heaven* (1988).
Flusser, D. "Hystaspes and John of Patmos." *Irano-Judaica* (1982) 12–75.
Frye, R. N. "Qumran and Iran: The State of Studies." *Christianity, Judaism and Other Greco-Roman Cults* (1975) 3.167–73.
Glasson, T. F. *Greek Influence in Jewish Eschatology* (1961).
Hinnells, J. R. "The Zoroastrian Doctrine of Salvation in the Roman World." *Man and His Salvation* (1973) 125–48.
Hultgård, A. "Das Judentum in der hellenistisch-römischen Zeit und die iranische Religion—ein religionsgeschichtliches Problem." *ANRW* 2 (1979) 512–90.
Kobelski, P. J. *Melchizedek and Melchireša'* (1981).
Shaked, S. "Qumran and Iran: Further Considerations." *IOS* 2 (1972) 433–46.
———. "Iranian Influence on Judaism: First Century B.C.E. to Second Century C.E." *CHJ* (1984) 1.308–25.
Winston, D. "The Iranian Component in the Bible, Apocrypha, and Qumran: A Review of the Evidence." *HR* 5 (1965–66) 183–216.

There is general agreement that Persian religion and tradition had an influence on Judaism over the centuries. The question is where this influence was and which of the developments in Judaism can be ascribed to Iranian influence, as opposed to the effect of Greek or other cultures or even to purely internal developments. There are a number of points to consider:

1. The problems of determining beliefs in the early Zoroastrian community. The early Persian literature is often difficult to understand because of philological and textual problems; also, a large section of the *Avesta* has been lost over the centuries.

2. The question of dating the Persian literature and theological developments. The preserved literature is, by and large, the product of the post-Islamic period in its present form (Bailey). It is not always easy to determine what is early and what is late. For example, scholars are agreed that certain of the *Gathas* (the earliest section of the *Avesta*) go back to Zoroaster himself, so that his teachings can often be determined. On the other hand, many of the areas of interest for Judaism were not pronounced on by Zoroaster in the extant authentic sayings and can be found only in very late sources, such as the *Bundahišn* and the *Denkart*.

Boyce has argued that much of this material is early, even though found only in late sources, because it was preserved unchanged in the oral tradition (e.g., 1987: 10). This may be so, but biblical and Judaic scholars would generally be cautious here, because such claims have also been made about biblical traditions but are now generally rejected. In addition, if large sections of the *Avesta* could be lost, how certain can we be that what is left has been passed down unchanged? Nevertheless, there is agreement among Iranologists that some beliefs and traditions do represent an early stage of Persian religion and may legitimately be compared with Second Temple Judaism.

3. The channel of transmission for such influence. Jews were a part of the Persian Empire, but one should be skeptical about the extent of religious influence caused by contact with the administration (Shaked 1984: 324–25). A more likely influence would be the experiences of individual Jews living among Persians in Persia and Babylonia. Another often overlooked source is the Greek accounts of Persians and Persian religion (Barr: 218–20). The Greeks were fascinated by such "Eastern sages" as the "magi" and wrote about them. It may in some cases be these or other accounts in Greek that exerted influence on Jewish writers, rather than direct contact with Zoroastrians.

4. The difficulty of demonstrating influence. Influence is most likely to have taken place in areas of Judaism that already showed some affinity with Persian thought. However, this makes demonstration more difficult, whether to prove or to refute.

With these points in mind, we can take a brief look at areas of alleged

Iranian influence. One area that has occasioned considerable discussion is that of Qumran (Shaked 1972; Frye). Although various points in Qumran theology have been suggested as examples of Iranian influence, one often mentioned is the dualism of the scrolls: the Sons of Light versus the Sons of Darkness, the good angels versus the wicked angels, and so forth. Sometimes this has been rejected with the assertion that the absolute dualism of Zoroastrianism does not compare with the Jewish belief in the sovereignty of God over the whole of creation; however, the Zoroastrian belief is actually closer to the Jewish belief than many realize (Shaked 1984: 315–16). Although a strong dualism had developed by the Sassanian period, the original view of Zoroaster set out in the *Gathas* seems not to have been too different from that at Qumran. Therefore, Iranian influence of some sort on the Qumran writings has been widely accepted.

Another area often discussed (also with regard to Qumran) is eschatology in general, including apocalypticism. This is a more problematic area, because the age of some points of Zoroastrian eschatology is difficult to determine. There is also the problem of weighing possible Iranian influence against that from the Hellenic side. For example, belief in the immortality of the soul looks similar to that found in Persian religion, and one could also make a case for a native development from the Israelite tradition. In the end, however, the most likely source (or the source of greatest influence, at least) for belief in the soul's immortality is Greek thought. In contrast, resurrection of the body has its closest parallels in Iranian tradition and probably developed under stimulus from that direction (cf. Barr: 223–24). Another area is angelology. Elements within Israelite religion were capable of producing the elaborate structure of the angelic and demonic world (e.g., "Satan"; cf. Day), but it was during the Persian period that the Jewish angelology and demonology, with their close parallels to the Zoroastrian "good spirits" (*Amesha Spenta*s) and "wicked spirits" (*Angra Mainyu*s), seem to have developed. Here again one might well think in terms of influence, not borrowings as such (see further Kobelski: 84–98).

Access to Iranian scholarship is particularly difficult for the nonspecialist, but recent assistance has come from Iranian scholars. A good overall guide with bibliography is given by Shaked (1984; cf. also Hultgård and Collins). The major research tools are the enormous history by Boyce (*1975–) and her shorter version (1979). However, one should be aware that Iranologists disagree considerably even on basic points, so Boyce's judgments need to be compared with those of other experts. Boyce's recent translation of many of the Iranian sources, along with accompanying commentary, is very useful (1984a).

2.3.11 The Rise of Sectarianism

Blenkinsopp, J. *Prophecy and Canon* (1977).

———. "Interpretation and the Tendency to Sectarianism: An Aspect of Second Temple History." *Jewish and Christian Self-definition* (1981) 2.1–26.

———. "A Jewish Sect of the Persian Period." *CBQ* 52 (1990) 5–20.

Redditt, P. L. "The Book of Joel and Peripheral Prophecy." *CBQ* 48 (1986a) 225–40.

———. "Once Again, the City in Isaiah 24–27." *HAR* 10 (1986b) 317–35.

———. "Israel's Shepherds: Hope and Pessimism in Zechariah 9–14." *CBQ* 51 (1989) 632–42.

Rofé, A. "Isaiah 66:1-4: Judean Sects in the Persian Period as Viewed by Trito-Isaiah." *Biblical and Related Studies Presented to Samuel Iwry* (1985) 205–17.

Talmon. S. "The Emergence of Jewish Sectarianism in the Early Second Temple Period." *King, Cult and Calendar in Ancient Israel* (1986) 165–201.

2.3.11.1 General

It is often suggested that religious sectarianism had developed (or perhaps only surfaced) by the early Persian period. The sectarianism of later times is much better attested (chap. 8), but many scholars have argued that various texts reflect tension within the Jewish community under Persian rule, perhaps by the early decades of the restoration. Hints of sectarianism have been found especially in Third Isaiah (Isaiah 56–66) and also elsewhere. Indeed, there have been attempts to find all-encompassing theories to bring into a coherent whole a variety of texts and to extrapolate a socioreligious situation (2.3.11.2–3). Although these are not generally thought successful, many of the texts used have also been interpreted by others as referring to conflicts within the community. To illustrate the problem of sectarianism, some recent studies may be referred to.

Both Talmon and Blenkinsopp (1981: 24) have seen the post-exilic situation as conducive to the creation of sects. Despite the divided kingdom under the monarchy, there was a national cohesion and identity, a united people with a central government and cultic establishment. After the exile the authority of the temple and priests was weakened, there was no king to enforce religious conformity, and thousands of Jews lived outside the homeland. The door was open to dissension and even to the creation of separate sects. (See 8.1 for a discussion of the definition of "sect.")

Blenkinsopp (1981) has argued that the interpretation of sacred traditions was a major factor in creating conflicts—even that the canonization process was a product of these conflicts and an attempt to reconcile different points of view (Blenkinsopp 1977). Especially revealing is the group referred to in Isa 66:5 as "those who tremble (*haḥărēdîm*) at my word" (Blenkinsopp 1990). Using this passage as a focal point, Blenkinsopp has identified similar ideas in Isa 66:1-4, 17; 65:13-16; 57:1-10; Mal 3:13-21; and Ezra 9–10. This has led him to associate these with a single group which is not antitemple as such but critical of the current priestly establishment, pietistic, eschatological, and temporarily severed from the central cult.

Rofé begins with Isa 66:1-4 but also branches out to other passages in Trito-Isaiah, Malachi, and Ezra-Nehemiah. He appears to come to conclusions similar to Blenkinsopp's. Interestingly, although both reject Hanson's reconstruction (Blenkinsopp 1981: 302 n.34; Rofé: 213 n.40), their result does not seem too far from his in certain major respects; that is, a pietistic, prophetic, eschatological sect is alienated from the corrupt priestly establishment, which it has criticized.

Redditt examined Joel, Isaiah 24–27, and Zechariah 9–14. Behind Joel he finds a marginalized prophetic group, which became exclusivistic, nonmessianic, and eschatological but not apocalyptic (Redditt 1986a). In his opinion a similar nonpriestly, nonmessianic group is reflected in Isaiah 24–27, but it is centered in Jerusalem (Redditt 1986b). He sees Zechariah 9–14 as made up of six basic collections, which a redactor took over and reworked to express his point of view. This individual was part of a community which lived outside Jerusalem and was in opposition to the hopes of the Jerusalemites. They thought the leaders as a whole (the "shepherds": priests, Davidides, prophets) were corrupt and looked for a cleansed Jerusalem, with the whole nation (not just the city or temple) as holy to God.

The specific hypotheses are less important than the common core: a variety of post-exilic texts (including Isaiah 56–66, Ezra-Nehemiah, Malachi, and perhaps Joel and others) indicate tensions within the Jewish community, which led even to the rise of opposing movements and sects. General comment follows later (2.3.11.4), but first, two theses about sectarian developments will now be treated individually and in detail. This is not because they are necessarily more significant or sounder than others already mentioned but because they have been worked out more extensively and have become widely known.

2.3.11.2 Morton Smith

Pietersma, A. Review of *Palestinian Parties and Politics*, by M. Smith. *JBL* 91 (1972) 550–52.

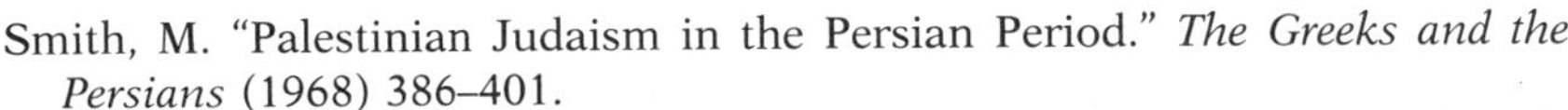

Smith, M. "Palestinian Judaism in the Persian Period." *The Greeks and the Persians* (1968) 386–401.
———. *Palestinian Parties and Politics That Shaped the Old Testament* (1971).
———. "Jewish Religious Life in the Persian Period." *CHJ* (1984) 1.219–78.

Smith's thesis was first expounded in his 1968 article and worked out in detail in his *Palestinian Parties and Politics*. It can be fairly simply stated in broad terms but requires considerable qualification and explanation at the detailed level, because despite initial appearances it is not a simple proposal. For much of the history of Israel, Smith sees the majority of Israelites as those who worshiped Yahweh along with other gods, as those for whom Yahweh was perhaps the major national "God of Israel" but who by no means regarded worship of Yahweh as exclusive or henotheistic. This broad, heterogeneous group, made up of all social groups and strata of society, Smith refers to for convenience as "the syncretistic party."

At some time in the ninth century another group appeared on the scene that believed that worship of Yahweh should be exclusivistic, that worshipers "should have no other gods before" Yahweh. These Smith refers to as the "Yahweh-alone party," which was also made up of members of various social groupings within Israel: ordinary Israelites, prophets, priests, and kings. Although this "party" may have been in existence for a long time, it first made itself felt about the time of Elijah and Elisha, who represented Yahweh-alone prophets. The first king clearly to adhere to this party was Asa, followed by his son Jehoshaphat. Some of the later kings, such as Hezekiah and Josiah, were adherents of this party, but most were not. It was this party's products, however, which were collected and edited during the exile to produce the core of the Old Testament. The diversity of the party is indicated by the literature: Deuteronomy, Deuteronomistic history, various psalms, collections of proverbs, the Holiness Code (Leviticus 17–27), various prophetic collections. The three main types of literature (prophetic, deuteronomic, priestly) show so little knowledge of each other that one must conclude the Yahweh-alone party was made up of various "minority parties."

Smith's thesis works most successfully for the pre-exilic period; indeed, it agrees in broad outlines with much Old Testament scholarship. It can hardly be disputed that much of the time Israel did not follow Yahweh exclusively and that any reforms to make the people do so (e.g., Hezekiah) were short-lived. The canonical prophets make it clear that many other prophets, as well as priests, did not not follow the Yahweh-alone view. Indeed, many of the prophetic and historical sections of the Old Testament contain a constant polemic against false worship. Other sources of information, such as theophoric names and archeological finds, indicate that non-Yahwistic worship was widespread throughout the pre-exilic period. Against the thesis may be noted a number of points.

1. Much of Israel's religious history is reduced to the opposition between these two movements, which is surely simplistic.

Smith's constant use of the terms "syncretistic party" and "Yahweh-alone" party may give the impression that he is thinking of tightly knit groups. Such is not the case, however, as he is careful to explain:

> Accordingly, in reckoning the parties which advanced the worship of Yahweh, we must include a widespread popular devotion to him which found its expression in syncretistic worship. This seems to have been rather the general attitude of the population than a party position. However, since it formed the background from which the minor parties distinguished themselves, we may for convenience list those who shared this common attitude as "the syncretistic party." . . . we do have knowledge of the reformations in the Israelite kingdoms and of the belief, there, that Israelites should worship *only* Yahweh. This belief seems to have been held by a number of groups who sometimes cooperated, but who differed in social make-up and motivation. For convenience' sake, however, we may speak of them together as "the Yahweh-alone party" (or "movement," if "party" suggest too strongly an organization). (27, 29)

Thus Smith sees not only a complicated situation in which the two movements cut across other social and party groupings but also one in which social and economic factors could be as important as religious ones.

In criticism of Smith, it can be said that the constant discussion in terms of religious worship sometimes allows other factors to be slighted. In spite of his care to delineate qualifications and complexities, everything is ultimately subsumed under the opposition between the two "parties." The simplification has the advantage of clarity, yet there is always the danger that any particular situation will be analyzed in these terms alone. Smith is not always able to avoid this, even though his comments indicate that he is often aware of it. As Pietersma notes, "What emerges from the literature itself and what Smith's book reflects (in spite of his theory) is a spectrum ranging all the way from syncretism to militant Yahweh-alone-ism" (551).

2. The usefulness of Smith's analysis for the pre-exilic period soon ceases in the post-exilic situation:

> The objective of the Yahweh-alone party had changed. What it wanted of the High Priest was no longer a purge of the cults of the other gods. Evidently these were not officially practiced; we may assume that the party's influence had been strong enough to prevent their resumption when the city's cult of Yahweh was restored. . . . But now a new issue had developed, a question of purity law. . . . From now on the conflict

> in Jerusalem centers on such legal questions, and converts to the party are described as "those who had separated themselves from the *impurity* of the peoples of the land." (110–11)

Even though one may well agree with the broad outlines of the thesis for the pre-exilic period, it has already become problematic at the beginning of the post-exilic period and becomes even more strained and unhelpful as one moves on. It is no longer a case of syncretists against Yahweh-alone groups but one of assimilationists against exclusivists. Neither of these, however, is necessarily a direct heir to Smith's original groupings. Indeed, it is not clear in many cases that the objections of the "exclusivists" necessarily had a religious basis.

In addition to these two major points, there are individual interpretations of specific passages that many will find problematic, such as the following two.

3. Zerubbabel and the returnees were members of the Yahweh-alone party, whereas the "people of the land" were partisans of the the syncretistic party; the priesthood was divided. In the struggle over the rebuilding of the temple, however, the priesthood was in a position to bargain with the two groups for its own ends. The result was a compromise between the priests and Zerubbabel's group, in which Zerubbabel was crowned as civil leader and allowed to rebuild the temple. In return the high priest, Joshua, was allowed to be associated with Zerubbabel's messianic claims (Zech 6:9-15), and a crown, contributed by Zerubbabel's followers, was hung in the temple to mark the agreement. The attacks on Joshua by Zerubbabel's followers (e.g., Zech 3:2) would now cease, as long as he "kept the law" (i.e., toed the Yahweh-alone party's line). Furthermore, the party would see to it that the people paid the priestly dues.

4. Zerubbabel was opposed not by the Samaritans, as the present text of Ezra 4 implies, but by the "people of the land," the Judeans, because they were not allowed to help in rebuilding the temple. This breach is possibly reflected in Zech 11:14. Zechariah 12:2-10 may not only suggest the results of this breach but also explain Zerubbabel's disappearance: he was possibly assassinated, perhaps even by other members of the Davidic family in alliance with the syncretistic party. Thus the history of Judah from this time until the coming of Ezra was dominated by the syncretistic party. The criticisms of the Yahweh-alone party can be found in Isaiah 56–66, Zech 12–14, and Malachi.

2.3.11.3 O. Plöger and P. Hanson

Albrektson, B. *History and the Gods* (1967).
Barr, J. "Story and History in Biblical Theology." *JR* 56 (1976) 1–17.

Carroll, R. P. "Twilight of Prophecy or Dawn of Apocalyptic?" *JSOT* 14 (1979) 3–35.
Grabbe, L. L. "The Social Setting of Early Jewish Apocalypticism." *JSP* 4 (1989) 27–47.
Hanson, P. D. *The Dawn of Apocalyptic* (1973).
———. "From Prophecy to Apocalyptic: Unresolved Issues." *JSOT* 15 (1980) 3–6.
Plöger, O. *Theocracy and Eschatology* (1968).
Roberts, J.J.M. "Myth versus History: Relaying the Comparative Foundations." *CBQ* 38 (1976) 1–13.

In his first German edition (1959) Plöger developed the thesis of a major polarity in the Jewish community in the last few centuries B.C.E. His starting point was the period of the Maccabean crisis. From the writings of this time, especially the book of Daniel, he deduced two opposed factions within Judaism: on the one side, the pro-Hellenistic, pragmatic, priestly governing hierarchy; on the other side, the Hasidim, an eschatologically minded group who had the vision of an idealized Judaism expressed in millenarian terms. The problem he addresses is that of the origins of these two groups: Is there evidence of an earlier evolutionary stage to these two quite divergent approaches in the Old Testament literature? Analyzing primarily the "Isaiah Apocalypse" (Isaiah 24–27), Trito-Zechariah (Zechariah 12–14), and Joel 3–4, Plöger thinks he can trace the predecessors of the Hasidim in the preceding century or two. The attitude of the theocratic group is deduced primarily from a look at the Priestly source (P) and the Chronicler (Chronicles, Ezra, Nehemiah). (*Kellermann has built on Plöger's analysis, although he has developed it in his own way in an interpretation of Nehemiah.)

Although Hanson hardly refers to Plöger, most reviewers have pointed out his heavy indebtedness to the latter for his basic thesis. However, Hanson's textual analysis overlaps Plöger's only in the case of Zechariah 12–14, whereas his way of expressing the thesis has particular differences of nuance and terminology: the post-exilic community in the quarter of a century or so between the return under Cyrus and the end of the sixth century witnessed a struggle between two basic groups. On the one hand there was the "hieratic group," comprising the temple hierarchy and supporters, who sought to control not only the cult but also leadership of the community. They were basically this-world oriented, trying to exercise practical political wisdom for survival under the Persian overlordship. Opposed to them, on the other hand, was the "visionary group," the heirs of Deutero-Isaiah. They had a different view of the cult and the state but were excluded from both temple and government by the hieratic group. Cut off from actual power, the visionary group began to see the solution to their difficulties in cosmic terms. Their prophetic vision becomes other-worldly and mythical, rather than located in terms of history in this world. In this period the roots of apocalypticism emerge in the proto-apocalyptic sections of the Old Testament.

Hanson finds support for his thesis primarily in the writings of Trito-Isaiah, Zechariah, and Ezekiel, which include the literary products of both the hieratic and visionary communities. Much of his monograph is an analysis of these writings (plus a few other texts) and a consideration of the implications of their message for the early post-exilic Jewish community. Hanson initially proceeds by attempting to date the various prophecies. Because there is little actual historical allusion, he develops what he terms the "contextual-typological" method of analyzing the prophetic texts. According to this, the different prophecies can be dated by the breakdown of old poetic forms and meters and the employment of later forms. Accompanying this he sees an increasing adoption of mythical and cosmic language, in place of the historical, mundane language of earlier prophecies.

The basis for the visionary group and its conflict with the temple establishment is found primarily in Isaiah 56–66 (32–208) and Zechariah 9–14 (280–379), for both of which Hanson gives detailed textual reconstruction, poetic analysis, and his own translation. The program of the post-exilic, hierocratic establishment is taken for granted by Hanson, indicated by both the significantly small space devoted to it (209–79) and the lack of detailed exegesis of the texts used.

Despite the rather different approaches of Plöger and Hanson, there is enough in common to critique them together, although differences will be noted where significant. The most important objections and weaknesses are these (the major review of Hanson has been that of Carroll):

1. There is a considerable danger in these approaches of circular reasoning. The hypothesis is first presented, then followed by textual exegesis, and finally the hypothesis and exegesis are connected. Even in the detailed exegetical treatments by Hanson, it is generally clear that the texts themselves are being interpreted in the light of his hypothesis; this impression is reinforced by the frequency with which he reiterates his hypothesis in his exegetical discussion. In many cases, the hypothesis is simply being imposed upon the text.

The dangers here could be counterbalanced with the use of passages that straightforwardly support the hypothesis; unfortunately, there is little that does this. It is interesting that perhaps the greatest clear support comes from Plöger's reading of Daniel, whereas the exegetical commentary of prophetic material seldom produces anything clear-cut. That is, Hanson and Plöger both give a possible interpretation of the material but hardly the only or even most likely one (cf. the use of some of the same texts by Smith [2.3.11.2] to support a rather different thesis). With so much left obscure, it is scarcely surprising that it is hard to demonstrate the thesis from Trito-Isaiah or Trito-Zechariah. Nevertheless, this difficulty must be faced and acknowledged.

2. No one questions that a variety of movements and polarities in the Jewish community existed during these centuries. Nevertheless, the sharp opposition postulated, with a significant part of the community supporting the priestly establishment and another large part carrying out a wholesale attack on it, seems rather overdone in the light of the undisputed historical data. Why would such a sharp dichotomy, with most of the community on either one side or the other, leave so little evidence in the period literature, except in difficult and obscure prophetic oracles?

3. The models used by both Plöger and Hanson are questionable. Plöger depends on a particular analysis of the situation during the Maccabean revolt, especially with regard to the Hasidim. Not only does his view of the Hasidim go far beyond the evidence, his whole perspective of the various strands of thought and action in the revolt should be challenged. (See chap. 5 and 8.2.1 for a further discussion.)

Hanson acknowledges dependence on sociological models taken from Weber, Mannheim, and Troeltsch (1980). As Carroll has noted, these models do not seem the most useful for the postulated situation in the early post-exilic Jewish community in Palestine (27–28). Further, a great deal of work has been done in sociological research since these pioneers. The view of the priestly establishment as pragmatic, this-worldly, and interested primarily in maintaining the status quo, whereas the visionaries are without power, see things only in idealistic terms, and are concerned with eschatology, is simplistic and not based on sound sociological research (Grabbe: 32–33).

4. The treatment of myth and history is important to both Plöger and Hanson, yet neither's effort can be considered valid in the light of recent study. Symptomatic of the problems in their interpretations is the fact that, starting from similar premises, Plöger and Hanson come to opposite conclusions about what literature is "historical" in approach. Plöger states that the Chronicler is not interested in history because there is no place for eschatology in his outlook (39–45); Hanson sees the views of the visionaries as the result of allowing their eschatology to be become mythologized (23–28)! Although some of the important studies on myth and history have appeared since Plöger and Hanson (Barr; Roberts), Hanson rejected the important work of Albrektson (Carroll: 21). These recent studies (Barr; Roberts; Albrektson; Carroll) all go against the categories of myth and history as used by Plöger and Hanson.

2.3.11.4 Analysis

There is undoubtedly an element of truth in the belief that sectarianism was present in the Persian period. It was probably in existence even in pre-exilic times, but it is not necessarily evident in the extant sources. The traumas of the post-exilic situation would likely have fueled the tendency to produce groups with different ideas about how to resolve a situation which no one seems to have found acceptable. Both sociological and religious factors would lead one to expect sectarian factions to emerge. Nevertheless, it is useful to point out the tenuous nature of some of the interpretations of sectarianism, to illustrate how little we know. There are several difficulties in trying to extract information on sects and other sociological movements of this time:

1. The paucity of information available increases the danger of over-interpreting the little that we have. For example, charges of corruption, slackness, deviance, and wickedness of the most perverse kinds are part of the stock rhetoric of the preacher. To turn Isaiah 59 into a source of sociological data or an objective evaluation of contemporary society, as has been done, is absurd.
2. There is a persistent trend to argue from silence; that is, if a concept is not mentioned (e.g., a messiah), then the group did not believe in it. Arguments from silence can be very important when a good deal of information is available, but they are treacherous when argued on the basis of a few often heavily edited verses.
3. Certain sociological "truths" are too frequently read into the data, often in the form of simple dichotomies (laity versus priests; Jews versus Samaritans; the apocalyptic versus establishment). For example, it is usually assumed that criticism of the priesthood automatically makes the group marginal, anticlerical, or cut off from the cultic establishment. This is not necessarily the case, as can easily be demonstrated from religious and social movements today, when some of the most acute criticisms come from within a movement itself. Preachers commonly claim (sometimes even in truth) to be directing their strongest sermons at themselves.
4. The relative probability of various theses must be carefully weighed. All sorts of hypotheses explain part of the phenomena gleaned from the texts of this period, but not all are equally likely. Producing new theories is an important part of scholarship, but so is testing and sifting out those that do not appear to be useful when a broader perspective is taken.
5. When all is said and done, the main source for information about

Jewish society at this time is still Ezra-Nehemiah. Perhaps connections can be established between the books and some of the prophetic material (Blenkinsopp's [1990] exploration of the term *haḥărēdîm* ["quakers"] is suggestive in this regard). Yet even these books are often far from clear, which highlights the difficulties with establishing any thesis in this area.

Therefore, the suggestions and speculations can be very interesting and even helpful in advancing knowledge, and the act of producing them should not be castigated. Nevertheless, each must be carefully scrutinized, and one must take care that even then such hypotheses do not become anything more than tentative. The danger is taking a particular thesis as the basis for further research, when it is really no more than informed speculation. As will be discussed later (chap. 8), we have reason to bemoan the few data preserved on the later sects, such as the Pharisees and Sadducees, and to warn of the dangers of overinterpretation. Nevertheless, when we consider what we know of them, it is a veritable embarrassment of riches compared with that left in the literature of the Persian period.

2.3.12 The Thesis of Frank M. Cross

Cross, F. M. "Aspects of Samaritan and Jewish History in Late Persian and Hellenistic Times." *HTR* 59 (1966) 201–11.

———. "Papyri of the Fourth Century B.C. from Daliyeh." *New Directions in Biblical Archaeology* (1969) 45–69.

———. Contribution to *Discoveries in the Wadi ed-Daliyeh,* edited by P. W. Lapp and N. L. Lapp (1974) 17–24.

———. "A Reconstruction of the Judean Restoration." *JBL* 94 (1975) 4–18.

Grabbe, L. L. "Josephus and the Reconstruction of the Judean Restoration." *JBL* 106 (1987) 231–46.

Cross's comprehensive theory was presented in his 1974 presidential address to the Society of Biblical Literature (1975), although various aspects of it had already been adumbrated in previous publications (Cross 1966; Cross 1969; Cross 1974). The basic arguments can be summarized as follows:

1. There are several lacunae in the list of Jewish high priests for the Persian period. This is indicated by the statistical average for a generation, which comes to about thirty-four years. According to

Cross, it should be closer to twenty-five years, suggesting that some names have dropped out of the list. These can now be filled primarily by means of information from several sources, which follow.

2. Papponymy (the naming of a child after his grandfather) was a common practice during this period. Therefore, we find several figures in a genealogy with the same name (e.g., there were three governors of Samaria named Sanballat to the time of Alexander). Important in arguing for papponymy is the presence of hypocoristic names (i.e., shortened forms or nicknames); for example, Johanan might appear as Honi (in Greek, Onias). Cross postulates that the presence of the same name repeatedly in the high priestly list was responsible for several scribal haplographies. The restoration of these will produce the proper statistical average for the generations.
3. Josephus is also important in restoring the names lost from the priestly genealogy. He preserves the name of a governor of Samaria (Sanballat III) not otherwise known from the Bible or recent discoveries. He describes an altercation between the high priest Johanan and his brother Joshua, in which the latter was slain. This caused the governor Bagoses, identified as the general of Artaxerxes III, to intervene. Josephus also describes the situation in which Manasseh, the brother of the high priest Jaddua, married Nicaso, the daughter of Sanballat (III). Sanballat built a temple at Gerizim for Manasseh about the time of Alexander.

The list of high priests as reconstructed by Cross (using conventional English forms) is:

	1.	Jozadak born before 587
father of	2.	Jeshua born ca. 570
father of	3.	Joiakim born ca. 545
(brother of	3.	Eliashib I born ca. 545)
(father of	4.	Johanan I born ca. 520)
(father of)	5.	Eliashib II born ca. 495
father of	6.	Joiada I born ca. 470
father of	7.	Johanan II born ca. 445
father of	8.	Jaddua II born ca. 420
father of	(9.	Johanan III born ca. 395)
(father of	10.	Jaddua III born ca. 370)
(father of)	11.	Onias I born ca. 345 (= Johanan IV)
father of	12.	Simon I born ca. 320

A major critique of Cross's thesis has been given by Widengren (*506–9):

1. The reconstruction depends on the assumption of papponymy as a prevalent usage among the high priests of this time. In attempting to demonstrate this, Cross must postulate two haplographies.
2. Even if we accept the assumption of two haplographies, the theory of papponymy still has difficulties: (1) despite the assumption of a haplography, Eliashib appears only twice; (2) the name Johanan appears once (by hypothesis), then disappears until the fourth generation, rather than the third; and (3) such hypocoristic forms as Jaddua and Onias are treated as if they were identical to Joiada and Johanan; that is, Jaddua is treated as if it were a clear papponymy of Joiada, even though the names are actually not the same.
3. Although the assumption of a new generation every twenty-five years is correct statistically, it is not necessarily justified historically. One cannot assume that every high priest married and had a male offspring by age twenty-five, especially in such a troubled period as this.
4. Cross argues that the Eliashib, who was a contemporary of Nehemiah, could not have been the brother of Joiakim, because he would have been too old in the time of Nehemiah; yet Neh 12:10 specifically says that Eliashib was the *son* of Joiakim.

To these may be added a fifth argument (Grabbe). Cross is actually heavily dependent on Josephus but assumes, without discussion, that Josephus has additional reliable information, even though Josephus has admittedly misinterpreted it. There is actually no evidence that Josephus had genealogical data beyond what can be found in the biblical text. He does have one additional tradition (about a quarrel between the high priest Johanan and his brother Jesus), which may be reliable, but that seems to be all. See further at 2.2.5.

2.3.13 Economic, Social, Demographic Factors

Albright, W. F. *The Biblical Period from Abraham to Ezra* (1965).

Blenkinsopp, J. "Temple and Society in Achemenid Judah." *Studies in the Second Temple* (1991) 22–53.

Finley, M. I. *The Ancient Economy* (1985).

Kippenberg, H. G. *Religion und Klassenbildung im antiken Judäa* (1978).

Kreissig, H. *Die sozialökonomische Situation in Juda zur Achämenidenzeit* (1973).

Scharbert, J. "*Bēyt 'Āb* als soziologische Grösse im Alten Testament." *Von Kanaan bis Kerala* (1982) 213–37.
Schottroff, W. "Zur Sozialgeschichte Israels in der Perserzeit." *Verkundigung und Forschung* 27 (1982) 46–68.
Tuplin, C. "The Administration of the Achaemenid Empire." *Coinage and Administration in the Athenian and Persian Empires* (1987) 109–66.
Weinberg, J. P. "Demographische Notizen zur Geschichte der nachexilischen Gemeinde in Juda." *Klio* 54 (1972) 45–59.
———. "Das *Bēit 'Ābōt* im 6.-4. Jh. v. u. Z." *VT* 23 (1973) 400–414.
———. "Die Agrarverhältnisse in der Bürger–Tempel–Gemeinde der Achämenidenzeit." *Acta Antiqua* 22 (1974) 473–86.
———. "Die soziale Gruppe im Weltbild des Chronisten." *ZAW* 98 (1986) 72–95.

2.3.13.1 The Persian Empire in General

See the general comments at 1.2.2. For a convenient survey, see Dandamaev/Lukonin (*96–222). The basic economic and social structures of the Persian Empire were simply a continuation of those extant under the Assyrian and neo-Babylonian empires, although naturally these structures varied from area to area. As with both previous and subsequent empires, the primary aim of the government was to promote a stable status quo, which allowed the collection of as much revenue as possible. Whereas previous empires had often done this by force, the Persians generally tried to keep the various entities in submission by certain concessions to local custom (e.g., respecting local cults and deities). Nevertheless, they did not hesitate to gain or maintain territory by military might.

The Persian desire to exploit the empire for the maximum amount of revenue meant the introduction of new measures. Darius I (re)organized the empire into twenty satrapies, with a fixed amount of annual tribute due from each one. This seems to have been carefully calculated on the ability of each to pay and was, on the whole, realistic. Taxation was systematic and thorough, but it appears to have been bearable for most payers. A further requirement that might have been economically crushing in certain cases was the maintenance of the army, for it was the obligation of the local people to provide for the army when its duties took it to their area.

The economy was largely agrarian. The term "Asiatic mode of production" is often used of the economic structure. Whether or not this is appropriate (1.2.2), production was characterized primarily by free peasant labor. That is, agrarian workers were not slaves, although they were often dependent in the sense of being bound to the soil by law or circumstances. Their condition may often have been no better than the slaves', but technically their status was different. Some owned their own land, but many worked as tenants on the estates owned by the aristocracy and the wealthy, working especially on royal lands. Slavery was characteristic of some areas, such as Babylon and certain other cultural centers, as well as perhaps many of the Greek areas of Asia Minor. The overall characteristic, however, was free or semi-free labor, not slavery. The real question is what situation prevailed in Judah; there are several possibilities, and the question is addressed in the next section.

One of the main economic factors affecting the Persian Empire throughout its two centuries was the requirement of tribute in precious metal. Rather than being coined and put into circulation, the metal was centrally hoarded so that silver and gold gradually became scarcer (*Olmstead: 297–99). One of the empire's main needs was to pay mercenary forces and influence decisions by potential enemies, in particular the Greeks. As time went on, the satrapies became increasingly drained of precious metal. To what extent this created hardship, as Olmstead suggests, is open to debate, because taxes were paid in kind as well as coin (*Dandamaev/Lukonin: 177–95). However this affected the individual, such taxation seems to have stifled the economy by encouraging the barter system, rather than the use of money.

A second factor that had an impact on the empire was the granting of large estates to loyal servants by the king. Toward the end of the empire there was a tendency to concentrate land in the hands of a few royal satraps and other Persian nobles (*Frye: 117). Some non-Persians were able to profit from the system, for example, the few successful banking houses, such as that of Murašu (2.2.3.5). These not only loaned money to pay taxes but also undertook the management of large estates for their clients (*Frye: 117). All in all, apart from Darius's satrapal organization, there do not seem to have been major changes under the Persians: the economic structures and systems that had developed in Mesopotamia over many centuries were largely continued.

2.3.13.2 The Province of Yehud

Considering Finley's cautions about the social and economic situation of the Greeks and Romans, for whom a larger measure of data has been preserved (e.g., 25–26), it would be foolish to attempt other than a very careful discussion about such matters in Judah (cf. 1.2.3). Nevertheless, there are sufficient data preserved to discuss some of the outlines of Judah's socioeconomic situation.

First, on the question of population, estimates have varied widely. Albright (87, 110) was willing to state that only about 20,000 inhabitants remained in Judah (about 10 percent of the population by many estimates; cf. Weinberg 1972: 45). This seems unduly influenced by the prejudice of the Old Testament writers, however, and there is a tendency in recent specialist works to argue that only a minority of the Judean population was taken captive, with the bulk of the people remaining in Judah itself (*Ackroyd 1968: 20–31; Kreissig: 101; Weinberg 1972: 45–47). Contrary to the picture in Ezra-Nehemiah, those who returned from Babylon were coming not to a wilderness but to an area heavily populated by their own people, who were not necessarily enthusiastic to see them return. It had been mainly the upper class and governing officials who were taken to Babylon, probably not least because they had been anti-Babylonian and perhaps pro-Egyptian (Weinberg 1972: 48–50).

Much of northern Judah (the area of Benjamin) had been untouched or only lightly damaged by the Babylonian armies. The people of this area seem to have been left to get on with their lives. The "poor of the land" (*dallat hā'āreṣ*) would even have welcomed the Babylonians, because many of them had now gained land to work, if not to own. Life may not have been easy, but it was looking up for many of those left. The account in Ezra-Nehemiah must be read against this background; what it treats in purely religious terms may in fact be a cover for major social and economic concerns (e.g., the "people of the land" are judged for their impiety, whereas their friction with the returnees may have been chiefly socioeconomic in origin).

The structure of Judah in the Persian period is now widely explained on the model of the *Bürger–Tempel–Gemeinde,* a community centered on a temple that the citizens control (Weinberg 1974; cf. the summary in Blenkinsopp). This model had three types: (1) Group A_1, in which the temple was the owner of the land but contracted part of it out to be worked by members of the community and administered part of it itself; (2) Group A_2, in which the theoretical ownership of land by the temple was waived and all farming was done by members of the community; and (3) Group B, in which the temple owned no land and carried on no commerce.

Judah clearly belonged to Group B. The actual concept of land possession centered on the *bêt 'ābôt* "(extended) family" (Weinberg 1974; Scharbert). The returnees would have made up the entire community, the indigenous inhabitants (the descendants of those not taken captive in 587/586) being excluded.

Although recognizing the heuristic value of Weinberg's thesis, Blenkinsopp has subjected it to critical analysis. One of the weaknesses that he notes concerns the number of inhabitants in the province, which Weinberg took to be about 200,000 or so. Exactly how many returned in the early post-exilic period depends in large part on how one evaluates and dates such lists as Ezra 2//Nehemiah 7. A number of recent discussions accept that the lists represent those who had returned from exile in the first few decades (2.2.1.5.1), although some would argue that it includes the returned population by the time of Ezra or Nehemiah (Weinberg 1972: 54). If the 42,000 of the list is correct, the membership of the *Temple–Bürger–Gemeinde* would make up about 20 percent of the population (Weinberg 1972: 52–53). As Blenkinsopp notes, a population as large as this is problematic. Much more critical work remains to be done on Weinberg's thesis.

The economy of Judah through this period was largely agrarian. Until Jerusalem and other towns flourished, it is unlikely there was much trade, because the cities served as important agricultural markets for the peasant farmers (Kreissig: 102, 107). Because the annual tribute paid to the Persian overlords had ultimately to be paid in coin, it has been suggested that it was necessary that each family produce a surplus for cash sale (Kippenberg: 51). If so, this could lead to specialization in such high-yield crops as olive trees and vines (Kippenberg: 51–53). This seems a matter of speculation, however, because it is possible that taxes could completely or in part be paid in kind. The bulk of the province was now located in the hill country and much of the land good for grain production was now lost; it is possible that Judah was not even self-sufficient in grain production (Kippenberg: 47). The one hint of international trade involving Judah (Ezekiel 27) indicates exclusively agricultural products. This suggests that handcrafts and other products of skilled workers did not play an important part in the Judean economy at this time, although such forms of trade existed in Jerusalem, if not elsewhere (Kippenberg: 47–49).

Nehemiah 5 is an important source for attempting to determine the economic situation of the mid-fifth century. The question is how to interpret the three groups of vv 2-5. Kreissig takes these as three different groups: (1) the day laborers, who mortgaged their children because this was all they had; (2) those who were smallholders, that is, who owned their own land; and (3) those who sold their children as slaves, because they were only tenant farmers and their lands were not their own (78–79). Kreissig sees a progression toward large estates (*latifundia*), with the wealthy Jews taking over the property, labor, and even bodies of the poor who could not afford to repay loans or interest. Kippenberg understands the situation somewhat differently: in his opinion the three groups represent three stages in one process (55–62). First, children were mortgaged to secure loans. When that route was exhausted, the land itself would be mortgaged. Finally, there was nothing left to do but sell the children into slavery. Kippenberg sees an important model in the reform of Solon in Athens (Aristotle, *Athen. Polit*. 5–9). The complaint of the Athenians was similar to that of those who came to Nehemiah. They wanted redemption from slavery, the elimination of debts, and the redistribution of land. Both Solon and Nehemiah enacted measures to secure the first two, but the third was resisted. Kippenberg also discusses at length the sabbatical and jubilee years of Leviticus 25, suggesting that the Holiness Code helped provide a religious sanction for the interests of the peasantry, thus creating solidarity between the priesthood and the smallholders (64–68). This also served to hinder—at least, to some extent—the developing class distinctions of the time.

2.4 SYNTHESIS

2.4.1 Overview

Any history of the Persian Empire must acknowledge that the sources are few, often biased, and leave out large periods of time. There are enormous gaps in data. We must distinguish between what is known, what can be reasonably inferred, what is more or less guesswork, and where even speculation is unjustified because nothing is known.

What applies to the writing of Persian history as a whole must be multiplied several times over when attempting to produce a history of Judah under Persian rule. The sources are episodic and thus insufficient for writing a connected history of Persian Judah. Moreover, almost all of them are written from a very particular point of view. We have hardly any inscriptional material for the Palestine of this time, and archeology can give only a rough framework in the absence of the necessary literary remains. The bulk of the source material consists of religious literature with its own individual perspectives, prejudices, and blind spots. It would be a mistake to take this literature at face value (although some histories still insist on doing so), but one who does not is often left with little more than question marks, speculation, and frustration. Even so simple a matter as a list of high priests for the period cannot be worked out; the one attempt to do so cannot be considered successful (2.3.12).

The one contemporary source that, by and large, is still undisputed is the Nehemiah Memorial (2.2.1.3). Despite its strong bias, it does give us a statement by an actual eyewitness to some of the events described. The prophecies of Zechariah and Haggai also seem to have some contemporary material, but the precise amount is debated (2.2.1.6.1). Even more of a problem is Isaiah 56–66, although many date large sections of it to the early Persian period (2.2.1.7). The Aramaic documents in Ezra 4–7, although widely accepted, are still problematic (2.2.1.2); in particular, a number of them are strongly redolent of Jewish theology. The criticisms apply not only to the Cyrus decree in Ezra 1, which has often been doubted, but also to the Aramaic documents themselves. Still, it seems unjustified at this point to conclude that the documents are forgeries: some may be genuine, most or all may be genuine decrees reworked by the Jewish writer(s), or some or all may be outright inventions. For the historian, the resulting uncertainty is disappointing, but the problem must be faced. Apart from the Nehemiah Memorial, the most accessible account (the books of Ezra and Nehemiah as a whole) is still very problematic and must be scrutinized carefully.

A further problem is often overlooked: the degree to which Achaemenid history is itself unknown or uncertain. It is commonplace to quote *Olmstead and go from there, without acknowledging the problems of access to historical events in the Persian Empire. In some cases there are considerable data from reliable sources (inscriptions, trustworthy Greek historians, archeology), but a great deal comes from piecing together the comments of Greek compilers such as Diodorus, whose ultimate source is the mendacious Ctesias and whose compilation is itself known only in part from a Byzantine epitomist. Such a frequently cited incident as the Megabyzus revolt is actually based on very doubtful information and may be nothing but a fiction (2.2.6.3; 2.4.3.2). Therefore, the status of the background history into which the history of Judah is fitted must always be kept in mind; that it is in Olmstead does not make the data reliable.

Despite these caveats, we are not completely ignorant. Something is known of Persian history, and something is known of the events and situation in Judah, which can be fitted into the broader sweep of history. The neo-Babylonian Empire (626–539 B.C.E.), despite the leadership of such dynamic individuals as Nebuchadnezzar II, was short-lived. In less than a century it was taken over by a vassal of its erstwhile ally, the Medes. For almost exactly two centuries the Persian Empire dominated both the Near East and the center of European culture in the Aegean.

When Jerusalem fell in 587/586, many of the population were taken captive to Babylon, but recent studies indicate that the bulk of the population remained in Palestine (2.3.13.2). Those taken to Babylon settled down, built up their communities, and became integrated into the society, as indicated by personal names in such sources as the Murašu documents (2.2.3.5). The result was a community with two centers, one in Palestine and one in Mesopotamia. The exact size of the community in Babylon is difficult to determine, although judging from the situation in later centuries under the Parthians, it was large and thriving. If so, it seems that those who returned to Palestine during the reign of Cyrus and in the intervening decades down to the time of Ezra and Nehemiah were very much in the minority when compared with either the indigenous Palestinian population or those who remained in the Babylonian region.

For those who chose to live in exile in the East, there was some opportunity of advancement under Persian rule. This is indicated by the Jewish court apologies, such as Esther (2.2.1.9.1) and Daniel 1–6 (5.2.3). One does not have to assume the historicity of the specific stories to appreciate that it was possible for a Jew to rise not only in society but also even in the Persian court—and to a rather high level. Such court novellas had a dual function: (1) to give courage to those who were not prospering but saw themselves as only aliens in a pagan environment, and (2) to provide models of how to behave in such circles, without compromising proper Jewish worship and religion.

Those who remained in or chose to return to Judah could gain some comfort from being in the Promised Land, but the realities of life were not particularly paradisiacal. The country was small, had a backward economy, and was surrounded by neighbors who at times could be hostile (but who, conversely, were sometimes treated with suspicion even when they appeared to be friendly). The economy was largely agrarian, and skilled handicrafts and manufacturing were at a minimum, at least in the early part of the post-exilic period (2.3.13.2). The best of the farmland was no longer within the borders of the province. The Shephelah had long been taken away, and even the southern area of Judah was now in the hands of Edomites or Arabs. Most of the country was made up of the Judean hill country. The soil and climate were suitable for vineyards and olive orchards. The tax system may also have tended to create specialization in crops which could be sold for cash rather than grown for the subsistence of the residents, but grain production would have been low in any case and may have been insufficient for the needs of the people themselves.

One benefit of the exile was that many of the farm tenants remaining in Judah came into land of their own with the deportation of the landlords in 587/586. Things may not have been easy for the "poor of the land" left by the Babylonians, but life was probably better for many of them than it had been under the Judean monarchy. They would not have been particularly enthusiastic about the return of their fellow Jews from exile if it looked as if they would have to revert to working as tenant farmers or even as day laborers, as many of them probably had before 587/586. Therefore, when we read of rivalries and clashes that are explained in religious terms in the Old Testament literature, we have to keep in mind that what is explained as religious may actually have been in part or even largely socioeconomic in origin.

The succession of high priests is particularly important, because Judah seems to have been a temple state and theocracy (2.3.1). It can be shown that Judah had its own governors for part of the time and was referred to as the "province of Judah" (*Yĕhûd mĕdîntāh*), but whether this was for the entire period or only from the time of Nehemiah (mid-fifth century) is a moot point (2.3.4). Some have argued that Judah was administered from Samaria in the first part of the post-exilic period. Even if Judah had a governor, the priests in general and the high priest in particular were of great importance in the administration of the country. The structure of administration initiated in the early post-exilic period was to continue for much of the history of the country during the Second Temple period.

2.4.2 The Early Persian Period and the Initial Return

2.4.2.1 Cyrus the Great (539[559]–530 B.C.E.

Cargill, J. "The Nabonidus Chronicle and the Fall of Lydia." *AJAH* 2 (1978) 97–116.

Grabbe, L. L. "Another Look at the *Gestalt* of 'Darius the Mede.'" *CBQ* 50 (1988) 198–213.

Graf, D. F. "Medism: The Origin and Significance of the Term." *JHS* 104 (1984) 15–30.

Petit, T. "L'évolution sémantique des termes hébreux et araméens *pḥh* et *sgn* et accadiens *pāḫatu* et *šaknu*." *JBL* 107 (1988) 53–67.

Cyrus was the son of the Persian king and his Median wife. On the Median side, Cyrus's great-grandfather had been the ally of Nabopolassar the Chaldean and had helped bring down the Assyrian Empire. The Persians were vassals of the Medes during Cyrus's youth and early adulthood. In 550, however, Cyrus led his army against his Median grandfather, Astyages, and defeated him, replacing the empire of the Medes with that of the Persians. It evidently appeared to outside observers that there had simply been a change of dynasty among the Medes (Graf), because the Persian Empire continued to be referred to as "Medes," and the term was an alternative to "Persian" for centuries afterward.

Becoming king over the Median Empire was only Cyrus's first step toward taking over the neo-Babylonian Empire. His next recorded operations were in Asia Minor, where he defeated Croesus, the king of Sardis, and took the city; the exact date is uncertain (*Nab. Chron*. 2.16 is often cited in this connection, but see now Cargill). Other expeditions east consolidated his territories until he was ready for the final assault on the heart of the Chaldean Empire. In 539 he launched a direct attack against Nabonidus, who was apparently expecting it. The Chaldean army was defeated at Opis, and Babylon itself fell without a battle on 12 October 539 (*Nab. Chron*. 3.15–16), although Cyrus himself was not present. The Persian entry into Babylon was led by the general Gubaru (Gobryas), who prepared the way for Cyrus's triumphal entry two weeks later. Gubaru himself evidently died only a few days after this (*Nab. Chron*. 3.22; cf. Grabbe: 200, 206–7).

Cyrus's initial actions were to ingratiate himself with both the Babylonians and the subject peoples. The temples were protected from looting in the conquest of Babylon itself. Cyrus left in place Nabu-aḫḫê-bulliṭ, who had been the chief administrative officer of Babylon under Nabonidus, but he had his own son Cambyses made king of Babylon (Grabbe: 199–204). This was evidently a mistake, because Cambyses held the office for less than a year before the title "king of Babylon" reverted to Cyrus, as revealed in various administrative documents. Exactly why Cambyses held the office for only a short period is uncertain but may have been due to undiplomatic actions on his part at the new year ceremony, which began Cyrus's first year of rule (cf. Oppenheim's thesis and its criticism by Boyce [*2.73 n.15a] and *Dandamaev 1989: 56–57).

The Cyrus Cylinder seems to have been produced in Cyrus's first year, when Cambyses was joint ruler. Although the cylinder is in Babylonian cuneiform and therefore was probably written by Babylonian scribes, it is clearly propaganda for Cyrus (2.2.3.2). Further pro-Cyrus propaganda is found in the "Verse Account of Nabonidus," which attacks Nabonidus as the opponent of the Marduk priestly establishment and hails Cyrus as the city's deliverer and champion (*ANET*: 312–15).

Because the *Nabonidus Chronicle* breaks off shortly after the conquest of Babylon, the detailed activities of Cyrus until near the end of his reign are no longer known. Although one must treat Cyrus's own statements with caution, it seems likely that he allowed a return of some of the Jews to Palestine. In his fourth year Cyrus made another Gobryas satrap of "Babylon and Ebir-nari"; this individual (probably not the same person who was the conqueror of Babylon [cf. Grabbe: 206–7; contra Petit: 65–67]) held the office until well into Cambyses' reign and possibly until the first years of Darius I. Although the preserved accounts do not agree with one another, Cyrus evidently met his death in a military campaign in 530 and was succeeded by the crown prince Cambyses.

2.4.2.2 Cambyses (530–522 B.C.E.)

Atkinson, K.M.T. "The Legitimacy of Cambyses and Darius as Kings of Egypt." *JAOS* 76 (1956) 167–77.
Brown, T. S. "Herodotus' Portrait of Cambyses." *Historia* 31 (1982) 387–403.
Dubberstein, W. H. "The Chronology of Cyrus and Cambyses." *AJSL* 55 (1930) 417–19.

Cambyses suffered from negative propaganda. The campaign to impugn his integrity found its way into the Greek histories, primarily Herodotus, and has also tended to affect the treatment of Cambyses in many modern histories (Brown). After a brief reign as king of Babylon in Cyrus's first year (2.4.2.1), Cambyses assumed an obscure role until the last year of Cyrus's reign, at which time he was elevated to a position of co-ruler and left in charge while Cyrus conducted his campaign into the Caucasus. With Cyrus's death in 530 B.C.E., Cambyses became king. The main achievement of his reign was the conquest of Egypt which, after several years of preparation, commenced in 525. Cambyses arranged with the local Arab tribes for supplies in his crossing of the desert in southern Palestine, and also managed to persuade the Egyptian admiral Udjahorresnet to revolt and support him (2.2.4). The new pharaoh Psammetichus III capitulated shortly after the frontier fortress of Pelusium fell.

From contemporary monuments it seems that Cambyses was quite respectful of the Egyptian cults, except for those that revolted against him (*Olmstead: 89–92; Atkinson: 170–71; *Dandamaev 1989: 81–82). He also took the traditional title of the pharaoh of Egypt, as rulers—both foreign and native—had always done and would continue to do until the coming of the Romans. The report that he killed the *apis* bull by stabbing it to death seems to be only a piece of anti-Cambyses propaganda, because records show that the bull which was alive at the time of his conquest did not die until several years later.

In 522 a revolt against Cambyses took place in Persepolis, led by an individual claiming to be Cambyses' brother Bardya (in Greek, Smerdis) (2.4.2.3). Cambyses immediately began the march back to Persia but died on the way; the exact cause of his death is uncertain because of differing traditions.

2.4.2.3 Darius I (522–486 B.C.E.)

Bickerman, E. J., and H. Tadmor. "Darius I, Pseudo-Smerdis, and the Magi." *Athenaeum* 56 (1978) 241–61.
Cameron, G. G. "The Persian Satrapies and Related Matters." *JNES* 82 (1973) 47–56.

Lecoq, P. "Observations sur le sens du mot *dahyu* dans les inscriptions achéménides." *Transeuphratène* 3 (1990) 131–39.

Although an able ruler, Darius was a usurper of the throne, in the opinion of some modern scholars. He was also an able self-promoter, primarily through the *Behistun Inscription* and its various versions, which circulated throughout the empire (2.2.3.3). The story Darius presents is that he rescued the throne after it had been taken over by an imposter claiming to be Cambyses' brother Bardya. Darius baldly tells us that it could not have been Bardya because Cambyses had already secretly executed him; instead, the imposter was a magus by the name of Gautama (*Beh. Inscr.* §§10–13:1.26–61). A similar story is found in Herodotus (3.61–79). According to both accounts, Darius led a party of seven noble Persians to remove the imposter. They succeeded, and by some means one was chosen to be king, the one who took the name Darius. (Darius was possibly a throne name; if so, we do not know his personal name.)

There are reasons to doubt this version of the story, despite the fact that it is found in both Persian and Greek sources. Herodotus's version only confirms that he knew of a tradition of the account which Darius himself propagated. Although there has been considerable debate on the subject (*Dandamaev 1976: 114–26; *Dandamaev 1989: 83–94; Bickerman/Tadmor), a number of modern scholars think that the rebel against Cambyses was indeed his own brother and that the story of his secret execution is a part of the slander against Cambyses. From the information preserved it seems that Bardya had a considerable popular following. Therefore, the conspiracy led by Darius had to use every means to support its own claims. In addition to his clear military ability, which crushed the many revolts that sprang up all over the empire in his first year, Darius sought to secure his throne by spreading the story that he had only removed a clever usurper and restored the throne to its rightful heirs.

Whatever faults may be laid at Darius's door, he reigned long, evidently as a good administrator. According to Herodotus, he organized the Persian Empire into twenty administrative and military satrapies (3.89–97). Attempts to reconcile Herodotus's list of satrapies with the "peoples" (*dahyāva*) mentioned in *Beh. Inscr.* §6:1.14–17 have not been successful, most likely because the Behistun list is probably not that of the formal satrapies (Cameron; Lecoq). Darius is also credited with reforming the traditional laws. It seems evident that he first introduced coinage into Persian usage, borrowing the concept from the Greeks. His coin, the "daric," became a medium of exchange in about 515 and continued in use until the time of Alexander.

For the rest of his long reign, much of Darius's energy went to other parts of the empire, but periodic events in the west of the empire must have been noted in Palestine, even if their exact portent is not now known. It is usually assumed that in 518 Darius himself led his army to Egypt, which submitted without battle; but Cook doubts his personal participation (*60–61). Thus Darius was possibly in the area of Palestine at a critical time during the rebuilding of the temple, but even if so, he remained there only a few months before returning to Persia. Any supposed visit to or communication with Judah at this time is speculation. Darius instituted the building of a canal from the Nile to the Red Sea which was finished in 512. At this time Libya was added to the empire as a new satrapy, a fact recorded on the stelae set up at the opening of the canal (2.2.3).

The next major event was the revolt of the satraps over the Ionian Greek area of Asia Minor, ca. 500. When this was finally put down by 493, it was clear that something had to be done about Greece proper if the Persian Empire was to be extended to Europe or even maintained in Asia. Therefore, preparations began for the conquest of Greece. Apart from his mention in the Bible, Darius has gone down in history as the invader of Greece and the one defeated at the battle of Marathon in 490. He lived only a few years beyond this, although he was evidently in the process of planning another invasion of Greece at the time of his death in 486.

2.4.2.4 First Return and Rebuilding of the Temple

Lust, J. "The Identification of Zerubbabel with Sheshbassar." *Ephemerides Theologicae Lovanienses* 63 (1987) 90–95.

Olmstead, A. T. "Tattenai, Governor of 'Across the River.'" *JNES* 3 (1944) 46.

Tuland, C. G. "'*Uššayyā*' and '*uššarnâ*': A Clarification of Terms, Date, and Text." *JNES* 17 (1958) 269–75.

Vaux, R. de. "The Decrees of Cyrus and Darius on the Rebuilding of the Temple." *The Bible and the Ancient Near East* (1971) 63–96.

One of Cyrus's first acts after conquering Babylon was to allow the return of the statues of the various gods to their native cities. In the last days of the neo-Babylonian Empire, Nabonidus, for a reason that is not completely clear, had brought many of the statues into Babylon. As part of Cyrus's self-propaganda to his newly conquered peoples, he had himself proclaimed as the choice of their particular god (e.g., the choice of Marduk, according to the Cyrus Cylinder [2.2.3.2], but the choice of Sin, according to a tablet from Nippur [de Vaux: 68–69]). According to Ezra

1:2-4, soon after the beginning of his reign Cyrus issued a decree authorizing—indeed, commanding—the return of the Jews to Palestine and the rebuilding of the ruined temple (2.2.1.2). This decree has seemed to many to fit with the propaganda of the Cyrus Cylinder and the actions related in the *Nabonidus Chronicle*. However, not only has the authenticity of Cyrus's decree been questioned, but also the evidence is that only a few Jews returned and probably over a period of years, not all at once. (The lists of returnees in Ezra 2 and Nehemiah 7 may be cumulative and are, in any case, not a list of those who returned in the first few years [2.2.1.5.1].) The circumstances are difficult to ascertain, and credence depends heavily on how trustworthy one thinks the story in Ezra 1 is. There is reason to doubt that Cyrus's benevolence was completely straightforward; however, he may have had special reasons for allowing the return of the Jews or at least no reason to forbid those who wanted to go back.

The initial return is said to have been under Sheshbazzar, who is referred to in one place as a "prince of Judah" (Ezra 1:8) but in another as having been appointed "governor" (*peḥāh*) of the area (Ezra 5:14). Under Sheshbazzar, the vessels captured from the temple half a century earlier were allowed to be returned and, with the approval of the Persian government, even the actual foundations of the temple were supposedly laid (Ezra 5:16). Here our information ceases. What happened to Sheshbazzar and why the rebuilding of the temple did not progress are not stated. A further problem is that other passages ascribe the refounding of the temple to Joshua and Zerubbabel, without any indication of previous activity (e.g., Haggai 1; Zech 4:1-10), and even the compiler of Ezra may have intended Sheshbazzar to be identified with Zerubbabel (Lust).

Ezra 2:1-2 states that Zerubbabel brought a group of Jews along, with Joshua as high priest, suggesting that this was shortly after Cyrus's decree in 538 (which ignores Sheshbazzar's alleged activities). Rather, Zerubbabel probably came some time later, certainly several years after 538 and possibly as late as the latter part of Cambyses' or early part of Darius's reign. What does seem likely is that he was governor and may even have succeeded Sheshbazzar (Hag 1:1; 2:2, 21). More problematic is the question of his work on the temple. According to Ezra 3–4, Zerubbabel and Joshua began work right after coming (nothing is said of any previous work done by Sheshbazzar), but the activity was stopped by directives from the Persians; after the prophecies of Haggai and Zechariah, however, the Jews began work again, ca. 520 (the second year of Darius). Their activities drew the attention of Tattenai, who was responsible for the subsatrapy of Ebir-nari (Olmstead), and he investigated Jewish authority to build. Fortunately, the Persian bureaucracy was able to produce documentation necessary to allow them to continue, and according to 5:1—6:15 they brought the work to a conclusion in about 516 B.C.E.

The books of Haggai and Zechariah give a somewhat different picture. The prophets complain that the temple lies in ruins and call on the people to build it (Haggai 1; Zech 4:1-8). There is no mention of previous activities by anyone (whether Sheshbazzar or Zerubbabel), and nothing is said about any opposition or about a Persian decree against the project. Zerubbabel and Joshua led the people in beginning the building, although, surprisingly, nothing is said about the completion of the work.

Thus we have three different accounts about the building of the temple: (1) by Sheshbazzar; (2) by Zerubbabel, with the work interrupted (Ezra 4–6); and (3) by Zerubbabel, without interruptions (Haggai, Zechariah). Although one could forcibly harmonize these accounts (as does Tuland), such heavy-handed literalism would ignore the nature of the sources. We are dealing not with historical narratives but with three theological accounts that, incidentally, contain some historical data.

The only information about the completion of the temple is the statement in Ezra 6:15 that it occurred in Darius's sixth year (516 B.C.E.). This appears only in the narrative section of Ezra 1–6 and is confirmed nowhere else. Furthermore, the resources available were unlikely to have been sufficient to allow completion so soon. Neither Joshua nor Zerubbabel is mentioned in connection with the ceremony over the temple's completion. Speculation that Zerubbabel and, possibly, Joshua were removed by the Persian authorities because of messianic pretensions is interesting but unsubstantiated (2.3.3). Haggai and, to a lesser extent, Zechariah seemed to see Zerubbabel as a potential Davidic king over a new Jewish state, but this proves nothing about Zerubbabel's own aspirations. Considering the confidence placed in him by the Persians in choosing him as governor, he was probably more of a realist than the prophets; although he may have suffered as a result of messianic stirrings in some quarters, more likely he fulfilled his term of office in the normal way. Nevertheless, that neither he nor Joshua is referred to in the dedication of the temple is curious. This may be due to the tendentiousness of the editor of Ezra, it may show that his information breaks off at this point, or it may indicate no real knowledge of the actual situation in the first place (2.2.1.1).

After this, darkness falls over the history of Judaism for the next sixty to eighty years. Attempts have been made to illuminate this period by assigning various biblical texts to it, but such attempts have met with little success. The documents quoted in Ezra (4:6-22) indicate that attempts were made to rebuild the walls of Jerusalem during the reigns of Xerxes and Artaxerxes. If genuine, these reports suggest that the walls were destroyed by external forces within the Persian Empire.

Whatever the external pressures, there was evidently much strife within the Jewish community itself. The religious and social situations were most likely complex, with various factions and rivalries. There is undoubtedly some degree of truth in the dichotomies proposed by different individuals (2.3.11), but the reality was probably much more complicated. The sections of Zechariah mentioning Zerubbabel and Joshua together suggest a competition between them, although whether it existed in actuality or only in the mind of the editor is another question (2.3.3). Most commentators believe that the prophet called Trito-Isaiah lived and proclaimed in the early post-exilic period, even though all the material in Isaiah 56–66 is not to be assigned to him (2.2.1.7). Whether he was hostile to—or was a member of a group hostile to—the temple establishment is a matter of speculation because the cultic statements in the collection are capable of more than one interpretation.

Archeological evidence is minimal in the way of specific data, but together with certain biblical texts, some things may be suggested cautiously about the economic and social situation of the time. Zechariah, Haggai, and Malachi all indicate a period of considerable agrarian and economic hardship. There seem to have been difficulties with harvesting and storing enough for sufficiency, much less a surplus to sell. If much of the material of Isaiah 56–66 belongs to this general period, then it confirms the economic difficulties, as well as paints a picture of religious uncertainty. Archeological study also shows a widespread area of destruction in Benjamin and southern Samaria at about this time (2.2.7.3). There have also been attempts to postulate a revolt in Palestine and to see this as background to the Aramaic letter of Ezra 4:7-22 (2.3.7). The problem is that so little of the literature can be connected with archeology in anything more than a very speculative way.

2.4.3 From Zerubbabel to Nehemiah

2.4.3.1 Xerxes I (486–465 B.C.E.)

Kuhrt, A., and S. Sherwin-White. "Xerxes' Destruction of Babylonian Temples." *Achaemenid History* (1987) 2.69–78.

Stolper, M. W. "The Governor of Babylon and Across-the-River in 486 B.C." *JNES* 48 (1989) 283–305.

Xerxes was not the eldest son of Darius, although he was the eldest born after his father came to power, and his mother was Atossa, a daughter of Cyrus. This is why by the year 498 he had been designated crown prince. Just before Darius's death Egypt revolted, and it fell to Xerxes to put the rebellion down. This he did in his first year (485/484). Whether the Egyptian campaign had any significance for the Palestinian area is uncertain, but there is evidence of widespread destruction in Benjamin and southern Samaria about this time (2.2.7.3). How to interpret this information is difficult (see also 2.4.2.4). There is no evidence that Xerxes himself ever went to Egypt (*Dandamaev 1989: 182).

Much has been written about Xerxes' relationship with Babylon. In 484 Babylon slew its satrap and revolted under a rebel leader, but this was put down within a few weeks. A more serious revolt took place in 482, and according to most handbooks, Babylon was severely punished: the wall built by Nebuchadnezzar was destroyed, the temples at Esagila and elsewhere demolished, and the huge gold statue of Marduk taken away to be melted down. The ruins were supposedly not fully cleaned up until the time of Alexander. It is also alleged that about this time, Xerxes removed the phrase "king of Babylon" from his titulature. Much of this has been discounted by recent study (Kuhrt/Sherwin-White). Despite Babylon's punishment, the temples and cult continued to function. As for Xerxes' titulature, his usage represents a transitional phase that probably had nothing to do with Babylon's revolt.

Ebir-nari may have been divided from Babylon as a separate province at this time (but see Stolper's discussion). Several years later Xerxes led the invasion against Greece that resulted in defeats at Salamis in 480 and Mycale in 479. After this, Xerxes retired from military activity and spent most of the rest of his reign building the new capital of Persepolis. He was assassinated in a palace coup in 465.

Of the Achaemenid rulers, Xerxes appears the most concerned about matters of religion in his inscriptions. Of particular interest is the famous "*daiva* inscription," which tells how Ahura Mazda aided him in conquering a country that worshiped the *daiva*s (evil deities). Xerxes claims to have destroyed the *daiva* sanctuary and forbidden *daiva* worship (Xerxes Persepolis Inscription H [XPh §46b:35–41 = Kent: 150–51]; *Boyce: 2.173–77); yet the precise meaning of this inscription is controversial, and its significance has eluded scholars.

2.4.3.2 Artaxerxes I (465–424 B.C.E.)

At the beginning of his long reign Artaxerxes put down a number of revolts. The story is that Artabanus, the leader of the successful palace coup against Xerxes, favored Artaxerxes even though he was the youngest son of Xerxes. Not long afterward, Artabanus was himself killed in an assassination attempt. A third son, who was satrap of Bactria, revolted as soon as he heard of Artaxerxes' succession to the throne but was defeated.

Only a few years later, in 460, Egypt rebelled under Inarus with the aid of Athens. The revolt was suppressed by Megabyzus, and the Athenian fleet was defeated by the new Egyptian satrap, Arsames. Although some of the rebel forces managed to flee into the delta and continue their resistance there, Egypt was basically back in Persian hands by 454. The struggle with Athens went on, but only a few years later, in 449, the peace of Callias was concluded. This was a mutual hands-off agreement between Athens and Persia and brought an end to hostilities with the Greeks for several decades. According to Ctesias, shortly after this Megabyzus, the satrap of Ebir-nari, revolted because the Egyptian rebels who had surrendered to him in good faith had been executed by the king. There are now reasons to doubt the reliability of this story, especially because Ctesias's reasons for the revolt are rather dubious (2.2.6.3). Whatever the truth of the Megabyzus revolt, most of the rest of Artaxerxes' reign seems to have been peaceful.

Many scholars believe that Ezra came to Jerusalem in the seventh year of this Artaxerxes (458 B.C.E.). If so, the mission may well have had the Egyptian revolt as a background (but see 2.3.6). It was almost certainly in 445, Artaxerxes' twentieth year, that Nehemiah's commission as governor over Judea commenced. The problem with providing a setting for this is that little is known of Artaxerxes' reign after 449: much of our information for this period is from Greek sources, and they refer to Persia and Persians only when the Greeks were directly affected. Olmstead has seen the Megabyzus rebellion as the background of Nehemiah's commission, assuming that although Jerusalem was preparing to take part in the revolt, Nehemiah was able to intervene both to avoid revolt and to accomplish the building of the city's defenses (*313–17). As noted, the problem is that the question of the Megabyzus rebellion is a sticky one. Furthermore, the book of Nehemiah gives no hint of such a background for the building of the wall.

2.4.3.3 Nehemiah's Mission

Lightstone, J. N. *Society, the Sacred, and Scripture in Ancient Judaism* (1988).

Ezra 6 ends with the completion of the temple (the date 516 B.C.E. [Ezra 6:15] is unlikely). Whatever the date, our knowledge ceases in the early years of Darius, and more than sixty years pass before we are given further information. Ezra 7 begins with the seventh year of Artaxerxes (7:7-8), which would be 458 if Artaxerxes I is intended. The rest of the book of Ezra is devoted to the activities of Ezra the priest and scribe, but as the next section shows, the matter is not straightforward. Therefore, it seems best to deal with Nehemiah's activities first and come back to the question of Ezra.

Our knowledge of Nehemiah comes primarily from his own testimony, the Nehemiah Memorial (sometimes referred to as his "memoir" or "autobiography" [2.2.1.3]). This gives a certain immediacy and authority to his statements but also cautions the reader to expect a one-sided and biased account. Nehemiah's mission was political; he was sent as the officially appointed Persian governor over Judah. As such, he was able to undertake tasks with a boldness that the Jewish community as a whole could not do without a degree of risk. His most important achievement was to rebuild the defensive walls of Jerusalem. The central question is why the walls had not already been rebuilt, since almost a century had passed since the first Jews were allowed to return from Babylon.

There are several possible answers. One is that the wall had been rebuilt but then destroyed by a military activity or civil disturbance about which we have no information. Although attempts to find literary evidence for such an event have not been generally accepted (2.3.7), archeological evidence does indicate that some sort of destruction took place in the areas of Benjamin and southern Samaria sometime in the 480s (2.2.7.3). It may be that the ruined wall which Nehemiah repaired was not the wall destroyed by Nebuchadnezzar in 587/586 but a subsequent wall breached during a period of fighting only a few decades before Nehemiah's time for which no literary account has survived. Or it may be, as others have speculated, that the correspondence of Ezra 4 belongs between the missions of Ezra (assuming his was in 458) and Nehemiah (in 445). This would represent a situation only a few years old at the time of Nehemiah's coming.

According to his memorial (2.2.1.3), Nehemiah seemed to anticipate trouble in the rebuilding of the wall from the beginning. This would fit well with the interpretation that the correspondence of Ezra 4:8-23 concerned events from only a few years earlier. Nehemiah's tour of the walls of Jerusalem was done stealthily at night, as if he expected spies to be reporting on his activities (Neh 2:11-16). Opposition from Sanballat and Tobiah is mentioned from the time of Nehemiah's arrival (2:10); as soon as work on the wall began, they made a charge against the Jews identical to that in Ezra 4: "What is this that you are doing? Are you rebelling against the king?" (2:19).

Beyond this one statement, the opposition of Sanballat and Tobiah, as well as of Geshem the Arab, is nowhere clearly explained. Nor is Nehemiah's hostility to them. He describes their activities and statements in the most negative and unreasonable terms. Nehemiah's memorial is personal and completely one-sided, as one would expect. He does not even bother to clarify the positions of his opponents; one would gather from Nehemiah that they were simply mean and jealous pagan opponents, and Tobiah seems to be designated an Ammonite "slave" (2:10, 19). In fact, Sanballat was the governor of Samaria, appointed by the Persians, and Geshem was a king of the Arabs, as has been inferred from inscriptions (2.3.5.4). Tobiah was a Jew whose family held territory across the Jordan in the old area of the Ammonites (see discussion of the Tobiads at 4.3.2). The term "slave" or "servant" (*'ebed*) could be used in reference to high officials who were "servants" of the king; it was evidently in this sense that the term correctly applied to Tobiah, but the title seems to be used sarcastically by Nehemiah, as a slur. Therefore, the opposition to Nehemiah consisted of Persian officials and local rulers and nobles, not the rabble one would assume from the Nehemiah Memorial.

The precise aim of Nehemiah's opponents is not clear, although one can surmise that it was a matter of politics. It was not just a case of outside opposition. In addition to Tobiah, Jews at Jerusalem, some of them evidently part of the aristocracy, were displeased with Nehemiah and aided Sanballat and his colleagues. Shemaiah attempted to persuade Nehemiah to take security measures, which would be seen as cowardly (6:10-13). Although it is not explicitly stated, the context suggests that Shemaiah was a prophet. The prophetess Noadiah and other prophets are also said to have spoken similar things to intimidate Nehemiah (6:14).

Various nobles, relatives of Tobiah, corresponded with him and reported on Nehemiah's activities (6:17-19). Moreover, these same nobles were not afraid to speak well of Tobiah to Nehemiah in person. This suggests a complex situation. On the one hand, they were in contact with Nehemiah and perhaps not entirely opposed to him, but, on the other hand, they evidently regarded him as something of an extremist and one unnecessarily antagonistic to the local Jewish nobility. Their communications with him may have been intended simply to moderate his enmity against Tobiah and perhaps even to bring about a reconciliation, which would be better for the Jews as a whole. If so, they were not "enemies" but only part of the local Jewish leadership who saw things differently from Nehemiah. From their point of view, cooperation between the Persian authorities and indigenous leadership probably would be preferable to the confrontational style adopted by Nehemiah.

Viewed in this light, a rather different picture emerges from the one in the book of Nehemiah. Until the arrival of Nehemiah, Sanballat and others such as Geshem apparently had had good relations with the Jewish leadership in Jerusalem, undoubtedly to mutual advantage. Exactly why building a wall around Jerusalem threatened that relationship is not clear. Perhaps the threat was not the wall but Nehemiah as governor. He wanted to close the Jewish community to the surrounding environment and make it exclusivistic and inward-looking. Perhaps the wall was only symbolic of this changed attitude, although in fact it would have been easier to isolate Jerusalem by a defensive wall that allowed the entrance of goods and persons to be closely monitored. Nehemiah saw the intercourse with the surrounding peoples in a completely negative light (see below). Although not all the references to events in the book of Nehemiah may belong to his own time, there are a number of statements that do, as well as his own decrees and rulings, some of which are discussed below.

One of the first acts undertaken after building the wall was to register the people by family (7:5). This was only a prelude to resettlement in Jerusalem of many of those living in outlying areas, the ultimate aim being to have a full one-tenth of the population living in Jerusalem itself (11:1-2). Soon after celebrating the Feast of Tabernacles, a fast was called for the purpose of confession of sins and separation from the "foreigners" (9:1-2). This fast day ended in a signed declaration to follow God's law and to separate from the "peoples of the land" (10:1, 29-32 [Eng. 9:38; 10:28-31]). In the mind of Nehemiah and his supporters, obedience to God's law carried an automatic concomitant of being separate from the surrounding peoples. This point is further emphasized in 13:1-3. To stop intermarriage between Jews and others, Nehemiah resorted to drastic measures, such as flogging and other forms of corporal punishment (13:23-25). The final measure mentioned in Nehemiah concerns the son of the high priest, who had married the daughter of Sanballat. Nehemiah is said to have driven the high priest's son from Jerusalem. (Whether this episode is a part of the Nehemiah Memorial is a debatable point [2.2.1.3], but it illustrates the attitude of mind of Nehemiah's adherents, even if it is not in Nehemiah's own words.)

According to the books of Ezra and Nehemiah, attitudes and actions such as the opposition to intermarriage are a necessary part of being a loyal Yahwist; but it must not be assumed that all took this point of view. On the contrary, many who undoubtedly considered themselves pious individuals and full-fledged heirs to the Yahwistic tradition did not see eye to eye with Nehemiah (cf. Lightstone: 21–43). This was not just the case among the nobility, as already noted (Neh 6:17-19), but also true for members of the high priesthood itself. After a twelve-year period of rule, Nehemiah had only to be absent for a short time for the high(?) priest Eliashib to allow his relative Tobiah to set up an office in the temple court (Neh 13:4-9). Eliashib clearly did not agree with Nehemiah's exclusivistic point of view. How can he, as apparently the holder of the highest ecclesiastical office, be accused of lack of zeal for worship of Yahweh?

On the contrary, it seems that Nehemiah was the odd man out and able to enforce his will only because of his powers as the officially appointed governor.

Further evidence that Nehemiah's was not the only view among Yahwists is found when the background of Sanballat is investigated further. So far it has only been noted that Sanballat was governor of Samaria, and one would infer from the book of Nehemiah that he was a pagan. Extrabiblical evidence confutes this implication. From both the Wadi Daliyeh papyri and the Elephantine papyri (2.2.2), it seems clear that the governorship of Samaria was kept in one family for a period of time. A Sanballat was governor during the time of Nehemiah about 445 B.C.E., and his sons seem to be performing the same function some decades later (see below). A seal from Wadi Daliyeh, dated ca. 350, mentions an individual (name partially lost) who was governor and the son of a Sanballat, showing that there were at least two individuals by that name and that they and their sons inherited the governorship.

More specifically, among the Elephantine papyri are copies of a letter from the colony, about their ruined temple, which mentions the Jerusalem high priest (Cowley: nos. 30–32), some decades after the time of Nehemiah (407 B.C.E.). At the end of the letter, the following statement is made (30.29; cf. 31.28, Porten's translation [2.2.2]):

> Moreover, we sent in our name all the(se) words in one letter to Delaiah and Shelemiah sons of Sanballat governor of Samaria.

Although the letter to Delayah and Shelemyah is unfortunately not preserved, this brief reference tells us several things. First, it confirms that Sanballat was not just a resident of Samaria but its governor; second, the office was evidently hereditary, because his sons seem to be fulfilling the office in either an official or de facto capacity for their father, who was by now rather aged or possibly even deceased; and third, Sanballat was a worshiper of Yahweh, as indicated by the *-yah* element in their names. Therefore, the cooperation between Sanballat and Tobiah the Jew was not unusual, because they shared the same basic religious outlook. The outlook of Ezra and Nehemiah is therefore not one of true worshipers of Yahweh against surrounding pagans but rather of one sort of Yahwist against another sort. In this area, at least, Smith's model of exclusivists versus assimilationists has merit (2.3.11.2).

Nevertheless, in one area Nehemiah undoubtedly gained the gratitude of many Jews: the economic problems that many of them were suffering at the time, as described in Neh 5:1-3 (2.3.13.2). Here there seems good reason to think that members of the wealthier classes were exploiting the less well-off. Nehemiah had no reason to think well of the former because most of his opponents seem to have been from their ranks; however, he may paradoxically have come to the aid of the very "people of the land" who were not rigorous in their observance of the law as Nehemiah and his supporters would interpret it. Indeed, this is why simplistic dichotomies (assimilationist versus exclusivist, visionary versus hierocratic establishment, etc.) are not likely to conform to reality; many issues cut across expected or hypothesized dichotomies such as this.

2.4.3.4 The Place of Ezra and His Activities

The subject of Ezra is not easy (2.3.8). There are several queries: Who was he? What was his mission? When did it take place? All sorts of answers have been given, and this variety illustrates the difficulty in approaching Ezra. A great deal depends on how one evaluates the authenticity of the decree of Artaxerxes (Ezra 7:12-26) and the "Ezra source" (2.2.1.2; 2.2.1.4). If there was no Ezra source, as some allege, or if it was tendentiously rewritten by the editor, then the historical Ezra becomes problematic. By contrast, if the authorization by Artaxerxes is basically accurate, this is important information, even if there was no Ezra source.

Therefore, more important than when Ezra came is why and even whether (2.3.8), although the questions may be related. The authorization in Ezra 7, allegedly coming from Artaxerxes, implies that Ezra was to set up the "law of the God of heaven" as the law of Judah, as well as to bring temple vessels, gifts, and an allowance from the Persian administration for the temple. We also know, however, that the temple had long been rebuilt and the cult restored, with the temple vessels stolen by Nebuchadnezzar long since returned, whereas the Judean priesthood and community were hardly ignorant of many of the traditions that at some point became a part of the Pentateuch. Therefore, Ezra would not be coming to set up a theocracy, restore cultic worship, or proclaim a completely unknown law to a people bereft of religion. Furthermore, Ezra was not the high priest, although he seems to have taken that prerogative; nor was he said to be civil governor in the same way that Nehemiah and probably others, such as Zerubbabel, had been, although he seems to have acted that way in part.

The question, then, is what Ezra hoped to accomplish. We hear nothing about his setting up religious courts or investigating Jewish worship throughout the satrapy of Ebir-nari (despite 7:25-26, which is suspect anyway). In the preserved account Ezra's only real activity concerns mixed marriages. Was this the whole reason for his mission? Why would he want to come with authority concerning a long-established cult, with a functioning high priest, unless he was convinced that something was amiss? In other words, does the account in Ezra 7–10 hide a priestly dispute in which Ezra's faction attempted to bring the priesthood of Jerusalem into line with the faction's concepts? Such may be indicated in the question of mixed marriage, because the "guilty" priests head the list (Ezra 10:18). This is not to suggest that only the priests were involved, for a list of ordinary Jews is included. It implies, however, that the practice of mixed marriage continued because the local serving priests did not teach against it.

This episode is really the only specific act of importance ascribed to Ezra. The account may have been curtailed, because it breaks off abruptly without any natural conclusion; but in the light of the material preserved, one gains the impression that the main purpose of Ezra's journey was to address the problem of mixed marriages. The question comes up almost as soon as he arrives in Jerusalem (9:1). If this was Ezra's purpose, Smith's model of exclusivists versus assimilationists seems helpful at this point (2.3.11.2).

If we assume that there was a mission of Ezra to Jerusalem to address this situation, when did it take place? Choosing one of the three chief alternatives (2.3.6) is problematic, unless one can be convinced that we have reliable data. All three assume that the "seventh year of Artaxerxes" (7:7-8) is an accurate datum which only needs interpreting (or emending). Nevertheless, the issue is more complex than that. Ackroyd (*1988: 41–42) has noted that the "seventh year" follows on the "sixth year" of the previous chapter (6:15). Is the number "seven" here only a stereotypical number? If so, no reliance should be placed on it for chronological purposes.

Moreover, any dating that puts Ezra and Nehemiah in Jerusalem at the same time is problematic (*Clines: 16–17). If they overlapped, then why is each not mentioned in the memoir of the other? That the editor has had to emend the tradition at Neh 8:9 and to associate Ezra and Nehemiah (as most commentaries point out) shows that the separate traditions did not have them overlapping. It is difficult to believe that both Ezra and Nehemiah dealt with the same problem, mixed marriages, if both were in Jerusalem at the same time. This seems to rule out Bright's dating (2.3.6.2). It would also seem to refute the traditional dating, which puts Ezra and Nehemiah together; however, according to the interpretation of some scholars (e.g., *Clines: 15; *Williamson 1985: xxxix), Ezra's mission was accomplished in a short time and he returned to Babylon, so that he and Nehemiah did not overlap. The dating that puts Ezra in 398 B.C.E. also seems to fit the data.

Nonetheless, to choose one of these dates requires one to make assumptions about the reliability of the Ezra material. There are too many uncertainties to be so confident. There may well have been an Ezra, and he may well have come to Jerusalem; but when, if, and why cannot be answered with any degree of confidence at this time. The definite answers to these questions that are given by many scholars seem arbitrary in the present state of scholarship on the subject. All we can speak of are possibilities.

2.4.3.5 Darius II Ochus (424–404 B.C.E.)

Stolper, M. W. "Bēlšunu the Satrap." *Language, Literature, and History* (1987) 398–402.

Artaxerxes left as heir his only legitimate son, who became Xerxes II. After a rule of only forty-five days, however, he was assassinated by another of Artaxerxes' sons, this one by a concubine. In a few weeks the pretender was himself displaced by Ochus, yet another of Artaxerxes' sons by a concubine, who took the throne name of Darius (II). Under him, the Persians began to intervene in the Peloponnesian War to keep the Greeks divided for their own advantage. Playing a major part in this was the skilled diplomat Tissaphernes. The success of Darius's diplomats in keeping the pressure on the Greeks and off the Persian Empire is all the more remarkable in that several revolts broke out within the empire at this time (such as the revolt of the Medes and of the eunuch Artoxares). The plan of "divide and conquer" followed by Tissaphernes and his fellow satrap Pharnabazus, although apparently working quite well, was derailed because of Darius's second son, Cyrus (or, according to the anecdotal account of Ctesias, because of Darius's queen Parysatis). Cyrus was put in charge of Asia Minor in about 408 and, by means of military aid and funds, enabled the Spartans to bring Athens to submission in 404. In the short run the policy may have been seen to demonstrate Persian strength; in the long run it rebounded on Persia.

From Darius's reign we find preserved one of the small windows into the Jewish communities of the time. In 419 the Passover decree was issued, giving permission for Jewish worship in the community at Elephantine (2.2.2). Some time later in 410 B.C.E. the Jews' Egyptian neighbors, during the absence of the Persian governor, took the opportunity to destroy the temple of Yah(o), apparently because they resented the blood sacrifices of the Jews. Letters were sent to the high priest at Jerusalem, who ignored them, to Bagohi, governor of Judah, and to Delayah and Shelemyah, sons of Sanballat and governors of Samaria, who transmitted the petition to the governor of Egypt, Arsames (Cowley: nos. 30–32).

Permission was eventually given to resume worship, although for a cult not including animal sacrifice, but whether the temple was ever rebuilt is uncertain. The satrap of Ebir-nari at this time (ca. 407–401 B.C.E.) was the Babylonian Belšunu, son of Belusuršu (Stolper).

2.4.3.6 Artaxerxes II Memnon (404–359 B.C.E.)

Arsaces, the eldest son of Darius II, became Artaxerxes II. His long reign of forty-five years was marked by some successes but also by almost continuous revolts, with various Greek city-states involved in most of them. These revolts began soon after he took the throne, with the rebellion of his brother Cyrus. At the coronation ceremony, Cyrus was alleged to have been implicated in an assassination plot against Artaxerxes but managed not even to lose his office as satrap. Nevertheless, using Greek mercenaries, he began a revolt soon after returning to his satrapy. Because one of these Greek soldiers was Xenophon (2.2.6.4), we have a detailed account of at least part of the revolt. Cyrus was defeated and killed in 401. When Tissaphernes came to take over Cyrus's old satrapy the next year, however, the Ionian cities refused to acknowledge his rule and called on Sparta for aid. The result was a lengthy conflict with the Spartans who were led by their king, Agesilaus; and it was further complicated by the Athenians' attempts to revive their empire. This culminated in one of Artaxerxes' major achievements, the King's Peace of 386 with the Greek states, which acknowledged Persian control of most of the Ionian Greek cities. Artaxerxes was able to renew this treaty several times, until 367.

Egypt had already revolted in 405, in the last days of Darius II, and the rebellion of Cyrus the Younger prevented a concentrated attempt by the Persians to retake Egypt. Egypt managed to stay independent by enlisting Greek aid at various times. The King's Peace temporarily cut off help from Athens, but Nekhtenebef (in Greek, Nectanebo I [380–363 B.C.E.]), the first king of the new Thirtieth Dynasty, was an able ruler. In 373 Pharnabazus led an abortive expedition against Egypt. His successor, Datames, prepared for another invasion but was forced to postpone it because of a rebellion nearer home in Cataonia. When making preparations a second time for an invasion, Datames himself rebelled (ca. 368). This was soon followed by revolts among other governors in Asia Minor and Syria, the so-called Satraps' Revolt. Egypt, under its new king Tachos (363–360 B.C.E.), launched an attack into Coele-Syria. Then the invasion collapsed when the Egyptian people revolted against Tachos, because of high taxes, and supported his nephew who became Nectanebo II (360–343).

Tachos surrendered to the Persians and was well treated by Artaxerxes. With Tachos out of the way, the revolting satraps could be picked off one by one. Sometime about 359 order was restored.

Thus, in spite of considerable internal dissension, Artaxerxes managed to keep his empire intact over his long reign, but he did not fulfill his plans to retake Egypt. Furthermore, many of the satraps, especially those in Asia Minor, acted as semi-independent rulers, maintaining private armies, fighting with one another, colluding with the Greeks, and even revolting against the king when his instructions conflicted with their own ambitions.

2.4.4 The Last Part of Persian Rule

2.4.4.1 Artaxerxes III Ochus (359–338 B.C.E.)

Ochus, a satrap and commander of his father's armies in the last years of his rule, became Artaxerxes III. He was able to centralize power as had not been done for a long time, ordering the more distant satraps to disband their private armies. Most obeyed this order, but Artabazus in Phrygia and Aroandas (in Greek, Orontes) of Mysia refused and rebelled. The former, however, was soon forced to flee to Philip II of Macedon, whereas the latter seems to have remained quiet although not officially reconciled with Artaxerxes. This left the way open for Artaxerxes to tackle the major prize, Egypt.

The campaign against Egypt was not easy and took close to ten years. In 350, the first invasion ended in defeat for the Persians. Then Phoenicia revolted in 349 in what is sometimes referred to as the Tennes Rebellion, named after the king of Sidon who played an important part. This revolt was put down in 345, with the execution of Tennes and the destruction of Sidon as an example to other rebels. Egypt finally capitulated in 342, although Nectanebo escaped and fled to Upper Egypt. Artaxerxes himself led the final Egyptian campaign, but an important commander was a eunuch by the name of Bagoas (Bagohi). Bagoas is said to have been virtual ruler in the last days of Artaxerxes' reign and eventually poisoned the king. With Artaxerxes' death, Egypt once again revolted against Persian rule. It was during Artaxerxes' reign that Philip II of Macedon united Greece under his control. Through much of his reign, however, it was to Philip's advantage to be on friendly terms with Artaxerxes, and the latter may have died without knowing of Philip's plans for the invasion of Persia.

2.4.4.2 Arses (338–336 B.C.E.)

The story is that Bagoas could not himself be king because he was not an Achaemenid, but he thought Arses, a son of Artaxerxes III, would do his bidding (Diodorus 17.5.3–6). Arses may have taken the throne name of Artaxerxes IV. When Arses proved difficult and even tried to take Bagoas's control away from him, the story is that Bagoas killed him.

2.4.4.3 Darius III Codommanus (336–331 B.C.E.)

The Achaemenid chosen by Bagoas was a grandson of the brother of Artaxerxes III. He was already in his mid-forties and had distinguished himself in a campaign against the Cadousii. Bagoas allegedly realized that this was a man he could not control, but Bagoas was himself poisoned before he had a chance to dispose of the new king. As Darius began his reign, Philip of Macedon had actually begun the preliminary phases of his invasion of Persia, but Philip's assassination cut the effort short. It was left to Philip's son Alexander to defeat Darius III and end the Achaemenid Empire (4.4.2).

2.4.4.4 Events in Judah

The book of Nehemiah breaks off around 430 B.C.E. From then until the coming of Alexander, only a few fragments of information are preserved, unless Ezra should be dated to 398. The letters from Elephantine show that a man named Johanan was high priest in Jerusalem about 407; he is widely identified with the Johanan of Ezra 10:6. Josephus also preserves an independent tradition that a high priest Johanan killed his brother Joshua in the temple (2.2.5). If this has a factual basis, as is not unlikely, it gives another bit of information. The problem is when to date it. I would identify the high priest with the Johanan (and the governor Bagohi who is also in the tradition) of the Elephantine papyri, thus putting the episode about 400, although others want to put it close to the end of Persian rule (2.2.5).

Archeological evidence indicates a destruction which affected the Shephelah and Negev about 380 B.C.E. (2.2.7.3). This could be explained on the basis of a successful Egyptian revolt from Persian rule about 400. Egypt controlled the southern part of Palestine until about 380, when the Persians retook the area, even though Egypt itself remained independent. There are also some late traditions that some groups of Jews were resettled from Palestine around the middle of the fourth century. This has been connected with the rebellion of the Sidonian king Tennes (2.3.9), but the literary evidence is not strong. The archeological evidence is also problematic, because any destruction in this period would be difficult to distinguish from that of the time of Alexander's conquest. Therefore, if Judah was involved in the Sidonian revolt, then we have no clear information on the subject.

If Ezra is dated to 398, the last sixty years of Persian rule in Judah are a blank. If he is dated to 458, the last century of Persian Judah—half of the Persian period—is for practical purposes unknown to us. We also have to accept that he may have come at some other time or possibly not at all.

2.4.5 Religious Developments

Cody, A. *A History of Old Testament Priesthood* (1969).

Gese, H. "Zur Geschichte der Kultsänger am Zweiten Tempel." *Abraham unser Vater* (1963) 222–34.

Gunneweg, A.H.J. *Leviten und Priester* (1965).

Hasel, G. F. *The Remnant* (1974).

———. "Remnant." *IDBSup* (1976) 735–36.

Hausmann, J. *Israels Rest* (1987).

Kellermann, D. לֵוִי *TWAT* (1984) 4.499–521.

Knibb, M. A. "The Exile in the Literature of the Intertestamental Period." *Heythrop Journal* 18 (1977) 253–72.

The Jewish community in Palestine from the time of Cyrus (commonly referred to as the "post-exilic period") saw itself as linked to and a continuation of the nation that came to an end with the fall of Jerusalem in 587/586 B.C.E. This was indeed the case; nevertheless, there were many differences between the two eras, and some of these differences had major consequences. The changes are significant enough that one can speak of a new entity—Judaism. It has long been the custom to speak of "Judaism" as the religion after the exile, as distinguished from the one before 587. This demarcation has too often in the past been one of value judgment and even theological apartheid, as if Judaism were somehow a deterioration or inferior development of the earlier, "pure" Israelite religion. Such absurdities have no place in the work of either the historian or the historian of religion. Although the theologian can and must make value judgments, the consequences of using theological discussion as a guise for religious chauvinism and outright prejudice have been shown all too clearly by modern history.

To the historian, however, it is still valid from a purely descriptive point of view to attempt to identify demarcations in religious development. The "Second Temple period"—the time from Cyrus to the fall of Jerusalem under Titus—has specific common characteristics that allow one to discuss it as a self-contained entity, to be distinguished from both Israel before 587 B.C.E. and Judaism after 135 C.E., even though the end of one era grades into the other and the transition points are best seen from a distance.

One of the most important changes with the destruction of the First Temple was the loss of the native monarchy, which had religious as well as national consequences. The king had been an important figure in religious life (regardless of whether one accepts the elaborate mytho-cultic theories associated with Mowinckel and others). Now there was no king, and much theological energy went into explaining why there was no Davidic successor and what was to follow from this fact. Thus we have the beginnings of what for convenience is often referred to as "messianism"—the history of speculations about a royal or priestly leader chosen by God (8.3.5).

Closely associated with this was the status of the Jewish state in the Land of Israel. Statehood as such was lost, even though for much of its last century and a half the kingdom of Judah was only a vassal of one of the great powers (Egypt or one of the Mesopotamian empires). Further, a significant number of its people had been taken captive to distant lands. How was this low state of God's people to be explained? For many the answer had to be religious in nature (cf. *Ackroyd 1968; Knibb). The last king had sinned; previous kings had sinned; the people had sinned; the nation had sinned; God was punishing/correcting/abandoning God's people. These were only some of the explanations; there were at least a few who saw the attempt to impose Yahwism exclusively as the problem (Jer 44:15-19).

One theological idea used to explain the situation was the concept of the "remnant" (Hausmann; cf. Hasel 1976), an idea with a long history in both ancient Near Eastern literature and the Old Testament (Hasel 1974). Although the concept of remnant originally emphasized the completeness of destruction (only a remnant was left), it took on the more positive idea of being the foundation for a new people. That is, the purified, even "holy" remnant was the seed or root from which the new growth came. This explanation helped to put a more positive interpretation on an unprecedented disaster, although how many Israelites would have taken much comfort in it at the time is an interesting question. In the post-exilic period, however, it would serve to strengthen the new community of those returned from exile.

A complication to all this was that only some of the population had been deported. Many people (probably the vast majority, although even approximate figures are not available [2.3.13.2]) had remained in the land. What was to be gleaned from this? Were they the righteous and those deported the sinners? Some seem to have thought so (Ezek 11:15). In the eyes of some later writers, however, when a few thousand returned from Babylonia and other areas, these were true Israel (2.4.3.3). The books of Ezra and Nehemiah more or less disregard the indigenous population, except occasionally to castigate it. For the writer(s) of these books, the "people of the land" were not a part of the community, except as they conformed to the demands of the leadership "chosen by God" (i.e., chosen by God in the eyes of the writers).

This particular view now dominates the tradition, making it difficult to determine other points of view at the time. Nevertheless, here and there we do seem to have data which have not been brought completely into line with the theological editing. The prophet Haggai had no objection to members of the indigenous community taking part in rebuilding the temple; indeed, he seems to have expected it (Haggai 1). In later centuries the "people of the land" would be seen as the Jews who were not strictly observant according to the demands of certain sects (8.2.15). Therefore, from the data known, these people were most likely Jews, not pagans as the books of Ezra and Nehemiah seem to suggest.

We also know that both priests and prophets were numbered among those not in full agreement with the views of either Nehemiah (2.4.3.3) or Ezra (10:15). This indicates a complicated situation, rather than the simple binary oppositions put forward by a number of theories (cf. 2.3.11). The priests on the whole were associated with the *golah* (those who had returned from captivity), with whom the authors of Ezra and Nehemiah also identified. There were those, apparently, who opposed the current priesthood and temple cult even at this early stage and would have been opponents of the priests. There undoubtedly was also friction between those already in the land and the priesthood. By contrast, some priests happily intermarried with the native population within a few generations, and the wives did not all come from the pagan inhabitants of Philistia and the like (contrary to the picture of Ezra 9–10; Neh 13:23-27). Some priests as well as prophets were unhappy about the activities of Nehemiah, and not necessarily just those who had intermarried (2.4.3.3)—no doubt Nehemiah's winsome personality had something to do with this.

We hear a good deal about prophets in the early part of the Persian period. It has often been argued that prophecy took on a different form at this time. No doubt there is some truth to this, but it is also a distortion, because prophecy in pre-exilic Israel existed in a variety of forms. Prophets could be supportive of the priestly establishment (Haggai;

Zechariah) or critical of it (some passages of Trito-Isaiah). They could oppose as well as support the "official" rulership, such as Nehemiah (2.4.3.3). In short, prophecy took on as large a variety of forms and functions in this period as it had in pre-exilic times, and the question of "false" prophecy was just as acute. What we also see developing (whether from prophecy or other sources) is apocalypticism (4.3.3). The question of definition still plagues scholarly study of this phenomenon, so it is difficult to say when apocalyptic literature first formally appeared. Nevertheless, the elements that are generally agreed to make up the phenomenon of apocalypticism can be found in literature of the Persian period, and the genre apocalypse may have been in existence by this time, even if the major developments are first clearly attested in the Greek period.

The temple cult naturally has a long history, dating from the founding of the First Temple. Nevertheless, many of the forms that we associate with the temple under the monarchy may actually be post-exilic developments. The detailed organization ascribed to David in Chronicles is probably much closer to what pertained in the early centuries of the Second Temple period. Such developments continued, as is indicated by the occasional reference in later literature (Josephus, *Ant.* 12.3.3–4 §§138–46; Ben Sira 50:1–21). The precise origin of the Levites and their relationship to the priests is debated (cf. Cody; Gunneweg; Kellermann); however, there is general agreement that in post-exilic times, the Levites were in an inferior position, caring for the fabric of the temple structure and similar mundane duties but not presiding at the altar. In the literature of the Persian period, we also see a development in the ranks of the Levites: various groups of temple personnel (e.g., the singers, doorkeepers, and Netinim) who were originally kept separate in their categories (cf. Ezra 2:40-58, 70//Neh 7:43-60, 73; Ezra 7:24; 10:23-24; Neh 10:29 [Eng. 10:28]; 11–12) gradually became assimilated to the Levites. They were eventually included in the enumeration of Levitical clans, although this was a lengthy process, extending well into the following centuries (cf. 2.2.1.8; Gese; Cody: 175–92; Gunneweg: 204–18).

One of the perpetual problems is knowing to what extent the regulations of the Pentateuch were actually applied and to what extent they represent an idealization that had only temporary or even no place in the actual temple activities. Whatever functions the king had were now transferred or dropped, and the high priest became a much more important figure (2.3.1).

3 THE JEWS AND HELLENIZATION

3.1 INTRODUCTION AND BIBLIOGRAPHICAL GUIDE

Avi-Yonah, M. *Hellenism and the East* (1978).
Burstein, S. M., ed. *The Hellenistic Age from the Battle of Ipsos to the Death of Kleopatra VII* (1985).
Goodman, M. *State and Society in Roman Galilee,* A.D. *132–212* (1983).
Hengel, M. *Judaism and Hellenism* (1974).
———. *Jews, Greeks and Barbarians: Aspects of the Hellenization of Judaism in the Pre-Christian Period* (1980).
———. *The "Hellenization" of Judaea in the First Century after Christ* (1989).
Kuhrt, A., and S. Sherwin-White, eds. *Hellenism in the East* (1987).
Momigliano, A. *Alien Wisdom* (1975).
———. "Greek Culture and the Jews." *The Legacy of Greece* (1981) 325–46.
Rajak, T. "The Hasmoneans and the Uses of Hellenism." *A Tribute to Geza Vermes* (1990) 261–80.
Samuel, A. E. *From Athens to Alexandria* (1983).
Starr, C. G. "Greeks and Persians in the Fourth Century B.C.: A Study in Cultural Contacts before Alexander." *Iranica Antiqua* 11 (1975) 39–99; 12 (1977) 49–115.
Tarn, W. W., and G. T. Griffith. *Hellenistic Civilisation* (1952).
Walbank, F. W. *The Hellenistic World* (1981).

The question of Hellenization and the Jews has long been a debate in scholarly study. This chapter addresses the issue by looking at the process of Hellenization over a wide area of space and time. The effects of Hellenization on the Jews can best be understood by looking at the broader context of which Judaism forms a small part, rather than focusing exclusively on the Jews and their reactions. To concentrate on the Jews in isolation is to distort the picture, which has been one of the major problems with understanding Judaism in some periods. For these and other reasons, this chapter gives a wide sweep and will leave the details of Jewish history to other chapters; therefore it also takes a slightly different format. The original sources for the data and evaluation of Hellenization are too extensive to be examined here; instead, this chapter considers primarily the major secondary studies and their critics.

A classic account of Hellenization is Tarn/Griffiths, now somewhat dated. Walbank is aimed at a popular audience but is produced by a noted scholar in the field and has a useful bibliographical guide. Avi-Yonah's study is by a well-known Israeli classicist, although unfortunately the work was not fully completed at the time of his death. Momigliano, another noted classicist, has addressed the subject of the Jews in the Hellenistic age in a number of essays. Kuhrt/Sherwin-White is practically unique as a full collection on the subject of Hellenization in the East (although a number of valuable individual articles on the subject have appeared over the years). Goodman and Starr are specialized studies that make important contributions to the subject at various points. Rajak's article came to my attention only when this chapter was complete, but she seems to make a number of points parallel to mine. Discussion of the subject can also be found in a number of the bibliographical items listed at 4.1 and 5.1.

3.2 MAJOR STUDIES

3.2.1 Martin Hengel

3.2.1.1 Hengel's Basic Thesis

Hengel's magnum opus, which appeared in English in 1974, is probably the most significant work to deal with Judaism in its relationship to Hellenism, although it builds on and is influenced by earlier authors, especially Bickerman. Although limiting himself formally to the period from Alexander to the Maccabean revolt, Hengel discussed the later period in passing at many points. Further, his monographs of 1980 and 1989 filled in specific aspects of the post-Maccabean period.

Hengel's major work is a highly concentrated book that cannot easily be summarized. His central thesis relates to the cause of the suppression of Judaism as a religion under Antiochus IV, and in this he comes out forcefully on the side of the proposal already advanced by E. J. Bickerman (5.3.2.4). In reaching that conclusion he examines the entire process of Hellenization and concludes, among other things, that Judaism and Hellenism were not mutually exclusive entities (*1974: 1.2–3) and that from "about the middle of the third century B.C. *all Judaism* must really be designated '*Hellenistic Judaism*' in the strict sense," so that one cannot separate Palestinian Judaism from Hellenistic Judaism (*1974: 1.103–6).

To demonstrate this thesis, Hengel does not merely advance a series of arguments or proofs. Rather, by thoroughly describing Judaism during this period and by setting out its context in the Hellenistic world of the time, Hengel forces the conclusion that the Jews of Palestine were not successful in—indeed, made little attempt at—holding themselves aloof from the dominant culture. Judea under the Ptolemies and Seleucids was a part of the wider Hellenistic world, and the Jews of Palestine were as much a part of this world as the other peoples of the ancient Near East. Therefore, to disprove Hengel one would have to give positive evidence that the Jews wanted to resist all aspects of the Hellenistic culture, were able to distinguish between "Hellenistic" and "native" elements, and prevailed in their resistance. Hengel has successfully put the burden of proof on any who would challenge the view that Palestinian Judaism was a part of Hellenistic Judaism of the time. Although a summary cannot do justice to the detailed study, Hengel's major points and arguments may be condensed as follows:

1. The Jews of Palestine, far from being isolated, were thoroughly caught up in the events of their time, particularly in the rivalry between the Ptolemaic and Seleucid kingdoms. Palestine itself was a disputed territory, claimed by the Seleucids with some legality but nevertheless under Ptolemaic rule for the century before 200 B.C.E.
2. Ptolemaic (and later Seleucid) administration reached to the lowest levels of Jewish society. Every village was supervised by the Greek administration and its officials saw that the various taxes were paid. Although natives were often delegated as supervisors at the lower levels, Greeks and Greek-speaking natives were much in evidence, especially at the higher levels.
3. International trade was a feature of the Hellenistic world; indeed, trade with the Aegean had brought many Greek influences to the Phoenician and Palestinian coasts long before the time of Alexander. Palestine itself was an important crossroads in the trade between north and south and between Egypt and Arabia.
4. The language of trade and administration was Greek. The use of Greek for official purposes is quite visible by the middle of the third century, and its direct influence on the Jews can be deduced from a variety of sources.
5. Greek education also had an influence on Jews and Jewish education.
6. Greek influence on Jewish literature is documented as early as

Alexander's conquest and can be illustrated from literature in Hebrew and Aramaic, as well as those works composed directly in Greek. Evidence of the influence of Greek philosophy arises in such quintessentially Jewish circles as Qumran and in writings such as *1 Enoch*.

7. The "anti-Greek" forces that followed on the Maccabean crisis did not succeed in erasing the pervasive Greek influence of the previous century and a half, and Jewish Palestine, even as it gained basic independence under the Hasmoneans, remained a part of the Hellenistic world.

In his later writings Hengel's overall position has seemed to remain the same, although he has nuanced it somewhat to answer some of the criticisms (see 3.2.1.2). He recognizes that in the period before 175 B.C.E. "we only have very fragmentary and sporadic information about the Jews in Palestine and in the Diaspora" (*1980: 51). He also accepts that Hellenization was perhaps a lengthier process than originally allowed:

> A more thorough "Hellenization", which also included the lower classes, only became a complete reality in Syria and Palestine under the protection of Rome. . . . It was Rome which first helped "Hellenism" to its real victory in the East . . . (*1980: 53)

3.2.1.2 Criticisms of Hengel

Feldman, L. H. "Hengel's *Judaism and Hellenism* in Retrospect." *JBL* 96 (1977) 371–82.

———. "How Much Hellenism in Jewish Palestine?" *HUCA* 57 (1986) 83–111.

Millar, F. "The Background to the Maccabean Revolution: Reflections on Martin Hengel's *Judaism and Hellenism*." *JJS* 29 (1978) 1–21.

Momigliano, A. Review of *Judentum und Hellenismus*, by M. Hengel. *JTS* 21 (1970) 149–53.

Of the many reviews of Hengel's work—some of them by well-known specialists in the Hellenistic period and even in Hellenistic Judaism—the majority have been impressed by his breadth of learning and by his basic arguments about the Hellenizing of Judaism. Criticism has tended to focus on two areas: Hengel's support of Bickerman's thesis (5.3.2.4) and the extent of Hellenization in the pre-Maccabean period. The major rejection of Hengel's thesis about Hellenization has come from Feldman (1977; 1986). In his 1977 review he summarized Hengel's work in twenty-two points and then attacked each point as invalid or as not supporting Hengel's thesis in a significant way. His 1986 article covered some of the same ground but in a more diffuse way. There is no doubt that Feldman makes some important criticisms and has drawn attention to areas where Hengel is weak or where the data do not strongly support his argument. Unfortunately, Feldman vitiates the impact of his arguments with two major flaws. First, he seems to make a strong, underlying assumption that being Hellenized means ceasing to be a proper Jew. Second, his arguments against Hengel often depend on interpretations that would not be accepted by the majority of specialists.

With regard to the first flaw, note the following statements by Feldman:

> even after the Maccabees the degree of Hellenization was hardly profound, and . . . , indeed, there were far more who were attracted to Judaism as proselytes than deviated from it through apostasy and intermarriage. (1986: 85)

> But even in Lower Galilee, the people, as portrayed by Josephus, were deeply religious in theory and in practice, and presumably only minimally affected by Hellenism. (1986: 95)

> Moreover, Hellenization could not have been truly profound, for we hear of few apostates. . . . (1986: 105)

Feldman seems to be making the tacit assumptions that Hellenization means apostasy and intermarriage, and that those who are deeply religious could have been only minimally Hellenized. Neither of these assumptions would be accepted by many scholars; indeed, they are clearly contradicted by the prime example of Philo (7.2.2).

With regard to the second flaw, here are some examples from Feldman's 1977 contribution: he states in point 1 that there is no evidence that Palestinian Jews served as mercenaries; however, this seems unreasonable skepticism. Because we know that Jews did serve as mercenaries and at times rose to high rank (cf. 5.4.7), why should it be doubted that this included Palestinian Jews? Feldman's point 5 states that "aside from the highly assimilated—and highly exceptional—family of the Tobiads," there is little evidence of Greek commercial influence. Why should we assume that the Tobiads were exceptional or that they were more assimilated than many other upper-class Jews? Such upper-class individuals were the exception in any society of the time, but why must this fact be dismissed rather than used (within recognized parameters)? In other cases Feldman actually goes against the current scholarly consensus in order to challenge Hengel (e.g., in point 21 he dates *1 Enoch* 12–36 much later than is generally done, whereas at point 22 he doubts the identity of the Qumranites as Essenes). Other doubtful points occur in Feldman's 1986 article, for example, that only Gentiles attended events in the various amphitheaters and sports stadiums erected by Herod and others (104) or that the ossuary inscriptions in Greek were only to prevent non-Jews from molesting the graves (88).

Feldman does make a number of important points, probably the most valuable of which is to cast doubt on the speed with which Judaism was Hellenized. Other contributors have also noted this (cf. Hengel's response noted above). Some of Feldman's criticisms are less significant but no less valid for that: for example, many will agree with him that Qohelet does not bear clear marks of Greek influence (cf. 4.2.5.1). Nevertheless, Feldman's complete rejection of Hengel's thesis seems unjustified. As noted (3.2.1.1), the major strength of Hengel's work is that it sets out a context in which the Jews were bound to be influenced by Greek culture and in which Hellenization was inevitable, barring a strong, conscious effort to reject all Greek influences. Therefore, Feldman must do more than simply disprove individual points made by Hengel or claim that some of Hengel's specific arguments are not proved beyond all doubt. Instead, he needs positive proof that the Jews maintained consistent countermeasures to Hellenization, but this he does not advance. More problematic is what seems to be simply a reluctance to accept the idea of Palestinian Jews being Hellenized.

Millar's article seems primarily directed against the thesis that the persecutions were initiated by the "Hellenizing party" of the Jews and will not be discussed here (cf. 5.3.2). However, his attitude toward the thesis about the Hellenizing process in Palestine is not completely clear. On the one hand, Millar states, "only new evidence could improve Hengel's portrayal of Hellenism in Judaea itself" (p. 3). On the other hand, he writes, "it is precisely the nature of the first phase of the Hellenising movement after 175 B.C. . . . which shows how *un*-Greek Jerusalem had remained up to that moment" (p. 9). In his conclusion, he states, "the evidence shows how un-Greek in structure, customs, observance, literary culture, language and historical outlook the Jewish community had remained down to the earlier second century, and how basic to it the rules reimposed by Ezra and Nehemiah had remained" (p. 20). Perhaps the problem is one of definition of terminology, for one could argue that the Jewish community was "faithful" to its tradition while nevertheless undergoing the Hellenizing process which affected all other parts of the ancient Near East. To be Hellenized does not necessarily mean to become Greek, as I will discuss in 3.4.

Hengel's weakest or most controversial theses (aside from his thesis about the causes of the religious suppression in Jerusalem) are three:

1. Whereas Greek influence on Jewish literature in Greek is easy to demonstrate, it is more difficult to show regarding literature in the

Semitic languages. For example, Hengel takes the view that Qohelet shows knowledge and terminology of Greek popular philosophy, a thesis developed at greater length by his pupil H. Braun. By contrast, scholars such as O. Loretz have argued that there is nothing in Qohelet that cannot be explained from pre-Hellenistic, ancient Near Eastern tradition (4.2.5.1). In other examples, although one can find Greek parallels and make a cogent case for Greek influence, one cannot prove that other potential sources are not equally possible. Therefore, Hengel's arguments, which are generally quite strong with regard to Jewish literature in Greek, become less certain and more likely to be disputed in the area of Hebrew and Aramaic literature.

2. Many of the examples Hengel uses actually belong to the post-Maccabean period, partly because our knowledge of the Ptolemaic period is so problematic (Momigliano). In many cases it seems legitimate to extrapolate to the earlier period (e.g., the evidence of the Qumran scrolls); also, it shows that the crisis that arose in Jerusalem was primarily not one of Hellenizing but one of religious suppression. Nevertheless, Hengel is not always careful to make clear that Hellenization was a dynamic process, so that some developments may have come about only in post-Maccabean times, whereas the exact path of Hellenization in Judea during the Ptolemaic period may not be as clear as he implies.
3. In the way he selects and presents examples Hengel appears to exaggerate the place of Greek education and language in Palestine. The examples used go only so far. That is, they demonstrate that some Jews had a reasonable knowledge of Greek and many more had a smattering of it, but the actual number of Jews who could be considered monolingual or bilingual in Greek in Palestine was probably less than Hengel seems to conclude. In any case, the evidence is not conclusive for a pervasive use of Greek throughout Jewish society in Palestine. As for the question of education, we simply have almost no information about education at all in Judea at this time, much less education in Greek.

3.2.2 Victor Tcherikover

Tcherikover, V. A. [V. A. Tscherikower]. "Palestine under the Ptolemies." *Mizraim* 4–5 (1937) 9–90.
———. *Hellenistic Civilization and the Jews* (1959).
Tcherikover, V. A., A. Fuks, and M. Stern. *CPJ* (1957–64).

In his 1959 volume Tcherikover gave a lengthy description of the Hellenization process and a detailed history of the Jews in the Hellenistic period, down to the Maccabean revolt. There is not the focus that one finds in Hengel, but many of the things which Hengel says had already been said in one form or another by Tcherikover. (Indeed, Tcherikover develops another thesis about the cause of the religious persecution under Antiochus, of which Hengel took scarce account [5.3.2.5].) His more detailed studies (1937; Tcherikover, et al.: 1957–1964) are a mine of information about various aspects of Ptolemaic Egypt, of which Hengel has also made thorough use.

Tcherikover argued in a somewhat conventional way about the aims of the Hellenizers. He also saw the development of the Hasmonean state as basically a class struggle between the masses (represented by the Pharisees) and the upper-class aristocracy and priests (represented by the Sadducees). He finally concluded that Judea could not be a Hellenistic state without compromising its principles:

> Their aim was *to build a Hellenistic state on a Jewish national foundation*. This, however, was to prove impossible. Judaism and Hellenism were, as forces, each too peculiar to itself to be able to compromise within one country. A Hellenistic state could not be founded on the Jerusalem theocracy. (1959: 264–65)

He made it clear, however, that these conclusions concerned *political Hellenism*, not Hellenistic culture:

> Power [under Herod's rule] was gathered in the hands of Greeks and Hellenizing Jews; but simultaneously Hellenism ceased to be a problem of inner Jewish history; Hellenization assumed an individual form and no single Jewish party or group sought to draw Jews from their religion or propagate Hellenism among them by force. The political period of Hellenization had passed and gone for good, only the cultural influence of Hellenism remaining. Generations of proximity to the Greeks had not passed over the Jews of Palestine without leaving considerable traces in their literature, language, law and all other aspects of their civilization. (1959: 265)

3.2.3 Saul Lieberman and H. A. Fischel

Fischel, H. A. *Rabbinic Literature and Greco-Roman Philosophy* (1973).
———, ed. *Essays in Greco-Roman and Related Talmudic Literature* (1977).
Lieberman, S. *Hellenism in Jewish Palestine* (1962).
———. "How Much Greek in Jewish Palestine?" *Biblical and Other Studies* (1963) 123–41.
———. *Greek in Jewish Palestine* (1965).

S. Lieberman, a rabbinic scholar of great renown, wrote several works about the Greek influences on that most Semitic environment, rabbinic Judaism. In his book on Hellenism (1962) he investigated literature that he dated between the first century B.C.E. and the fourth C.E. Subjects included literary editing and textual preservation, hermeneutical rules, and specific statements about "Greek wisdom." His earlier pioneering work on Greek (2d ed. 1965) looked mainly at the second, third, and fourth centuries C.E. and concluded that there was enormous Greek influence on the rabbis.

Fischel follows very much in the footsteps of Lieberman. In addition to his Ph.D. thesis investigating a specific aspect of rabbinic literature in relation to the Hellenistic world, his collection of essays (1977) is especially enhanced by an important prolegomenon and an annotated bibliography of works that have examined Greek influence on rabbinic literature. He also has a frank discussion about those who minimize the Greek impact on the world of the rabbis and the reasons for it. Fischel's approach seems in harmony with that of Hengel.

3.2.4 Morton Smith

Smith, M. "Palestinian Judaism in the First Century." *Israel: Its Role in Civilization* (1956) 67–81.

———. *Palestinian Parties and Politics That Shaped the Old Testament* (1971).

In a wide-ranging yet concise chapter (chap. 3), Smith (1971) gives a cogent description of how the Hellenistic world differed from "classical" Greek culture, an important distinction because many have used the term "Hellenization" simply as a synonym for "Greek," without considering the important changes that occurred with the development of Hellenization. Further, these differences were not just evident for the Hellenistic empires of the Near East but applied equally to the Aegean and to Greece itself. Smith notes that all the points listed below are characteristic of the Near Eastern empires (except 3), rather than of classical Greek civilization:

1. Landholdings of the Hellenistic period were primarily large estates (usually of the king or his officials), not small holdings (but cf. 1.2.2 on this question).
2. Government was located primarily in the monarchy, which governed a large territory or empire, rather than in the small city-states. The Greek foundations preserved the myth but not the substance of independent rule.

3. Written laws played a greater part than unwritten custom during the Hellenistic period.
4. The cult of the city god(s) of the classical period gave way to the imperial cult plus a variety of local (but nonpolitical) or individual cults.
5. Private citizens were more important to the classical city-state, tying individual endeavors in commerce, art, and philosophy closely to politics. In the Hellenistic world the individual (even the wealthy person) was more concerned with private affairs than with politics.
6. Members of both the army and the administration tended to be professionals in the Hellenistic world, rather than amateurs, as in classical Greece.
7. The arts and sciences of the Hellenistic period were characterized by professional preoccupation and systematization; hence the large production of handbooks, collections, and imitations of classical models.

3.3 EXAMINATION OF SELECTED EXAMPLES

3.3.1 Language

Doty, L. T. "The Archive of the Nanâ-Iddin Family from Uruk." *JCS* 30 (1980) 65–90.

Millar, F. "The Problem of Hellenistic Syria." *Hellenism in the East* (1987) 110–33.

Pugliese Carratelli, G., and G. Garbini. *A Bilingual Graeco-Aramaic Edict by Asoka* (1964).

Rostovtzeff, M. "Seleucid Babylonia: Bullae and Seals of Clay with Greek Inscriptions." *YCS* 3 (1932) 1–114.

In the post-Alexandrian centuries "Greek" became less an ethnic designation and more one of education, especially in good Greek style. There is evidence that many educated and upper-class Orientals were knowledgeable in the Greek language. The question is how far this knowledge penetrated. Although it is often asserted that Greek became the official language of the conquered territories, this seems mistaken (*Kuhrt/Sherwin-White: 5–6, 23–25): the Seleucid Empire was multilingual, and local languages continued to be used in official documents (with perhaps a few exceptions; e.g., slave-sale documents after 275 B.C.E. were issued only in Greek [Doty: 85; Rostovtzeff: 65–69]).

A similar situation pertained in Egypt (*Samuel: 105–17). Although Egypt is famous for its finds of papyri in Greek, the accumulating evidence suggests that at least as much material was produced in Demotic during the same period of time. There was a flourishing native literary tradition in all sorts of genres, not just temple literature, during this time. More significant, though, is the amount of Demotic papyri relating to the administration. The native Egyptian legal system was still administered alongside Greek justice, but the Demotic documents embrace more than the legal sphere; they encompass bureaucratic activity up to a fairly high level. Contrary to a frequent assumption, Egyptians could and did rise to high positions in the administration, and much of the work of the bureaucracy was done in bilingual mode. In short, a great deal of business and everyday life was conducted in the Egyptian language by Egyptians at all levels of society.

A major question is interpretation. One can point to such examples as the Armenian king Artavadses, who cultivated Greek learning and even wrote Greek literature; at a birthday celebration, the *Bacchides* of Euripides was performed for his court (Plutarch, *Crassus* 33). The Buddhist king Asoka erected inscriptions in good Greek (as well as Aramaic) in the remote area of Kandahar (Pugliese Carratelli/Garbini). But what conclusion should be drawn from this? Can such examples be taken as typical? Hengel states, "Galilee, completely encircled by the territories of the Hellenized cities . . . , will similarly have been largely bilingual" (*1989: 14–15). Goodman gives a more nuanced and somewhat less categorical view (*64–68). Although recognizing that Greek had its place in Galilee, he notes that it was not dominant and that Aramaic—not Greek—was the lingua franca: "In Upper Galilee and probably in the area around Lake Tiberias, Greek was only a thin strand in the linguistic cloth" (*67–68). Was Galilee bilingual? Not if one means that Greek was widely used everywhere. The presence of some Greek usage does not necessarily deserve the designation "largely bilingual."

Greek did function as a lingua franca in many parts of the Hellenistic East, as Aramaic had done under the Assyrian, neo-Babylonian, and Achaemenid empires. Although royal inscriptions and many other types of documents were issued in Greek, there was no attempt to make Greek the sole language of administration. Traders no doubt found some acquaintance with Greek useful not only in dealing with officialdom but also for getting around in areas with a multitude of local languages. If a buyer or seller knew a second language, however, then in many parts of the Seleucid Empire that language was more likely to be Aramaic than Greek.

The complexity of the penetration of Greek is illustrated by two examples. An ostracon in Aramaic from as early as the middle of the third century B.C.E. contains two Greek words (4.2.7.4). Another ostracon from

Khirbet el-Kom in the Idumean area, dated about 275 B.C.E., is bilingual in both Greek and Aramaic (4.2.7.2). By contrast, there is only one formal bilingual inscription known so far in the entirety of Syria, that from Tel Dan ca. 200 B.C.E. (4.2.7.4; cf. Millar: 132). Therefore, although Hengel's demonstration in his various writings of the widespread use of Greek cannot be doubted, the significance of this is not so easily assessed. The use of Greek seems to have been confined to a particular segment of the population, namely, the educated upper class. To what extent it penetrated into the lives of the bulk of the population is difficult to determine; however, the number of Jews outside the Greek cities who were fluent in Greek seems small.

3.3.2 Religion

Avi-Yonah, M. "Syrian Gods at Ptolemais-Accho." *IEJ* 9 (1959) 1–12.

Griffiths, J. G. "Hellenistic Religions." *The Encyclopedia of Religion* (1987) 252–66.

Oden, R. A. *Studies in Lucian's De Syria Dea* (1976a).

———. "The Persistence of Canaanite Religion." *BA* 39 (1976b) 31–36.

Smith, J. Z. "European Religions, Ancient: Hellenistic Religions." *Encyclopaedia Britannica* (1985) *Macropaedia* 18.925–27.

Teixidor, J. *The Pagan God* (1977).

Waldmann, H. *Die kommagenischen Kultreformen unter König Mithradates I. Kallinikos und seinem Sohne Antiochos I* (1973).

Information about the religions of Syria is skimpy, except for the "Syrian goddess" (*Syria Dea*) described by Lucian (Oden 1976a). Nevertheless, the data available do indicate that native cults of Syria and Phoenicia survived and thrived during the Hellenistic period, amid strong Greco-Roman cultural influence (Teixidor). As Teixidor notes:

> Near Eastern religions maintained their traditional character during the last centuries of the first millennium B.C. . . . Popular religion must have remained practically unchanged in Greco-Roman times, for the inscriptions do not reflect the impact of new fashions. (5–6)

This is illustrated by an inscription at Ptolemais dedicated to Hadad and Atargatis, two Syrian gods. The dedication is in Greek, the man who dedicated it has a Greek name ("Diodotos son of Neoptolemos") that was normally borne by ethnic Greeks, and the cult seems new to this area (Avi-Yonah).

This basic continuity does not mean that there were no developments in the native religions. One of the main changes was the move from nationalistic cults, which in some cases became even more conservative in the homeland, to salvation religions in the wider Greco-Roman world, with emphasis on personal conversion and individual salvation (Smith). Isis worship was a prime example of the change from a native Egyptian cult to a widespread personal religion that drew on many different nationalities in the Roman Empire. In their homeland, though, the native cults were not suppressed or displaced by the Greek cults.

There was a degree of syncretism, but this should not be exaggerated because many of the changes were natural developments, not complete mergings with Greek worship. What at first might look like syncretism often consisted only of the identification of native deities with Greek deities, without a major change in the character of the Oriental cult (cf. Avi-Yonah: 6; also 5.3.4). Where there was genuine syncretism, it was more likely to be in the Greco-Roman "diaspora" than in the homeland. An interesting example of deliberate syncretism, however, is the cult reform by Mithridates I and Antiochus I of Commagene. They claimed to trace their ancestry back to both Alexander the Great and Darius the Persian. Their new cult was an amalgam of the two traditions, Greek and Persian, which included worship of "Zeus Oromasdes" (Zeus + Ahura Mazda), presided over by priests in Persian dress (Waldmann: 59–79; *Burstein: text 48).

3.3.3 Babylonia

Kuhrt, A. "Berossus' *Babyloniaka* and Seleucid Rule in Babylonia." *Hellenism in the East* (1987) 32–56.

Sarkisian, G. K. "Greek Personal Names in Uruk and the *Graeco-Babyloniaca* Problem." *Acta Antiqua* 22 (1974) 495–503.

Sherwin-White, S. "A Greek Ostrakon from Babylon of the Early Third Century B.C." *ZPE* 47 (1982) 51–70.

———. "Ritual for a Seleucid King at Babylon?" *JHS* 103 (1983) 156–59.

———. "Seleucid Babylonia: A Case Study for the Installation and Development of Greek Rule." *Hellenism in the East* (1987) 1–31.

Spek, R. J. van der. "The Babylonian City." *Hellenism in the East* (1987) 57–74.

The cities of Babylon and Uruk provide useful evidence about Hellenization in Mesopotamia. Alexander originally made Babylon the capital of his empire. It has often been assumed that, with the founding of Seleucia-on-the-Tigris, Babylon declined to the point of desolation. The founding of Seleucia was probably done deliberately to provide a new Hellenistic center, but Babylon continued not only to survive but to thrive (Sherwin-White 1987: 18–20; van der Spek: 65–66). The native tradition of kingship, in which the Seleucid ruler acted in the same capacity as the old native Babylonian kings, is attested as continuing and seriously supported by at least some of the Seleucids (Sherwin-White 1983; Sherwin-White 1987: 8–9, 28–29; Kuhrt: 51–52, 55–56).

Neither Babylon nor Uruk is certainly known to have been a polis in the early Greek period, although evidently some Greeks were there (cf. Sherwin-White 1982; Sherwin-White 1987: 20–21; van der Spek: 66–70, 72–74). The Greek names found in cuneiform sources fall into four periods that seem to correspond with the history of the city under Greek rule (Sarkasian; van der Spek: 60–74): stage 1: Greek residents but no involvement with the native inhabitants (Greek names practically absent); stage 2 (223–187 B.C.E.): Greeks begin to take part in civic life, with some intermarriage (limited Greek names among the Babylonians); stage 3 (middle of second century): influx of more Greeks, probably because of the policy of Antiochus IV (Greek names more frequent); and stage 4 (after 140): the Arsacid conquest halts the Hellenization process (Greek names continue sporadically for a time but gradually die out).

3.3.4 Syria and Phoenicia

Barr, J. "Philo of Byblos and His 'Phoenician History.'" *BJRL* 57 (1974–75) 17–68.

Millar, F. "The Phoenician Cities: A Case-Study of Hellenisation." *Proceedings of the Cambridge Philological Association* 209 (1983) 55–71.

———. "The Problem of Hellenistic Syria." *Hellenism in the East* (1987) 110–33.

The subject of Hellenization in Syria is very important, because it formed Judea's immediate environment. Hengel has also emphasized the part played by Phoenicia and Philistia as the intermediaries of Greek culture to Judea (*Hengel 1974: 1.32–35; *Hengel 1980: 28). Millar has produced two seminal essays that address the question directly. One of his major points is that, because of the paucity of evidence and perhaps apart from Phoenicia, it is difficult to draw general conclusions about Hellenization for the Syrian area (1987: especially 111–13, 129–31). After extensive discussion, Millar concludes on a rather negative note: "The enigma of hellenistic Syria—of the wider Syrian region in the hellenistic period—remains" (1987: 129). The paucity of data is true not only for the Hellenistic period but also for the Achaemenid period: you cannot talk about changes after Alexander if you do not know what conditions were like before him.

This lack of remains can lead to widely differing interpretations of what little there is. Hengel, for example, places a good deal of emphasis on the writers and philosophers who came from the Syrian region, including such individuals as Meleager of Gadara (*1974: 1.84–86; *1980: 118). Millar, by contrast, comments with regard to Meleager, "But there is nothing in the quite extensive corpus of his poetry to show that he had deeply absorbed any non-Greek culture in his native city" (1987: 130).

This does not mean that only a negative conclusion can be drawn from Millar's study. As the editors note in their introduction, "His careful examination of a scattered body of material is susceptible to a more positive interpretation than he himself allows" (*Kuhrt/Sherwin-White: x). One of the facts which does emerge is the strong continuation of the native culture in that area, which clearly was neither generally submerged by the Greek nor absorbed into it. Millar has also produced evidence of changes under Hellenism, which included the spread of Greek culture in specific ways.

In Phoenicia we have a useful example of how Hellenization could penetrate the culture yet not displace the native traditions. The influence of Greek culture actually began well before Alexander (Millar 1983: 67; *Hengel 1974: 1.32–35). Although the precise course of Hellenization is difficult to document (cf. Millar 1983: 60), the cities of the region gradually evolved into Greek *poleis* (Millar 1987: 123–24). Nevertheless, it is also clear that Phoenician culture continued at all levels, both in Phoenicia itself and in its colonies overseas. We find Phoenician names alongside Greek ones, and some individuals have both sorts. Coins have both Greek and Phoenician writing. Philo of Byblos wrote a work (supposedly based on the work of the ancient author Sanchuniathon) that preserves many details of Canaanite religion from antiquity, yet Philo's work is itself thoroughly Greek in form (Barr). Therefore, the major Phoenician cities were Hellenized in some sense, yet they also remained Phoenician, with a strong continuation of their past.

3.3.5 Pergamum

Hansen, E. V. *The Attalids of Pergamon* (1971).

Pergamum is an interesting study in deliberate Hellenization. The process began with Philetaerus (283–263 B.C.E.) and continued under his successors, who became independent dynasts. Attalus I (241–197) attempted to turn Pergamum into the Athens of Asia. The kingdom was organized as a Greek city-state, and the capital of Pergamum became a showcase for Hellenistic architecture and art. This is exemplified in the famous altar celebrating the subjugation of the Gauls (Celts), which symbolized Pergamum as the champion of Hellenistic civilization against barbarism. An interesting illustration of this is the letter of Eumenes II (197–160) to the Ionian league, in which he states, "I . . . having revealed myself as the common benefactor [*euergetēs*] of the Greeks, undertook many great struggles against the barbarians" (quoted from *Burstein: text no. 88, lines 7–10). All in all, the Attalid dynasty was active in promoting the city as a Greek cultural and intellectual center.

Nevertheless, the Greek facade is hardly the whole picture. Despite the appearance of being a Greek polis, Pergamum was governed by a king. Most of the countryside was treated as royal property, with the peasants no doubt continuing with life as they had done for centuries. The tamed Gauls (Galatians) were used in the army, but Hellenization of their upper classes came about only gradually. Thus despite the active "missionizing" for Greek culture, Pergamum seems in many ways to be a miniature of the contradictions of the Hellenization process, with the contrasts and the coexistence of the old and new side by side.

3.3.6 Art and Architecture

Colledge, M. "Greek and Non-Greek Interaction in the Art and Architecture of the Hellenistic East." *Hellenism in the East* (1987) 134–62.
Hornblower, S. *Mausolus* (1982).

Architecture is a whole study in itself. Colledge, however, is an easily accessible example that illustrates the process of Hellenization. The Persians had a sophisticated artistic culture, which drew on a long Eastern tradition (Colledge: 135–36; *Starr 1977: 49–59). Greek influence had begun in the Persian Empire, partly because Greek artists were sometimes used, a prime example being the famous mausoleum of the satrap Mausolus (Hornblower: 223–74). (Contrary to some assumptions, the beauty of such places as Persepolis was not due solely or primarily to Greek artisans: Colledge: 136; *Starr 1977: 57.) After Alexander's conquests, a "mixed style" that combined both native and Greek elements developed with time and eventually became predominant. However, both pure native and Greek styles existed happily side by side as well as with the mixed style long after it had developed. Such sites as Ai Khanum show fine examples of all three styles in juxtaposition. Of what did Greek influence consist? Was only the pure Greek style Hellenistic? Or only the mixed style? A static definition is difficult, yet one would have no trouble putting the whole process under the rubric of "Hellenization."

Samuel indicates a similar situation with art in Egypt (*101–5). Apart from a few examples of sculpture produced by the "mixed school," the Greek and Egyptian styles were kept separate. Egyptian art was very conservative. Some innovation occurred in the Greek sphere, but it too was conservative and did not generally borrow motifs from Egyptian style. Thus, art in Egypt during Ptolemaic rule was either purely Egyptian or purely Greek, with very little mixture of the two.

3.3.7 Resistance to Hellenization

Collins, J. J., ed. *Apocalypse: The Morphology of a Genre* (1979).
Eddy, S. K. *The King Is Dead* (1961).
Flusser, D. "Hystaspes and John of Patmos." *Irano-Judaica* (1982) 12–75.
Johnson, J. H. "Is the Demotic Chronicle an Anti-Greek Tract?" *Grammata Demotika: Festschrift für Erich Lüddeckens zum 15. Juni 1983* (1984) 107–24.
La Barre, W. "Materials for a History of Studies of Crisis Cults: A Bibliographic Essay." *Current Anthropology* 12 (1971) 3–44.
Lloyd, A. B. "Nationalist Propaganda in Ptolemaic Egypt." *Historia* 31 (1982) 33–55.
Peremans, W. "Les révolutions égyptiennes sous les Lagides." *Das ptolemäische Ägypten* (1978) 39–50.
Worsley, P. *The Trumpet Shall Sound: A Study of "Cargo" Cults in Melanesia* (1957).

The reactions against Hellenization were complex and diverse, but the Jews were by no means the only people to fight it. Although much of the evidence has no doubt disappeared, enough survives to show that there were anti-Hellenistic moves of various sorts among a wide range of the Near Eastern peoples. The most obvious form of resistance was armed rebellion against Greek political domination and the attempt to restore native rule. The Jewish state stands out because it successfully gained independence, whereas most other rebels met with failure; yet the Jews of Palestine were not the only ones to aspire to independence or to attempt to gain it by force of arms. Among the Egyptians in particular there were a number of uprisings, although none was successful (cf. Peremans).

Gaining independence from Greek rule did not necessarily mean overthrowing Hellenistic culture or rooting out all Greek elements or influences, as is made clear by the example of the Hasmonean state, which threw off the Seleucid yoke but made no attempt to eliminate the overt Greek elements in Palestinian culture. On the contrary, Judea under Hasmonean rule was typical of Hellenistic kingdoms of that general period. In this, one may compare modern "nativistic movements": they often react against some cultural elements of colonial powers simply because they are symbolic of oppression (La Barre: 20–22), yet many elements taken over from the colonizers will be accepted, either because they have become so well integrated that they are no longer recognized as foreign (cf. Worsley: 23) or because they are useful or symbolically neutral to the movement.

Another sort of anti-Greek reaction was the production of anti-Greek propaganda, generally literary. We find a whole genre from the Hellenistic period produced by a variety of peoples, often taking the form of oracles or *ex eventu* prophecies. In Egypt there were prophecies predicting the overthrow of Greek rule, including the *Oracle of Bocchoris or the Lamb* and the *Potter's Oracle* (Eddy; Collins: 168–70). (The *Demotic Chronicle* is also often added to this list, but Johnson has recently argued that it is anti-Persian rather than anti-Greek; see also 2.2.4.) From Persia came the *Oracle of Hystaspes* (Eddy; Collins: 210; but Flusser argues that it is Jewish). The Jews produced fake *Sibylline Oracles* (9.2.3.2; Collins: 46–47). This literature itself was a way of kindling hope and venting frustration. What effect it had from a practical point of view is uncertain; probably little in most cases, although there may have been times when it served to inspire the native peoples to active resistance and revolt.

3.4 SYNTHESIS

3.4.1 Hellenization in General

Bernard, P. "Aî Khanum on the Oxus: A Hellenistic City in Central Asia." *Proceedings of the British Academy* 53 (1967) 71–95.

Roueché, C., and S. M. Sherwin-White. "Some Aspects of the Seleucid Empire: The Greek Inscriptions from Failaka, in the Arabian Gulf." *Chiron* 15 (1985) 1–39.

An older view emphasized the Greek influence on the original civilizations of the ancient Near East and the dominance of Greek institutions. Such an attitude can be found in the classic work by Tarn (*Tarn/Griffiths) and is also the prevalent view in the first edition of volume 7 of *CAH* (although Rostovtzeff gives a more nuanced approach in his articles in that volume). Recent work has not only recognized the Greco-centric view of so much older scholarship but also has found evidence in new discoveries, as well as old, that the earlier cultures were far from obliterated under Greek rule (especially *Kuhrt/Sherwin-White).

The spread of Greek institutions and culture to the remotest parts of the Greek Empire can be seen in the Greek remains in such unlikely places as Ai Khanum (Bernard) and the island of Failaka (ancient Icarus) in the Persian Gulf (Roueché/Sherwin-White). The presence of Greek communities, as indicated by inscriptions, architecture, and literary remains, shows that no region could escape the influence of Greeks. The question is to what extent the Greek presence produced merging, adoption, or change in the indigenous cultures. A "mixed culture" (*Verschmelzung*) was slow in coming in most cases, if it ever occurred.

Hellenization was a long and complex phenomenon. It cannot be summarized in a word or a sentence. It was not just the adoption of Greek ways by the inhabitants of the ancient Near East or of Oriental ways by Greeks who settled in the East. Hellenistic civilization was sui generis and must be considered from a variety of points of view, because it concerned many different areas of life: language, custom, religion, commerce, architecture, dress, government, literature, and philosophical ideals.

Hellenization represented a process as well as a description of a type of culture. Whatever Alexander's ideals may have been, his successors were highly Greco-chauvinist. Pride of place in society was to go to Greeks alone; the natives were usually at the bottom of the pyramid. Greek ideals were preserved in the Greek foundations, and citizenship and membership of the gymnasium were jealously guarded and were the exclusive privilege of the Greek settlers. Orientals might live in the Greek cities, but they were not citizens and were generally barred from becoming so. There was no interest in cultural imperialism as such by the Greek rulers.

Over a period of a century or so after Alexander's death, however, the situation gradually began to change. Local nobles and chieftains were often of use in the Ptolemaic and Seleucid administrations, and they employed Greek secretaries. A good example of this is the Jewish noble Tobias, for whom we have a number of letters in Greek from the Zenon archive (4.2.1; 4.3.2). These individuals also were likely to see the need to have their sons given a Greek education. Thus it is that by early in the Greek period, we find educated Orientals who have some knowledge of Greek. Individuals such as Manetho in Egypt and Berossus in Babylon were writing treatises in Greek by the early part of the third century. In the Tobiad romance Joseph and, later, his son Hyrcanus (second half of the third century) deal with the Ptolemaic court on an equal footing

(4.3.2); there is no indication that they communicate by translator or that their educational background is considered inferior. There are indications of the impact of the Greek language even early in the Greek period (e.g., the bilingual ostracon from Khirbet el-Kom [4.2.7.2]).

During this time a shift also took place in the definition of "Hellene." The term originally referred to physical ancestry; however, many of the new settlers in the Orient were Macedonians and others who were looked down upon by the inhabitants of Athens. The criterion soon became one not of genealogy but of education: a Greek was one who had a Greek education—a Greek was one who had a command of the niceties of the Greek language. This concept was extremely important in breaking down the barriers between the settlers and the natives, as the natives began to acquire a Greek education. It was a slow process, but gradually Orientals made their way into the exclusive ranks of the ephebate (candidature for citizenship) and citizenry. With a Greek education and the adoption of a Greek name, it would often have been difficult to tell who was a descendant of Alexander's soldiers and who was from the losing side.

The phenomenon of Orientalization of the Greeks was another complicated process, which affected various parts of the Hellenistic world differently. For example, in Egypt the Ptolemaic kingship quickly assimilated to the pharaonic tradition. Each new ruler was considered a son of the sun god, Re, and given a variety of traditional Egyptian names and titles. In the hieroglyphic inscriptions no distinction is made between the Ptolemies and the native Egyptian pharaohs of previous generations. Nevertheless, the dealings of the Ptolemies with other states and with Greek cities was done in the normal Greek way, and the court was typically Hellenistic. Although the Seleucids perhaps did not have the same pressure as the Ptolemies to conform to Oriental models, they were treated in the inscriptions as heirs of Nebuchadnezzar and played their part in the traditional Babylonian ceremonies of kingship (3.3.3). Hellenistic kingship as an institution owed much to the earlier Near Eastern monarchies and the traditions that had developed around them.

The differences between the Ptolemaic and Seleucid empires and modes of administration are also revealed in the specific way in which the Jewish state was treated. The pressure to adapt to Greek ways was fairly general and diffuse under the Ptolemies. Because the Seleucids put a good deal of emphasis on Greek foundations, however, under them there was pressure to engage in more specific and more communal measures: instead of individuals choosing to conform to Greek culture, it would be advantageous to make a collective decision that would involve a large group of Jews in one specific action, namely, for the Judean capital to elect to become a Greek foundation. This would be the decision not of an individual made for the advantage of him and his family alone, but of a governing body (or national leader) with consequences for a large group of people or even the entire nation. This was precisely what happened within the first quarter-century after Seleucid rule began over Judea.

The life of the average person was not strikingly affected. The poor peasant continued to work the land, only noting that he had a new landlord or had to pay taxes to a new regime. We must not forget, however, that the day-to-day life of the bulk of the population in the Near East probably changed little between the third millennium B.C.E. and the eighteenth century C.E. The coming of the Greeks did not radically change their lives, but neither did the coming of the Assyrians, the Persians, the Romans, the Arabs, the Turks, or the British. Nevertheless, there were constant reminders of the new culture, most obviously in the language of administration and commerce. Anyone who wished to engage in trade probably found it advantageous to gain some acquaintance with Greek, and those who could afford it would be under pressure to provide some sort of Greek education for their offspring. The native languages continued to be used in administration, however, and most people could get by quite well without any knowledge of Greek.

As an analogy, consider the Anglicization of India in the nineteenth century or the Westernization of Japan in the post-World War II era. Anglo-India was a complex synthesis of the two cultures, with administration and communication dominated by the English culture and language but the life of the ordinary Indian continuing much as always. Moreover, the influence worked both ways. The English who lived in India soon adopted a way of life and cultural tradition that was often quite different from that in Great Britain, and they came to occupy a sphere which was neither that of the average Indian nor that of the home country. This reverse influence of India on Britain was less pronounced than the Anglicization process but nevertheless significant, especially in such spheres as food and linguistic borrowing. One might compare modern India, in which English is widely used, is generally the language of the bureaucracy (despite moves to oust it in favor of Hindi), and is spoken by many educated Indians, and yet the number of English speakers has recently been estimated at an astonishingly low figure. Similarly, the modern Japanese businessman is Western in dress and mode of life when abroad, with English the most likely means of communication, yet conduct in the domestic sphere in Japan in many ways may be little different from that of fifty or one hundred years ago (as Japanese feminists have complained). In many areas Japan has become very Westernized, but one can hardly conclude that the native customs and culture have been ousted or submerged.

Therefore, the terms "Hellenize" and "Hellenization" can refer to more than one thing. The first is the general situation after Alexander. Much remained the same, at least for the time being, but there was a qualitative change overall. Greece, Asia Minor, Egypt, and Mesopotamia now all fell under the rubric "Hellenistic"—they made up the Hellenistic world. All Eastern peoples, the Jews included, were a part of this world.

The second is the cultural phenomenon, with its complex set of elements derived from both Greek and Near Eastern sources. It was neither "Greek" nor "Oriental," but neither was it homogenized. Some loci (regions, social and economic classes, institutions) were almost purely Greek, whereas others remained unadulteratedly native, and there were mixtures of various sorts. The balance of the different elements and their relationships were not static, however, but constantly changing and developing. Therefore, Hellenistic culture can only be adequately described as a process. From this point of view, the Jews were Hellenized. There is no indication that the Jews were different from the other peoples in this world, both in adopting specific Greek elements and practices and in preserving their own cultural heritage.

Third is the question of the extent to which individuals adopted or conformed to specific Greek practices. The Hellenistic world included far more than the culture of classical Greece, but one could be said to be "Hellenized" if an effort was made to adhere to Greek ideals and customs. From this point of view, individual Orientals—including individual Jews—might be more Hellenized than others.

Therefore, on the one hand, Hellenization was a centuries-long process in which all were engaged and from which no one escaped. All peoples of the Near East, the Jews included, were part of the Hellenistic world, were included in this process, and were, from this point of view, Hellenized. On the other hand, one can speak of degrees of Hellenization, in the sense of how far individuals went in consciously imitating and adopting Greek ways. From such a perspective it is legitimate to talk of a particular individual as being "more Hellenized" or "less Hellenized" than another, and Hellenization in this sense represents a spectrum encompassing many shades of Greek influence, from the limited to the intense. It is important to make clear which context is being referred to in speaking of Hellenization, although many writers fail to make such distinctions and talk as if it were all or nothing, as if someone were Hellenized or not.

3.4.2 Conclusions about the Jews and Hellenization

Although there are many points to be debated in current study, Hengel's dictum is increasingly accepted: we can no longer talk of Judaism versus Hellenism or of Palestinian versus Hellenistic Judaism. To do so is to create an artificial binary opposition and to reduce an enormously complex picture to stark, unshaded black and white. It is also to treat a lengthy process as if it were a single, undifferentiated event—as if conception, pregnancy, birth, childhood, and adulthood could be simultaneous. At the risk of repeating remarks made in the previous section, six points relate to the Jews specifically.

First, Hellenism was a culture, whereas Judaism was a religion. Some aspects of Hellenistic culture were irrelevant to Jewish religious views. Other aspects were viewed as irrelevant by some Jews but highly subversive by others. From any point of view, particular aspects of Hellenistic culture, especially those in the religious sphere, had the potential to bring about major transformations of Judaism. The stark dichotomy of "Hellenizers" and "Judaizers" of 1 Maccabees has been used too simplistically and thus has caused gross distortion (5.3.3; 5.4.3.2). It assumes a narrow, prejudicial definition of a loyal Jew, with no allowance made for those of a different opinion. It is as if, to take a modern analogy, the only form of Judaism allowed to be "Jewish" were Orthodox Judaism. This may indeed be the view of some Orthodox Jews, but it is hardly the perspective of Conservative, Reform, Liberal, Karaite, Falasha, and other forms of Judaism. It is not the job of the historian to adopt the denominational prejudice of the sources.

Second, those called "Judaizers" (or, misleadingly, "orthodox" in some modern works) were not totally opposed to all aspects of Hellenistic culture. They opposed specific things affecting their religion, although this opposition sometimes used—or reacted to—cultural symbols as a means of expressing its loyalty to a particular form of Judaism. (One might compare a common reaction among "nativistic movements," in which overt elements of the colonial culture are attacked, even though much has been absorbed without conscious recognition [3.3.7].)

Third, the attitudes of those called "Judaizers" seem to have covered a wide spectrum, represented by the Hasidim, the Maccabees, those who refused to defend themselves against their enemies, the partisans of Onias, and those who wrote Daniel 7–12; the same is true of the so-called Hellenizers (5.3.3). As far as we know, none of them rejected the label "Jew," not even Menelaus and his followers, whom many would regard as the most extreme of the Hellenizers. Nevertheless, to be "Hellenized" did not mean to cease to be a Jew. Take, for example, Philo of Alexandria, a man with a good Greek education, who wrote and thought in the Greek language (probably knowing no Hebrew), lived a life whose daily habits did not differ from those of the Greek citizens of Alexandria, and yet who thought himself nothing less than a loyal and pious Jew (7.2.2). We might also ponder the message of the *Letter of Aristeas* that Jews can be a part of the Hellenistic world without necessarily compromising their Judaism. A final example is the Jason who became high priest; he evidently considered himself a full and faithful Jew (5.4.3.2), yet he was the one who obtained permission for Jerusalem to become a Greek foundation. That some Jews may have judged him an apostate is irrelevant to his self-designation or his own Jewish identity.

Fourth, the native cultures continued to thrive, to a greater or lesser extent, all over the Near East, not just in Judea. Greek remained a minority language and did not displace the many local languages or the old lingua franca, Aramaic (3.3.1). Hellenization as a process—not just a static culture—continued with the coming of the Romans and the growth of their empire.

Fifth, it is indeed true that Jews were unique and did not lose their identity in the face of Hellenization—a fact with which some writers on the subject seem obsessed—but one could make the same statement about many of the native peoples. Each ethnic group was unique and was just as attached to its own identity, culture, native language, and traditions as were the Jews. In many cases this attachment also included particular religious cults, which were as important to the ethnic groups in question as Yahwism was to the Jews. One can readily accept the Hellenization of the Jews without denying their uniqueness, loyalty to religion, careful maintenance of tradition and custom, or continual contribution to Hebrew and Aramaic literature.

Sixth, in accommodating to Hellenistic culture the Jews always maintained one area that could not be compromised without affecting their Judaism, that of religion. In the Greco-Roman world only the Jews refused honor to gods, shrines, and cults other than their own. Thus even those Jews who were most at home in the Hellenistic world, such as Philo or the author of Pseudo-Aristeas, found themselves marked—and marked off—by this fact. For the vast majority, this was the final barrier that could not be crossed; we know from antiquity of only a handful of examples of Jews who abandoned their Judaism. Therefore, however Hellenized they might be, observant Jews could never be fully at home in the Greek world.

4 ALEXANDER, THE DIADOCHI, AND THE PTOLEMIES

4.1 BIBLIOGRAPHICAL GUIDE

Bagnall, R. S. *The Administration of the Ptolemaic Possessions Outside Egypt* (1976).
Bickerman, E. J. [E. Bikerman]. *Institutions des Séleucides* (1938).
———. *From Ezra to the Last of the Maccabees* (1962).
———. *The Jews in the Greek Age* (1988).
CAH[2]. Vol. 7.1: *The Hellenistic Age* (1984); Vol. 7.2: *The Rise of Rome to 220 B.C.* (1989); Vol. 8: *Rome and the Mediterranean to 133 B.C.* (1989).
Cary, M. *A History of the Greek World, 323 to 146 B.C.* (1963).
CHJ. Vol. 2: *The Hellenistic Age* (1989).
CPJ: Vols.1–3.
Grimal, P., ed. *Hellenism and the Rise of Rome* (1968).
Hengel, M. *Judaism and Hellenism* (1974).
Hornblower, S. *The Greek World 479–323 B.C.* (1983).
Rostovtzeff, M. *The Social and Economic History of the Hellenistic World* (1941).
Schalit, A., ed. *The Hellenistic Age* (1972).
Tcherikover, V. [V. Tscherikower]. "Palestine under the Ptolemies (A Contribution to the Study of the Zenon Papyri)." *Mizraim* 4–5 (1937) 1–90.
———. *Hellenistic Civilization and the Jews* (1959).
Will, E. *Histoire politique du monde hellénistique (323–30 av. J.-C.* (1979–1982).
Will, E., et al. *Le monde grec et l'Orient* (1975).

For events in Jewish history, the best sources are probably Tcherikover (1959), Schalit, and *CHJ* 2; unfortunately, most of the articles in *CHJ 2* were almost fifteen years old when published. On the broader aspects of Seleucid and Ptolemaic history, the most up-to-date references are Will and the new edition of *CAH* 7. Useful older works include Cary and Grimal. Hornblower includes the first part of this period, namely, Alexander and his conquests.

Because we know little about specific political events, other areas of historical study have always been emphasized for the Ptolemaic age more than for other periods. Two such areas of study are the social and economic, for which we have more abundant information than for some other periods. Tcherikover (1959) has good coverage of this in a readily accessible form, but his earlier work (1937) is more detailed. Fundamental to any study of social and economic matters of this time is the massive work of Rostovtzeff. Many important documents for the Jews in Egypt are published, with bibliography and commentary, in *CPJ*. Bickerman (1988) contains important coverage of political, social, literary, and cultural events by a master of the period; unfortunately, this posthumous publication gives little in the way of references to original or secondary literature, making it difficult for the student or nonspecialist to use. Occasionally Bickerman's earlier work (1962) has a reference where the later one does not, although it too is sparsely documented.

4.2 SOURCES

4.2.1 Zenon Papyri

Harper, C. M., Jr. "A Study in the Commercial Relations between Egypt and Syria in the Third Century before Christ." *AJP* 49 (1928) 1–35.
Rostovtzeff, M. *A Large Estate in Egypt in the Third Century* B.C. (1922).
Vincent, L. H. "La Palestine dans les papyrus Ptolémaiques de Gerza." *RB* 29 (1920) 161–202.

Among the papyri discovered at Darb el-Gerza in Fayum (the ancient Philadelphia) in Egypt during World War I was the archive of an individual named Zenon. This Zenon was the agent of Apollonius, the finance minister of Ptolemy II. In 259 B.C.E. Apollonius sent Zenon on a lengthy tour of Palestine and southern Syria to take care of various sorts of business. After his return Zenon continued to correspond with individuals whom he had met in his travels. Therefore, the archive contains documents from Egypt and Palestine not only for the year 259 but also for several years afterward. The result is a wealth of material that throws light on the trade, administration, culture, and (only to an extent) historical events in Palestine for this period. It has taken several large collections to finish publication of the papyri, not to mention numerous individual studies. The documents relating specifically to the Jews have been published separately with commentary (*CPJ:* 1.115–30), whereas a good summary of the major implications for Palestinian history is given by Tcherikover (*1937; *1959).

4.2.2 Hecateus of Abdera

Diamond, F. H. *Hecataeus of Abdera: A New Historical Approach* (1974).
———. "Hecataeus of Abdera and the Mosaic Constitution." *Panhellenica* (1980) 77–95.
Gauger, J.-D. "Zitate in der jüdischen Apologetik und die Authentizität der Hekataios-Passagen bei Flavius Josephus und im Ps. Aristeas-Brief." *JSJ* 13 (1982) 6–46.
GLAJJ: 1.20–44.
JWSTP: 169–71.
Mendels, D. "Hecataeus of Abdera and a Jewish 'Patrios Politeia' of the Persian Period (Diodorus Siculus XL, 3)." *ZAW* 95 (1983) 96–110.
Murray, O. "Hecataeus of Abdera and Pharaonic Kingship." *JEA* 56 (1970) 141–71.
Schürer: 3.671–77.
Stern, M., and O. Murray. "Hecataeus of Abdera and Theophrastus on Jews and Egyptians." *JEA* 59 (1973) 159–68.
Wacholder, B. Z. *Eupolemus* (1974) 85–96.

One of the most interesting pieces of information is the alleged account of the Jewish nation by Hecateus of Abdera, a writer at the beginning of the Ptolemaic period. There are a number of questions about his account, which has provoked a lengthy list of studies. The recent commentary and discussion by Stern (*GLAJJ*: 1.20–46) covers most of the issues and the bibliography to 1974, although he did not have access to Diamond's study (1974); see also the important recent article by Mendels. An extensive quotation regarding the Jews is given below at 4.4.5.

There are basically two questions that have arisen about Hecateus's account: (1) Are the fragments in Josephus genuinely the work of the Hecateus quoted in Diodorus? and (2) What is the source of Hecateus's account of the Jewish nation? The first question has been debated extensively without any assured conclusions (see *GLAJJ*: 1.20–46; Gauger); however, some defend the quotations in Josephus as truly from Hecateus. As to the source of the description of early Hellenistic Judah, both Diamond and Mendels argue for a Jewish source of information, rather than direct observation by Hecateus. Others such as Murray would suggest that Hecateus consulted Jews, perhaps even priests (Stern/Murray: 168). According to Mendels, Hecateus's source represents a point of view widespread in particular priestly circles (hence the statement that the Jews had never had a king) and basically in line with that taken in Ezra-Nehemiah. This description was then assimilated to the Greek "native constitution" (*patrios politeia*) pattern, which explains the Greek coloring of the description. Still, the basic description of the situation in Judah is accurate for the time of its writing, probably the late fourth or early third century.

4.2.3 Josephus

As with the later Persian period, Josephus has little information on the time from Alexander to Antiochus III. He devotes a fair amount of space to this period, but the reliable historical content is limited. A section at the beginning of the period about Alexander (*Ant.* 11.8.1–6 §§304–45) is based mainly on the Alexander legend and is pure fiction (4.2.5.9), although it has been combined with anti-Samaritan material. The anti-Samaritan information could have been transmitted as a part of the Jewish Alexander legend, but more likely Josephus received the Samaritan story separately and combined it with the legend of Alexander's coming to Jerusalem. Another long section is only a close paraphrase of the *Letter of Aristeas* (*Ant.* 12.2.1–15 §§11–118); not only is the original extant but also it is usually dated to the late second century B.C.E., rather than the Ptolemaic period, making the information in it problematic for illustrating Judah during Ptolemaic rule (4.2.5.6). This is followed by a major section on the Tobiads (*Ant.* 12.4.1–11 §§157–236), which probably depends on some sort of family history or chronicle (4.2.4). Although there is a large romantic element in the Tobiad section, it still contains some useful information about a family that was very influential on Palestinian politics in the Ptolemaic and Seleucid periods. It should be noted, however, that Josephus has dated this to the reign of the wrong Ptolemy (see 4.3.2 for a discussion). Interspersed between these blocks of material are some bits and pieces about Alexander, the Diadochi, and the Ptolemies, which Josephus had probably picked up from reading Hellenistic historians. For example, there is a quotation from Agatharchides of Cnidus about the taking of Jerusalem by Ptolemy I, an event otherwise unknown (*Ant.* 12.1.1 §6; given more extensively in *Ag. Ap.* 1.22 §§209–11). Several quotations are said to be from Hecateus of Abdera (*Ag. Ap.* 1.22 §§183–204), although this is disputed (4.2.2). Also of some interest is a letter to the Spartans that claims a distant kinship between them and the Jews (*Ant.* 12.4.10 §§225–27; see 5.3.6).

4.2.4 History of the Tobiads

Goldstein, J. A. "The Tales of the Tobiads." *Christianity, Judaism and Other Greco-Roman Cults* (1975) 3.85–123.

In a lengthy section Josephus discusses the exploits of individuals from the same family, primarily Joseph b. Tobias and his son Hyrcanus (*Ant.* 12.4.1–11 §§157–236). Although Josephus at no point mentions a specific source, it has long been accepted that he is closely following a written source that concerned itself with the Tobiad family. Two major questions arise: What is the nature of this source? and How reliable is it as history? The first question is difficult to answer. Goldstein has recently argued that it is pro-Ptolemaic Jewish propaganda written by Onias IV. Although his suggestion is not unreasonable, it is tied up with his very speculative views about Josephus's aims and methods of writing history. As for the second question, most scholars seem to accept that the story contains many novelistic and otherwise incredible elements, but they consider that in outline it is still usable as a historical source for the activities of the Tobiad family.

4.2.5 Other Jewish Literature

Critical introductions with extensive bibliographies for many of the writings of this section can be found in the *Encyclopaedia Judaica* (1971).

4.2.5.1 Qohelet (Ecclesiastes)

Braun, R. *Koheleth und die frühhellenistische Popularphilosophie* (1973).
Crenshaw, J. *Ecclesiastes* (1988).
Loretz, O. *Qohelet und der alte Orient* (1964).
Reif, S. Review of *Koheleth*, by C. Whitley. *VT* 31 (1981) 120–26.
Whitley, C. F. *Koheleth: His Language and Thought* (1979).
Whybray, R. N. *Ecclesiastes* (1989).

The book of Ecclesiastes is now commonly referred to by its Hebrew name of Qohelet (also spelled Koheleth), which is traditionally translated as "preacher" (Eccles 1:1 and passim). Although it cannot be dated precisely, the lateness of its Hebrew has led most scholars to place it at about the third century B.C.E., that is, in the Ptolemaic period. The only recent dissenter is Whitley, who thinks that it was written after Ben Sira in the second century, his argument being that Qohelet presupposes certain passages in Ben Sira (122–46). Most scholars have generally argued that the influence is the other way around, and no one seems to have been convinced by Whitley's arguments (cf. Reif). Although scholars have thought they could find contemporary references in the text, there has been little agreement about what these are (cf. Whybray: 8–11); and even though there is nothing against a Ptolemaic background, most such suggestions assume we know more about the society and economy of Ptolemaic Palestine than we actually do.

The central importance of Qohelet is for the state of religion and ideology and their development in Judea in this period. This book is in many ways unique in early Jewish literature in the way it challenges conventional thought. This seems true despite the widely differing interpretations of the book (cf. Whybray with Crenshaw). Thus it may tell us more about one writer than about Judaism in general; yet even a "voice crying in the wilderness" contributes to the total picture, and Qohelet is a valuable document. It has often been argued that the book shows the influence of Greek thought (e.g., Braun), but this also is strongly disputed (e.g., Loretz). What one can say is that the thought of Qohelet is fully compatible with the thought of the Hellenistic period, without assuming a direct influence upon the book from Greek philosophy or literature (cf. Whybray: 5–13).

4.2.5.2 Ben Sira (Ecclesiasticus)

JLBM: 55–65.
JWSTP: 290–301.
Sanders, J. T. *Ben Sira and Demotic Wisdom* (1983).
Schürer: 3.198–212.
Skehan, P. W., and A. A. Di Lella. *The Wisdom of Ben Sira* (1987).
Stadelmann, H. *Ben Sira als Schriftgelehrter* (1980).

The book of Joshua ben Sira has often been referred to by its Greek title, Ecclesiasticus. It was translated by the author's grandson and can be approximately dated by the preface to his Greek translation, which gives the date as the "thirty-eighth year of (Ptolemy VIII) Euergetes," which most scholars accept as 132 B.C.E. This would put the original composition in the general period of 190–175 B.C.E. Information in the book itself indicates that it was finished after the conquest of Palestine by Antiochus III (50:1–24), but there is no reference to the Maccabean revolt, which confirms the period of time mentioned above. Although the book was composed or, at least, completed in the Seleucid period, the overall situation gleaned from it seems to be that current during Ptolemaic rule. Therefore, the book provides important information on such subjects as the administration and social structure of the country, the priesthood, religious beliefs and outlook, and the opinions of the "scribal class" on a variety of issues.

4.2.5.3 Tobit

Deselaers, P. *Das Buch Tobit* (1982).
JLBM: 30–35.

JWSTP: 40–46.
Schürer: 3.222–32.
Zimmermann, F. *The Book of Tobit* (1958).

This is the story of a pious Jew blinded during an act of charity, his son Tobias, and a cousin named Sarah, who also suffers until she is married by Tobias. The setting of the story is ostensibly the exile of the Northern Kingdom in the land of the Assyrians, which suggests that it most likely originated in the eastern Jewish Diaspora. Its dating is uncertain, however, and cannot be put more exactly than between about 500 and 200 B.C.E. The reason for this period of time is that Tobit presupposes the existence of the Second Temple (14:5) but seems not to know of the Maccabean revolt. Although there are no certain historical allusions in the book, it gives a number of insights into Judaism and reveals its concerns for the period in which it was written. Some of the topics discussed are (1) temple worship (1:4-6); (2) tithing (1:6-8); (3) the "negative Golden Rule" (4:15); (4) angelology/demonology (3:7-9; 5:4-5; 12:6-21); (5) magical practices (8:1-3); and (6) an ascetic view of sex (only for procreation [8:7]).

4.2.5.4 3 Maccabees

JLBM: 169–72.
JWSTP: 80–84.
Parente, F. "The Third Book of Maccabees as Ideological Document and Historical Source." *Henoch* 10 (1988) 143–82.
Schürer: 3.537–42.
Tcherikover, V. A. "The Third Book of Maccabees as a Historical Source of Augustus' Time." *Scripta Hierosolymitana* 7 (1961) 1–26.

Despite its title, 3 Maccabees is ostensibly set during the reign of Ptolemy IV (221–204 B.C.E.). The first few verses (1:1-7) describe the battle of Raphia (217 B.C.E.), in which Antiochus III was defeated by the Egyptians and forced to retire from Coele-Syria (4.4.4). In the next section of the book (1:8—2:24) Ptolemy comes to Jerusalem and attempts to enter the Holy of Holies but is refused. He then returns to Egypt and initiates a persecution of the Alexandrian Jews; however, they are miraculously delivered (2:25—6:22), and the king repents of his plan and acknowledges the God of heaven (6:23-29). The Jews are allowed a festival, and the king issues a decree in their favor (6:30—7:23).

Recent study has indicated that the work is itself later than the Ptolemaic period, possibly as late as Augustan times (Tcherikover; Parente), but it does draw on some genuine Ptolemaic sources. Its account of the battle of Raphia, although brief, seems to have a good basis (Tcherikover: 2–3; Parente: 147–48). The basis of the story about the persecution of the Jews may lie in actual events from the time of Ptolemy VII Euergetes (145–116 B.C.E.), despite the legendary nature of the story in its present form (Tcherikover: 7–8; *CPJ*: 1.21–23), although it could reflect the situation at the time of its final editing, perhaps in the Augustan age (Parente). Therefore, even though the present form of 3 Maccabees may date from the Hasmonean or even Herodian times, portions of it probably reflect, to a greater or lesser extent, historical events from the time of Ptolemaic rule over Judea.

4.2.5.5 Judith

Craven, T. *Artistry and Faith in the Book of Judith* (1983).
JLBM: 105–9.
JWSTP: 46–52.
Moore, C. A. *Judith* (1985).
Schürer: 3.216–22.
Shedl, C. "Nabuchodonosor, Arpaksad und Darius: Untersuchungen zum Buch Judit." *ZDMG* 115 (1965) 242–54.

The setting of Judith is the time of Nebuchadnezzar. The story recounts the deliverance of an Israelite town besieged by Nebuchadnezzar's general, Holophernes. Judith, a pious widow, volunteered to enter the enemy camp, then seduced Holophernes and cut off his head to end the siege. The actual time of the writing is difficult to specify because there are historical remembrances that point to the early Persian period (Shedl), the time of Artaxerxes III, and the Maccabean revolt (cf. Moore: 38–49, 67–70). The Maccabean-Hasmonean period is probably the most favored dating. There is little that the book would add to our knowledge of actual events, even if its precise historical setting could be determined. Its contribution is, instead, on the side of Jewish religious and social history during the Persian period or Greek period. The book is, without good reason, often associated with Pharisaism (cf. Moore: 60–63, 70–71). The characteristic piety of the book (fasting, prayer, almsgiving) is by no means unique to Pharisaism; indeed, there seems a tendency to add the adjective "Pharisaic" to any occurrence of piety in early Jewish literature. By contrast, none of the traits unique to what is known of the Pharisees occurs in the book (8.2.2). There is, in fact, nothing particular in the book to associate it with any of the known sects of early Judaism (cf. Craven: 120–21).

4.2.5.6 *Letter of (Pseudo-)Aristeas*

Hadas, M. *Aristeas to Philocrates* (1951).
JLBM: 165–69.
JWSTP: 75–80.
Pelletier, A. *Lettre d'Aristée à Philocrate* (1962).
Schürer: 3.677–87.
Tcherikover, V. A. "The Ideology of the Letter of Aristeas." *HTR* 51 (1958) 59–85.

This work ostensibly explains how the Pentateuch came to be translated into Greek: Ptolemy II wanted copies of all the important works of literature among the non-Greeks to be included in his famous library at Alexandria. Aristeas brought the Jewish law to the notice of Ptolemy's minister, Demetrius, and recommended that such a "famous" book be translated and included in the library. Messengers were dispatched to Jerusalem to obtain copies of the law and to find skilled translators. After a lengthy description of Jerusalem and the temple, the *Letter* tells us that the high priest Eleazar sent seventy-two translators to Alexandria to render the Scriptures into Greek. They brought with them a number of beautiful copies of the Torah. At the Egyptian court they were elaborately entertained and their wisdom tested and found superior by Ptolemy. They did the translation, and the Pentateuch in Greek was accepted by the Jewish community in a public ceremony.

The letter is a fake. It was not written by an official of the minister Demetrius; and most specialists agree that it does not tell the true origins of the Greek Old Testament (4.3.4). Rather, it is a piece of Jewish propaganda, probably on behalf of the LXX version, and likely written after the reign of Ptolemy II. Exactly when it was written is a matter of debate. Perhaps the most popular date is the last decades of the second century, that is, during Hasmonean times. Some scholars, however, put its composition during the Ptolemaic period, whereas others date it just before the Maccabean revolt. The dating is important as it affects the question of whether the work has authentic material for Ptolemaic times in its description of Judah and Jerusalem. It obviously presents an idealized picture of Judea as a utopian state; also, some of its description of the temple appears to be based on the LXX Pentateuch. Elements of the narrative, however, may represent a genuine remembrance of the pre-Maccabean state. More specific study needs to be done on this issue, although it would be difficult to check its information in detail. If the *Letter* was written in the late second century, then one would need solid reasons for having confidence that it contained accurate information about Judah and the temple in Ptolemaic times, although it might be useful for the Hasmonean state.

4.2.5.7 Ethiopic Enoch *(1 Enoch)*

Black, M. *The Book of Enoch or I Enoch* (1985).
Charles, R. H. *The Book of Enoch* (1913).
JLBM: 46–55, 145–51, 214–23.
JWSTP: 395–406.
Knibb, M. A. *The Ethiopic Book of Enoch* (1978).
Milik, J. T. *The Books of Enoch: Aramaic Fragments of Qumran Cave 4* (1976).
Schürer: 3.250–68.
VanderKam, J. C. *Enoch and the Growth of an Apocalyptic Tradition* (1984).

In its present form *1 Enoch* is a complex book with five internal divisions, each probably produced at a different time. Recently published finds from Qumran suggest that parts of the book were generated early in the Greek period. *The Astronomical Book* (*1 Enoch* 72–82) is probably the earliest section and most likely from early in the Hellenistic period. *The Book of Watchers* (chaps. 1–36) also forms a unit in the present book, although it probably had a complicated tradition history. The story of the fall of the angels (chaps. 6–11) in its present form centers on two angelic leaders, Shemihazah and Asael; however, the Asael tradition is probably a later addition. Nickelsburg has suggested that the background of chapters 6 through 11 is the Diadochi period, when "giants" with their armies continually marched through Palestine (*JLBM*: 51–52). If his analysis is correct, chapters 1 through 36 and 72 through 82 were complete by about the end of the Ptolemaic period and would thus present the thinking of one section of Palestinian Judaism for this period.

The last section of *1 Enoch* is made up of two separate works. The first (83–90) consists of two apocalypses: the *Book of Dreams* (83–84) and the *Animal Apocalypse* (85–90). The *Book of Dreams* is about a warning in visions to Noah of the impending flood. No indication of the date is found in it, but it seems to be a unit with the *Animal Apocalypse,* which can be dated fairly precisely. The latter gives a review of Israel's history, using the figures of various animals (sheep and oxen for Israelites; unclean animals for pagans). It culminates in an account of a large ram, who is universally identified with Judas Maccabeus (90:9-12), but the apocalypse must have been written before 161 because there is no indication of Judas's death. The *Animal Apocalypse* is a useful indication of the events during the suppression of Judaism and the subsequent revolt, as well as of the attitudes of some of the contemporaries of the events.

1 Enoch 91–105 is in the form of an epistle. It begins with the *Apoca-*

lypse of Weeks (91:1-10, 18-19; 92:1—93:10; 91:11-17), which surveys history as an *ex eventu* prophecy within a schematic framework of ten weeks. The time of the end comes at the end of the seventh week. Most of the rest of the "epistle" is made up of admonitions about moral and religious conduct, with many parallels to Old Testament passages. Although this section has frequently been dated to the Hasmonean period, there are no clear historical allusions. The *Apocalypse of Weeks* has been thought to indicate the time of the end before the Maccabean revolt (Schürer: 3.255–56), and there is no reason why it could not have arisen in the early second century, rather than later Hasmonean times (*JLBM*: 149–50).

The dating of the *Similitudes* or *Parables* (chaps. 37–71) is very controversial. There is a recent tendency toward the first century C.E., though without agreement on whether before or after 70.

4.2.5.8 Demetrius the Chronographer

For discussion, see 5.2.10.1.

4.2.5.9 The Jewish Alexander Legend

Büchler, A. "La relation de Josèphe concernant Alexandre le Grand." *REJ* 36 (1898) 1–26.
Cohen, S.J.D. "Alexander the Great and Jaddus the High Priest according to Josephus." *AJS Review* 7–8 (1982/83) 41–68.
Flusser, D. *Sefer Yosippon* (1978–80).
Grabbe, L. L. "Josephus and the Reconstruction of the Judean Restoration." *JBL* 106 (1987) 231–46.
Kazis, I. J. *The Book of the Gests of Alexander of Macedon* (1962).
Marcus, R. "Appendix C. Alexander the Great and the Jews." *Josephus* (1934) 5.512–32.
Momigliano, A. "Flavius Josephus and Alexander's Visit to Jerusalem." *Athaeneum* 57 (1979) 442–48.
Pfister, F. *Eine jüdische Gründungsgeschichte Alexandrias* (1914).

Certain figures in history have tended to attract traditions and to become surrounded with an ever-growing body of legendary material—King Arthur, for example. Some of these figures in the ancient Near East produced bodies of literature which proliferated to such an extent that multiple versions in diverse languages have come down to us; examples of this are Ahiqar and the Alexander legend. The Alexander romance has little to do with history, even though there is a historical figure and a core of known events from Alexander's life underlying the legendary superstructure. This legend was generally given in the name of one of the genuine Alexander historians, Callisthenes, but this is a false ascription. The Pseudo-Callisthenes romance does not represent a unified tradition, and other legendary material is known whose relationship to Pseudo-Callisthenes is uncertain.

The Jewish version of the Alexander legend does not differ from Pseudo-Callisthenes in much of its overall structure, but there is one episode not present in the non-Jewish versions but found in certain Jewish sources without the rest of the Alexander legend. This is the story of Alexander's visit to Jerusalem, which is known in at least four versions: Josephus (*Ant.* 11.8.1–6 §§304–45), the Babylonian Talmud (*b. Yoma* 69a), Josippon 10, and the medieval Hebrew *Gests of Alexander* (Kazis). Some of the later accounts could be based on Josephus, although certain differences suggest that we probably are dealing with independent versions. As Tcherikover points out, the itinerary and timetable of Alexander are known in detail from the extant Alexander historians (*1959: 42–50). Not only is it unlikely that they would have omitted a visit of Alexander to Jerusalem, but also there is simply no place in Alexander's advance down the Mediterranean coast that fits such an event. Immediately after the fall of Tyre, he received messengers with an offer of terms from Darius. He refused these and went directly down the Phoenician coast to Gaza, which he besieged because it refused entry to him. When it fell after a two-month siege, he went straight on to Egypt. If Alexander had visited Jerusalem, it would have been on his return from Egypt; yet Josephus states that the visit was right after the siege of Gaza.

In any event, why would the Alexander historians have omitted a trip to Jerusalem? For Alexander to visit the holy places of other peoples was not unusual: his reason for besieging Tyre was that the city refused his request to worship at the temple of "Hercules" (the god Melqart) there, and later he made a special effort in crossing a stretch of desert to visit the Egyptian shrine in the oasis at Ammon. Because the Alexandrian historians mentioned these events, they would have mentioned a visit to Jerusalem. It seems rather that the Jewish tradition is itself modeled in part on the trip to Ammon (Pfister: 20–30). In addition, the basic Alexander legend contains an account of his visit to Rome, which appears to be a close parallel to the Jerusalem episode: both have an ethnic capital, a high priest, the prostration of Alexander to that priest because of a dream, and Alexander having sacrifices offered for himself in the sanctuary (Büchler).

In sum, modern scholars are practically unanimous in dismissing Josephus's story of Alexander's visit to Jerusalem as pure imagination with no historical basis. Furthermore, one should be leery of using details from the story as if they have substance despite the fictional nature of the whole, especially because these details are not consistent in the various versions of the story (Grabbe: 242–43).

4.2.5.10 Daniel 11

This is important because of the accurate (if sometimes allusive) information on events in Ptolemaic and Seleucid history for the third and early second centuries B.C.E. See 5.2.3 for a discussion.

4.2.6 Greek Historians

Lesky, A. H. *A History of Greek Literature* (1966).

The historians discussed below provide much of our knowledge of the background to Jewish history. For further scholarship, see *CHCL*, Lesky, and *OCD*. For specific references to the Jews and Jewish history in the Greek writers, see the extracts and commentary in *GLAJJ*.

4.2.6.1 Alexander Historians

Pearson, L. *The Lost Historians of Alexander the Great* (1960).

In addition to Pearson's detailed investigation, an up-to-date discussion about both ancient sources and modern secondary studies for Alexander the Great is Hornblower (*314–16). There are two main Alexander traditions: the more reliable one is in the *Anabasis* of Arrian, who depends chiefly on the accounts of Ptolemy I and Aristobulus of Cassandria. The "vulgate" tradition is an embellished and generally less reliable stream of tradition that is found in such accounts as Diodorus and the Roman writer Quintus Curtius, although Arrian himself sometimes quotes from it. The vulgate tradition also became the basis for the Alexander legend found in Pseudo-Callisthenes (4.2.5.9). Plutarch (4.2.6.4) also has a life of Alexander, drawn eclectically from a variety of sources.

4.2.6.2 Diodorus Siculus

For a general introduction to Diodorus, see 2.2.6.6. His account of Alexander (book 17) depends on the "vulgate" Alexandrian tradition (4.2.6.1) and is thus less reliable than other accounts. For the next part of the

Hellenistic period, however, he provides a detailed history of the Diadochi from 323 to 303 (books 18–20), probably drawing on Hieronymus of Cardia and Diyllus of Athens. Indeed, Diodorus is still the main source of information for the events of this period; however, after book 20 his history is only partially preserved, and the extant information is not as detailed.

4.2.6.3 Polybius

Walbank, F. W. *A Historical Commentary on Polybius* (1957–1979).

A Greek who spent many years in Rome as a hostage, Polybius (ca. 200 to post-118 B.C.E.) wrote a history of the Hellenistic world and the rise of Rome from the First Punic War to the Roman conquest of Greece (264–146 B.C.E.). In the opinion of many historians, the quality of his historical writing is second only to Thucydides among ancient historians. It is therefore unfortunate that only books 1 to 5 are preserved intact and the rest survive only in fragments or extracts made by Byzantine writers.

4.2.6.4 Plutarch

For a general introduction to Plutarch, see 2.2.6.8. His *Lives* includes one of Alexander, which is valuable for sources no longer extant but problematic because Plutarch also draws on the vulgate tradition (4.2.6.1). He also has lives of various individuals of the Hellenistic period.

4.2.6.5 Porphyry

For Porphyry's comments on the book of Daniel and history, see 5.2.3.

4.2.7 Papyri, Inscriptions, Coins

4.2.7.1 Elephantine Papyrus (Cowley No. 81)

Harmatta, J. "Irano-Aramaica (Zur Geschichte des frühhellenistischen Judentums in Ägypten)." *Acta Antiqua* 7 (1959) 337–409.

On the Elephantine papyri in general and for bibliography, see 2.2.2. Cowley's papyrus 81 (probably some sort of business account) is long but fragmentary and difficult. Cowley thought it might be from the Ptolemaic period because of the Greek names and put it about 300 B.C.E. because of the paleography. It has now been given a lengthy treatment and reconstruction by Harmatta, who dates it to about 310 because (1) it seems to use two standards of coinage, which ceased after Ptolemy I became king in 306; (2) it indicates that private individuals could still conduct trade, whereas it later became a royal monopoly; and (3) the price of wheat seems to fit what is known of this time. If Harmatta is accurate, this could be a valuable economic text, apparently dating from the period of the Diadochi.

4.2.7.2 Khirbet el-Kom Ostraca

Geraty, L. T. "The Khirbet el-Kôm Bilingual Ostracon." *BASOR* 220 (December 1975) 55–61.
———. "Recent Suggestions on the Bilingual Ostracon from Khirbet el-Kôm." *AUSS* 19 (1981) 137–40.
———. "The Historical, Linguistic, and Biblical Significance of the Khirbet el-Kôm Ostraca." *The Word of the Lord Shall Go Forth* (1983) 545–48.
Skaist, A. "A Note on the Bilingual Ostracon from Khirbet el-Kôm." *IEJ* 28 (1978) 106–8.

Six ostraca found in 1971 in the area of Edom seem to have belonged to a moneylender. Four are in Northwest Semitic, one is Greek, and one is bilingual. The bilingual ostracon is dated to "year 6," probably the sixth year of Ptolemy II's reign, 277 B.C.E. The ostraca show that Greek was already well established alongside the local language. The person who is listed in the bilingual as having borrowed money had the Greek name Nikeratos; however, his patronymic was Sobbathos, which seems to be a Grecized form of the Semitic name "Shabbat." If so, this local Edomite had adopted a Greek name and wanted to have his receipt for debt recorded in Greek as well as the native language.

The exact identity of the Semitic language is uncertain. Much of the text could be either Hebrew or Aramaic; however, there are both Aramaic forms (a plural form ending in *-n*) and Hebrew forms (*ben* and the verb *ntn*, though both readings have been disputed). This has led Geraty to label the language as Edomite, a not unreasonable identification, although it requires the assumption that the Edomites had their own language rather than Aramaic at this time.

4.2.7.3 Decree of Ptolemy II

*Bagnall: 11–24.
Bagnall, R. S., and P. Derow. *Greek Historical Documents: The Hellenistic Period* (1981).
Lenger, M.-T. *Corpus des ordonnances des Ptolémées* (1964).

Liebesny, H. "Ein Erlass des Königs Ptolemaios II Philadelphos über die Deklaration von Vieh und Sklaven in Syrien und Phonikien (PER Inv. Nr. 24.552 gr.)." *Aegyptus* 16 (1936) 257–91.
*Rostovtzeff: 1.340–51.

Among the Rainer papyri in Vienna is one with parts of two decrees by Ptolemy II Philadelphus, issued about his twenty-fourth year, that is, 260 B.C.E. (now SB 8008 = Lenger: 21–22; see also Liebesny). The legible parts read as follows (the words in brackets are textual restorations):

> [Col. 1 = left col., lines 1–10] --- to the *oikonomos* assigned in each hyparchy [*hyparcheia*], within 60 days from the day on which the [ordinance] was proclaimed, the taxable and tax-free [livestock] . . . and take a receipt. And if any [do not do as] has been written above, [they shall be deprived of] the livestock and shall be [subject to the penalties] in the schedule. [Whatever] of the livestock was unregistered up to the proclamation of [the ordinance shall be free of taxes] for former years, of the pasture tax and crown tax and the other penalties, but from the 2[5]th year they shall pay the sum owing by villages. . . . As for those . . . who make a registration in the name of another, the king will judge concerning them and their belongings shall be confiscated. Likewise, ---
>
> [Col. 1, lines 17–21] Those holding the tax contracts for the villages and the komarchs [*komarchas*] shall register at the same time the taxable and tax-free livestock in the villages, and their owners with fathers' names and place of origin, and by whom the livestock are managed. Likewise they shall declare whatever unregistered livestock they see up to Dystros of the 25th year in statements on royal oath.
>
> [Col. 1, lines 23–28] And they shall make each year at the same time declarations and shall pay the sums due as it is set out in the letter from the king, in the proper months according to the schedule. If any do not carry out something of the aforesaid, they shall be liable to the same penalties as those registering their own cattle under other names.
>
> [Col. 1, lines 29–32] Anyone who wishes may inform (on violations), in which case he shall receive a portion of the penalties exacted according to the schedule, as is announced in the schedule, and of the goods confiscated to the crown he shall take a third part.
>
> [Col. 1, line 33—col. 2 = right col., line 11] By order of the king: If anyone in Syria and Phoenicia has bought a free native person or has seized and held one or acquired one in any other manner --- to the *oikonomos* in charge in each hyparchy within 20 days from the day of the proclamation of the ordinance. If anyone does not register or present him he shall be deprived of the slave and there shall in addition be exacted for the crown 6000 drachmas per head, and the king shall

judge about him. To the informer shall be given . . . drachmas per head. If they show that any of the registered and presented persons were already slaves when bought, they shall be returned to them. As for those persons purchased in royal auctions, even if one of them claims to be free, the sales shall be valid for the purchasers.

[Col. 2, lines 12–15] Whoever of the soldiers on active duty and the other military settlers in Syria and Phoenicia are living with native wives whom they have captured need not declare them.

[Col. 2, lines 16–26] And for the future no one shall be allowed to buy or accept as security native free persons on any pretext, except for those handed over by the superintendent of the revenues in Syria and Phoenicia for execution, for whom the execution is properly on the person, as it is written in the law governing farming contracts. If this is not done, (the guilty party) shall be liable to the same penalties, both those giving (security) and those receiving it. Informers shall be given 300 drachmas per head from the sums exacted. (Bagnall/Derow: 95–96)

4.2.7.4 Other Inscriptions and Ostraca

Biran, A. "Tel Dan." *RB* 84 (1977) 256–63.
Cross, F. M. "An Aramaic Ostracon of the Third Century B.C.E. from Excavations in Jerusalem." *EI* 15 (1981) *67–*69.
Horsley, G.H.R. *New Documents Illustrating Early Christianity* (1981).

Two miscellaneous items are interesting because of what they tell us about the linguistic situation during the Ptolemaic period. The first is the Aramaic ostracon published by Cross. It is only a (tax?) list of commodities in Aramaic, but two of the six items of vocabulary are Greek borrowings. If the ostracon is correctly dated to the mid-third century B.C.E., then this is an example of how quickly the Greek language was already penetrating the language of Jerusalem only a few decades after the Greek conquest (but cf. 3.3.1).

The Tel Dan inscription is a bilingual in Greek and Aramaic, dated around 300. The writer is evidently not Jewish because the inscription is a dedication "to the god in Dan (plural)" (*theōi tōi en danois*). It is apparently the only formal Greek-Aramaic bilingual in the Syrian area before the Roman period (3.3.1).

4.2.7.5 Coins

All of the Yehud coins, some of which date from the Ptolemaic period, are discussed at 2.2.7.2.

4.2.8 Archeology

Arav, R. *Hellenistic Palestine* (1989).
Bull, R. J. "er-Ras, Tell (Mount Gerizim)." *Encyclopedia of Archaeological Excavations in the Holy Land* (1978) 4.1015–22.
Dentzer, J. M., F. Villeneuve, and F. Larché. "Iraq el Amir: Excavations at the Monumental Gateway." *Studies in the History and Archaeology of Jordan* 1 (1982) 201–7.
Halpern-Zylberstein, M.-C. "The Archeology of Hellenistic Palestine." *CHJ* (1989) 2.1–34.
Horowitz, G. "Town Planning of Hellenistic Marisa: A Reappraisal of the Excavations after Eighty Years." *PEQ* 112 (1980) 93–111.
Kuhnen, H.-P. *Palästina in griechisch-römischer Zeit* (1990).
Lapp, N. L., ed. *The Excavations at Araq el-Emir.* Vol. 1 (1983).
Lapp, P. W. " 'Iraq el-Emir." *Encyclopedia of Archaeological Excavations in the Holy Land* (1976) 2.527–31.
McCown, C. C. "The 'Araq el-Emir and the Tobiads." *BA* 20 (1957) 63–76.
Pummer, R. "Samaritan Material Remains and Archaeology." *The Samaritans* (1989) 135–77.
Stern, E. "The Walls of Dor." *IEJ* 38 (1988) 6–14.
Will, E. "Un monument hellénistique de Jordanie: Le Qasr el 'abd d' 'Iraq al Amir." *Studies in the History and Archaeology of Jordan* 1 (1982) 197–200.

For general comments on archeology, see 1.1.1. The standard studies on the subject are now Kuhnen and Arav (unfortunately, Halpern-Zylberstein's article was already fifteen years out of date when published). There is no clear break between the late Persian and the early Hellenistic periods; as important as Alexander's conquest and the wars of the Diadochi were to history, they left little impression on the artifactual record (Kuhnen: 38). Precise dating of finds during this part of the Hellenistic period is difficult. The Ptolemaic period is sparsely documented in major excavations, the main site being Marisa in Idumea (Horowitz). Most of the other Hellenistic sites represent the Seleucid and Hasmonean periods (Samaria; Beth-Zur; Jerusalem). Other sites in Palestine include Dor (Stern) and Tel Dan (4.2.7.4), but neither of these seems to have had Jewish inhabitants during this period.

Araq el-Emir, the residence and center of the Tobiad family, is something of a puzzle. According to Josephus, it was built by Hyrcanus Tobiad (late third or early second century); however, two inscriptions of the name "Tobiah" found there have been dated much earlier, even as early as the fifth century by some epigraphers, and the Tobias of the Zenon papyri was in this region long before Hyrcanus (4.3.2). According to P. Lapp (1976) and the later excavators (in N. Lapp 1983), the main buildings are confirmed for the time of Hyrcanus, although there is some scattered evidence of a third-century habitation. P. Lapp suggested that the inscriptions can also be traced to the time of Hyrcanus and that the earlier Tobiad habitation was at a separate site, but others still think that the Tobias of the Zenon papyri was here (cf. Will in N. Lapp: 151; Dentzer, et al.: 207 = N. Lapp: 147). There is also considerable debate about the function of the structure called the Qasr el-'Abd. Although P. Lapp and others definitely think it was a temple (cf. Arav: 107–10), this view has not commanded a consensus among archeologists; the most recent soundings seem to go against the temple idea (Will: 199–200; also N. Lapp: 151–53).

It has long been maintained that Building B, the building commonly identified as a Samaritan temple or altar on Mt. Gerizim (Tell el-Ras), is also to be dated to the early Hellenistic period; furthermore, it has been equated with the temple referred to by Josephus as having been built by Sanballat in the time of Alexander (2.2.5). New excavations by I. Magen have suggested that this picture needs radical revision (as reported by Pummer: 167–74). There are actually two sites on Gerizim, Tell el-Ras and the main peak. On the main peak is a Hellenistic city, now in the process of being excavated. The Hellenistic pottery found on Tell el-Ras was actually brought in as fill in antiquity. This pottery caused earlier excavators to misdate Building B to the Hellenistic period. In addition, the new excavations have so far found no trace of a Samaritan temple. If further work confirms these interpretations, Josephus's story (already questionable for other reasons) of a temple built by Sanballat will be disproved.

4.3 HISTORICAL PROBLEMS AND STUDIES

4.3.1 Government and Administration

Bar-Kochva, B. *The Seleucid Army: Organization and Tactics in the Great Campaigns* (1976).

Bengtson, H. *Die Strategie in der hellenistischen Zeit* (1944, 1952; 1964_2).

A good summary of the Ptolemaic administration in Egypt is given by Bagnall (*3–10). Egypt had been divided into nomes at an early period, and the nome continued to be the major administrative unit under the Ptolemies. Three officials of equal rank, answering directly to the financial minister (*dioikētēs*) in Alexandria, were put over each nome: the nomarch, who had responsibility for agricultural production; the *oikonomos*, who was responsible for finances; and the royal scribe (*basilikos* *grammateus*), who supervised the keeping of records. At first the military was an institution equal to the administrative branch but separate from it. It was generally organized around military colonies (*klēroi*) in the local areas; the settlers of the colonies not only served in external wars but also carried out the necessary internal policing (cf. Bar-Kochva: 20–47). Thus in each nome there was a general (*stratēgos*) with military authority and the three civil officials mentioned above. With time, however, the military commander began to take a greater hand in affairs of the nome and became the dominant official, even displacing the nomarch. This was probably not only because of his policing powers but also because there was originally no single civic official in charge.

The Ptolemies seem to have governed Palestine and Syria simply as another region of Egypt rather than as a separate entity. Whether there was a governor over the entire area has been debated. Tcherikover saw no evidence in the external sources (*1937: 38–39; *1959: 60–61), but others have argued that there was one (Bengtson: 3.166–71; *Rostovtzeff: 1.344–45). Bagnall (*219) notes that the first potential evidence for such a governor comes after the battle of Raphia (217 B.C.E.) and suggests the likelihood that all major areas except Cyrene had a *stratēgos* as governor by the reign of Ptolemy IV (222–205 B.C.E.). In any case, there was a financial administrator over the entire area (*Bagnall: 15). If a regional administrative center existed, then it was probably in Akko (cf. *Hengel: 1.20); the central administration was in Alexandria. This means that Palestine was viewed merely as a part of Egypt and administered more or less as if it were another nome. Things were more complex than this in practice, however, whatever the theoretical point of view (*Tcherikover 1937: 54–57), for the inhabitants of Palestine were not accustomed to unquestioning subservience, as were the natives of Egypt. To the masses of Egypt, the Ptolemies were just other pharaohs to be served and obeyed, but Syria and Palestine were made up of different peoples with a variety of traditions and national aims. The Ptolemies were not able to carry out high-handedly anything they wished with regard to Syria and Palestine but had to make adjustments in their administrative policy to avoid alienating the people and creating serious opposition within their own borders. The coastal cities of both Phoenicia and Palestine traditionally had been under Phoenician control; under the Ptolemies they were allowed for the most part to incorporate as Greek foundations and to keep an outward form of their historical semi-independence. The local rulers, princes, and sheiks were also recognized and enlisted as allies of the administration. Nevertheless, they could still be unruly and had to be dealt with much more carefully than native Egyptians would have been.

The Egyptian Empire was divided into hyparchies (*hyparchiai*), the hyparchy being the primary administrative unit. However, we do not know the size of these (*Bagnall: 15); they may have corresponded to the subdivisions of satrapies (*mĕdînôt*) of Persian times (see 2.3.4 and the Rainer papyrus [4.2.7.3]), but this does not necessarily tell us much. It is possible that the entirety of Coele-Syria was regarded as a hyparchy, or it may have been divided into several such. An *oikonomos* handled the finances of a hyparchy: the function of the hyparch is more difficult to determine. *Hyparchos* meant only "subordinate officer" in general and may not have been the title of the governor over the hyparchy (*Bagnall: 14–15). The basic administrative unit was the village (*komē*), however, and the Ptolemaic administration carefully supervised this level as well as the higher ones. Each village had a civil mayor (*komarches*) who was probably a local man, but there were also royal officials. As the Rainer papyrus indicates, tax farming and other royal supervision was carried out at the village level as well as higher up, because the primary concern of the Ptolemaic administration was the cultivation and harvesting of revenue from the region (4.3.6). To accomplish this supervision, government officials were in every city and village, so that the Egyptian government did not lack the means of control and supervision down to the lowest level. Although it is not clear that there was a regional governor between Alexandria and the individual towns and villages, as there was under the Persians, there does seem to have been a financial minister (*oikonomos* [Rainer papyrus]), as noted above, who was presumably responsible for overseeing the collection of revenues for the region.

As a part of this de facto policy of allowing local rulers to occupy positions of authority, the high priest in Jerusalem continued to maintain his nominal headship of the country, giving Judea a degree of self-government as well as religious autonomy. Both the offices of civil and religious leadership were in the hands of the high priest; however, from an early time he was advised by—and perhaps shared authority with—a council made up of priests and leading individuals (*presbouteroi*, "elders") who formed the local aristocracy. This council bears the standard name of *gerousia* (council of the elders) in the Greek sources. Exactly when the gerousia became important in Judah's history is not certain, although it may well go back to the Persian period. Because of the decree of Antiochus III we know it was significant by the beginning of the second century at the latest (5.3.1). The importance of the high priest for secular as well as religious oversight is indicated not only by Hecateus of Abdera (4.2.2) but also by the actions of the high priest Onias II at the time of Joseph Tobiad (Josephus, *Ant.* 12.4.1 §§157–59), by the decree of Antiochus III, and by the comments of Ben Sira about the high priest Simon (50:1–21). Hecateus does not mention the council, but it is the major point of

Antiochus's decree. This indicates that Judea at this time was a theocracy (2.3.1). Although Hecateus may well represent the views of a particular segment of the priesthood in the late fourth century, this view seems to correspond to the pictures of both Persian and early Seleucid times, suggesting that no major changes took place during this period of more than two centuries. Judah was a theocracy under the Persians and remained so under the Ptolemies.

This does not mean that one cannot expect to find many small changes within this basic framework over the decades. Although a Persian governor over Judah was in place during the early and middle Persian period (2.3.4), if not later, it is possible that this office was sometimes held by the high priest himself. For example, the name "Hezekiah the governor" (*hpḥh yḥzqyh*) has been found on a coin of the late Persian period (2.2.7.2). Some have identified him with the *archiereus* ("high priest" or "chief priest") named Ezekias (Greek form of Hezekiah), whom Ptolemy I wished to return with him to Egypt (Josephus, *Ag. Ap.* 1.22 §§187–89). If so, this could mean that Ezekias held both offices; the evidence is slender but intriguing. In any case, there does not seem to have been any governor over Judea appointed by the Ptolemies. By contrast, the high priest was apparently responsible for handing over specific tribute (*Ant.* 12.4.1 §§157–59). Although Josephus's account makes it sound almost as if this were a tax on the private wealth of the high priest, it seems more likely that this payment was from public funds. Whatever the local tax administrators collected, there was still an overall payment of tribute for the country, for which the high priest had the responsibility of collection. Joseph Tobiad was able to have this particular office (*prostasia*) transferred to himself; this shows that the precise functions of the high priest varied at times, even though his basic position as head of Judea remained.

4.3.2 The Tobiad Family

Büchler, A. *Die Tobiaden und die Oniaden* (1899).
Gressmann, H. "Die ammonitischen Tobiaden." *SPAW* (1921) 663–71.
Mazar, B. "The Tobiads." *IEJ* 7 (1957) 137–45, 229–38.
Momigliano, A. "I Tobiadi nella preistoria del Moto Maccabaico." *Quinto contributo alla storia degli studi classici e del mondo antico* (1975) 597–628.
Plöger, O. "Hyrkan im Ostjordanland." *ZDPV* 71 (1955) 70–81.

As noted above (4.2.4), Josephus seems to have had some sort of Tobiad family history or chronicle available to him, which serves as the source of *Ant.* 12.4.1–11 §§157–236. Despite ingenious suggestions, the exact nature of this source is still uncertain. Two things can be said with some confidence: (1) it was probably a written source; and (2) there is a large element of romance in the account, especially with regard to Hyrcanus. By contrast, much of it fits so well with data already known that one is justified in using it cautiously for an attempted reconstruction of some aspects of Jewish history under the Ptolemies.

Mazar has produced a plausible history of the Tobiad family back to pre-exilic times. He believes that the Tobiads were an upper-class, landowning family, already well established across the Jordan in the old area of Ammon in the time of the Judean monarchy. Even if this should be doubted, however, there is good reason to see the Tobiah of the book of Nehemiah as one of the patriarchs of the family (2.4.3.5). Therefore, the "Ammonite slave" to whom Nehemiah contemptuously refers (Neh 2:10, 19) was the head of an important Jewish family who served the Persian king, probably in an official capacity. The exact site of their holdings is not stated but may well have been the same area as that occupied by a Tobiad fortress of a later time, now known from archeological excavations (4.2.8). This fortress is located at the site of Araq el-Emir in modern Jordan, not far from the Jordan River. An inscription in Aramaic lettering reads *Twbyh,* "Tobiah," and has been dated paleographically to the fifth or sixth century B.C.E., though some put it later. If the early dating is correct, he is probably an ancestor of the Tobiads known from the Hellenistic sources.

Mentioned in the Zenon papyri (4.2.1) is an individual named Tobias (*Toubias*), who seems to have been in charge of a military cleruchy near the site of his estate and an important person in the local area. He was important enough for Zenon to have visited him on his journey in 259 B.C.E., where he received hospitality for his entourage. Later, Tobias wrote to Apollonius several times and once dispatched a gift of rare wild animals to Ptolemy II via Apollonius. Following is a letter about a gift of slaves sent to Apollonius:

> Toubias to Apollonios greeting. If you and all your affairs are flourishing, and everything else is as you wish it, many thanks to the gods! I too have been well, and have thought of you at all times, as was right. I have sent to you Aineias bringing a eunuch and four boys, house-slaves and of good stock, two of whom are uncircumcised. I append descriptions of the boys for your information.
>
> Goodbye. Year 29, Xandikos 10.
>
> (*CPJ*: 1.126)

There are several interesting things revealed to us about Tobias from the Zenon papyri. First, he was of sufficient status not only to provide hospitality to the representative of a high state official in Egypt but also

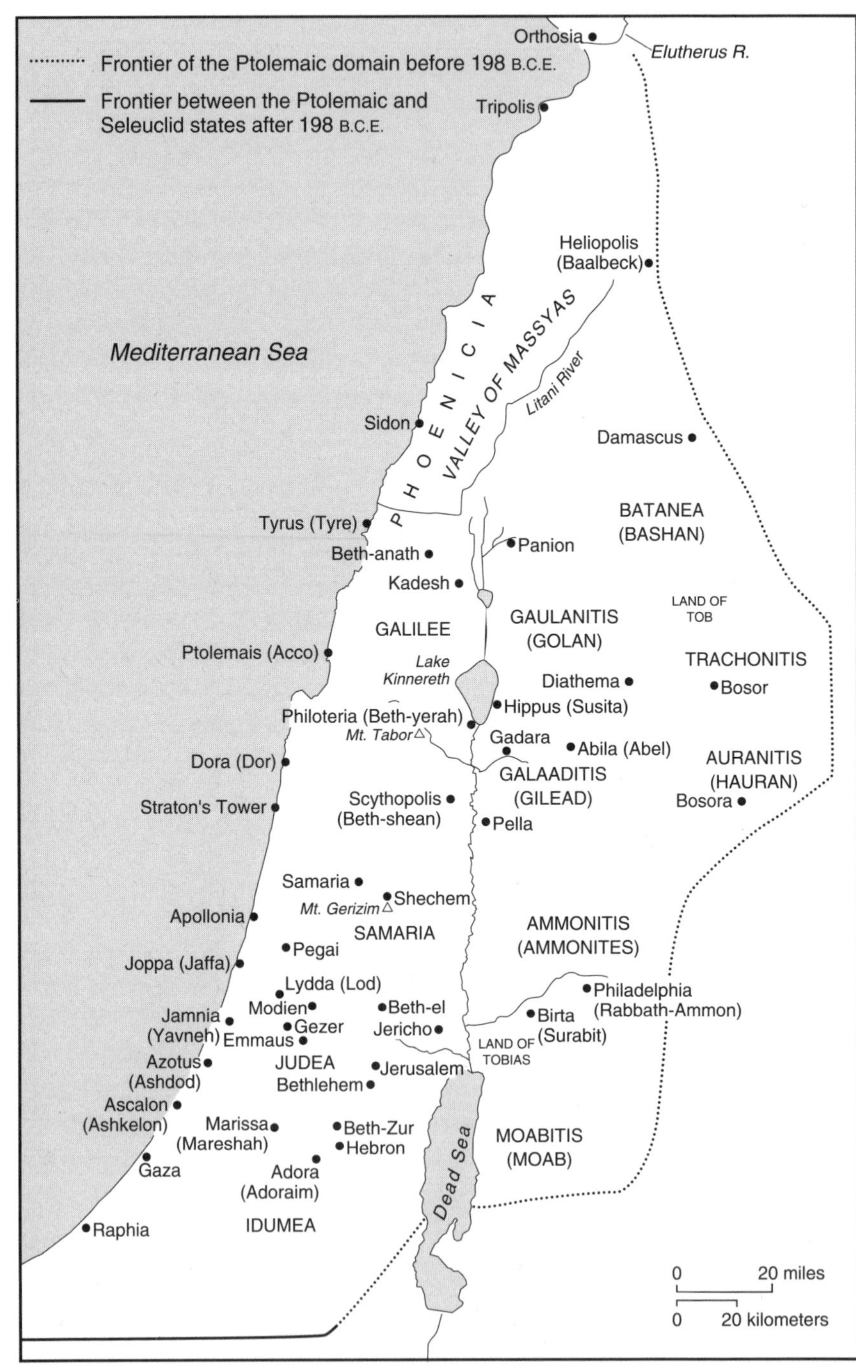

Map 3. Palestine under the Ptolemies and the Seleucids

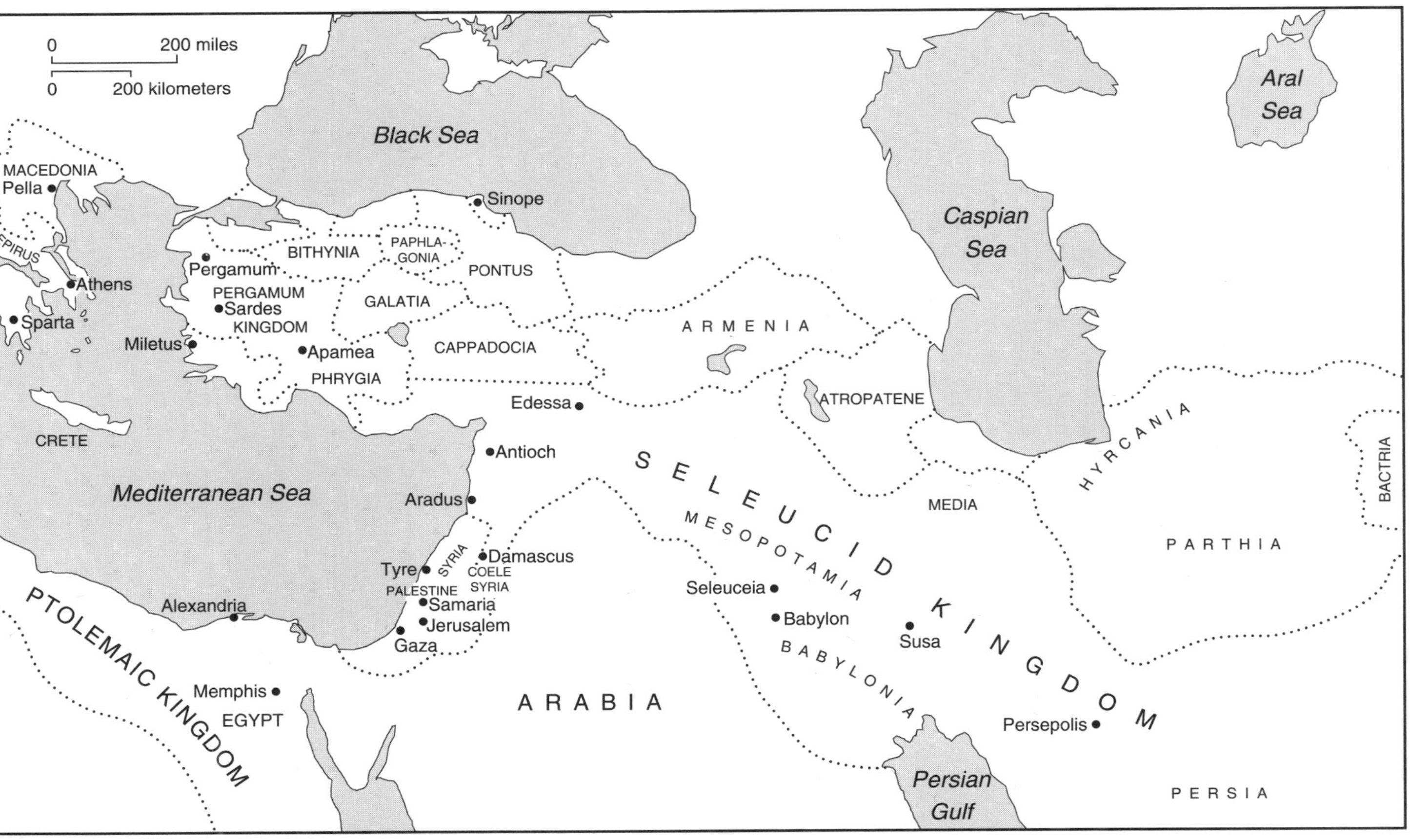

Map 4. The Hellenistic World

to send gifts to the king himself. Second, Greek was the normal written medium of communication. Although Tobias would have had a Greek scribe to do the actual writing, the indication is that Tobias himself had some knowledge of the language. Third, a broad-minded tolerance of the social conventions of Greek society is apparent in his willingness to use the conventional phrase "many thanks to the gods." Even if this phrase was the product of the scribe, Tobias would still have been aware of its use and evidently saw no reason to change it.

We do not know of this Tobias's relationship to Jerusalem, but if the family reconstruction commonly accepted is correct, then the Tobiad family had a close connection with Jerusalem, even if its family estate was in Transjordan. This is the case with Joseph, the next Tobiad whom we know of through Josephus. There is a chronological problem here, because Josephus dates his rise to power to the reign of Ptolemy V Epiphanes (ca. 204–180 B.C.E.); however, certain details within his own narrative are at odds with this (e.g., Joseph is an old man after only twenty years as a tax farmer, although he began this job as a young man [cf. *Ant.* 12.4.2 §160 with 12.4.7 §196]), not to mention the impossibility of this dating with other facts known of the history of the time: the tax-farming rights for Coele-Syria are controlled by Ptolemy V even after this area had been taken from him by Antiochus III. Joseph dies after twenty-two years as a tax farmer, at the time of the accession of Seleucus IV in 187 B.C.E. (*Ant.* 12.4.10 §§223–24), which means that he began his career in 209, several years before Ptolemy V came to the throne. Joseph begins his career in opposition to Onias (II), who was succeeded by Simon (II); from Ben Sira 51:1-4 we can gather that Simon was high priest at the time of the transfer of Palestine to the Seleucids (200 B.C.E.), suggesting that Onias's career ended before Ptolemy V came to the throne. Therefore, most scholars feel that Josephus has misdated Joseph's career and should have put it in the reign of Ptolemy III Euergetes (246–221 B.C.E.), rather than Ptolemy V Epiphanes.

If this dating is correct, Joseph was probably the son of the Tobias of the Zenon papyri. It is at this time that we first hear of rivalry between the Tobiad family and the high priestly family, the Oniads. The high priest of Jerusalem, who was named Onias (usually referred to as Onias II), was reluctant to pay the tribute to Egypt. The narrative in Josephus states that this was because of his being mean and tightfisted. Would that history could be so simplistically explained by appeal to such personal traits! On the contrary, it is far more likely that Onias had a reasonable political motive for his approach to the payment. The simplest explanation, now widely accepted, is that Onias was a pro-Seleucid who was hoping for a change of political fortune, which would render the payment to Egypt unnecessary. The conflict between the Ptolemies and Seleucids suggested that Judea might not always be under Ptolemaic control.

Onias was Joseph Tobiad's uncle (Joseph's mother being Onias's sister), but Joseph nevertheless saw advantages in the situation and immediately intervened to see that the tribute was paid. In so doing he presented himself as a champion of the people. This not only showed up Onias but suggested to the Ptolemaic ruler that Joseph could be a useful power in Palestine. Therefore, when he bid for tax-farming rights to Palestine, the king was quite willing to grant them, not least because Joseph promised to double the sum previously collected. For twenty-two years Joseph pursued his career, becoming quite wealthy and influential under the Ptolemaic administration.

Much of the Tobiad legend given by Josephus centers on Hyrcanus. This young man was ambitious and apparently quite willing to use others to gain his own ends. Therefore, he is pictured on his trip to the Ptolemaic court as freely and high-handedly using his father's wealth to impress the court. This was not merely for his own indulgence, however, but was a means of gaining favor and building prestige, so that the Egyptian king would be willing to grant favors in return. The indication is that Hyrcanus replaced his father as the king's tax farmer for Palestine. Not surprisingly, Hyrcanus's exploits alienated his father as well as his brothers. The result was that he was unable to establish himself in Jerusalem as he wished but had to retire to his estate across the Jordan. (Josephus states that Hyrcanus was the one who built the estate, which archeological evidence tends to confirm, but there are some complications to this assessment [4.2.8].) According to Josephus, the accession of Antiochus IV to the Seleucid throne was the occasion for Hyrcanus to commit suicide.

In assessing the Tobias legend, it is clear that many of the story's details are incredible (e.g., the 16,000-talent tribute that Joseph promised to collect from Syria and Palestine), whereas others are the stock in trade of romantic fiction (e.g., Hyrcanus's precocious wit). If the outline of the story seems credible, however, then we have an account of Joseph, a member of a leading Jewish family with its base in Transjordan. He managed to become tax farmer for Palestine, probably under Ptolemy III in the latter part of the third century B.C.E. This office was likely to have been gained at some expense to the power of the high priest, who was the nominal head of the Jews in Palestine. Joseph's son Hyrcanus took over his office, whether by normal inheritance or intrigue, and maintained his pro-Ptolemaic stance. Many of the details regarding Hyrcanus's conflict with his brothers are also credible, such a quarrel itself being likely because of the political situation, as even Josephus indicates (*Ant.* 12.4.11

§§228–29). By this time the dynamic Seleucid ruler Antiochus III was on the scene. Hyrcanus's brothers seem to have viewed the Ptolemies as a part of the order about to pass away, so they threw their lot in with the Seleucids, as did the high priest Simon II. Their quarrel with Hyrcanus was not just personal but arose from being on quite different political sides. Hyrcanus banked on Palestine's remaining in Egyptian hands; the brothers, on its passing to the Seleucids.

Hyrcanus's brothers turned out to be correct: Palestine was under Seleucid rule by 200 B.C.E. Hyrcanus himself had lost his power base, which depended on his having a position in the Ptolemaic administration, and retired to his estate in Transjordan, where he allegedly maintained himself by raiding the neighboring Arabs. Nevertheless, Hyrcanus seems to have maintained some influence in Jerusalem. According to 2 Macc 3:11, he had money on deposit in the temple, which the finance minister of Seleucus IV attempted to confiscate for the imperial treasury. (He is referred to as Hyrcanus, son of Tobias, but this may be a generic designation or even a slip of the pen.) Although Onias II and Joseph had been rivals, Hyrcanus evidently reached an agreement with Onias III, who attempted to keep his money safe from the Seleucid minister. This time a Tobiad and an Oniad were on the same side, but only because the Tobiad family was split. A little later, members of the Tobiad family were apparently to play a significant role in the events leading up the Maccabean revolt (5.4.3.2). These events did not include Hyrcanus, however; whether Hyrcanus's life and influence came to an end with such a melodramatic gesture as suicide is questionable, but the story indicates that Hyrcanus was off the scene by the time of the events under Antiochus IV.

4.3.3 The Rise of Apocalypticism

Charlesworth, J. H., with J. R. Mueller. *The New Testament Apocrypha and Pseudepigrapha: A Guide to Publications* (1987) 20–24.

Collins, J. J., ed. *Apocalypse: The Morphology of a Genre* (1979).

———. *The Apocalyptic Imagination* (1984).

Grabbe, L. L. "The Social Setting of Early Jewish Apocalypticism." *JSP* 4 (1989) 27–47.

Hanson, P. D. "Apocalypticism." *IDBSup* (1976) 29–31.

Hellholm, D., ed. *Apocalypticism in the Mediterranean World and the Near East* (1983).

Knibb, M. A. "Prophecy and the Emergence of the Jewish Apocalypses." *Israel's Prophetic Tradition* (1982) 161–65.

Kvanig, H. S. *Roots of Apocalyptic* (1988).

Lambert, W. G. *The Background of Jewish Apocalyptic* (1978).

Müller, H.-P. "Magisch-mantische Weisheit und die Gestalt Daniels." *Ugarit-Forschungen* 1 (1969) 79–94.
———. "Mantische Weisheit und Apokalyptik." *VTSup* 22 (1972) 268–93.
Sanders, E. P. "The Genre of Palestinian Jewish Apocalypses." *Apocalypticism in the Mediterranean World* (1983) 447–59.
Smith, J. Z. "Wisdom and Apocalyptic." *Religious Syncretism in Antiquity* (1975) 131–56.
Stone, M. E. "Lists of Revealed Things in the Apocalyptic Literature." *Magnalia Dei* (1976) 439–43.
VanderKam, J. C. *Enoch and the Growth of an Apocalyptic Tradition* (1984).
———. "The Prophetic-Sapiential Origins of Apocalyptic Thought." *A Word in Season* (1986) 163–76.
Yarbro Collins, A., ed. *Early Christian Apocalypticism: Genre and Social Setting* (1986).

The roots of apocalypticism go back a long way, both in ancient Near Eastern tradition (Kvanig; VanderKam; Lambert) and in Israel to well before the exile. A variety of origins have been proposed over the years. Apocalypticism has often been thought to derive from prophecy, but in recent years suggestions concerning its roots have included wisdom, especially mantic wisdom (Müller 1969; 1971). Any suggestion must take account of the fact that apocalypticism is not unique to Israel but is found widely over the ancient Near East, especially in the Hellenistic period (Smith). It is becoming common to see multiple elements in apocalypticism, although the recent study by VanderKam (1986) notes that prophecy and mantic wisdom share many elements.

One problem is how to define apocalypticism. A good deal of work has been done on the genre of apocalypse. Despite the widely used definition worked out by the Society of Biblical Literature seminar on the subject (Collins 1979), there is still not complete agreement (cf. the criticisms of Sanders, Knibb, and Charlesworth, as well as Collins's reply [1984: 8]). The debate continues (Yarbro Collins: especially 1–96; see also Grabbe: 42 n.14), but most scholars now see the genre limited to a fairly narrow group of early Jewish and other writings. The apocalypse as a literary type probably developed sometime during the Persian period (some scholars consider even such Old Testament prophetic passages as Zechariah or Isaiah 24–27 to be apocalyptic), but we have none preserved on which there is general agreement. Therefore, the oldest accepted apocalypses seem to date from the Greek period, but some passages of *1 Enoch* probably come from early during this time, possibly even the time of the Diadochi.

Scholars often speak as if apocalypticism were limited to apocalypses; in fact, a number of literary genres can carry apocalyptic messages (cf.

Grabbe: 28–30). Although actual apocalypses are perhaps rare outside a handful of Jewish writings, apocalypticism is found in a number of Near Eastern writings that are not themselves apocalypses (Smith). There is also a tendency to assume the production of apocalyptic writings was limited to certain situations (e.g., times of crisis, marginal groups, deprived individuals), whereas they can arise in a variety of social situations (Grabbe: 30–33). The sociological study of apocalypticism has really only begun.

4.3.4 Translation of the Bible into Greek

Brock, S. P., et al. *A Classified Bibliography of the Septuagint* (1973).
Jellicoe, S. *The Septuagint and Modern Study* (1968).
Schürer: 3:474–93.
Swete, H. *An Introduction to the Old Testament in Greek* (1914).
Tov, E. *The Text-Critical Use of the Septuagint in Biblical Research* (1981).
———. "The Septuagint." *Mikra* (1988) 161–88.

One of the most significant events for Judaism as a religion was the translation of the Hebrew Scriptures into Greek. Exactly when and how this came about is unknown, although it seems clear that different parts were translated at different times. According to the legend in the *Letter of Aristeas* (4.2.5.6), the translation was done for Ptolemy II's library. This seems most unlikely—Greeks were not generally interested in the native literature—and modern scholarship has largely rejected this account. More likely, the Pentateuch was translated as a unit by Egyptian Jews for their own liturgical needs. The mid-third century (which happens to fall within Ptolemy II's reign), however, seems a reasonable date and is widely accepted. The Jewish writer Demetrius (5.2.10.1) already used the LXX as the basis for his exegesis, which would put it in existence before 200 B.C.E., assuming that his reference to Ptolemy IV is authentic. Translation of the rest of the books now found in the Jewish canon was probably finished by 100 B.C.E. or not long afterward, but the time and place of their completion are uncertain.

The LXX translation is significant for two reasons. First, it made the biblical material available to the increasing number of Jews whose first language was Greek and who knew little or no Hebrew. The LXX became the Bible of the Greek-speaking Jews to the extent that its very letter was considered inspired and was used for detailed exegesis by such writers as Philo of Alexandria (7.2.2). Second, it attests to the variety of biblical texts circulating during the centuries before the fall of Jerusalem. In some sections the LXX is quite different from the MT, which became the standard Hebrew text of the Old Testament. Discoveries at Qumran now support what had often been argued by scholars, namely, that the LXX, where different, often attests a different Hebrew *Vorlage*.

For a complete bibliography to 1969, see Brock, et al.; this can be updated with the annual listing of publications in the *Bulletin of the International Organization for Septuagint and Cognate Studies*. Jellicoe's is the basic introduction, but it needs supplementing from the older work by Swete.

4.3.5 Letter of Antiochus III to Zeuxis

Bickerman, E. J. "Une question d'authenticité les privilèges juifs." *Studies in Jewish and Christian History* (1980) 2.24–43.

Cohen, G. M. *The Seleucid Colonies* (1978).

Gauger, J.-D. *Beiträge zur jüdischen Apologetik* (1977).

Marcus, R. "Appendix D. Antiochus III and the Jews." *Josephus* (1943) 7.743–66.

Momigliano, A. Review of *Beiträge zur jüdischen Apologetik*, by J.-D. Gauger. *Classical Philology* 77 (1982) 258–61.

Schalit, A. "The Letter of Antiochus III to Zeuxis regarding the Establishment of Jewish Military Colonies in Phrygia and Lydia." *JQR* 50 (1959–60) 289–318.

According to Josephus (*Ant*. 12.3.4 §§148–53), Antiochus wrote a letter to his governor in Phrygia and Lydia to stop the revolutionary activities there by bringing in Jewish military colonists. The first part of the letter reads as follows:

> King Antiochus to Zeuxis, his father, greeting. If you are in good health, it is well. I also am in sound health. Learning that the people in Lydia and Phrygia are revolting, I have come to consider this as requiring very serious attention on my part, and, on taking counsel with my friends as to what should be done, I determined to transport two thousand Jewish families with their effects from Mesopotamia and Babylonia to the fortresses and most important places. For I am convinced that they will be loyal guardians of our interests because of their piety to God, and I know that they have had the testimony of my forefathers to their good faith and eagerness to do as they are asked. (§§148–50)

This decree seems to show the king as highly impressed by the Jews as a people, and it attests to their usefulness as military colonists. Not surprisingly, there have been questions as to whether the decree is authentic or just another piece of Jewish propaganda (see Marcus for discussion and older bibliography). Nevertheless, its genuineness has been argued for by a number of important scholars (Schalit; Bickerman; Tcherikover [*1959: 287–88]), and it has been accepted by others as a usable historical source (e.g., Cohen: 5–9). But in a detailed study Gauger has recently come out against it (3–151), arguing that Josephus was not quoting a Greek author but instead saw the letter in a Jewish source. Momigliano, although recognizing the quality of Gauger's study, did not find himself convinced.

4.3.6 Socioeconomic Questions

Davies, J. K. "Cultural, Social and Economic Features of the Hellenistic World." *CAH*[2] (1984) 7.1.257–320.

Kreissig, H. *Wirtschaft und Gesellschaft im Seleukidenreich* (1978).

*Will, et al.: 2.495–565.

The initial impression is that scholarship is richly blessed with original documents concerning the economic situation of Ptolemaic Egypt. In one sense this impression is true, and one for which the researcher can be thankful; however, there are still major questions that cannot yet be given a satisfactory answer, and the abundant papyrological sources at times only delineate the range of possibilities and may do nothing more than whet the appetite.

Thanks to the papyri, especially the Zenon papyri, we have an important window into the economic situation of Palestine in about the middle of the third century. The papyri tell us especially about matters of trade and commerce. Palestine was apparently treated more or less like any other Egyptian nome by the Ptolemaic government (4.3.1) and was an important source of those commodities Egypt itself lacked. Wherever possible, trade and communication were by sea, and Palestine possessed important ports at Gaza, Strato's Tower (Caesarea), Jaffa, and Ptolemais (Akko). Much of the traffic between Syria and Egypt was carried on by Nile boats (Greek *kelētes*, *kubaiai*) rather than large seagoing vessels. Because much still had to be carried by caravan, Palestine also served as a transit center for overland routes from Phoenicia, Mesopotamia, and Arabia. For example, one papyrus contains a long list of items, including honey, wine, cheese, nuts, and potter's earth, named as products brought from areas outside Syria (*P. Zen*. 59012); however, such items usually came from territories in Asia Minor and Cyprus, which belonged to the Ptolemies. The major item from Arabia was incense, for which Gaza served as the trade center. Mendes, in Egypt, was a manufacturing center for unguents, most of the raw materials evidently coming to it through Gaza (*Tcherikover 1937: 25–27).

The agricultural products of Syria that were most important to Egypt were wheat, wine, and oil; although Egypt itself produced some of these products, they were not always of equally high quality. The Ptolemaic financial administration saw to it that most agricultural products were strictly regulated and taxed; however, the papyri indicate that much of the trade was actually in government hands, with the merchants involved only as middlemen (*Tcherikover 1937: 20–23). It appears that the bulk of the imported grain was from royal estates in Syria, which explains not only how it moved without restriction but also why it was imported even though Egypt itself produced a good deal of grain. Oil was also a government monopoly, even though merchants were allowed to handle the actual importation; once the merchants brought oil into Egypt, they had to sell it for a fixed price to the government.

Slaves are the Syrian export most often mentioned in the Zenon letters. They seem to have been in short supply in Egypt, judging from the high prices they fetched. The expectation of profits would explain why the slave trade from Syria was so brisk. The slaves were primarily children and young women, which suggests that they were not intended for hard labor in agriculture. Rather, their primary function seems to have been service in the households of their owners. Prostitution of female slaves is specifically mentioned in the papyri (e.g., *PSI* 406; see also *WHJP*: 6.91), but boys may also have been imported for this purpose, even though that is not referred to in the extant papyri. There is also an indication that slaves were used in the wool industry (*Tcherikover 1937: 18).

An important document that relates particularly to slavery but also contains information on administration and taxation is the Rainer papyrus (SB 8008; see 4.2.7.3). Several points emerge from this document. The extension of the bureaucracy to the lowest level, the village, is evident. All property was noted and records kept for tax purposes; incentives encouraged the reporting of violators among one's neighbors, for the informant received a portion of the penalties and one-third of any confiscated goods. We get a brief glimpse of the myriad of taxes in the passing reference to the "pasture tax" and the "crown tax," as well as to the role played by tax farmers in seeing that all property was registered and the taxes collected. With regard to slaves, the promulgation of such a decree suggests a widespread practice of enslaving free individuals. This would naturally cause concern on the part of the government, because illegal enslavement would reduce the available peasant population for working the royal estates and contributing to the tax revenues.

4.4 SYNTHESIS

4.4.1 Overview

The first part of the Hellenistic period is better documented than is the period of Persian rule. The Alexander historians have left full accounts of Alexander's conquests, and the activities of the Diadochi are recorded in detail. When it comes to the third century and the Ptolemies and Seleucids, however, there are some large and exasperating gaps, although certain periods are reasonably well recorded.

Alexander's brief period of rule (336–323) was occupied mainly with conquest and military activity, leaving only the last few years to work on the problems of organization in his new empire. There was no clear successor at his death, which resulted in approximately forty years of struggle among various of his generals (the Diadochi) for control of the vast territory from Macedonia to India. By about 300 B.C.E. the division was threefold, which the events of the next twenty years did not significantly alter: Greece and Macedonia were ruled by the Antigonid dynasty; Asia Minor, northern Syria, and the entire area to the east of the Euphrates by the Seleucids; and Egypt, Cyprus, and some small areas in Asia Minor by the Ptolemies. Much of the third century (ca. 280–200) was taken up with controversy between the Seleucids and the Ptolemies over Coele-Syria (southern Syria and Palestine). In a treaty of 301 this region was assigned to Seleucus; however, Ptolemy had just seized it and refused to return it. Because Ptolemy had been very helpful to Seleucus in the past, the latter did not press his claim, but the Seleucid Empire continued to regard the region as rightfully theirs. The result was the series of Syrian wars, in which the Seleucids attempted to take the territory back.

This forms the backdrop to the history of Judea during the early Greek period. There are gaps in the history of the Hellenistic kingdoms for this time, but we still know a good deal of the broader picture. For Palestine specifically, however, we have probably even less information than for the time of Achaemenid rule. The real question is if one can write a history of Judah under Ptolemaic rule, because our knowledge of specific events for the century and a quarter between Alexander and Seleucid domination is so skimpy. It is not difficult to situate Judah in the general history of the Ptolemaic Empire, both politically and economically, but to find a plausible background for the state is not the same as writing its history. Josephus is not of much help except with regard to the Tobiad family, and the valuable Zenon papyri tell us much about economic matters at a particular time but little about economic developments or political events.

Therefore, in some ways the Ptolemaic period is even less known than the Persian; all we have are a few fragments—a keyhole here and there for a brief glimpse into what is otherwise closed. We are attempting to reconstruct the mosaic of third-century Jewish history from a few odd pieces. We can try, but the cogency of the result remains a very subjective judgment.

4.4.2 Alexander and His Conquests (336–323 B.C.E.)

Alexander was only twenty when his father, Philip II, was assassinated in 336, but he was quickly acclaimed by Philip's trusted generals Antipater and Parmenion and by the army. His immediate concern was to secure Greece, because of fears that treaties imposed by Philip would not necessarily be adhered to after his death. Any question about Alexander's leadership ability was soon answered by his brilliant maneuvers in swiftly squelching the anti-Macedonian developments in Thessaly and cowing the rest of Greece. Before the end of 336, he had been formally elected head of the Corinthian League, which included all the important states of Greece except Sparta.

By early 335 Alexander faced a variety of threats to his rule. The first was from Celtic tribes in Thrace. Then the democratic party at Thebes seized power and was promised support by Athens and other states. A Greek revolt seemed imminent. Alexander acted quickly and mercilessly: Thebes was taken and razed, and its inhabitants were sold into slavery. The lesson was all too plain to the other Greek states, which hastily fell in line. Thus by the end of 335 Alexander was able to return to Macedonia and prepare for the invasion of Persia.

Alexander crossed the Dardanelles in the spring of 334 with a force of about thirty thousand, and five thousand cavalry troops. Their first encounter with the Persians was at the crossing of the Granicus River. The Persian army was smaller than the exaggerated figures of later legend; the Greek invasion had, in fact, caught the Persians by surprise. Many of the cities of Asia Minor were Greek but were ruled by Persian-appointed tyrants or oligarchies. Because of Alexander's proclaimed policy of restoring democracy, popular uprisings in many of these cities established democratic governments which promptly declared for Alexander. In his advance south through Ionia, only in Miletus did he have to besiege a city. After this, Caria also resisted, and the new Persian commander-in-chief, Memnon, held Halicarnassus; but Alexander took the latter city before the end of 334. In early 333 he marched to Ancyra and then turned south toward the Cilician Gates. Had the Persians properly secured this pass, they could have stopped him, but once again Alexander pushed ahead of his main force and reached the Gates long before he was expected. He was able to take them and cross the Tarsus before the Persians could mount a proper defense.

So far Alexander had met little effective opposition from the Persians. One of their strengths should have been their fleet; however, Alexander's strategy was to ignore the fleet, partly because he simply could not afford the cost of maintaining his own fleet. Instead, he concentrated on land conquest, although his strategy included taking some of the important coastal bases. It would have been impossible to occupy all of them, of course, but there was little likelihood that the Persians could induce Greece to defect, and it was impossible to cut off all communications from there to Alexander. In addition, as Greek cities were liberated their ships quietly left the Persian fleet and went home. In the end Darius himself finished the job by taking away all but fifteen hundred men for the army he was gathering to oppose Alexander.

The crucial battle with Darius was at Issus in the autumn of 333. Alexander had set up camp in Issus and moved south after leaving his sick and wounded there, assuming that Darius was at Sochi. His intelligence was wrong, however. Darius attacked Issus in Alexander's rear and wiped out those he had left behind; he then positioned his army to wait for Alexander. Although the Persians inflicted considerable damage on Alexander's phalanx in the subsequent battle, the result was disastrous for Darius. He escaped, but his family—wife, mother, and daughters—was captured, and most of his Greek mercenaries deserted and made their way to Egypt.

Alexander continued south toward Phoenicia and Egypt. Except for Tyre, the Phoenician cities welcomed him, and Damascus fell without a fight. This gave the Greeks Darius's war chest, which had been sent to Damascus before the battle of Issus, and Alexander's acute shortage of funds was finally resolved. Darius himself sent messengers with proposed terms for negotiation, but Alexander's reply was calculated to be unacceptable to the Persians. By taking Phoenicia, Alexander delivered the final blow to the Persian fleet. Tyre refused his request to offer a sacrifice at the temple of "Hercules" (the city god, Melqart), however, and a seven-month siege was necessary. Tyre fell in midsummer of 332, and the Greek army moved on down the coast. The Jewish account of a visit to Jerusalem at this time is legendary (see below and 4.2.5.9). Gaza also refused entry and had to be besieged, falling after two months.

Egypt submitted without resistance late in 332. Alexander spent the winter there, arranging the government of this valuable satrapy, founding the city of Alexandria, and visiting the famous oracle of Ammon in Siwa. In the spring of 331 he was back in Syria to punish a revolt in Samaria (see below); then he marched across the Euphrates and Tigris toward the Persian heartland. Darius met him at Gaugamela on 1 October 331. Just as at Issus, Darius fled the scene at the first sign of Persian faltering, even though there was plenty of fight left in his troops, which initiated an unnecessary rout. The Persians had not lacked either military skill or formidable forces; their weakness was Darius as commander-in-chief. If he had left the command to some of his most able satraps, then the invasions would have been much more difficult for the Greeks. As it was, the fate of the Persian Empire was sealed, and it was only a matter of time until Darius himself was taken. Alexander went on to Babylon, where he was welcomed, and to Persepolis, where he burned Xerxes' palace in a gesture of revenge for the invasion of Greece one hundred and fifty years before. He reached Ecbatana in the middle of 330. Darius had fled there after Gaugamela but now had moved eastward, where he was attempting to raise a new army. Alexander pursued but found that the Persian king had already been assassinated by one of own satraps.

With Darius dead, Alexander proceeded formally to succeed him. This was an important step, because Alexander was not just king of Macedonia who now also ruled over the Persians. Rather, he took both the tiara and many of the customs of the Persian monarchy. This became a source of friction to the Greeks, some of whom had criticized Alexander as early as the time of his consultation of the oracle at Ammon. The custom the Greeks most objected to was obeisance (*proskynēsis*), which they interpreted as prostration, an act reserved for the gods. Alexander's actions not only were contrary to the fairly egalitarian tradition of the Macedonians but also, in the opinion of many, verged on impiety. Several individuals were later to pay with their lives for not showing sufficient enthusiasm for the new custom (e.g., Callisthenes).

In 329 Alexander moved farther into the eastern realms of the Persian Empire, founding cities and subduing the natives, although some of the wild nomadic tribes were not easy to subjugate. The city foundations were partly to serve as a military presence in areas still far from tamed. In the summer of 329 Alexander caught up with Darius's slayer, the satrap Bessus, and had him executed. Bessus was succeeded by Spitamenes, and it took the Greeks another year and a half to defeat him. Northern India (modern Pakistan) was reached in 326, and Alexander began his conquest of this area. His soldiers mutinied at this point, however, and refused to go any farther, so it is still questionable how successful he would have been in the invasion of India. In 325 he sent his fleet home via the Indus and Persian Gulf and himself marched with the army back through Beluchistan, a tactical error that caused him to lose a good many men.

Back in Babylon, he set about consolidating his rule. Whether he would have been as successful in peace as in war is debatable. In the remaining year or two of his life there were mutinies and executions because of unhappiness among many Greeks who did not approve of his "Orientalizing" policy or his manner of rule. A major issue was his requirement of deification by the Greek cities, although the exact nature of this command is unclear; another was the order for the Greek cities to accept back their exiles. This all ended abruptly in 323, when Alexander died at Babylon at the age of 32.

Exactly what happened in Judea during Alexander's conquest is largely unknown. As noted, he marched rapidly south down the Mediterranean coast (though delayed by the sieges of Tyre and Gaza) with the object of reaching Egypt as soon as possible. In 331 he pushed north up the coast toward the Euphrates and the Persian heartland. At no point did Alexander show interest in the interior of the country. Josephus gives the story that Alexander came to Jerusalem to punish Judea for refusing assistance in the siege of Tyre, but instead ended up honoring the high priest; however, this is only a variant of the Alexander legend and has no basis in fact (4.2.5.9). Too much is known of Alexander's itinerary and timetable to give this story any credence, and there are clear signs of Jewish apology in the account. Alexander no doubt received the fealty of the Judean nation on his way to or from Egypt, as he did that of other peoples, but representatives would have come to him, probably at Jamnia, not he to them in Jerusalem.

The only event relating to the interior of Palestine from Alexander's time is the rebellion of Samaria. The Samaritans had submitted to the Macedonians, as had the other smaller nations of Syria, but then the city of Samaria rebelled, burning Andromachus, the governor left in charge by Alexander. The Greek response was understandably severe: the city was taken, the inhabitants slaughtered or sold into slavery, and the site turned into a Macedonian colony. The Wadi Daliyeh papyri (2.2.2) seem to be the archives of individuals fleeing from the destruction of Samaria, who took refuge in caves near the Jordan but were nevertheless tracked down by the Greek soldiers and slaughtered. The few citizens who escaped the destruction of Samaria apparently moved to the area of ancient Shechem and settled there.

4.4.3 The Diadochi (323–281 B.C.E.)

The four decades of the Diadochi (from Greek *diadochoi*, "successors") were years of continual fighting and frequent territorial and political change. Only an outline is given here, which concentrates on some of the major personalities and particular situations at crucial points during the period.

When Alexander died, his Persian princess, Rhoxane, was pregnant. Although Perdiccas was Alexander's confidant and most obvious successor, the army proclaimed Philip's half-wit son (Alexander's half-brother) Philip III, with the proviso that if Rhoxane had a son, then he would rule jointly with Philip. Antipater had been left in charge of Macedon but had been recalled to Babylon just before Alexander died. Antigonus was over Phrygia, Lysimachus over Thrace, and Ptolemy over Egypt. Ptolemy did not believe the empire would survive Alexander and had already begun surreptitiously to carve out a kingdom in Egypt. Seleucus was over the elite guard.

The initial situation altered drastically within several years (322–321). Revolts broke out immediately, including a revolt of mercenaries in Bactria and the Lamnian War in Greece. Perdiccas set out to pacify the rest of Asia, but Antigonus refused to cooperate. Perdiccas's position was further weakened by Philip III's marriage to the daughter of Olympias (Alexander's mother). When Perdiccas went against Antigonus to force obedience, the latter fled to Antipater and formed a coalition with him. Perdiccas began his campaign of bringing the others in line by an attack on Ptolemy, ostensibly over Alexander's body, which Ptolemy had stolen and taken to Egypt. After an initial defeat, Perdiccas's ambitions were brought to an abrupt halt: he was murdered by Seleucus and other of his companions. By 321 the situation was the following: Seleucus was given Babylon, and Ptolemy continued to hold Egypt; Antipater was the leading figure in Asia, with Antigonus, his lieutenant; Rhoxane had borne a son, Alexander.

The next phase covered 321–317 B.C.E. Antipater died in 319, but instead of naming as successor his son Cassander, he passed on the succession to another of Alexander's former officers, Polyperchon. By this time Antigonus had basically established his rule over Asia. Cassander, who had been left in charge of Greece and Macedonia, made an alliance with Antigonus to defeat Polyperchon. Olympias attempted to play politics by having Philip III and his wife killed, but she was, in turn, killed by Cassander, who also imprisoned Rhoxane and her son. By 317 Cassander had control of Macedonia and Greece, and Antigonus held

Asia (although Seleucus remained in Babylon). Ptolemy continued to hold Egypt.

More fighting occupied 317–311. Antigonus marched to Babylon for an accounting from Seleucus, who did not wait for him but fled to Egypt, where with Ptolemy's help he organized a coalition against Antigonus. Much of the rest of the period of the Diadochi can be summarized as a contest between Antigonus (and later his son) on one side and a coalition headed by Seleucus and Ptolemy on the other side. The allies divided the territory and issued an ultimatum to Antigonus to accept it; when he refused, war resumed. One of the important events of the war was the battle of Gaza in the summer of 312 between Ptolemy and Antigonus's son Demetrius. Ptolemy's victory paved the way for Seleucus to return to Babylon (marking the start of the Seleucid era which was widely used in antiquity). Antigonus was able to turn most of Greece against Cassander, but his attempts to recapture Babylon ended in stalemate. Finally, the treaty of 311 gave the following division of territory: Antigonus over Asia; Lysimachus over Thrace; Ptolemy over Egypt; and Cassander as regent over Macedonia until Alexander came of age. Seleucus had de facto possession of Babylon.

The next round of fighting (311–301) was important because it ended in a division of Alexander's empire, which was often mistakenly remembered as if it had been a permanent division (cf. Dan 11:3-4). In 310 Cassander had Alexander and Rhoxane killed, but over the next few years, most of Greece fell to Antigonus and Demetrius. These two were also able to dislodge Ptolemy from Cyprus in 306, but an offensive against Egypt failed. Antigonus took the title "king" in 306, as did Ptolemy in 305, and then Cassander, Lysimachus, and Seleucus. In 302 the alliance was reformed against Antigonus, who was killed at the battle of Ipsus. The division of 301 was not the last word but was significant: Cassander still had Greece (with his brother over Caria and Cilicia); Lysimachus had the rest of Asia and Thrace; Seleucus was given Armenia and Syria, as well as Babylon. However, as well as holding onto Egypt, Ptolemy (excluded from the negotiations for not taking sufficient part in the battle) seized southern Syria and Palestine, even though the treaty assigned them to Seleucus. This was to remain the Ptolemaic kingdom for the next century.

The final round of fighting (301–280) ended with the death of the last of the Diadochi. Demetrius was at first without a country but managed to form an alliance with Seleucus, which allowed him to retake Athens in 294. He succeeded because Cassander had died in 297 and his sons were fighting between themselves over Macedonia. When one of the sons called on Demetrius for help, Demetrius gave it at first but then had the son slain and himself proclaimed king. His mastery of this "Greek kingdom" was short-lived, however, partly because of his plans to extend his own territory. Opposed by an alliance led by Lysimachus, he was driven from Greece in 287 and ended his life in 283, after defeat and capture by Seleucus. This left Lysimachus over the whole of Greece, a danger that Seleucus quickly countered. Lysimachus was defeated and killed in the battle of Cyrus in 281. Seleucus then proclaimed himself king of Macedon but was killed by a disaffected son of Ptolemy, Keraunos, who became king of Macedon. At his death, the dynasty passed to Antigonus Gonatas, a son of Demetrius. Thus despite his lack of success, Antigonus's memory was nevertheless perpetuated in the rule of the Antigonid dynasty over Greece. The basic threefold division of Alexander's empire—Greece and Macedonia under the Antigonids, Syria and Mesopotamia under the Seleucids, and Egypt under the Ptolemies—remained for two centuries, until it was finally ended by the Romans.

During the wars of the Diadochi, Palestine was fought in and over many times. We have no details for the most part but can assume that this had a devastating effect on the population and economy of the country. It has been conjectured that the "giants" (offspring of women and angels) who devastate the earth in *1 Enoch* are symbols of the Diadochi, whose military activities seemed to threaten human life in the country (*JLBM*: 51–52). The only direct evidence about Judea at this time is possibly that given in a single reference by Josephus, who states that Ptolemy I took Jerusalem on the Sabbath by pretending to enter to sacrifice at the temple (*Ant.* 12.1.1 §§3–10; *Ag. Ap.* 1.22 §§209–12). The source is Agatharchides of Cnidus who is quoted as follows:

> The people known as Jews, who inhabit the most strongly fortified of cities, called by the natives Jerusalem, have a custom of abstaining from work every seventh day; on those occasions they neither bear arms nor take any agricultural operations in hand, nor engage in any other form of public service, but pray with outstretched hands in the temples until the evening. Consequently, because the inhabitants, instead of protecting their city, persevered in their folly, Ptolemy, son of Lagus, was allowed to enter with his army; the country was thus given over to a cruel master, and the defect of a practice enjoined by law was exposed. That experience has taught the whole world, except that nation, the lesson not to resort to dreams and traditional fancies about the law, until its difficulties are such as to baffle human reason. (*Ag. Ap.* 1.22 §§209–11)

Josephus goes on to say that Ptolemy took many captives, not only from Judea but also from Samaria, and settled them in Egypt. Later, many other Jews were attracted to Egypt and immigrated there. This caused some rivalry between the Jews and Samaritans in Egypt over the question of which temple should receive their offerings.

Specifics concerning when and why Ptolemy captured Jerusalem are not given in the brief information we have on the subject; however, Josephus quotes Hecateus of Abdera (4.2.2) to the effect that after the battle of Gaza (312 B.C.E.), Ptolemy I asked Ezekias (Hezekiah), the *archiereus* (either the high priest or a chief priest), to accompany him back to Egypt. A good number of other Jews asked to go with him. Interpreting this passage is difficult, partly because of the question of its authenticity and partly because the identity of this Hezekiah is uncertain. Some scholars have identified him with Hezekiah the governor of Judah, known from coins in the late Persian period, an interesting suggestion but very speculative (2.2.7.2).

4.4.4 Ptolemaic Rule to 200 B.C.E.

Galili, E. "Raphia, 217 B.C.E., Revisited." *Scripta Classica Israelica* 3 (1976/77) 52–126.

The rest of the century was dominated by the Syrian wars, continual fighting between the Ptolemaic and Seleucid Empires over Coele-Syria. As noted in 4.4.3, the council of victors after the battle of Issus (301 B.C.E.) had awarded Coele-Syria to Seleucus because Ptolemy had not participated in the battle. However, Ptolemy occupied the area up to the Eleutherus River, north of Tripolis, and refused to concede the territory. The Seleucids spent the next century trying to regain what they viewed as rightfully theirs, but had only temporary successes until the Fifth Syrian War. In addition to Coele-Syria, the Ptolemies controlled Cyprus, various cities on the coast of Asia Minor, some Aegean islands, and Cyrenaica. The Seleucid Empire, much larger and more diffuse, began to disintegrate almost immediately. The eastern part of Iran was soon troublesome and was lost permanently with the rise of the Arsacid dynasty ca. 251 B.C.E. (except for the brief period ca. 209–187, when Antiochus III established hegemony again). Furthermore, because of Seleucid weakness, certain kingdoms in Asia Minor managed to establish and maintain independence for shorter or longer periods (e.g., Pergamum, Pontus, and Cappadocia).

Ptolemy II Philadelphus (282–246) was a long-lived and productive ruler who was associated as co-ruler with his father on the throne in 285. Seleucus I was assassinated in 281; his successor, Antiochus I (281–261), had difficulties securing his throne (in the so-called Syrian War of Succession, ca. 280–279 B.C.E.), and Ptolemy II seems to have taken advantage of Antiochus's temporary weakness to extend his possessions. Antiochus's troubles continued in the Celtic invasion of 278–277. He defeated the Gauls decisively in the "Elephant Battle," sometime between 275 and 270, but they continued to cause difficulties. The First Syrian War (274–271 B.C.E.) began with the revolt against Egypt of Magas, the governor of Cyrenaica, in which he involved his father-in-law, Antiochus. Although Magas was able to maintain independence for almost twenty-five years, the war seems to have caused little change with regard to Seleucid and Ptolemaic territories.

In the next decade Egypt was involved in the Chremonidean War (ca. 267–261 B.C.E.), trying to counter Macedonian influence in Greece. Whether Antiochus also participated is uncertain, although the loss of Ephesus to Ptolemaic rule in about 261 suggests that he was. Antiochus I died in 261, and his successor, Antiochus II (261–246 B.C.E.), was the instigator of the Second Syrian War (ca. 260–253 B.C.E.). Antiochus II actually gained territory in Asia Minor, and Ptolemy lost further land to the king of Macedonia and to Rhodes. A settlement between the two brought peace for the rest of the lives of both Ptolemy II and Antiochus II. Ptolemy was also able to regain Cyrenaica by arranging for his son to marry Magas's daughter.

The Third Syrian War, or Laodicean War (246–241 B.C.E.), originated with a rivalry between two sons of Antiochus II for the Seleucid throne. Antiochus's son by his first wife, Laodice, was recognized in Asia Minor as Seleucus II; however, a son (name unknown) by his second wife, Berenice, was accepted as the new ruler elsewhere and was also supported by the new Egyptian king, Ptolemy III. Ptolemy advanced through Syria without opposition, taking Seleucia and Antioch. He proceeded across the Euphrates into Mesopotamia, but a revolt in Egypt forced him to return. At some point during his advance, the Seleucid pretender and Berenice were murdered in circumstances now unknown. Seleucus II's claim to the throne was then recognized in Babylon, but he left western Asia Minor under his brother Antiochus Hierax as he moved to secure his throne in Syria and the east. The treaty ending the war left various territories in Ptolemaic hands, including parts of the southern and western coasts of Asia Minor and Seleucia and Antioch.

The conclusion of the Third Syrian War was the beginning of the so-called War of the Brothers (ca. 241–236) between Antiochus Hierax and Seleucus II. After a quarrel with his brother, Antiochus proclaimed himself king over the Seleucid realms. To what extent he was supported in this by Ptolemy III is not clear, but he probably had Egyptian support. Antiochus defeated Seleucus in a major battle near Ancyra (ca. 240/239), but peace was concluded before 236, which allowed Antiochus to retain control over his territory. After further squabbles, Antiochus Hierax was murdered in 226, and Seleucus II died about the same time. Seleucus III (226/225–223 B.C.E.), who succeeded to the throne, wished to reassert Seleucid rule over Asia Minor. He attacked Attalus I (241–197), king of Pergamum, which had gained independence during the War of the Brothers. Seleucus III was killed in a conspiracy during the campaign.

His younger brother became the new king, Antiochus III (223–187 B.C.E.), later called Antiochus the Great. His reign marked a gradual shift in the balance of power that had been maintained for a century. Because Antiochus was only twenty at the time of his accession, another member of the Seleucid family, Acheus, served as a general in Asia Minor, and Molon became governor over the eastern satrapies. It was not long before both subordinates rebelled and created problems for Antiochus. However, Antiochus seemed primarily concerned with trying to take Coele-Syria in what became known as the Fourth Syrian War (221–217 B.C.E.), waged against the new Egyptian king, Ptolemy IV Euergetes (221–204 B.C.E.). Antiochus made little headway at first and instead returned to take personal command against Molon, who had defeated the generals sent against him. Not only did Antiochus defeat Molon, but Acheus seems to have caused no further trouble. This left Antiochus free to turn against Coele-Syria once more. Things seemed to go well for a time. From 220 to 218 the Seleucid armies pushed continually southward, delayed mainly by various Egyptian diplomatic maneuvers. Ptolemy used this period to assemble and train a large force. The decisive battle came in 217 at Raphia, in Palestine, at which Antiochus was defeated and forced to abandon his gains in Coele-Syria (cf. Galili).

The next fifteen years were marked by Antiochus's attempts to consolidate his empire in the west. In 216 he made an agreement with Attalus I of Pergamum, the erstwhile ally of Acheus, leaving Acheus isolated. Antiochus then pushed Acheus back into Sardis, where Acheus was defeated and killed in 213. Ptolemy IV died in 204, succeeded by Ptolemy V Epiphanes (204–180 B.C.E.). Antiochus III saw his chance and initiated the Fifth Syrian War (202–200 B.C.E.). In spite of clever generalship on the part of Scipio, the Egyptian commander, the Ptolemaic cause was lost at the battle of Paneion in 200. Coele-Syria was now in Seleucid hands, after a century of effort. Judea had changed rulers, and the immediate result seemed favorable, although little immediate difference in circumstance could be seen. The importance of the change in government was to come a quarter of a century later under Antiochus III's son, Antiochus IV.

4.4.5 Judea under the Ptolemies

In 301 Ptolemy once more took Palestine and this time retained it for the next century, no doubt a welcome event for most Jews, at least initially, because it inaugurated a period of peace and stability. The Ptolemaic possessions in Palestine and Syria were governed as if they were only another province of Egypt, administered from Alexandria but with Egyptian agents in the various cities and villages to see that the appropriate taxes were paid and the Ptolemaic interests served (4.3.1). Whether there was one governor over the entirety of Coele-Syria is debated, but the basic unit of administration and taxation was the village. Each village had its officials and tax agents, bringing Ptolemaic supervision to the lowest level of society and making it difficult for the individual to avoid the multitude of taxes that weighed on him.

Although Egypt was a rich country, attractive to foreign settlers, the area of Syria and Palestine was important for the Egyptian economy (4.3.6). To the Ptolemies the region was just another milk cow, providing goods and revenues. It was valuable for two reasons: for its various products and as a trading center. The variety of agricultural products exported to Egypt was large, the main ones being wheat, wine, and oil. Some of the export probably came from royal estates in the region, but the trade of all these products seems to have been regulated as a state monopoly. Another important product from Egypt's point of view was slaves, both for employment in the households of nobles and to work in the wool trade. This encouraged the illegal enslavement of private individuals, and at least one royal edict attempted to stop the practice (4.2.7.3). The region also served as a transit area for trade from Asia Minor and other areas north and from Arabia. Gaza was the major center for the incense trade, which was also a royal monopoly.

Josephus states that Ptolemy I found the Jews useful as soldiers and used them in his garrisons (*Ant.* 12.1.1 §8). This fits the policy of the Ptolemaic (as well as Seleucid) kings and seems to be borne out by other sources. The basic means of providing defense of the country was by military colonies, usually referred to as "cleruchies" (Greek *katoikiai* or *klērouchoi*; the settler's plot of land was a *klēros;* the individual settler was a *katoikos*). They served not only as a reserve to be drawn on in time of war but also as a local police force; hence they were often settled in troubled areas as a way of bringing them under control (4.3.1). The Tobias of the Zenon papyri was head of such a military cleruchy, although the actual settlers in his colony seem to have been a mixed group and not just Jews (4.3.2).

Judah evidently continued as a theocracy, just as it had under the Persians. The Ptolemaic administration was primarily interested in revenue. As long as the Jews paid their taxes and did not threaten rebellion, they were allowed to continue their traditional mode of government and their other customs. This is described in detail by Hecateus of Abdera (4.2.2), who, on the balance of evidence, provides valuable insight into the Jewish nation at the beginning of the Ptolemaic period. Because of its importance, Hecateus's account is worth quoting at length:

> (4) . . . He [Moses] picked out the men of most refinement and with the greatest ability to head the entire nation, and appointed them priests; and he ordained that they should occupy themselves with the temple and the honours and sacrifices offered to their God. (5) These same men he appointed to be judges in all major disputes, and entrusted to them the guardianship of the laws and customs. For this reason the Jews never have a king, and authority over the people is regularly vested in whichever priest is regarded as superior to his colleagues in wisdom and virtue. They call this man the high priest, and believe that he acts as a messenger to them of god's commandments. (6) It is he, we are told, who in their assemblies and other gatherings announces what is ordained, and the Jews are so docile in such matters that straightway they fall to the ground and do reverence to the high priest when he expounds the commandments to them. . . . (7) He [Moses] led out military expeditions against the neighbouring tribes, and after annexing much land apportioned it out, assigning equal allotments to private citizens and greater ones to the priests, in order that they, by virtue of receiving more ample revenues, might be undistracted and apply themselves continually to the worship of God. (Diodorus Siculus 40.3.1–7)

There are three points to note here. First, the nominal head of the country was the high priest. He not only held the chief religious office but also seems to have had the major administrative responsibility. The Tobiad romance (4.2.4) suggests that about the middle of the century the high priest held the office of official representative of the Jews to the Ptolemies (*prostasia*), an office taken from him and transferred to Joseph Tobiad, according to one interpretation of the story (4.3.2; *Tcherikover 1959: 132–34). Second, the priests evidently also undertook other civil functions, such as serving as judges. Third, the priests, either as a group or individually, are said to own land, contrary to the Pentateuch. This fits with later evidence that individual priests possessed estates.

How much Jewish literature was produced during this time is unknown, but some writings can be dated to the early Hellenistic period with relative certainty. This literature in many cases fits the traditional genres known from earlier periods of Israel's history. For example, in the category of wisdom is the book of Qohelet (4.2.5.1), most likely written during the third century. Some have suggested that Qohelet reflects Greek influence, but this is disputed by others; most of its content can be understood as a logical development of the earlier Israelite wisdom tradition, without any appeal to Greek influence. Similarly, the book of Ben Sira (completed in the early second century, but much of it possibly belonging to the Ptolemaic period) shows no clear Greek impress, even though this has been argued (4.2.5.2). Apocalyptic sections are already evident in some of the later prophets (e.g., Zechariah, in whole or in part; cf. 4.3.3). Sections of *1 Enoch* may well mirror the horrors of the Diadochi wars (4.2.5.7). Other books that may be from this time, such as Tobit and Judith, also seem to exemplify genres and elements known from the Hebrew tradition.

Nevertheless, the Greek language soon started to make its mark, even in the early Hellenistic period (3.3.1). The Yehuda coins of that time show the style of the coins of Ptolemy I (2.2.7.2). A moneylender's receipts could have been in Greek as well as in the local language soon after the accession of Ptolemy II, judging from the Khirbet el-Kom ostraca (4.2.7.2). The correspondence of the Jewish nobleman Tobias was regularly in Greek, which suggests some sort of Greek education, even though he undoubtedly employed a Greek secretary. The major achievement in Jewish Greek literature was the translation of the Pentateuch into Greek, probably about the middle of the third century, although this was most likely done in Egypt, not Palestine. Other Jewish writers in Greek could have been Palestinian, not just Alexandrian. Demetrius's commentary on portions of the Old Testament seems to know only the LXX (5.2.10.1).

The semilegendary story of the Tobiads (4.2.4; 4.3.2) is the only source of political history for the period. According to this account, the high priest Onias (commonly designated Onias II) refused to pay a tribute of twenty talents. The reason given is unlikely (i.e., that he was just miserly!). The suggestion that he was expecting or hoping for a transfer of rule to the Seleucids is a cogent one. In any event, his nephew Joseph Tobiad enlisted support from the people, borrowed money from friends in Samaria and, by political skill and bribery, managed to obtain the tax-farming rights for Coele-Syria. Modern scholarship dates his activities to the reign of Ptolemy III (rather than Ptolemy V, as Josephus's account has it).

Joseph retired after a career of some two decades, to be replaced by his youngest son, Hyrcanus. According to the story, Hyrcanus angered his father and brothers by using his father's money to obtain the tax authority that his father had possessed. This, however, probably represents a romantic interpretation of a situation very much governed by political circumstances, because the time at which Joseph ended his career and Hyrcanus began his was just before the Fifth Syrian War (202–200 B.C.E.).

Evidently, Hyrcanus's brothers (and, perhaps, the father, Joseph, by this time) were pursuing a pro-Seleucid policy in expectation of Antiochus III's taking over rule of the region. The new high priest, Simon (II), also seems to have supported the Seleucids (cf. Ben Sira 50:1–4). Hyrcanus continued to be pro-Ptolemaic, however, and benefited briefly from this stance with certain favors from the Egyptian king. As soon as Antiochus was victorious, though, there was little for Hyrcanus to do but retire to his fortress across the Jordan and maintain himself by raiding Arab territory. The Jews were now under Seleucid rule, which was to have profound consequences within the next half-century.

4.4.6 Religious Developments

Crenshaw, J. "The Birth of Skepticism in Ancient Israel." *The Divine Helmsman* (1980) 1–19.
Glasson, T. F. *Greek Influence in Jewish Eschatology* (1961).
Grabbe, L. L. "The Scapegoat Ritual: A Study in Early Jewish Interpretation." *JSJ* 18 (1987) 152–67.
———. "The Social Setting of Early Jewish Apocalypticism." *JSP* 4 (1989) 27–47.
Stone, M. E. "The Book of Enoch and Judaism in the Third Century B.C.E." *CBQ* 40 (1978) 479–92.

Whereas general consensus holds that religious change occurred in the early part of the Greek period, specific changes are not easy to determine because little of the relevant religious literature can be precisely dated. Therefore, the following list includes mutations or innovations that likely occurred in the century or so after Alexander; but more exact dating is not usually possible.

Although the roots of apocalyptic literature definitely are earlier than the Greek conquest, the first agreed-on Jewish apocalypses (parts of *1 Enoch*) seem to be from the early part of Greek rule (4.2.5.7). The Greek period was a time when apocalypticism flourished, and not only among the Jews (4.3.3). Thus, even if full-blown apocalyptic literature was written under the Persian Empire, it blossomed into a major tradition within Judaism in Hellenistic times. How to fit apocalypticism into the structure of Judaism at this time is an interesting question. It is evident that apocalyptic speculation took place and apocalyptic literature was produced under the Ptolemies. What part did it play in Jewish thinking? The problem is that literature which seems to be describing actual Jewish society (Josephus; Ben Sira; Zenon papyri; Hecateus; *Letter of Aristeas* [?]) is silent about apocalyptic movements—or even enthusiasms—among the people. Does this mean that the producers of such literature were only marginal, perhaps a disenfranchised "visionary" party or peripheral conventicles (Plöger; Hanson [2.3.11.3])?

Although this is one possibility, several considerations argue against it. Apocalyptic interest and speculation are not limited to marginalized or revolutionary groups. On the contrary, it can have a full place in established society and religion without requiring overt action on the part of the believer (Grabbe 1989). As a subordinate people, the Jews were not likely to advertise their expectations that God was going to overthrow kings and make nations drink the wine cup of God's wrath. Yet belief in such things no doubt sustained many Jews in the difficult Ptolemaic times, as they have various peoples through the ages. Priests and elders were no less subject to such apocalyptic curiosities, and a strong priestly contribution to the writings and speculation during this time is very likely. Some may not have believed in it (Ben Sira?); others would not have taught it, except perhaps in a circumspect manner. In any case, the execution of future judgment was usually thought to be in the hands of God, without requiring militant human action. Such an explanation would recognize the strong apocalyptic strands in Judaism at this time while also explaining why the life of the people does not seem to have been overly agitated by such ideas.

In the area of eschatology, several theories have been offered for the origin of the concept of the soul, including Persian ideas and native developments within Judaism itself (2.3.10; 8.3.5). Because one can make a case for each of these, the question is one of determining the balance of probability. The idea of the "soul" could arise from ideas found already in the Old Testament, such as the frequent word *nefeš* ("soul," "life," "person"), or perhaps *nĕšāmāh* ("breath"), although neither of these equates to "soul" in the Platonic or Pythagorean sense that the soul is the person, which may or may not be attached to a body. What is clear is that just about the time of the establishment of Greek rule, an idea akin to the Platonic concept begins to appear in Jewish literature. This concept is well developed by the turn of the era, but it begins to appear in *1 Enoch* in sections probably dated as early as the third century B.C.E. One could argue for native developments under Greek influence or even under both Greek and Iranian influence; however, the developed concept is so much like the Greek notion of the immortal soul that a Greek origin or heavy Greek influence seems the most likely explanation. Interestingly, the belief so often thought characteristic of Jewish eschatology, the resurrection of the body, is not clearly attested until the second century (Dan 12:2).

An issue that was of concern in writings as early as Ezekiel 18 and 33 and Jeremiah 18 is the origin of and responsibility for evil. If God is sovereign over all, then how is the presence of evil to be explained? Zoroastrianism had resolved the dilemma by positing two coeval spirits, one good and one evil. This concept had its influence in various circles (2.3.10), but it was never taken over as a system. An idea central to some systems of Judaism was that of fallen angels. This myth first appears in full-blown form in *1 Enoch* 6–11 (although such an idea may already lie behind Gen 6:1-4 [4.2.5.7]). Angels sinned by cohabiting with human women, producing giant, bastard offspring, which wrought destruction and bloodshed on the earth. After their death, the spirits of these giants continued to roam the earth as wicked spirits. In time this myth was united with the old Israelite idea of the Adversary (Satan) as a member of the heavenly court (Grabbe 1987). Thus even though God was the originator of all things, God was still not the author of sin, which arose from a portion of God's creation.

What is often referred to as "skeptical wisdom" (Crenshaw) has a long tradition in ancient Near Eastern literature. The book of Job is often included in this category, although Job is difficult to date (2.2.1). A prime representative of the genre, however, which is generally dated to the third century, is the book of Qohelet or Ecclesiastes (4.2.5.1). Whether or not the arguments about Greek influence on the book are accepted, Qohelet represents a radically new element within Jewish literature, with few parallels. It may be the masterpiece of a solitary genius, yet the elements it has in common with other Near Eastern literature suggest the culmination of a tradition, not a completely new departure. Depending on how radically one interprets the message, the book seems to fit an age under the spell of heady new influences and ideas, but one in which Judaism was not yet threatened by persecution. Nevertheless, it is not repeated in the extant Jewish literature; indeed, the contrast between Qohelet and the conventional wisdom of the roughly contemporary Ben Sira is striking. Perhaps the experience of the Hellenistic reform and the Maccabean revolt put an end to any environment that could nourish such religious questioning.

5 SELEUCID RULE, THE MACCABEAN REVOLT, AND THE HASMONEAN PRIEST-KINGS

5.1 BIBLIOGRAPHICAL GUIDE

Bar-Kochva, B. *Judas Maccabaeus: The Jewish Struggle against the Seleucids* (1989).

Bickerman, E. J. *The God of the Maccabees* (1979).

Bringmann, K. *Hellenistische Reform und Religionsverfolgung in Judäa* (1983).

*CAH*². Vol. 7.1: *The Hellenistic Age* (1984); Vol. 7.2: *The Rise of Rome to 220 B.C.* (1989); Vol. 8: *Rome and the Mediterranean to 133 B.C.* (1989).

Cary, M. *A History of the Greek World 323 to 146 B.C.* (1963).

Cary, M., and H. H. Scullard. *A History of Rome* (1975).

CHJ. Vol. 2: *The Hellenistic Age* (1989).

Crawford, M. H. *The Roman Republic* (1978).

Efron, J. *Studies on the Hasmonean Period* (1987).

Fischer, T. *Seleukiden und Makkabäer* (1980).

Goldstein, J. A. *I Maccabees* (1976).

———. *II Maccabees* (1983).

Grimal, P., ed. *Hellenism and the Rise of Rome* (1968).

Gruen, E. S. *The Hellenistic World and the Coming of Rome* (1984).

Harrington, D. J. *The Maccabean Revolt* (1988).

Hengel, M. *Judaism and Hellenism* (1974).

Mørkholm, O. *Antiochus IV of Syria* (1966).

Schalit, A., ed. *Hellenistic Period* (1972).

Schürer: 1.125–242.

Schwartz, S. "Israel and the Nations Roundabout: 1 Maccabees and the Hasmonean Expansion." *JJS* 42 (1991) 16–38.

Sievers, J. *The Hasmoneans and Their Supporters* (1990).

Tcherikover, V. A. *Hellenistic Civilization and the Jews* (1959).

Will, E. *Histoire politique du monde hellénistique (323–30 av. J.-C.* (1979–1982).

Will, E., et al. *Le monde grec et l'Orient* (1975).

Woude, A. S. van der. Review of *Studies on the Hasmonean Period*, by J. Efron. *JSJ* 20 (1989) 91–94.

Two standard works which have been around for some time are Bickerman and Tcherikover, both indispensable even if one does not agree with their particular theses. Tcherikover also writes on the Maccabean revolt and its background in Schalit. As useful as Schalit is, the text of most of the articles dates from the late 1950s; only occasionally are the notes and bibliography updated. Hengel has a lengthy section on the period before and during the Maccabean revolt (1.267–309), although much else relates to this time indirectly. Mørkholm's monograph is specifically on Antiochus, but of necessity it covers a great deal related to the revolt directly.

Despite its title, Bar-Kochva's monograph is not a complete study of Judas Maccabeus; rather, it concentrates on his military campaigns, with detailed commentary on the passages that describe battles. Bar-Kochva is unexcelled as a military historian of this period, and his work is extremely important not only for the campaigns of the Maccabean revolt but also for Seleucid military history in general. He also covers a number of important, miscellaneous points in the appendixes and notes. On the subject of chronology, however, I have argued against his reconstruction (5.3.7). Bringmann tackles some important aspects of the Hellenistic reform and the revolt, especially chronology and the cause of the persecution. Sievers has now given an important critical study of the first Hasmoneans and their supporters. Harrington is aimed primarily at students but incorporates a good deal of recent scholarship and has a good annotated bibliography. The recent article by Schwartz is an example of the type of study very much needed for the Maccabean period.

The best background study of Seleucid history is Will (see also Will, et al.). For Roman history at this time, Gruen is excellent, and Crawford gives a useful, brief introduction; see also Cary/Scullard. Surveys of various aspects of Seleucid history and rule are found in the new edition of *CAH*. Also useful in English is the volume edited by Grimal from the *Fischer Weltgeschichte*.

5.2 SOURCES

5.2.1 1 Maccabees

Abel, F.-M. *Les libres des Maccabées* (1949).
*Bar-Kochva: 151–70.
*Goldstein 1976.
JLBM: 114–17.
JWSTP: 171–76.
Neuhaus, G. O. "Quellen im 1. Makkabäerbuch? Eine Entgegung auf die Analyse von K.-D. Schunck." *JSJ* 5 (1974) 162–75.

Schunck, K.-D. *Die Quellen des I and II Makkabäerbuches* (1954).
Schürer: 3.180–85.
*Sievers: 1–4.

The most extensive source for the events in Judea during the forty years from about 175 to 135 B.C.E., 1 Maccabees was written by an anonymous author sometime during John Hyrcanus's reign (135–104 B.C.E.), probably before 125 B.C.E. (*Bar-Kochva: 162–64). Although the original was presumably in Hebrew, only the Greek version is extant. Of the sources for the Maccabean revolt, 1 Maccabees has often been judged the most trustworthy, largely because of its matter-of-fact narrative, lacking overt elements of miracle or supernatural intervention. Recently, however, scholars recognized the underlying *Tendenz* of the writing, and they now consider the appearance of straightforwardness to be one of the arts of the narrator. It is now generally accepted that 1 Maccabees was to some extent the official version of the Hasmonean dynasty and thus an account from the Maccabean point of view.

The author's precise sources are not clear. Schunck has given a detailed source analysis, but this has been criticized by Neuhaus, who reflects the current move away from confident identification of multiple sources. No doubt Neuhaus is correct in dismissing the idea that one can find a different source for practically every episode within the book. Nevertheless, some source proposals may be more widely accepted than others. For example, the use of a Seleucid chronicle of some sort has long been accepted in scholarship and is suggested by the presence of date formulas at various points that differ from those normally found in Jewish sources (Schunck; *Bickerman: 9–12, 101–3). Bar-Kochva has argued that the author was an eyewitness to a number of the battles described and was able to obtain reports from participants in others (*158–62, but note the objections of Schwartz [*37 n.64]).

Of particular importance are a number of Jewish, Seleucid, and Roman documents quoted at various points in the text. The authenticity of these documents has been the subject of much debate. Most are widely accepted as genuine, although it must be recognized that in many cases they were translated from Greek into Hebrew and then back into Greek, which may have caused changes or potential misunderstandings. The points debated are the treaty with Rome during the time of Judas (1 Macc 8:23-32) and the letter from the king of Sparta (12:20-23). On these, see 5.3.5–6.

Most of the secondary literature to 1975, including information on critical editions of the Greek text, is found in Goldstein (*1976: 175–86);

however, because he does not attempt to represent all points of view, older commentaries still must be consulted for interpretations that differ from his. An especially well-done older commentary is Abel.

5.2.2 2 Maccabees

Abel, F.-M. *Les livres des Maccabées* (1949).
*Bar-Kochva: 170–85.
Doran, R. *Temple Propaganda: The Purpose and Character of 2 Maccabees* (1981).
*Goldstein 1983.
Habicht, C., ed. *II. Makkabäerbuch* (1976).
JLBM: 118–21.
JWSTP: 176–83.
Momigliano, A. "The Second Book of Maccabees." *Classical Philology* 70 (1975) 81–88.
Schürer: 3.531–37.
*Sievers: 4–10.

According to its preface, 2 Maccabees is an epitome of a much larger work by Jason of Cyrene, a writer otherwise unknown. The account is parallel in part to 1 Maccabees, but it covers a much briefer period of time (ca. 175–161 B.C.E.), is more detailed about the events preceding the suppression of the Jewish religion, and often gives a different perspective on various issues. Because of the explicit appeal to the supernatural at various points in the account, scholars often considered 2 Maccabees much inferior to 1 Maccabees. Recent scholarship sees a more nuanced picture. Second Maccabees is more overtly theological in its aim; its chronology is often confused and less trustworthy than 1 Maccabees. The long descriptions of martyrdom in chapter 7 are suspect in certain details (although some religious executions did indeed occur). However, the information about the events during the "Hellenistic reform" is much more detailed than in 1 Maccabees, and there are other data at various points not found elsewhere.

Of special interest are the original documents quoted, most of which are not found in 1 Maccabees. The authenticity of several of these has been widely accepted: the first letter prefacing 2 Maccabees (1:1-9) and part or all of the documents in chapter 11. Arguments have also been made for and against the authenticity of some of the others. See further at 5.3.5.

As with 1 Maccabees, the sources used (other than the documents explicitly quoted) are not clearly identified A number of scholars (most recently Goldstein [*1976: 90–103; *1983: 37–41]) have suggested that a common source underlies both 1 and 2 Maccabees. The disagreements between the two seem to be rather striking, however, and many of the agreements can be explained as the result of knowledge of the actual events rather than a common source. Therefore, the theory of a *Grundschrift* for both books seems to require a good deal more argument to be accepted as cogent. Most of the secondary literature to 1982 is found in Goldstein, but, as with 1 Maccabees, he does not necessarily summarize previous scholarly positions and many of his interpretations are very speculative. Therefore, one still must supplement Goldstein with older commentaries, such as Abel. The German translation by Habicht also has detailed notes on many passages.

5.2.3 Daniel

Archer, G. L. *Jerome's Commentary on Daniel* (1958).
Beaulieu, P.-A. *The Reign of Nabonidus, King of Babylon 556–539 B.C.* (1989).
Braverman, J. *Jerome's Commentary on Daniel* (1978).
Bunge, J. G. "Der 'Gott der Festungen' und der 'Liebling der Frauen': Zur Identifizierung der Götter in Dan. 11,36-39." *JSJ* 4 (1973) 169–82.
Charles, R. H. *A Critical and Exegetical Commentary on the Book of Daniel* (1929).
Collins, J. J. *The Apocalyptic Vision of the Book of Daniel* (1977).
Davies, P. R. *Daniel* (1985).
Goldingay, J. E. *Daniel* (1989).
Grabbe, L. L. "Another Look at the *Gestalt* of 'Darius the Mede.'" *CBQ* 50 (1988) 198-213.
Hartman, L. F., and A. A. Di Lella. *The Book of Daniel* (1978).
Hieronymus (Jerome). *Commentariorum in Danielem* (1964).
Humphries, W. L. "A Life-Style for Diaspora: A Study of the Tales of Esther and Daniel." *JBL* 92 (1973) 211–23.
JLBM: 19–30, 83–90.
Lebram, J.C.H. "Perspektiven der Gegenwärtigen Danielforschung." *JSJ* 5 (1974) 1–33.
———. "König Antiochus im Buch Daniel." *VT* 25 (1975) 737–72.
McNamara, M. "Nabonidus and the Book of Daniel." *ITQ* 37 (1970) 131–49.
Montgomery, J. A. *A Critical and Exegetical Commentary on the Book of Daniel* (1927).
Moore, C. A. *Daniel, Esther and Jeremiah: The Additions* (1977).
Rowley, H. H. *Darius the Mede and the Four World Empires in the Book of Daniel* (1935).
Schürer: 3.245–50.
Soden, W. von. "Eine babylonische Volksüberlieferung von Nabonid in den Danielerzählungen." *ZAW* 53 (1935) 81–89.

The "tales of Daniel" (Daniel 1–6) are of a different character and probably originated in a different time and place from the "apocalypse of Daniel" (Daniel 7–12). They are similar to Esther and such deutero- or noncanonical books as Tobit and Ahiqar, in that they are tales about a heroic figure who is adviser to the king in an ancient Near Eastern court. They portray a series of contests and conflicts that demonstrate this figure's wisdom and piety and, ultimately, serve as a model for Jews of the Diaspora (Humphries).

Although some have argued that all of Daniel should be assigned to Maccabean times, many now propose that Daniel 1–6 developed over a period of time and was essentially in its present form before the Maccabean revolt (Collins: 7–11). The Maccabean author did not compose these chapters but simply took them over and added his material. This does not mean that the material in 1–6 is historical; on the contrary, much of it is manifestly legendary, although it is often built around a historical core. Thus, there was a Nebuchadnezzar and Belshazzar (Beaulieu), but the Nebuchadnezzar of Daniel 3 and 4 is probably a reflex of Nabonidus, not the historical Nebuchadnezzar (von Soden; McNamara), and the Belshazzar of Daniel 5 was never king and was not killed in the conquest of Babylon (which actually occurred without a battle). "Darius the Mede" of Daniel 6 (Eng. 5:30—6:28) is more problematic. It has often been thought that he represented Darius I but also incorporated elements of Cyrus (Rowley: 54–60); however, there are reasons why this is unlikely, and Darius the Mede is probably only a literary creation for theological purposes (Grabbe). The suggestion that he represents Cyrus's general Gubaru is now almost certainly disproved.

Scholarship has long recognized that Daniel 7–12 was written during the Maccabean revolt but before the Jews retook the temple area, that is, about 166/165 B.C.E. (Fischer is a notable exception in arguing for ca. 160/159 B.C.E. [*140] .) Various elements within this section represent the period around the time of the Maccabean revolt, and 11:45 predicts the death of Antiochus IV in a way unlike what actually occurred, showing that it was a genuine but inaccurate prediction. The importance of Daniel 7–12 is that it gives the view of a writer contemporary with the events. Where it can be checked, it seems to record events accurately (if briefly) and in correct order. The symbolic language of the book, however, often makes it difficult properly to interpret its allusions and determine the actual happenings behind the symbols. Nevertheless, any discussion of this important period of Jewish history must take these chapters of Daniel fully into account.

It is often asserted that Daniel 7–12 owes its authorship to Hasidic circles. However, not only is little known about the Hasidim (8.2.1), but also some elements within the book seem to be at variance with the views of this group. Especially important is the attitude expressed toward active resistance to persecution. We know that the Hasidim were willing to fight against the Seleucids; indeed, they are referred to as "mighty warriors" (1 Macc 2:42). The author of Daniel, however, believed in passive resistance only, with martyrdom as the way to fight the forces of evil. In this Daniel has some affinities with the *Testament of Moses* (Collins: 198–210).

Daniel 11 is important because it seems based on an accurate portrayal of the interactions between the Seleucid and Ptolemaic rulers, although the account is given under the guise of prophecy. It is generally assumed that some sort of chronicle made during Ptolemaic times underlies this chapter. Although the historical description is in symbolic language, it is generally clear what event is being referred to. However, the value of the account is somewhat diminished because it must be interpreted by information from other historical sources. Nevertheless, it provides some useful information, especially when used in conjunction with the lost account of Porphyry, which is often quoted or paraphrased in Jerome's commentary on Daniel.

The Neoplatonic philosopher Porphyry (ca. 232–305 C.E.) included a valuable commentary on Daniel 11 and other parts of Daniel in his work *Against the Christians*. Porphyry's exact source is uncertain but seems to have been basically reliable. Although the work as a whole has been lost, it is frequently cited and quoted by the church father Jerome (Hieronymous, ca. 342–420 C.E.) in his commentary on Daniel. A convenient English translation of Jerome's commentary is given by Archer (although he uses the old Migne text rather than the more reliable one in CCL). See also the selections and commentary in *GLAJJ*: 2.444–75.

5.2.4 Josephus

*Bar-Kochva: 186–93.
Cohen, S.J.D. *Josephus in Galilee and Rome* (1979).
*Sievers: 10–14.

In *War* 1.1.1–2.2 §§31–53 Josephus has a brief account of the Maccabean revolt. Although short and evidently somewhat muddled, it is nevertheless valuable because it seems to be independent of our other extant sources. The tendency among scholars has been to ignore the picture given in *War* as confused. Undoubtedly there is truth to this charge because the representation of Onias, Jason, and Menelaus as brothers (and of Menelaus as also bearing the name Onias) is less credible than the more complicated depiction of 2 Maccabees. Nevertheless, Josephus explicitly notes the involvement of the Tobiads in the machinations to obtain the high priesthood, a point ignored by both 1 and 2 Maccabees. Moreover, any independent evidence is useful in countering the systematic bias of the two major sources. Josephus's information is probably from Nicolaus of Damascus (5.2.5).

Antiquities 12.5.1 §237—13.7.4 §229 provides a much longer account of the Maccabean revolt and Hasmonean rule to the coming of the Romans than the *War.* His primary source for the Maccabean conflict was 1 Maccabees, which he closely paraphrased; however, his account contains frequent minor differences that are usually due to his own reworking of the data, including his own surmises and inferences (for discussion and bibliography, see Cohen: 44–47). He also added information at several places (e.g., 12.5.5 §§257–64; 13.2.4–3.4 §§59–79; 13.4.5–9 §§103–22) that came from another source or sources. Scholars generally agree that Josephus did not know either Jason of Cyrene or 2 Maccabees (contra Goldstein [*1976: 55–61; *1983: 26–27 nn.79–80, 549]). Because Josephus's account does not closely parallel 1 Maccabees after 13:42 (*Ant.* 13.6.7 §214), it has been suggested that his version did not contain 13:43—16:24, although other explanations are possible. Once he ceased to use 1 Maccabees, Josephus's primary source appears to have been Nicolaus of Damascus (5.2.5). For this part of Josephus's history there is considerably more text in *Antiquities* than in *War,* but the actual data are not usually significantly greater, suggesting that the bulk of *Antiquities* represents rhetorical expansion, not further information. New sources of information are occasionally drawn on, however, and thus supplement the data from Nicolaus (e.g., the lost *History* of Strabo).

5.2.5 Nicolaus of Damascus

GLAJJ: 1.227–60.

Jacoby, F. "90. Nicolas von Damascus." *Die Fragmente der griechischen Historiker* (1926–58) 2A.

Shutt, R.J.H. *Studies in Josephus* (1961) 79–92.

Stern, M. "The Greek and Roman Literary Sources." *The Jewish People in the First Century* (1974) 1.18–36.

Wacholder, B. Z. *Nicolas of Damascus* (1962).

Nicolaus of Damascus was a secretary to Herod the Great. If he was not of Greek origin, he was at least trained in the Greek rhetorical tradition, which skill he used before Augustus in arguing the case of Archelaus after Herod's death. He wrote a universal history in 144 books, most of which has perished. Because he had access to documents in Herod's archives, however, his work evidently contained a good deal on Jewish history and was therefore a valuable source for Josephus for the Hasmonean and Herodian periods. Most of what survives from Nicolaus is known through Josephus, but portions of his works are known through other sources (see Jacoby).

For the period of Hasmonean rule, Nicolaus seems to have been Josephus's main source (5.2.4), in both *War* and *Antiquities*. Although in *Antiquities* Josephus used 1 Maccabees for the Maccabean revolt and the period down to the rulership of Simon, Nicolaus was probably his source for this period in *War* (which does not seem to use 1 Maccabees), as well as for the information in *Antiquities* that does not agree with 1 Maccabees. Josephus's use of Nicolaus is universally agreed upon, but when it comes to a detailed picture of exactly how his work was used, there is wide diversity of opinion. This is because the few preserved fragments of Nicolaus's original work make it difficult to compare the original with Josephus's version.

5.2.6 Qumran Scrolls

Bar-Adon, P. "Another Settlement of the Judean Desert Sect at 'En el-Ghuweir on the Shores of the Dead Sea." *BASOR* 227 (1977) 1–25.
Brooke, G. J. *Exegesis at Qumran* (1985).
———, ed. *Temple Scroll Studies* (1989).
Brownlee, W. H. "The Wicked Priest, the Man of Lies, and the Righteous Teacher—The Problem of Identity." *JQR* 73 (1982–83) 1–37.
Callaway, P. R. *The History of the Qumran Community* (1988).
Collins, J. J. "The Origin of the Qumran Community: A Review of the Evidence." *To Touch the Text: Biblical and Related Studies in Honor of Joseph A. Fitzmyer, S. J.* (1989) 159–78.
Cross, F. M. *The Ancient Library of Qumran* (1961).
Davies, P. R. *1QM, the War Scroll from Qumran: Its Structure and History* (1977).
———. *Qumran* (1982).
———. *The Damascus Covenant: An Interpretation of the "Damascus Document"* (1983).
———. "Eschatology at Qumran." *JBL* 104 (1985) 39–55.
———. *Behind the Essenes: History and Ideology in the Dead Sea Scrolls* (1987).
———. "How Not to Do Archaeology: The Story of Qumran." *BA* 51 (1988) 203–7.
Dimant, D. "Qumran Sectarian Literature." *JWSTP* (1984) 483–550.
Fitzmyer, J. A. *The Dead Sea Scrolls: Major Publications and Tools for Study* (1990).

Horgan, M. P. *Pesharim: Qumran Interpretations of Biblical Books* (1979).
JLBM: 122–42.
Knibb, M. A. *The Qumran Community* (1987).
Koester, C. "A Qumran Bibliography: 1974–1984." *BTB* 15 (1985) 110–20.
Levine, B. A. "The Temple Scroll: Aspects of Its Historical Provenance and Literary Character." *BASOR* 232 (1978) 5–23.
Milik, J. T. *Ten Years of Discovery in the Wilderness of Judaea* (1959).
Murphy-O'Connor, J. "La genèse littéraire de la Règle de la Communauté." *RB* 76 (1969) 528–49.
———. "The *Damascus Document* Revisited." *RB* 92 (1985) 223–46.
Pardee, D. "A Restudy of the Commentary on Psalm 37 from Qumran Cave 4." *RevQ* 8 (1972–73) 163–94.
Qimron, E., and J. Strugnell. "An Unpublished Halakhic Letter from Qumran." *Biblical Archaeology Today* (1985) 400–407.
Schiffman, L. H. "The New Halakhic Letter (4QMMT) and the Origins of the Dead Sea Sect." *BA* 53 (1990a) 64–73.
———. "*Miqṣat Ma'aseh Ha-torah* and the *Temple Scroll*." *RevQ* 14 (1990b) 435–57.
Schürer: 2.575–83; 3.380–469.
Stegemann, H. "Is the Temple Scroll a Sixth Book of the Torah—Lost for 2,500 Years?" *BAR* 13, no. 6 (Nov./Dec. 1987) 28–35.
———. "The Literary Composition of the Temple Scroll and Its Status at Qumran." *Temple Scroll Studies* (1989) 123–48.
Vaux, R. de. *Archaeology and the Dead Sea Scrolls* (1973).
Vermes, G. *The Dead Sea Scrolls: Qumran in Perspective* (1977).
———. *The Dead Sea Scrolls in English* (1987).
Yadin, Y., ed. *The Scroll of the War of the Sons of Light against the Sons of Darkness* (1962).
———, ed. *The Temple Scroll* (1983).

The finds from the caves on the northwestern shores of the Dead Sea, near the ruins known as Khirbet Qumran, have revolutionized our understanding of certain aspects of Jewish history in the late Second Temple period. Even to begin to outline their contribution to scholarship would take too much space here, but there are a number of useful summaries that do this. Especially important is the bibliographical guide by Fitzmyer. Introductions can also be found in Davies (1982), Dimant, Vermes (1977), Schürer, and Cross, although one must be aware that there is much more controversy on many points than some introductions indicate. The most useful collection of the scrolls in English translation is Vermes (1987; but see also the selection with detailed notes in Knibb). Although the Qumran scrolls pertain to many aspects of Jewish culture and religion, only a few points will be noted here. For further information on original editions and translations, secondary studies, and exhaustive bibliographies, see especially Fitzmyer, supplemented by Koester, and 8.2.5.

5.2.6.1 The Documents

A variety of texts were found in the area of Qumran, many of which still have not been published: fragments of every book of the Hebrew Bible except Esther, portions of the Apocrypha and Pseudepigrapha (cf. 5.2.7; 5.2.8; 4.2.5.2–3, 7), other Jewish writings heretofore unknown, and writings which seem to be a product of the community itself (sometimes referred to as Qumran "sectarian writings"). Only the more important texts of the last category will be surveyed here, because these give us some insight into the history of the Qumran group and occasionally even into its relationship with wider history.

Two works seem to be manuals for the organization and running of the community: the *Community Rule*, sometimes called the *Manual of Discipline* (1QS), and the *Damascus Document* (CD). Although these are parallel in part, there are also important differences between them which have been explained in various ways (e.g., that the two rules are for two different groups, such as 1QS for Qumran and CD for other settlements). Recently, Murphy-O'Connor (1969; 1985) and Davies (1983) have argued that some of the differences, as well as some of the confusing passages within each document, can be explained as due to their tradition history; that is, the manuals were revised over time, with later changes sometimes causing clashes with directives from an earlier stage.

The *War Scroll* (1QM) describes an eschatological military campaign between the forces of good and the forces of evil. Both human beings and angelic powers take part, and eventually good triumphs over evil. Although the fighting itself is presented in a very stylized and unworldly way for the most part, the work reflects a genuine knowledge of military matters (Yadin 1962). Davies (1977) has argued that an original edition was revised in the first century C.E. and reflects the attitude of the community to the developing crisis between Jews and Romans.

The Commentaries, or Pesharim (from Hebrew *pešer,* "interpretation"), contain a number of important historical allusions, although the correct understanding of these allusions is more widely debated than is sometimes indicated in surveys. One of the most important of the Pesharim is the *Commentary on Nahum* (4QpNah), which mentions two Seleucid kings by name. The *Habakkuk Commentary* (1QpHab) is important for its references to the internal history of the sect, as well as to the "Kittim," who seem to be the Romans. The *Commentary on Psalm 37* (4QpPs[a]) is also important for its internal references. See 5.2.6.3 for a discussion of possible historical allusions. For a study of the Pesharim in general, see Horgan and Brooke (1985).

Other documents have potential value because of their references to either external history or the internal development of the sect, but they are much more difficult to interpret. For example, the *Hymns* (1QH) are thought by many to have been written in part by the founder of the sect, but their precise meaning is often obscure. This has not prevented some scholars from attempting to use them for historical reconstruction (cf. the criticisms of Davies 1987: 87–105). It is debatable whether the other scrolls are a product of the community or were taken over by the community from some other source. For instance, many take the *Temple Scroll* (11QT) to be a Qumran composition (e.g., Yadin), but others disagree (e.g., Levine; Stegemann 1987; Stegemann 1989).

5.2.6.2 The Archeology

Very important for both the history of the community and the archeological picture of Judea is the archeological survey carried out at Qumran (de Vaux; cf. Davies 1982: 36–69). It is important, however, to distinguish between the actual data and their interpretation by archeologists and others.

Qumran was inhabited off and on for almost a millennium. Discounting evidence of prehistoric occupation in some of the caves, the first major occupation took place during the time of the Israelite monarchy. The site is probably referred to in some Old Testament passages (perhaps as the "City of Salt" in Josh 15:61-62), but the precise identification is disputed. Qumran was most likely only a fortress or military installation. The site was abandoned at some point, probably toward the end of the monarchy, and left vacant for several centuries.

The main periods of occupation are identified by phases Ia, Ib, and II (using de Vaux's terminology). Phase Ia was a very small settlement, comprising only a few dozen individuals at most. This period cannot be dated precisely, but both coins and pottery indicate the last part of the second century B.C.E., although the beginning of the first century B.C.E. cannot be excluded. Phase Ib represents a considerable expansion in building with no break in habitation. The community came to include perhaps as many as two hundred inhabitants. The dating of this phase depends on the dating of phase Ia, which was probably only of short duration. Coins suggest that phase Ib covered the first two-thirds of the first century (about 100–31 B.C.E.). The reason for including 31 B.C.E. is the evidence of an earthquake, followed by a period of abandonment; because Josephus mentions a major earthquake in 31 B.C.E., this dating is usually accepted. However, it is not clear whether the earthquake caused the abandonment or was coincidental. There is also the possibility that the damage ascribed to the earthquake was caused simply by a shift of the unstable soil of the plateau on which the settlement stood, making the dating even more problematic.

Phase II began near the turn of the era and seems to have been brought to an end by the Romans, as evidenced by Roman arrowheads uncovered in a burn layer (i.e., about 1–68 C.E.). The population of the community seems to have been about the same in number as in phase Ib. The layout of the buildings was also similar, with some modifications. These and other indications suggest that the community of phase II was a continuation of that of phase Ib. Phase II was followed by phase III, which represents a short occupation by Roman forces, probably only until about 73 or 74 and the fall of Masada. Some coins also suggest a brief occupation during the Bar-Kokhba revolt, probably by Jewish fighters.

5.2.6.3 Historical Data

From the historian's viewpoint, the scrolls appear to provide information for (1) some events of Judean history, and (2) some aspects of the internal history of the Qumran sect (for discussion on the sect's identity, see 8.2.5.4.1). For example, a figure mentioned in a number of passages is the "Wicked Priest." This figure has generally been taken to be one of the Hasmonean priest-rulers, such as Simon (Cross: 149–52) or Jonathan (Vermes 1987: 31), or even a succession of Hasmonean rulers (Brownlee 1982–83). Also featured is the "Man of Lies." Is he to be identified with the Wicked Priest, as is often thought, or is he someone else? The founder and leader of the sect is called the "Teacher of Righteousness" (*môrēh haṣṣedek*). A number of passages have been widely interpreted as referring to the internal development of the sect (e.g., CD 1:1—2:1) or to interaction between the community and the Hasmoneans (especially the *Habakkuk Commentary*). Certain groups are referred to as "the wicked of Ephraim and Manasseh" (4QpPs[a] 2:17), which have been widely identified with the Sadducees and Pharisees. Similarly, the "Seekers after Smooth Things" (4QpNah 1:2, 7; 2:2; etc.) are often taken to be the Pharisees. One should be cautious, however, because these are stereotyped terms that could be applied to a variety of enemies (Pardee 1972–73); it would be a mistake to use such data to reconstruct the history of the Pharisaic movement. As Davies has pointed out, the *Hymns* may have been a source for stereotyped expressions that had different meanings at different times and in different contexts, even if a particular passage seems to have a clear referent (1987: 87–105).

The problem is that many widely accepted interpretations depend on several assumptions, which have been strongly challenged in recent years by Murphy-O'Connor and Davies, about the nature of the evidence and the associated methodological problems: (1) that the scrolls are the product of the community, rather than earlier works simply adopted or reworked by the sect; (2) that the veiled allusions in the scrolls can be correctly interpreted (e.g., the Wicked Priest and the Man of Lies); (3) that the archeological data can be interpreted by the development of the sect as it is assumed from the literary sources; and (4) that paleography is an exact enough science to allow fairly close dating of the preserved MSS. As Davies has noted, one would expect the archeological data to have precedence over the literary information, rather than vice versa (1985: 46).

More secure are references that mention historical personages by name. For example, as noted above, the *Commentary on Nahum* (4QpNah) says that King Demetrius came against a "furious young lion" (1:5) who "hangs men alive" (1:7–8). This strongly suggests Alexander Janneus and an incident during his rule involving Jewish opponents and the Seleucid king Demetrius III (5.4.9). Furthermore, the "Kittim" are now almost universally identified with the Romans. Nearly thirty years ago it was stated that other Hasmonean figures (e.g., Alexandra Salome, Hyrcanus, the Roman governor Aemilius Scaurus [Milik: 73]) are mentioned by name in a calendar, but the document with these names has yet to see the light of day. It has also been alleged that the as yet unpublished *Halakic Letter* (4QMMT) is a letter from the community (the Teacher of Righteousness?) to its opponents (Jonathan or Simon Maccabee?) and will provide important clues to the history of the community (Qimron/Strugnell); however, if the unofficial transcription in circulation is anything to go by, then other, quite different interpretations are possible. Therefore, in using the scrolls to reconstruct Judean history at this time, one should probably be much more cautious and tentative than is often recognized. There are still major problems to be sorted out with regard to Qumran and its literature.

5.2.7 *1 Enoch* 83–105

For discussion and bibliography, see 4.2.5.7.

5.2.8 Book of Jubilees

Charles, R. H. *The Book of Jubilees or the Little Genesis* (1902).
Doran, R. "The Non-dating of Jubilees: Jub 34–38; 23:14-32 in Narrative Context." *JSJ* 20 (1989) 1–11.
Endres, J. C. *Biblical Interpretation in the Book of Jubilees* (1987).

Goldstein, J. A. "The Date of the Book of Jubilees." *PAAJR* 50 (1983) 63–86.
JLBM: 73–80.
JWSTP: 97–104.
Knibb, M. A. *Jubilees and the Origins of the Qumran Community* (1989).
Pummer, R. "The *Book of Jubilees* and the Samaritans." *Eglise et théologie* 10 (1979) 147–78.
Schürer: 3.308–18.
VanderKam, J. C. *Textual and Historical Studies in the Book of Jubilees* (1977).
———. "The Putative Author of the Book of Jubilees." *JSS* 26 (1981) 209–17.
———, ed. *The Book of Jubilees* (1989).

This book claims to be a revelation to Moses on Sinai. In fact, it paraphrases much of Genesis 1—Exodus 12 but includes many different details and interpretations. All events are dated according to a forty-nine-year jubilee cycle (hence the name), and a solar calendar is presupposed. In a list of Sabbath instructions and regulations (*hălākôt*) in 50:6-13, a number of parallels are found between Jubilees and instructions in the *Damascus Document* (CD 10:14—11:18) at Qumran. To the historian, interest in the work lies in its interpretation of the biblical text and in additional material which provides insight into the state of Judaism—or one sort of Judaism—during that time.

There is general agreement that Jubilees dates from the second century B.C.E., but precise dating is uncertain. VanderKam argues for a date of 161–140, based on battles of the patriarch Judah that he argues are thinly veiled descriptions of battles fought during the Maccabean revolt (1977: 207–85). Goldstein correctly notes that the alleged parallels are far from obvious but then uses the same dubious method to date the book to 169–167 on the basis of presumed (but less than obvious) parallels with the "Hellenistic reform." Nickelsburg similarly dates Jubilees to 168. Although many passages in the book can be associated with the period immediately preceding, during, or soon after the Maccabean revolt, most of them could also fit other times. Doran has pointed out the uncertainty of some of the most important proposed historical allusions and how easily they can be differently interpreted. Beyond a general second-century date, no precise time of composition can be said to have been established (cf. Schürer: 3.311–13).

5.2.9 *Third Sibylline Oracle*

Portions of the *Third Sibylline Oracle* were probably composed as early as the second century B.C.E. and tell us something about the Jewish community in Egypt. For a discussion, see 9.2.3.2.

5.2.10 Fragmentary Jewish Greek Writings

Attridge, H. W. "Jewish Historiography." *Early Judaism and Its Modern Interpreters* (1986) 311–43, esp. 311–16.
Collins, J. J. *Between Athens and Jerusalem* (1986).
Doran, R. "The Jewish Hellenistic Historians before Josephus." *ANRW* 2 (1987) 20.1.246–97.
Holladay, C. R. *Fragments from Hellenistic Jewish Authors.* Vol. 1: *Historians* (1983); Vol. 2: *Poets* (1989).
OTP: 2.775–919.
Walter, N. "Judische-hellenistische Literatur vor Philon von Alexandrian (unter Ausschluss der Historiker." *ANRW* 2 (1987) 20.1.67–120.

The fragmentary Jewish writings in Greek are generally treated as a collection, even though the accident of their preservation is their only common feature. Most of what is preserved has come from a first-century B.C.E. collection by Alexander Polyhistor, whose writing (now lost) was, in turn, drawn on by Eusebius, Clement of Alexandria, and other Christian writers. The writings represent diverse literary genres and were probably produced over a wide period of time and geographical area. Several most likely belong to the period from 200 to 63 B.C.E., although it is often difficult to be certain about provenance. A number cannot be dated more specifically than to the period between the conquest of Alexander and the time of Alexander Polyhistor. In addition to the individual bibliographies listed below, articles on many of the writings are found in the *EJ*.

5.2.10.1 Demetrius the Chronographer

Bickerman, E. J. "The Jewish Historian Demetrius." *Christianity, Judaism, and Other Greco-Roman Cults* (1975) 3.72–84.
JWSTP: 161–62.
Schürer: 3.513–17.

Only a few fragments of this writer's work on chronography are preserved. One of them mentions "Ptolemy the Fourth" (221–204 B.C.E.). If this is correct (although many scribal errors have been attributed to these fragments), then it would put Demetrius in last part of the third century. The only version of the Bible he seems to know is the LXX, showing that this translation of the Pentateuch was already extant by his time (4.3.4). The few bits of his work that survive show a rationalistic exegesis which attempts to sort out difficulties, especially as they relate to chronology. His work fits the spirit of Hellenistic historiography, in which traditions and legends were scrutinized and remolded into history.

5.2.10.2 Eupolemus

JWSTP: 162–66.
Schürer: 3.517–21, 528–31.
Wacholder, B. Z. *Eupolemus: A Study of Judaeo-Greek Literature* (1974).

Eupolemus composed a work which was apparently titled *History of the Kings of Judah*. He is widely accepted as being the Eupolemus b. John who was active as a Hasmonean ambassador to Rome (1 Macc 8:17; 2 Macc 4:11). The preserved excerpts are all on this period of Old Testament history and thus give no direct evidence about Eupolemus's own times. Nevertheless, they show how the Old Testament account of Israel's early history was interpreted, cherished, and used as a model for the ideals of many Jews during the rise of the Hasmonean state.

5.2.10.3 Artapanus

JWSTP: 166–68.
Schürer: 3.521–25.

Nothing is known about Artapanus, who could be from the third century rather than the second or early first. The preserved fragments show an embellishment of the biblical narrative similar to Eupolemus's writings, in which the biblical personages are magnified and turned into heroes. Thus Abraham teaches the Egyptians astrology, and Moses becomes an Egyptian general who conquers the Ethiopians. A major point of interest is that Artapanus accommodated Israel's history to pagan customs. For example, Moses is alleged to have appointed the particular gods to be worshiped by each nome in Egypt. This has led some scholars to argue that Artapanus was a pagan, not a Jew, but this is generally rejected because his writings seem too chauvinistic for a non-Jew. What his writings do show is the extent to which some Jews were ready to take a "broad-minded" view toward the surrounding Greek culture.

5.2.10.4 Aristobulus

JWSTP: 274–79.
Schürer: 3.579–87.
Walter, N. *Der Thoraausleger Aristobulus* (1964).

Aristobulus most likely wrote in the second century because the King Ptolemy to whom he dedicated his work is usually identified with Ptolemy VI (180–145 B.C.E.; see *OTP*: 2.832–33). His work is of interest because it seems to be the first time allegory was used extensively as a device in biblical interpretation by a Jewish writer. Aristobulus claimed that Plato drew on the Old Testament for his views on legislation, which further indicates the interaction of Jews with the surrounding Greek culture. The use of allegory to interpret Homer was widespread and the suggestion of Near Eastern priority to the Greeks was a device used by a number of native writers.

5.2.10.5 Ezekiel the Dramatist

Jacobson, H. *The "Exagoge" of Ezekiel* (1983).
JWSTP: 125–30.
Schürer: 3.563–66.

Ezekiel also probably lived after 200 but may have lived as early as the third century. The surviving fragments of his work concern the life of Moses and are said to be from a play on the exodus called the *Exagoge*. Two points of interest stand out. One is his use of a Greek literary vehicle for an Old Testament tradition. The other is at least one example of trying to explain a discrepancy in the biblical text (the question of the ancestry of Moses and Zipporah and how they could be contempories). The Bible was read and pondered, but it could also be repackaged in a form more suitable for those immersed in Greek culture.

5.2.11 *Testament of Moses*

Collins, J. J. *The Apocalyptic Vision of the Book of Daniel* (1977).
JLBM: 80–83, 212–14.
JWSTP: 344–49.
Nickelsburg, G.W.E., ed. *Studies on the Testament of Moses* (1973).
Schalit, A. *Untersuchung zur "Assumptio Mosis"* (1989).
Schürer: 3.278–88.

The date of completion of this book is more certain than most. Because it mentions Herod's death but not his sons' deaths (6:2-9), it must have been completed between 4 B.C.E. and about 30 C.E. Its review of history, however, has a significant section relating to the Maccabean revolt (chaps. 8–9), which has led Nickelsburg to argue that an original was composed during Hasmonean times and was then updated in the early first century C.E. (1973: 34–37).

The *Testament of Moses* is important for its attitude toward the Antiochean persecution—passive resistance and martyrdom rather than active military measures against the oppression. In this, it shows clear affinities with the book of Daniel and may well have originated in similar circles (Collins: 198–210); these circles were not necessarily those that supported the Maccabean cause.

5.2.12 Other Jewish Literature

A number of other Jewish writings seem to have emerged during the period 200–63 B.C.E. Scholars attribute some listed earlier, such as Judith (4.2.5.5), to this period. Ben Sira (4.2.5.2) was completed after 200, although it also reflects the general culture of late Ptolemaic rule in Palestine. Many scholars argue that the *Letter of (Pseudo-)Aristeas* (4.2.5.6) was also completed during the later second century.

Such writings do not usually provide information on specific events in Israel's history but are important for understanding the religion and culture, even if their precise significance is often a matter for discussion. Not all the writings one could mention are from Palestine or relate to the Jewish state, but even those that do not are of value for Jewish communities in other areas.

5.2.13 Greek Historians

Lesky, A. H. *A History of Greek Literature* (1966).

The following writers provide general information on the history of the period, although Jewish history is seldom specifically mentioned. All the authors are in the Loeb Classical Library, which provides a convenient text and translation; an up-to-date introduction with bibliography can be found in *CHCL*; see also *OCD* and Lesky. The specific passages on Jews and Judea are collected in *GLAJJ*. Other important sources include Diodorus Siculus (2.2.6.6), Pompeius Trogus (2.2.6.7), Plutarch (2.2.6.8), and Polybius (4.2.6.3).

5.2.13.1 Strabo

Strabo (ca. 64 B.C.E. to after 21 C.E.) wrote an important history that has now been lost, although it seems to have been drawn on by Josephus (5.2.4). However, his *Geography* survives and provides some useful information on Palestinian history as well as geography (16.2.28–46 §§759–65). The source from which he drew his information may have been describing the situation before Alexander Janneus, because he refers to the destruction of the city by Janneus (16.2.30) but says nothing about its rebuilding in 61 B.C.E.

5.2.13.2 Livy

Briscoe, J. *A Commentary on Livy, Books XXXI–XXXIII* (1973).
Ogilvie, R. M. *A Commentary on Livy, Books 1–5* (1965).

The history of Rome by Livy (64 B.C.E.–17 C.E.) covered the years to 9 B.C.E. With Tacitus, Livy is one of the best Roman historians, but, like Tacitus, much of his work has perished. Books 41 to 45 are complete and cover 178–167 B.C.E., an important period for Jewish history. There are also extensive fragments and summaries of the lost books.

5.2.13.3 Appian

Writing in Greek, Appian (flourished ca. 150 C.E.) produced a history of Rome to the time of Trajan. Only eighteen of the twenty-four complete books survive, although there are also fragments of the others. Of special importance for Jewish history is the *Syriakē* (book 11), which describes events in the eastern Mediterranean.

5.2.13.4 Cassius Dio

Millar, F. *A Study of Cassius Dio* (1964).

Dio began his history of Rome (in Greek) in 229 C.E. and eventually included events up to that date. He is often a useful source, because he had access to important writers whose work has been lost (e.g., portions of Tacitus). Unfortunately, many of his books, including those that cover most of the Maccabean and Hasmonean period, are known only from fragments or from the epitome of the Byzantine writer Joannes Zonaras. The years 68–10 B.C.E. of his history are complete (books 36–54).

5.2.14 Archeology, Inscriptions, and Coins

5.2.14.1 Decrees of Antiochus III

Bertrand, J. M. "Sur l'inscription d'Hefzibah." *ZPE* 46 (1982) 167–74.
Fischer, T. "Zur Seleukideninschrift von Hefzibah." *ZPE* 33 (1979) 131–38.
Landau, Y. H. "A Greek Inscription Found near Hefzibah." *IEJ* 16 (1966) 54–70.

A stela found near Hefzibah in Israel contains several decrees issued by Antiochus III between 202 and 195 B.C.E. The decrees concern protecting the local people from having soldiers billeted on them or from being ejected from their houses, which would be given over to quartering soldiers. The decrees reveal the realities of the area during and just after the Fifth Syrian War (4.4.4). They have been compared with Antiochus's decree regarding Judea and Jerusalem, quoted by Josephus (*Ant.* 12.3.3–4 §§138–46; see 4.3.1). For ease of reading, the following excerpt does not have minor restorations indicated:

> [IVa 20–26] To the great King Antiochos, memorandum by Ptolemaios, *stratēgos* and chief-priest. I propose, if you approve, King, ---------- to [Kle(?)]on and Heliodoros the *dioiketai* respecting the villages belonging to me as property and hereditary tenure and respecting those which you ordered to be assigned (to me), that nobody should be allowed to quarter under any pretence, or to bring in others or to commandeer the draught animals or to eject the villagers. The same (letter) to Heliodoros. [V 27–33] King Antiochos to Marsyas greetings. There announced to us Ptolemaios the *stratēgos* and chief-priest, that man[y of those] travelling through lodge by violence in his villages and do many other acts of injustice, not caring for the qua[rters(?) (prepared) by] us. Relating to this now take care that they not only be restrained but also punished tenfold if damages are done. The same (letter) to Lysanias, Leon, Dionikos. (Landau: 61; translation modified in light of Fischer)

5.2.14.2 Jerusalem Inscription

This is a fragmentary inscription recently published in *SEG* (30 [1980] 483–84: no. 1695), although it apparently first appeared in a Hebrew article by Applebaum in 1980. It has been little discussed so far. Applebaum (as quoted in *SEG*) suggested that it was a votive inscription of the Seleucid garrison at Jerusalem. The *SEG* editors labeled Applebaum's reconstruction and interpretation "clearly fanciful" but made no further suggestion for the inscription. Goldstein (*1983: 112) also found Applebaum's interpretation "unconvincing" but suggested that the stone might have been brought from elsewhere, perhaps a military colony in Samaria. According to Bar-Kochva (*119 n.12), however, the mineral composition and other characteristics indicate that the stone was local to Jerusalem. The preserved text is fragmentary and damaged in places; it contains no clear reference to the Akra, even though Applebaum apparently included the Akra in his reconstruction to fill one of the lacunae.

5.2.14.3 Coins and Seals

Avigad, N. "A Bulla of Jonathan the High Priest." *IEJ* 25 (1975) 8–12.
Fischer, T. "Johannes Hyrkan I. auf Tetradrachmen Antiochos' VII.?" *ZDPV* 91 (1975) 191–96.
Hanson, R. S. "Toward a Chronology of the Hasmonean Coins." *BASOR* 216 (1974) 21–23.
———. *Tyrian Influence in the Upper Galilee* (1980).
Jeselsohn, D. "Hever Yehudim—A New Jewish Coin." *PEQ* 112 (1980) 11–17.
Kindler, A. "The Jaffa Hoard of Alexander Jannaeus." *IEJ* 4 (1954) 170–85.
———. "Addendum to the Dated Coins of Alexander Janneus." *IEJ* 18 (1968) 188–91.
Meshorer, Y. *Ancient Jewish Coinage.* Vol. 1: *Persian Period through Hasmonaeans* (1982) 35–98.
Naveh, J. "Dated Coins of Alexander Janneus." *IEJ* 18 (1968) 20–25.
Rabin, C. "Alexander Jannaeus and the Pharisees." *JJS* 7 (1956) 3–11.
Rappaport, U. "The Emergence of Hasmonean Coinage." *AJS Review* 1 (1976) 171–86.
Sperber, D. "A Note on Hasmonean Coin-Legends. Heber and Rosh Heber." *PEQ* 97 (1965) 85–93.

According to 1 Macc 15:6, Simon was given the right to mint his own coins. The actual finds, however, have the names of Johanan, Judah, Jonathan, and Mattathias in paleo-Hebrew script; there is no archeological evidence for coins minted under Simon (coins earlier identified with his rule have now been shown to belong to the war in 66–70). The problem in identifying the extant coins is that more than one ruler bore the names Johanan (Hyrcanus I and II) and Judah (Aristobulus I and II). Therefore, it has been disputed whether the Johanan coins are to be ascribed to John Hyrcanus or Hyrcanus II and whether the Judah coins belong to Aristobulus I or Aristobulus II (Meshorer: 35–47; Rappaport). For nonspecialists to judge between the two is difficult, but the arguments can be summarized. Rappaport lists five points in favor of John Hyrcanus and Aristobulus I.

1. John Hyrcanus I was independent of Seleucid rule and would be expected to mint his own coins. Coins were an important medium of propaganda, especially silver coins whose minting would be a demonstration of independence. Rappaport argues, however, that the Hasmoneans as a whole did not use coins for propaganda; rather, they issued bronze coinage purely out of need. Silver coins were not produced because they were not needed; enough Seleucid silver was in circulation to meet the people's needs.
2. The archeological sequence at Beth-Zur and elsewhere shows the

coins of Hyrcanus following directly on Seleucid coinage dated to about 130 B.C.E. If the Johanan coins were issued under Hyrcanus II, this leaves an unexplained gap of 60 to 70 years.

3. Hyrcanus II was not given sufficient freedom by the Romans to mint his own coins until he became ethnarch in about 48 B.C.E.
4. The "Judah" coins are more likely those of Aristobulus I than Aristobulus II because the title "king" is not used on the inscription (as we would expect on those of Aristobulus II).
5. The early Hyrcanus coins replace the portrait found on Seleucid coins with a helmet, which takes up a large amount of space. Later coins show better use of space for symbols and inscription.

Meshorer has written more recently. His arguments against Rappaport include the following:

1. Hasmonean coinage cannot be earlier than 105–102 B.C.E. The argument revolves around some coins of Antiochus VIII that were supposedly struck in his twentieth year in Jerusalem (Rappaport denies they were struck in Jerusalem). Because Antiochus was not in control of Jerusalem at this time, we must conclude that these coins were actually struck by John Hyrcanus (or Alexander Janneus), who chose to mint a Seleucid imitation rather than produce his own. It is unlikely that he would have minted Seleucid coins once the distinctive Hasmonean coinage had been created. Therefore, Hasmonean coins were introduced after 105–102, that is, sometime in the reign of Janneus.
2. Under Antiochus VII a number of local areas produced Seleucid coins that used their own local symbols. Some of these coins (dated to about 131–129 B.C.E.) were struck in Jerusalem. Because the lily (a prominent symbol on later Jewish coinage) is found on these, Meshorer argues that these coins were minted by John Hyrcanus with Antiochus's authority. This helps confirm that Hyrcanus I was not producing his own coins.
3. Rappaport's archeological arguments are methodologically incorrect, failing to note the presence of post-130 Seleucid coins in the finds that he dates to the pre-130 period.
4. All the Johanan coins at Beth-Zur contain Greek letters or monograms that have been interpreted as those of Antipater, who was closely associated with Hyrcanus II.
5. No Johanan coins have been found at Samaria, even though John Hyrcanus was closely associated with that city. Coins of Alexander

Janneus, who was also associated with it, have been found there. The absence of Johanan coins in Samaria is therefore because these coins were minted by Hyrcanus II, who had little to do with the city.
6. No coins of Alexander Janneus have been found together with Johanan coins in Jerusalem, although Johanan coins have been found in later strata.
7. The Judah coins are an imitation of those minted by Alexander Janneus, who had been strongly influenced by the earlier Seleucid issues produced in Jerusalem. Therefore, the Judah coins were produced by Aristobulus II, not Aristobulus I.
8. There are too many die variants in the Judah coinage for the coins all to have been created during the one-year reign of Aristobulus I, which indicates that the Judah coins were minted by Aristobulus II.

This seems to be the latest published position of each scholar. More recently, however, Sievers reports some new developments based on a recent coin hoard acquired by the Hebrew University and some unpublished finds of excavations on Mount Gerizim (*152–54). Seleucid coins were found in both cases, but no Hasmonean coins other than those of "Johanan" were discovered. Both Meshorer and Barag conclude that the "Johanan" coins in the new finds are coins of John Hyrcanus I (from oral communications which Sievers was authorized to report). It remains to be seen what specialists will conclude when the full data become available, but it sounds as if present thinking comes down definitely on the side of Hyrcanus I as the first Hasmonean to mint his own coins.

One puzzle about the inscriptions on the "Jonathan" and "Johanan" coins is the phrase "congregation/council of the Jews" (*ḥbr yhwdym*). This sometimes appears as "[so-and-so], high priest and *hever* of the Jews." Sperber has argued that it refers to John Hyrcanus's taking over a title because of the opposition of the Pharisees. He assumes, however, that the coins belong to Hyrcanus I rather than Hyrcanus II, and he accepts the reports in rabbinic literature as reliable (see 1.1.4.2). Jeselsohn has drawn attention to the new find of a coin with the legend "*hever* of the Jews" alone, with no ruler's name. He also links this with the Pharisaic opposition to the Hasmoneans, this time in the reign of Alexander Janneus, and thinks that these coins were issued by the opposition to Janneus. Again, one of the major questions is the extent to which the opposition to Janneus was led by Pharisees (see Rabin; 8.2.2.1); however, one could accept Jeselsohn's suggestion that the *hever* was an institution abolished by Janneus without having to tie this to the Pharisees. Some coins have "Johanan head of the *hever* of the Jews" (*yḥnn r'š ḥbr yhwdym*).

According to Meshorer (1.66–67), Hyrcanus II adopted this title when he was designated "ethnarch of the Jews" under Julius Caesar (6.4.3).

5.2.14.4 Archeology

Arav, R. *Hellenistic Palestine* (1989).
Avigad, N. *Discovering Jerusalem* (1983).
———. "The Upper City." *Biblical Archaeology Today* (1985) 469–75.
Dequeker, L. "The City of David and the Seleucid Acra in Jerusalem." *Orientalia Lovaniensia Analecta* 19 (1985) 193–210.
Funk, R. W. "The 1957 Campaign at Beth-Zur." *BASOR* 150 (April 1958) 8–20.
Kuhnen, H.-P. *Palästina in griechisch-römischer Zeit* (1990).
Laperrousaz, E.-M. "Jérusalem à l'époque perse (étendue et statut)." *Transeuphratène* 1 (1989) 55–65.
Reich, R. "Archaeological Evidence of the Jewish Population at Hasmonean Gezer." *IEJ* 31 (1981) 48–52.
Sellers, O. R., et al. *The 1957 Excavation at Beth-Zur* (1968).
Tsafrir, Y. "The Location of the Seleucid Akra." *RB* 82 (1975) 501–21.
———. "The Desert Fortresses of Judaea in the Second Temple Period." *Jerusalem Cathedra* 2 (1982) 120–45.
Tushingham, A. D. "The Western Hill of Jerusalem: A Critique of the 'Maximalist' Position." *Levant* 19 (1987) 137–43.
Williamson, H.G.M. "Nehemiah's Walls Revisited." *PEQ* 116 (1984) 81–88.

For general comments and bibliography that are important for this period, see 1.1.1. A number of Seleucid and Maccabean sites are known (see the general surveys by Kuhnen and Arav), including Jerusalem, Beth-Zur, Gezer, Jericho, and Shechem. Although the ceramic evidence does not usually show sharp breaks during the Hellenistic period, dating is generally easier for this period because of the destruction during the Maccabean revolt, as well as finds of coins for the period (Kuhnen: 38–42). The important desert fortresses, better known for events during the time of Herod (Macherus, Alexandrium, Masada, Hyrcania), in most cases were actually Hasmonean foundations, as was the palace at Jericho (Tsafrir 1982). Although the history of Beth-Zur is known in some detail from the books of Maccabees, coordinating this knowledge with the stratigraphy has been a problem, giving rise to a variety of interpretations (cf. Arav: 67–71). Hellenistic remains from Jerusalem are rather scarce despite the extensive excavations, probably because later building activities tended to obliterate the earlier structures.

One problem that has exercised archeologists is the location of the Akra, which played such an important role in the Maccabean crisis.

According to Josephus, the Akra itself was destroyed, and even the hill on which it stood was leveled by Simon Maccabee. Despite fierce debate over the decades, recent scholarship has begun to accept that the Akra was located on the southeast hill of Jerusalem in the old City of David, probably on the north side but south of the Temple Mount, that is, in Josephus's Lower City (*Bar-Kochva: 445–65; Dequeker). However, Josephus's statement that the hill was leveled seems to be a legendary touch, for the hill on which the temple was erected was evidently always higher than that on which the City of David was located.

A second question concerns the area of settlement of Jerusalem at this time. The "maximalist" position assumes that the western hill (the Upper City) was already inhabited and a part of the city by the time of the Maccabees (Avigad), whereas the "minimalist" position maintains that only during Hasmonean rule did the western hill become incorporated into the city boundary (Tushington). It has even been argued that the western hill was already included inside the city wall as early as the time of Nehemiah (Laperrousaz), but at the moment the consensus is against it (cf. Williamson on the textual evidence).

5.3 HISTORICAL PROBLEMS

5.3.1 Antiochus III's Decrees concerning the Jews

Bickerman, E. J. "La charte séleucide de Jérusalem." *Studies in Jewish and Christian History* (1980a) 2.44–85.

———. "Une proclamation séleucide relative au temple de Jérusalem." *Studies in Jewish and Christian History* (1980b) 2.86–104.

Marcus, R. "Appendix D. Antiochus III and the Jews (*Ant*. xii. 129–153)." *Josephus* (1943) 7.743–66.

From the stela discovered near Hefzibah (5.2.14.1) we have original material illustrating the sorts of rulings made by Antiochus III during the fight for Palestine or shortly after he conquered it. The Jews are not mentioned directly; however, according to Josephus (*Ant*. 12.3.3–4 §§138–46), after his conquest of the area Antiochus issued proclamations that confirmed the rights of the Jews to practice their traditional customs and religion. Most scholars have accepted these decrees as authentic, even if there may have been some corruption of or tampering with them by Jewish scribes (Bickerman (1980a; 1980b); see Marcus for older literature). They fit Antiochus's known practice of affirming traditional customs and constitutions and honoring those people who had helped him or had otherwise gained his favor.

5.3.2 Causes of the Maccabean Revolt

As the discussion at 5.4.3 indicates, the exact course of events leading to the revolt is not certain, making any attempt to explain the oppression by Antiochus more difficult. The facile explanations so often found in handbooks frequently do not even note correctly the sequence of events leading up to the suppression of the temple sacrifices (e.g., they fail to note that the "abomination of desolation" [5.3.4] was not immediately associated with Antiochus's taking of Jerusalem but rather with an event some time later).

It must be kept in mind that a whole complex of dichotomies existed in the time preceding the revolt. There were pro-Seleucid and pro-Ptolemaic factions. There were the Tobiad and Oniad families (although these were actually related through intermarriage). And there were the promoters of Hellenism, in contrast to the rest of the people. These dichotomies do not line up neatly but intertwine in a complicated fashion; for example, there were pro-Ptolemaic Tobiads and pro-Seleucid Tobiads. The pro- versus anti-Hellenists were only a relative matter, because all Judaism by this time was as Hellenized as the rest of the ancient Near East (5.3.3; chap. 3).

Some of the major theories have been summarized in a convenient fashion by Bickerman (*24–31), Tcherikover (*175–85), and Bringmann (*99–111); what follows is my own formulation, which in some instances covers points not touched on by these scholars.

5.3.2.1 Ancient Views

*Bickerman: 9–23.

In 1 Maccabees the persecution is taken for granted. It is just assumed that "wicked" individuals, whether "heathen" or Jewish "apostates," will do such things without any particular motivation. A good deal of emphasis seems to be placed on the "arrogance" of Gentiles (e.g., 1:21).

Second Maccabees sees the major cause of the religious suppression in the sins of Israel itself. The Gentiles are seen as only a scourge in the hand of God to punish for such wrongs as the removal and murder of Onias III and the neglect of the temple by the priests (5:17-20; 6:12-16). It is presumed that the Gentiles will eventually be punished for their arrogance, but the emphasis falls on the "apostate" Jews.

On the pagan side, Tacitus presents a view that has also been popular in modern times, albeit in a slightly modified form: Antiochus was desirous of converting the Jews from their barbarism and exclusivistic religion to more enlightened and liberal views (Tacitus, *Hist.* 5.8).

5.3.2.2 Antiochus's Character

Habicht, C. "The Seleucids and Their Rivals." *CAH*[2] (1989) 8.324–87.

Antiochus's personal character as the explanation for the persecution arises from one of our earliest sources, the historian Polybius. He describes Antiochus's activities in a way which suggests that at least some of his actions would have appeared peculiar to his subjects (Polybius 26.1). The historian also cites the pun by which Antiochus was called *Epimanes* ("mad"), instead of Epiphanes. Although such an explanation can never be ruled out, it is not very useful because it ultimately admits no logical explanation; that is, the final answer is put down simply to the caprice of an unbalanced—or at least, unpredictable—individual.

In contrast, there is evidence that Antiochus was a very able ruler on the whole, and that a number of his actions are explained by his long sojourn in Rome. Some of his actions which would have seemed strange to the Syrians were normal among the Romans (*Goldstein 1976: 104–5). Further, Polybius's assessment of Antiochus is by no means wholly negative but has a positive side (e.g., 28.18). In his study of Antiochus, Mørkholm examines the question of the ruler's ability (esp. *181–91), and he summarizes the situation:

> The result of these considerations must be that Antiochus IV, in spite of some miscalculations, was actually a shrewd politician who may even deserve to be called a statesman. His campaigns in Egypt and Armenia show him to have been an able general too. If we review the Seleucid king list we may safely rate Antiochus IV well above average. (*187)

A similar assessment is given by Habicht (341–43).

5.3.2.3 Hellenization of Antiochus's Empire

Rigsby, K. J. "Seleucid Notes." *TAPA* 110 (1980) 233–54.

Among nineteenth-century scholars, Antiochus's Hellenizing policy was a favorite explanation for the religious suppression, and it still seems to be the explanation advanced in Schürer (1.147–48). The problem with this is that there is no evidence that Antiochus IV was a greater Hellenizer than his predecessors or that he actively promoted Hellenization for idealistic reasons. A number of Greek foundations (i.e., native cities allowed to organize themselves as *poleis*, "Greek cities") occurred during his reign. This has been reckoned as high as fifteen or so, but the actual number may have been rather fewer (Mørkholm: 115–18). In any case, they were fewer than under his predecessors Seleucus I and Antiochus I. After a hiatus of many decades in which few Greek cities were founded, Antiochus's father, Antiochus III, had resumed the practice, although in a number of cases under both Antiochus III and IV what occurred were refoundations rather than new foundations. More importantly, the initiation always came from the natives themselves. Far from being forced to adopt a Greek constitution, natives considered such a step an important privilege, for which they paid well into the king's coffers. Antiochus's encouragement of Hellenization was clearly given for political, not cultural or religious, reasons.

Jerusalem was a polis from 175 to 168 B.C.E., with no religious overtones. Even if Antiochus had been pushing a policy of Hellenization, it would have made no sense to force new religious measures on the Jews. To have done so to make Jerusalem a polis would also have been unusual, because the native cults of other sacred Oriental cities were not disturbed when allowed to incorporate (*Bickerman: 61–62; *Tcherikover: 471 n.9).

Antiochus no doubt wanted his empire unified, and the Greek incorporation of native cities would help to do this, but there is no evidence that he forced Hellenization or suppressed native customs. On the contrary, to have done so would have created not unity but discontent and strife; it would have been a "suicide" policy, as Bringmann notes (*103, 146). Appeal is often made to the statement of 1 Macc 1:41-43, that Antiochus sent a decree to all his subjects to abandon their native customs. Yet this statement is incredible for two reasons: (1) there is no corroborating evidence that such a decree was issued by Antiochus; and (2) there is no reason to think that the various peoples in the Seleucid Empire would abandon their local customs more easily than would the Jews. Why should the ancient nation of the Phoenicians give up its long established customs, its gods, and its culture more readily than its Jewish neighbors? On the contrary, even when the native peoples became "Hellenized," they continued to preserve their old culture alongside the Greek (*Bickerman: 61–68). Furthermore, there were many Jews in the Seleucid Empire outside Palestine, yet it is not clear that they suffered religious infringement or persecution (*Bickerman: 79–80).

A further argument often advanced for Antiochus's suppression of Jewish religious customs is that he promoted the cult of Zeus Olympius. It is true that Antiochus favored Zeus over Apollo, the latter having been the traditional patron of the Seleucid dynasty. Nevertheless, Seleucus I had been deified as Zeus Nicator, so Zeus was not new to the line (Rigsby: 233–38). Further, the frequent assertion that Antiochus issued coins with his own visage imposed on the image of Zeus is to be doubted (*Mørkholm: 130–31; *Hengel: 1.285–86 and notes). The ruler cult was practiced under Antiochus, but he did not originate it; he simply continued the custom of his predecessors. It seems at times to be tacitly assumed that Antiochus was attempting to set up some sort of pagan monotheism, but such an idea is anachronistic (*Tcherikover: 181–82). Above all, the god worshiped in Jerusalem was not the Greek Zeus but a Syrian god (5.3.4). Mørkholm's assessment is important:

> Antiochus IV was not a zealous Hellenizer, nor a religious innovator who tried to identify himself with Zeus Olympius. His persecution of the Jews had no religious basis, but must be regarded as [a] purely political measure. (*186)

5.3.2.4 Thesis of E. J. Bickerman

*Bickerman.
*Bringmann: 103–11.
Heinemann, I. "Wer veranlasste den Glaubenszwang der Makkabäerzeit?" *MGWJ* 82 (1938) 145–72.
*Hengel: 1.286–303.
*Tcherikover: 183–85.

One of the most important theories explaining the persecution was developed by Bickerman in 1937 in his *Gott der Makkabäer* (English translation *1979). Bickerman puts the blame solidly on the "extreme Hellenists," that is, Menelaus and the Tobiads (although at times Bickerman also refers to Jason in a way that suggests he was to be included with Menelaus). The "Hellenists" were attempting to create an enlightened Yahwism, in which the degenerate and anachronistic accretions (e.g., circumcision, food taboos, purity regulations) would be removed and the pristine original could once more shine forth. The barriers that had separated Jews from the surrounding world would then be removed. The reformed religion thus emerging was in many ways parallel with the Reform Judaism that arose in the nineteenth century (cf. *Bringmann: 110–11). Several statements in the primary sources are important for this argument: Dan 11:30 refers to the concourse of Antiochus with those Jews who "forsake the covenant," a statement paralleled in 1 Macc 1:11. According to Josephus, it was Menelaus who "had compelled his nation to violate their own laws" (*Ant.* 12.9.7 §385). Second Maccabees 13:3-8 also has Menelaus more or less putting Antiochus up to the religious suppression.

This theory has great ingenuity and has been accepted by Hengel (*1.287–303), yet it has also suffered extensive criticism from other eminent specialists (a fact to which Hengel gives far too little attention), especially Heinemann, Tcherikover (*183–85), and Bringmann (*103–11); see also Goldstein (*1983: 99–103). Tcherikover asks why Menelaus should be viewed as the fanatical ideologue that Antiochus was not. Menelaus was interested in power, not in an idealized, syncretistic religion. He was not a sophisticated philosopher or historian of religion. Although the account that associates him with temple robbery (2 Macc 4:39-42) may contain an element of slander, it suggests an individual more concerned with personal gain and advancement than with the ideals of religious innovation. Furthermore, although Menelaus is said to have led Israel to sin, and although the Jews themselves are blamed for the Hellenistic reform, only Antiochus's name is associated with the persecution; nor are any religious slogans connected with the reform. Hengel, in his defense of Bickerman, also seems to rely too much on the statements of hostile sources about the actual motives of the "renegades," instead of recognizing that we have inherited a very tendentious interpretation.

5.3.2.5 Thesis of V. A. Tcherikover

*Tcherikover: 186–203.

In addition to criticizing the theories of Bickerman and others, Tcherikover advances his own. He argues that resistance to Hellenization had developed in Jerusalem, led by the Hasidim. When Jason attempted to retake the city during Antiochus's second invasion of Egypt, Menelaus fled to the Akra; it was the Hasidic-led faction of the people that drove Jason out of the city and attempted to restore the status quo that had prevailed under Onias III. This revolt caused Antiochus to take and sack Jerusalem on his way back from Egypt, but the revolt must have flared up again after he left, and it was necessary to send Apollonius with troops to Jerusalem to install a military colony, or cleruchy. These troops, probably of Syrian origin, were also citizens of the polis of Jerusalem. They wanted to continue to worship their native deities but had no desire to offend the local god. Therefore, they set up their own worship in the Jerusalem temple. Menelaus could hardly refuse this, as it was part of the inherent logic of abolishing the old constitution; but in the eyes of pious Jews the temple was desecrated, and they ceased to worship there.

Many Jewish inhabitants of Jerusalem had already fled, either because their property had been confiscated or as a form of passive resistance. Desecration of the temple caused further Jewish resistance. Antiochus saw that religion was the basis of the new revolt. The Torah had become the watchword of Jewish resistance and had to be extirpated, so he issued decrees prohibiting the practice of Judaism in Palestine. (Tcherikover seems uncertain if Jews outside Palestine were affected; although not arguing that they were, he appears to allow that they might have been.) Therefore, the revolt was not a response to the persecution; rather, persecution was the response to the revolt.

Hengel's criticism of Tcherikover is valid but hardly does justice to the full range of Tcherikover's argument (*1.287; cf. *Goldstein 1983: 98–99). One weakness of Tcherikover's theory is the emphasis which he places on the role of the Hasidim. He reconstructs the Hasidim according to the model of the rabbinic sage (cf. *125–26, 196–97), but this is unjustified (see 8.2.1). Another weakness is Tcherikover's assumption that the only Hellenizers were from the upper class, whereas the common people were basically anti-Hellenistic; in fact, Tcherikover's description of the aims of Menelaus and the Tobiads seems to come close to representing them as ideologues, a representation which he denies Bickerman (*201–3). Finally, Tcherikover's assumption that the occupying force in Jerusalem was a cleruchy of native Syrian soldiers now seems unlikely (*Bar-Kochva: 92–105, 438–44).

5.3.2.6 Thesis of J. A. Goldstein

In a lengthy section of his introduction, Goldstein attempts to tackle the problem in a different way (*1976: 104–60). He points out that various foreign cults were frequently suppressed in Rome during the republican period. This was especially true of the Dionysus (Bacchus) cult. During the time he was a hostage in Rome, Antiochus would have seen several expulsions of foreign cults. Thus, when Antiochus became involved with the Jews, he identified their cult with that of Dionysus, an identification frequently made by outsiders. Because their religion seemed to be the basis of the Jews' revolts against him, Antiochus simply followed the Roman model and attempted to suppress the religion which he saw as the basis of the "Jewish problem." He also attempted to impose religious reform, a "return" to what he thought was the older and purer form of Judaism, without its ritualistic accretions. Menelaus is to some extent exonerated, because he did not agree with the imposed cult and delayed in implementing it until Antiochus sent other officials to do the job.

Goldstein's thesis attempts to resolve the major problem: Why would religious suppression accompany a political rebellion? Tcherikover pointed out that cults could be suppressed if they seemed to be the basis of revolution (*199), so Goldstein's idea is not prima facie improbable. Nevertheless, it makes Antiochus into an ideologue, which has already been shown to be problematic. A number of the criticisms leveled at Bickerman also apply here. Further, Goldstein's discussion is filled with the language of conjecture: "We may suppose . . ."; "Did Antiochus . . . ?"; "Could the Jews have . . . ?; "If this reconstruction is correct. . . ". One of his points was that Antiochus attempted to regulate the Dionysus cult, yet his sole argument was a tenuous interpretation of something to do with the Babylonian Nergal cult (*1976: 128–29). His interpretation of Daniel often depends on an emended reading. Much of the support for his thesis—ingenious and learned as it is—is of a similarly insubstantial nature. This hardly gives one confidence that there is a solid basis for Goldstein's argument, especially as the data are lacking at crucial points.

In a refreshingly self-critical section of his second volume, Goldstein considered problems with and criticisms of his original reconstruction (*1983: 98–112). His final thesis has much in common with Bickerman's: the imposed religion was a "heterodox Judaism," by which Goldstein means a type of polytheistic Judaism practiced in pre-exilic times at Elephantine and otherwise known from hints in the sources. Parallel to Tcherikover, he suggests that this religion was introduced by the garrison placed in the Akra (the "fortifiers of strongholds" in Goldstein's interpretation of Dan 11:39), which he argues was made up of Jewish soldiers (perhaps from Egypt) who practiced this sort of Judaism. The religion included the use of cult stones and pillars (*maṣṣēvôt*) in worship. These Jews were among those who advised Antiochus on his attempt to reform the Jerusalem cult. As will be obvious, a number of the criticisms of Bickerman and Tcherikover also apply to Goldstein's thesis.

5.3.2.7 Thesis of K. Bringmann

The most recent theory explaining the persecution has come from Bringmann in his well-argued monograph (esp. *120–40). His work is by and large a combination of the best insights of Bickerman and Tcherikover, but the resulting synthesis includes Bringmann's original contributions and thus represents a new thesis. The main elements include (in my formulation):

1. Antiochus was no crusading ideologue but a practical politician who needed money. He allowed Jason's "Hellenistic reform" because it brought money and because it seemed a way of resolving the

intra-Jewish conflict between Onias III and Simon the Tobiad (5.4.3.2).

2. Jason's reform did not in any way affect traditional Jewish worship. On the contrary, Jason and the priesthood had a major interest in maintaining the purity and sanctity of the temple, because it was the main source of revenue for the priests (including Jason himself [*74–82]).
3. When Menelaus displaced Jason, he had no reason to continue the Hellenistic reform because it was supported mainly by Jason's followers. Thus, far from taking Hellenization further, Menelaus actually brought Jerusalem's status as a polis to an end (*93–94).
4. Menelaus had promised Antiochus a good deal of money but was soon in difficulties about payment. A ready solution was to begin selling the temple vessels, but this brought a revolt of the people and the death of Lysimachus, Menelaus's brother. Menelaus had little support among the Jews but maintained his position by the help of Antiochus's troops.
5. During Antiochus's second expedition to Egypt, when Jason attempted to take back the priesthood by force, Antiochus intervened to drive off Jason's forces and then established a military colony in Jerusalem.
6. The military settlers may have been Syrian, although they could also have come from Asia Minor. They naturally brought their native worship of Baal Shamem ("lord of heaven") with them. The Jerusalem sanctuary was dedicated to Zeus, but this was no doubt simply the Greek term for Baal Shamem, who could also be identified with Yahweh. The presence of the troops and their cult made the sanctuary "unclean" in the eyes of most Jews.
7. Menelaus was no ideologue (contra Bickerman) but determined to maintain power at all costs. One way of doing this was to institute a new cult in the Jerusalem temple, which would break the tie with the old covenant and eliminate the constraints imposed by the hereditary priesthood. The peculiar measures in the new religion forced on Judea were created by Menelaus himself. He chose the Syrian cult for pragmatic reasons, but there were important differences in the religion he imposed, because the Syrians also practiced circumcision and avoided pork. In some ways the new measures stood Judaism on its head (e.g., sacrificing pigs, which had previously been forbidden). Antiochus accepted Menelaus's proposals partly because he had no choice but to support Menelaus and partly because he was unaware of their likely repercussions. He probably

did not have advisers knowledgeable in Jewish matters other than Menelaus.

Thus the religious measures owed something to the Syrian military cleruchy (because the basis of the cult was Syrian), as proposed by Tcherikover, and were largely instigated by Menelaus, as Bickerman argued. Nevertheless, the official decrees came from Antiochus, who issued them on Menelaus's advice. Antiochus's main concern, however, was to stabilize the province and bring it to heel under the high priest whom he officially designated.

Bringmann has benefited from the work of his predecessors, taking their insights while avoiding many of their drawbacks, and has produced an attractive thesis. This seems to explain most of the data in a rational way that also fits the general political and religious situation of the time. Nevertheless, one fundamental aspect still is not fully convincing: Why would Menelaus have created a religion which forced on the Jews practices that contravened such deeply ingrained elements of Judaism as circumcision and abstinence from pork? If his aim was simply to maintain power, then this seems a strange way of going about it. To his credit, Bringmann has partially dealt with the question, but not in a completely satisfactory way. Bar-Kochva has also argued against a military colony composed of Syrian troops (*92–105, 438–44), which undermines one aspect of Bringmann's thesis (points 6 and 7).

5.3.2.8 Socioeconomic Causes

The main discussion here is whether the Maccabean resistance was a class war, that is, a "peasants' revolt." See 5.3.9 for a discussion of this and other questions.

5.3.2.9 Conclusions

No theory to date has been able to command a consensus of scholars, despite the ingenuity of some hypotheses. Some suggestions can be ruled out, however, and some have more merit than others. The theories of the two giants—Bickerman and Tcherikover—have a great deal to commend them yet occasion some profound disagreements as well. Goldstein's first thesis may also have an important contribution to make, even though the theory as such seems improbable. The various explanations are not necessarily mutually exclusive, which points us toward some sort of synthesis. Bringmann has come up with an important synthesis, which may gain adherents as it becomes better known. Although it has loose ends (which theory does not?), it seems the best suggestion so far. In the absence of a consensus at the present time, the following points seem fairly solid:

1. The Jews were already a part of the Hellenistic world and no different from other *ethnoi* of the ancient Near East in the general process of Hellenization, which had begun with Alexander (cf. 3.4.1–2).
2. Antiochus's dealings with the Jews, as with other peoples, were on a political level and had political aims, not religious or ideological ones.
3. Jason's initial Hellenistic reform was met with enthusiasm by a significant (if minority) portion of the population and was not actively opposed by the rest.
4. Judaism as a religion was not impaired under Jason. Although in the eyes of some very conservative individuals Jason's actions may have looked impious, we have to keep in mind that 2 Maccabees was written in the aftermath of the religious persecutions and the Hasmonean successes. When the rhetoric is ignored and only the actual data examined, it is clear that the basic Jewish observances in and out of the temple continued. There was no devotion to pagan deities or any blatant breach of Jewish law.
5. Menelaus was a different sort of person. There is evidence that his actions eventually met with resistance from both the ruling council of the polis and the ordinary people who rioted and killed his brother Lysimachus.
6. Whatever the exact reason for Antiochus's anti-Judaism decrees, some Jews seem to have been involved somehow with these decrees. Antiochus was concerned with politics, and religious matters were only incidental to his principal goals, which were those of most politicians: money and power.

5.3.3 Who Were the "Hellenizers"?

The term "Hellenizer" is often bandied about in modern studies in a rather undifferentiated way. This is hardly surprising because such explicit or implied usage is found in the books of Maccabees. To the authors of these histories, "Hellenistic" and "Greek" were catchwords to condemn those people or things so labeled, and such usage is not absent in some modern writings. Nevertheless, careful consideration shows that a number of different phenomena have been lumped together in the terms "Hellenizer," "Hellenistic," and "Greek." The broad subject of Hellenization and the Jews is dealt with in chapter 3. The discussion here will focus on the identity of the so-called Hellenists in the context of the Hellenistic reform and the subsequent revolt.

One of the first problems we have is that of the sources. No surviving source speaks for any of the "Hellenizers"; all our significant sources are hostile and simply were not interested in giving a fair or complete account. We do not know directly either the objectives or aspirations of such individuals as Jason and Menelaus or how they justified these to themselves or others. Any conclusion is inferential at best. We can perhaps engage in reasonable speculation about Jason's aims (cf. *Hengel: 1.277–78), but we can hardly hope to do them justice. Menelaus is much more difficult to sympathize with, but many writers are content simply to repeat the accusations of the enemies of both Menelaus and Jason without weighing the evidence. What emerges from careful study is that there were clear differences between the activities of Jason and those of Menelaus; nor was the reaction of the common people identical to each. It would be useful to look briefly at each in turn.

Jason plainly had a program which he wished to carry out, namely, to make Jerusalem into a Greek polis, although we can only speculate about his motives. Although deposing his brother and taking the high priesthood was opportunistic, it is difficult to believe he was merely an opportunist. Perhaps he was an idealist who believed in some sort of rapprochement between the Jews and their neighbors (cf. *Bringmann: 67). It has been suggested that he had economic motives (*Tcherikover: 168–69; opposed by *Bringmann: 74). But whatever his reasons for the Hellenistic reform, it was a cultural and political matter, not a religious one. Jason had no desire to change the traditional cult or worship.

Menelaus could hardly have been more different from Jason. Although he performed the same trick that Jason did (i.e., buying the priesthood), his actions argue for a power play, pure and simple: offering Antiochus an impossible sum in exchange for the priesthood; stealing temple property and selling it; bringing about the murder of Onias III. No potentially idealistic motives emerge, at least from the data preserved, although we cannot be certain that he had none.

One complication in all this is the terminology used, for "Hellenistic" does not always mean "Greek," as one would expect. For example, the cult imposed by Antiochus at Jerusalem is referred to as "Greek" and associated with the name of a Greek god, Zeus Olympius, yet it is clear that this was not a Greek cult but a Canaanite-Syrian one (5.3.4). The name applied to the cult was Greek but the content was not. Similarly, the Samaritan temple at Shechem was dedicated to Zeus Xenios ("Zeus, hospitable" or "Zeus, friend of strangers"), yet there is no indication that a change of cult or religion took place. Rather, the Samaritans apparently continued to operate a cult very similar to that which had been banned in Jerusalem, but under a Greek label. Similarly, statements about "changing to Greek ways" (2 Macc 6:8; 11:24) actually have to do with leaving Judaism, rather than with adopting specifically Greek customs. Therefore, "Hellenistic," "Greek," and "Hellenize" are sometimes used in our sources simply to mean "non-Jewish" (*Bringmann: 141–45).

5.3.4 What Was the Cult in Jerusalem?

*Bickerman: 61–75.
———. "Les Maccabées de Malalas." *Studies in Jewish and Christian History* (1980) 2.192–209.
Nestle, E. "Der Greuel der Verwüstung." *ZAW* 4 (1884) 248.
Oden, R. A. "Ba'al Šāmēm and 'El." *CBQ* 39 (1977) 457–73.
Rigsby, K. J. "Seleucid Notes." *TAPA* 110 (1980) 233–54.

The nature of the cult imposed on the Jerusalem temple is not clear from the sources. Daniel speaks of an "abomination of desolation" (*šiqqûṣ šōmēm*: Dan 11:31; 12:11), but the precise significance of this is not immediately obvious. The following points emerge from 1 and 2 Maccabees:

1. The temple was dedicated to Zeus Olympius (2 Macc 6:2).
2. The primary cause of pollution and sacrilege was something erected on the altar of burnt offering (1 Macc 1:54; 4:43-47). This included a pagan altar (*bōmos*) on top of the original altar in the temple courtyard (1:59).
3. There was a monthly celebration of the king's birthday (2 Macc 6:7).
4. Worship of Dionysus took place on his feast day, with processions in his honor (2 Macc 6:7).

The first point to note is that there is no indication that an idol of any sort was placed in the temple, as would be expected with a Greek cult. It is almost inconceivable that the presence of such would have been ignored by Daniel or 1 and 2 Maccabees. Granted, there is a very late statement that a statue of Zeus Olympius was erected in the temple. The statement was made by the church father Jerome (*Com. in Dan.* to 8:9 and 11:31), allegedly quoting Porphyry, although it may have been

Jerome's own deduction. (Bickerman suggests this is only a reference to votive gifts, not a cult image [*67–68].)

Although the temple is said to have been dedicated to Zeus Olympius (2 Macc 6:2), this does not necessarily imply a change to a Greek form of worship. The Samaritan temple was also dedicated to Zeus without any change of cult (5.3.3). Despite being a particular devotee of Zeus Olympius, Antiochus IV made no attempt to impose the cult elsewhere (cf. Rigsby: 233–38). A century ago, Nestle first pointed out that the epithet "abomination of desolation" was most likely a Hebrew play on the name Baal Shamem ("the lord of heaven"; cf. Oden). It had become common to give Greek names to native deities, and Baal Shamem of the Phoenicians and others was frequently designated "Zeus" in Greek writings (*Bickerman: 62–65; Oden: 466–67). Bickerman argued that the cult was Syro-Canaanite, and this has been widely accepted (*Tcherikover: 194–95; *Goldstein 1976: 142–57, although cf. his reservations about Nestle's thesis). Part of the reason for this identification is that the imposed cult focused on the altar (*bōmos*), and one of the characteristics of Syrian religions was the practice of imageless, altar-based cults.

The celebration of the king's birthday was customary in the Seleucid Empire and is thus easily explained. More of a problem is the Dionysus worship. Was this a Greek cult? In view of the "Zeus" worship, it seems likely that "Dionysus" in this case is simply the Greek name for a Syro-Canaanite deity (cf. *Bickerman: 74; *Goldstein 1976: 153–55). Whether a goddess was also associated with the worship (*Bickerman: 73–74; *Goldstein 1976: 152–53) is perhaps debatable because the only evidence is from a later period (cf. Bickerman 1980); but such an inclusion would not be surprising because a consort goddess was frequently present.

Bringmann has noted, however, that there is more to be considered than just the imposition of a native Syrian cult. Elements of the forced new worship went against local Canaanite religion, particularly the sacrifice of swine and the prohibition of circumcision (*109–10, 130–32, 141). Therefore, he argues that it was "neither a Greek nor a pure Syrian cult" (*weder einen griechischen noch einen rein syrischen Kult* [*109]). This is one of the arguments used to support his view that the cult was Menelaus's own creation (5.3.2.7).

5.3.5 Documents in 1 and 2 Maccabees

*Bar-Kochva: 516–42.

Bickerman E. J. [E. J. Bikermann]. "Makkabäerbücher." *PW* (1930) 14.779–800.

———. "Ein jüdischer Festbrief vom Jahre 124 v. Chr. (II Macc $1_{1\text{-}9}$)." *ZNW* 32 (1933) 233–54.

———. "Une question d'authenticité: les privilèges Juifs." *Studies in Jewish and Christian History* (1980) 2.24–43.

Fischer, T. "Zu den Beziehungen zwischen Rom and den Juden im 2. Jahrhundert v. Chr." *ZAW* 86 (1974) 90–93.

Gauger, J.-D. *Beiträge zur jüdischen Apologetik* (1977).

Habicht, C. "Royal Documents in Maccabees II." *Harvard Studies in Classical Philology* 80 (1976) 1–18.

Momigliano, A. "The Second Book of Maccabees." *Classical Philology* 70 (1975) 81–88.

———. Review of *Beiträge zur jüdischen Apologetik*, by J.-D. Gauger. *Classical Philology* 77 (1982) 258–61.

Timpe, D. "Der römische Vertrag mit den Juden von 161 v. Chr." *Chiron* 4 (1974) 133–52.

Wacholder, B. Z. "The Letter from Judah Maccabee to Aristobulus: Is 2 Maccabees 1:10b—2:18 Authentic?" *HUCA* 49 (1978) 89–133.

Wirgin, W. "Judah Maccabee's Embassy to Rome and the Jewish-Roman Treaty." *PEQ* 101 (1969) 15–20.

A number of documents in the form of letters are quoted in 1 and 2 Maccabees. If authentic, these are valuable original sources, as is confirmed by the fact that they sometimes contradict the narrative in which they are embedded. The letters are as follows (numbers in parentheses in 2 Maccabees entries indicate letters that are discussed below):

1 Maccabees

8:23-32:	Treaty with Rome.
10:18-20:	From Alexander Balas to Jonathan.
10:25-45:	From Demetrius I to Jonathan.
11:30-37:	From Demetrius II to Jonathan.
11:57:	From Antiochus VI to Jonathan.
12:6-18:	From Jonathan to the Spartans.
12:20-23:	From King Areus of Sparta to the high priest Onias.
13:36-40:	From Demetrius II to Simon.
14:20-23:	From the Spartans to Simon.
15:2-9:	From Antiochus VI to Simon.
15:16-24:	Circular letter from Roman consuls.

2 Maccabees

1:1-10a:	From Palestinian Jews to Egyptian Jews on the observance of Hanukkah.
1:10b—2:18:	From Judas to the Egyptian Jews.

9:19-29:	From Antiochus IV to the Jews.
11:16-21:	From Lysias to the Jews (letter 1).
11:22-26:	From Antiochus V to Lysias (letter 2).
11:27-33:	From Antiochus IV to the Jewish *gerousia* and "the other Jews" (letter 3).
11:34-38:	From the Roman ambassadors to "the Jewish people" (letter 4).

Most of the letters in 1 Maccabees have now been accepted as genuine. The central dispute has centered on the treaty with Rome under Judas and the letter from the Spartan king Areus. According to 1 Macc 8:23-30, a treaty had been made with Rome in Judas's time, ca. 162 B.C.E.; 1 Macc 12:3 and 14:17-18 speak of a renewal of that treaty by Jonathan ca. 144/143, and 1 Macc 14:24 speaks of a treaty under Simon. The treaty under Judas has been doubted. Gauger in a lengthy study confirms that it is only an apologetic fiction, although he seems to accept the treaty made by Simon (155–328). However, Schürer argues for the authenticity of the treaty with Judas (1.171 n.33), as do Goldstein (*1976: 344–69), Fischer (92), Wirgin (17–18), Momigliano (1982), and Sievers (*68–70). The later treaties under Jonathan and Simon have been more readily accepted; however, there are some difficulties with the actual documents quoted (*Sievers: 116–18), so that one may accept the existence of such treaties but still reject the documents as inauthentic. Jonathan's correspondence with the Spartans is also now generally accepted (12:20-23), but questions remain. Did he possess a genuine letter from Areus, or was it a Jewish forgery, which Jonathan took to be genuine? See 5.3.6 on this question.

Of the two letters prefacing 2 Maccabees, the first (1:1-10 [Eng. 1:1-9]) is generally taken to be genuine. More of a problem is the one allegedly from Judas (1:10—2:18), because it seems to reflect the situation sometime after the retaking of the temple (Momigliano 1975: 84; *Goldstein 1983: 154–88; *Sievers: 6–7). Goldstein has also pointed out the chronological problems related to hearing the news of Antiochus's death and sending the letter to Egypt. Although Wacholder has recently argued for its authenticity, it seems most likely a forgery, often thought to be an attack on the temple at Leontopolis (Bickerman 1933: 250).

The letter of Antiochus IV in 2 Macc 9:19-27 has been accepted by a number of scholars because it does not prove what it is alleged to prove by the narrative in which it is set. Although it is introduced as a confession of sin by Antiochus, it in fact makes no such admission. Bickerman, for example, considers the title to have been changed (1980: 35) and, perhaps, interpolations to have been added (1930: 790); but he otherwise accepts it. Nevertheless, Momigliano is bothered because "the king puts his hope in heaven . . . , writes a prescript which is impossible for a king, and takes no account of the real situation in Judaea" (84). Therefore, he considers the letter to be modeled on an authentic document, perhaps a genuine letter to Antioch. Habicht also argues that it is a forgery (5–7).

The letters in 2 Maccabees 11 are almost universally considered genuine (Habicht: 12). However, Momigliano has pointed out that letter 2, the letter of Antiochus V to Lysias (11:22-26) is suspect, because there is no reason for it to have been sent to the Jews (84–85). It could have come as a copy, but then it should have had a cover letter. Why was the cover letter not quoted? Furthermore, why does 1 Macc 6:57-59 show no knowledge of it, and why does it not seem to have affected subsequent events? There are many who defend the letter (cf. *Bar Kochva: 523), but it is probably the most questionable of those in chapter 11.

One of the major problems with these letters concerns their dates and relationship to events, because they seem to have little to do with the context into which they have been inserted in 2 Maccabees 11. Although three of the letters are dated, letters 3 and 4 have the same date. This suggests that a copyist accidentally copied the date of one for the other, but which one is original is debated. A further complication is that the name of the month in letter 1 is otherwise unknown. Therefore, the sequence of the letters is placed differently by different scholars (e.g., Habicht: 3,1,4,2; *Tcherikover and *Bar-Kochva: 1,4,3,2; *Fischer: 3,4,2,1; *Bringmann: 1,3,4,2). A brief analysis of each letter helps our understanding.

Letter 1 (11:16-21). The year 148 S.E. would put this letter in the year autumn 165 to autumn 164 B.C.E.. The month "Dios Corinthios" is not otherwise known; however, the month Dios is the first month of the Macedonian calendar (October/November). Because it is thought that Antiochus may have added some extensions to month names, several scholars accept that this letter is dated to the month Dios, or about October 165 B.C.E. (*Bringmann: 44; *Bar-Kochva: 522–23). If so, then this is most likely the earliest of the four letters. Those, such as Habicht, who put it later must assume a corruption beyond restoration in the name. There are also those who reconstruct it as Dystros, or about February/March (*Tcherikover: 482 nn.21, 22).

A second problem is that of the addressees: the "multitude" (*plēthos*) of the Jews. The letter seems to have been sent to an unofficial group with whom Lysias wanted reconciliation. It has been argued that it was addressed to the "Hellenizers" or to Jews not primarily supporters of Judas (*Tcherikover: 216–18). Several reasons have been given as to why this was Judas's group, for example, that it was unlikely that Menelaus and his followers would have wanted religious rights restored (Habicht:

10; *Bar-Kochva: 521–22); however, none of these points makes it Judas's group exclusively. The points especially do not answer Tcherikover's argument that it was Menelaus's group which initiated the decrees, to be addressed to the mass of the Jews (who were not necessarily supporters of Judas), in order to weaken the hold of the Maccabean leadership (*216–18). (Because Menelaus could not be certain that the Jews would listen to him, he also enlisted the aid of a Roman delegation in the region.)

Letter 2 (11:22-26). Because this letter comes from Antiochus V, it must be dated after December 164, making it probably the latest of the four (assuming it is genuine, which most scholars do).

Letter 3 (11:27-33). Sent from Antiochus IV, this letter gives "until the 30th Xanthikos," that is, until sometime in March, as the deadline for Jews to benefit from a general amnesty. This date within the body of the letter does not seem to be disputed. The letter itself is dated 15 Xanthikos 148 S.E., or about the beginning of March 164 B.C.E.. This date fits well with Antiochus's own life, for he died less than a year later, in about December 164. The problem is that the date of the letter is the same as the date of letter 4; further, if Antiochus wrote a letter on 15 Xanthikos from somewhere in the eastern provinces, then it could hardly have reached Palestine and its intended recipients in time for them to do anything about the amnesty. A number of scholars think that the date "15 Xanthikos 148" has been accidentally copied from letter 4 (*Bringmann: 45–46). If so, letter 3 would have been issued toward the end of 165, or about the same time as letter 1. Others see the reverse of the argument, that is, that the date on letter 3 is correct but accidentally displaced that on 4 (*Tcherikover: 215; *Bar-Kochva: 528–29). This argument assumes that the date was the time when the letter left Antioch, but it ignores the problem of Antiochus's presence across the Euphrates.

Letter 4 (11:34-38). This letter comes from a Roman embassy in the region. One problem is the date, discussed above. The other problem is that the individuals named as making up the embassy are not otherwise known. Data on the embassies for this particular period are rather skimpy, however, and it is hardly surprising that the named persons are not otherwise attested; attempts to see the names as corruptions of known Romans in the area should probably be dismissed (*Gruen: 746; *Bringmann: 47–50; *Bar-Kochva: 532–33).

5.3.6 Supposed Kinship with the Spartans

Bickerman, E. J. [E. J. Bikermann]. "Makkabäerbücher." *PW* (1930) 14.779–800.
Cardauns, B. "Juden und Spartaner: Zur hellenistisch-jüdischen Literatur."

Hermes 95 (1967) 317–24.
Feldman, L. *Josephus and Modern Scholarship* (1984).
Katzoff, R. "Jonathan and Late Sparta." *AJP* 106 (1985) 485–89.
Schuller, S. "Some Problems Connected with the Supposed Common Ancestry of Jews and Spartans and Their Relations during the Last Three Centuries B.C." *JSS* 1 (1956) 257–68.
Wirgin, W. "Judah Maccabee's Embassy to Rome and the Jewish-Roman Treaty." *PEQ* 101 (1969) 15–20.

According to Josephus (*Ant.* 12.4.10 §§225–27), at the time of Onias I a letter came from the king of Sparta claiming kinship with the Jews through a common descent from Abraham. This information was supposedly found by the Lacedemonians in their archives. A similar story occurs in 1 Macc 12:5-23, except in this case Jonathan Maccabeus writes to the Spartans of their kinship, and a reply from Areios [*sic*] confirms this information. Three questions are raised by this information: (1) Was there actually correspondence to this effect between the Jews and Spartans? (2) What is the relationship between the accounts in Josephus and 1 Maccabees? and (3) What was the basis for this assumption of kinship?

There does seem to be a definite, close relationship between the texts of the letters in 1 Maccabees and Josephus, suggesting that 1 Maccabees is the source of the latter, even though Josephus has "corrected" the text in the light of his knowledge of Hellenistic usage. Whether there was actual correspondence is a moot point. It is more likely that the Jews wrote to the Spartans than the other way around. Many writers consider the letter from Areus to Onias to be an old piece of Jewish propaganda, although Jonathan may well have considered it genuine (e.g., Bickerman: 786). But recently several writers have suggested that the Spartans did have such a tradition, perhaps taken from Hecateus of Abdera's treatise *On Abraham* (Wirgin: 15–17; Feldman: 218–19; *Goldstein 1976: 455–62). Feldman suggests that the idea of such a kinship was drawn from the legend about Cadmus (a Phoenician), who sowed dragon's teeth from which armed men (*spartoi*, "sown men") sprang up; the term for "sown man" (*spartos*) is very similar to "Sparta" (*Spartē*).

5.3.7 Chronology

*Bringmann: 15–40.
Bunge, J. G. "Zur Geschichte und Chronology des Untergangs der Oniaden und des Augstiegs der Hasmonäer." *JSJ* 6 (1976a) 1–46.
———. "Die Feiern Antiochos' IV. Epiphanes in Daphne im Herbst 166 v. Chr." *Chiron* 6 (1976b) 53–71.

Grabbe, L. L. "Maccabean Chronology: 167–164 or 168–165 B.C.E.?" *JBL* 110 (1991) 59–74.
Ray, J. D. *The Archive of Ḥor* (1976) 14–20, 124–30.
Sachs, A. J., and D. J. Wiseman. "A Babylonian King List of the Hellenistic Period." *Iraq* 16 (1954) 202–11.
Schunck, K.-D. *Die Quellen des ersten und zweiten Makkabäerbuches* (1954).
Skeat, T. C. "Notes on Ptolemaic Chronology: II. 'The Twelfth Year Which Is Also the First': The Invasion of Egypt by Antiochus Epiphanes." *JEA* 47 (1961) 107–12.

In older sources the suppression of Jewish worship and the pollution of the temple are usually dated to 168–165 B.C.E. Since Bickerman's original treatment in 1937, however, the generally accepted dating has been 167–164. Bickerman argued that two systems of dating are used in 1 Maccabees: a Jewish dating, which began the Seleucid era with Nisan 311 B.C.E., and a Seleucid dating, which began with Tishri 312. Bickerman's contentions about two systems of dating were further buttressed by Schunck, who used them as a means of source analysis of 1 Maccabees. However, he disagreed with Bickerman on the Jewish dating, which he argued began with Nisan 312. Important new information became available with the publication of a cuneiform text by Sachs and Wiseman, which showed that Antiochus died in late November or December 164 B.C.E. We also now know that Antiochus's first invasion of Egypt most likely began in November 170 (Skeat), whereas he left Egypt after his second invasion at the end of July 168 (Ray: 14–20, 124–30). (Although all this necessitates a revision of some of Bickerman's dates, he apparently saw no reason to change his basic dating.)

Bringmann also dates the suppression of Jewish worship to 168–165, but he does so by arguing for a Jewish Seleucid era reckoned from Tishri 312 (*15–28); that is, in his opinion there is only one system of dating in 1 Maccabees (although this requires a peculiar interpretation of 10:21). In my study (originally written in 1973, published in 1991), I argue the following:

1. Two systems of dating are presupposed in 1 Maccabees (agreeing with Bickerman and Schunck against Bringmann), but they fit best with a Jewish Seleucid era beginning with Nisan 312 B.C.E. and a Syrian Seleucid dating beginning with Tishri 312 (in agreement with Schunck, against Bickerman). This requires no emendation of data.
2. The events preceding the suppression of Jewish worship point to the prohibition as starting at about the end of 168 B.C.E.
3. The sequence of events of the revolt, as recounted in 1 Maccabees,

shows that Antiochus IV died sometime after the temple had been retaken and cleansed by Judas. Because we know from a cuneiform text that Antiochus died about December 164, Judas must have taken the temple about a year earlier, in late 165 B.C.E.

4. This date is confirmed by the cycle of sabbatical years as it relates to the events described in 6:20-53.
5. Therefore, the "abomination of desolation" lasted 168–165, as proposed in the pre-Bickerman works (in agreement with Schunck and Bringmann) but contrary to most recent reference works.

5.3.8 The Temple at Leontopolis

Delcor, M. "Le temple d'Onias en Egypte." *RB* 75 (1968) 188–205.

Hayward, R. "The Jewish Temple at Leontopolis: A Reconsideration." *JJS* 33 (1982) 429–43.

Steckoll, S. H. "The Qumran Sect in Relation to the Temple of Leontopolis." *RevQ* 6 (1967–69) 55–69.

An interesting episode in the history of Judaism is that in which the hereditary high priest of the Jerusalem cult founded a breakaway temple in Egypt. The difficulty with analyzing what happened and why is the sometimes contradictory information found in the various accounts in Josephus (*War* 7.10.2–4 §§423–36; *Ant.* 12.5.1 §§237–38; 12.9.7 §387; 13.3.1–3 §§62–73). Notice the following:

1. The temple was founded by Onias III, the high priest deposed by Jason, according to *War* 7.10.2 §423, but by his son Onias IV, according to *Ant.* 12.9.7 §387.
2. It was in the nome of Heliopolis. This site is often identified with Tell el-Yehudieh and some of the remains there, although the archeology is perhaps less than clear-cut (cf. Schürer: 3.146 n.33).
3. It was similar to that in Jerusalem, according to one passage (*Ant.* 13.3.3 §72). Elsewhere, however, it is said to be unlike the Jerusalem temple, instead being in the form of a tower (*War* 7.10.3 §427). Although Hayward has suggested the two passages can be reconciled in that the Jerusalem temple was often compared to a tower, this contradicts Josephus's own statement that the one was different from the other.
4. The new temple outside Jerusalem was justified from a prophecy of Isaiah (perhaps Isa 19:18-22).
5. According to *Ant.* 13.3.2 §70, there was already a ruined temple on

the site, which Onias was allowed to cleanse and rebuild. The passage in *War* is silent on this.

Steckoll proposed a connection between the Qumran community and the Leontopolis temple. This was criticized by Delcor (and de Vaux, in a postscript to Delcor's article). Hayward has made some cautious comparisons, however, although some of these resemblances could be due simply to the common situation of both being communities of worship that were viewed as "heterodox" by the Jerusalem establishment.

5.3.9 Socioeconomic Matters

Bickerman, E. J. [E. Bikerman]. *Institutions des Séleucides* (1938).
Jeremias, J. *Jerusalem in the Time of Jesus* (1969).
Kippenberg, H. G. *Religion und Klassenbildung im antiken Judäa* (1982) 78–110.
Kreissig, H. "Der Makkabäeraufstand zur Frage seiner Socialökonomischen Zusammenhänge und Wirkungen." *Studii Clasice* 4 (1962) 143–75.
Mittwoch, A. "Tribute and Land-Tax in Seleucid Judaea." *Bib* 36 (1955) 352–61.

After the conquest by Antiochus III and the reversion of Palestine to Seleucid rule, there does not seem initially to have been any major change in the economic sphere. The basic tribute was probably the same under the Seleucids as under the Ptolemies. This is implied in the decree of Antiochus III, which allowed the Jews to continue under their native laws but also remitted taxes for a period of time because of help that the Jews provided for the Seleucid army (5.3.1). A similar conclusion can be drawn from later concessions made by Seleucid rulers to Hasmonean leaders (1 Macc 10:18-45; 11:30-37; 13:36-40). We get some idea of the annual tribute when we see the money offered by Jason for the high priesthood: the figure of 360 talents of silver (2 Macc 4:8) was probably a raising of the normal annual tribute of about 300 talents (*Bringmann: 115). (Jason offered another 80 talents as well, plus a further 150 to make Jerusalem into a polis.)

By 200 B.C.E. there are indications that the traditional theocracy that had been in place since Persian times had developed somewhat. The letter of Antiochus III mentions the several components of the Jerusalem establishment: the *gerousia* (council of elders), the priests, the scribes, and the temple singers. Especially important is the development of the gerousia, which is mentioned in the letter for the first time. Its composition is debated. Hengel argues that it was made up of priests (*1.25–26);

however, Jeremias has seen it as a body of laymen (223). Kippenberg agrees with Jeremias and thinks it shows the development of a Jerusalemite aristocracy (83–85).

When Jerusalem became a polis, it was primarily the native aristocracy that was enrolled as citizens. There were no doubt many advantages in having a Greek foundation and in being a citizen of it. An obvious one is that it would have reinforced the position of the aristocracy by officially confirming their privileges. It also seems likely that the new status would make Jerusalem more attractive for trade.

A major question about the Maccabean revolt is to what extent socioeconomic matters played a part. No doubt they played an important role after it developed, but were they the cause? Was it, for example, a peasants' revolt? Although this has been argued by Kreissig and also seems to be endorsed by Kippenberg (88–90), it is not supported by the sources. The sequence of events shows that there was no resistance to the "Hellenizers" until Lysimachus began to sell the temple vessels, and then the opposition came from the gerousia and the people of Jerusalem (5.4.3.2). Under the religious suppression, opposition was led by the Maccabees, who were hardly peasants. Peasant revolts may have been led by members of the upper classes, and many of the Maccabean supporters may have been peasants, but the catalyst was the religious persecution. Once the Seleucids were willing to withdraw the measures and allow religious freedom again, the support for further resistance fell away. A genuine peasants' revolt would not have been stopped by such concessions.

This does not mean that support for the revolt did not arise from a number of motives. The Maccabean movement at some point became one of independence, and many of their supporters may have been motivated at least in part by hopes of improving their socioeconomic position (cf. Mittwoch). Nevertheless, one must keep in mind that for many years there was little popular support for the independence movement. When the Maccabean leadership eventually took control and achieved its goal, it no doubt became clear that the socioeconomic position of many Jews was going to be improved. However, in the years following the return to religious freedom, many seem to have doubted that resistance had any hope of success, and present peace was more important and secure than the vague hope of improved conditions following the ravages of a prolonged and unpromising war against Seleucid rule (5.4.5).

As time went on, however, the Maccabean movement was able to obtain tax concessions from the Seleucid rulers, which were no doubt welcome. With independence the Hasmonean state still required finances. It is not clear how these were collected and on whom they fell. Not only the state apparatus but also the standing army, which was retained to continue expanding the borders of Judah, would have been a considerable cost (and eventually led to the hiring of mercenaries toward the end of Hasmonean rule). Nevertheless, the revenues from the newly conquered territories no doubt brought in substantial wealth. Furthermore, many Jews would have been settled on land in the new territories (6.3.7). The result was almost certainly that the average Jew was better off under the Hasmoneans than under Seleucid rule, even the peasants and others on the lowest level of the socioeconomic plane. The summary of Simon's reign in 1 Maccabees therefore had a large degree of truth, despite the utopian language borrowed from Scripture: "They tilled their land in peace, the ground gave its increase. . . . Each man sat under his vine and fig tree" (14:8, 12).

5.4 SYNTHESIS

5.4.1 Overview

5.4.1.1 Sources

For the first part of this period several sources are available, even if they are sometimes episodic, but this multiplicity seems only to complicate matters, because the sources differ widely in certain important areas. Josephus is the principal source for the transfer of Palestine to Seleucid rule. He also has some information on the intrigues for the high priesthood at the beginning of Antiochus's reign, but the main source for this is 2 Maccabees. Concerning the suppression of Judaism and the subsequent revolt, all the principal sources have information (although Josephus at this point is primarily dependent on 1 Maccabees). Second Maccabees ceases just before the death of Judas in 162/161. From this point to the end of Hasmonean rule, we are dependent on essentially no more than one source at any given time (5.2.1; 5.2.4).

Down to the reign of Simon, the major—and practically the only—source is 1 Maccabees (Josephus is almost entirely a paraphrase of it). During the reign of Simon, however, Josephus begins to deviate from 1 Maccabees and thus forms an independent witness. Then, however, 1 Maccabees itself runs out, and we have only the longer account in Josephus's *Antiquities*, along with the generally parallel but shorter account in *War*. Therefore, from the time of Simon most histories, including Schürer, are little more than a paraphrase of Josephus. This is unfortunate but inevitable. There is no other detailed source and one can only follow Josephus, with occasional supplementary material from coins and the Greek historians. One may find fault with Josephus's picture at various points, but this does not change the basic situation. All it means is that the historian ends up rejecting some of the meager data still extant.

Thus, the synthesis that follows is based chiefly on 1 and 2 Maccabees, as far as these are extant, with some contributions from Daniel and Josephus. When 1 Maccabees comes to an end, however, the main source is *Antiquities*, and references are normally given only when they are to some other source. Although *War* often does not have the same detail as the later work, it also does not usually contradict it; therefore, differences are generally noted except when they seem completely trivial.

5.4.1.2 Seleucid and Roman History (200–63 B.C.E.)

Davies, J. K. "Cultural, Social and Economic Features of the Hellenistic World." *CAH*[2] (1984) 7.1.257–320.
Musti, D. "Syria and the East." *CAH*[2] (1984) 7.1.175–220.

Seleucid history is an important backdrop to much that happened to the Jews. Antiochus III ("the Great") finally took Syro-Palestine, which the Seleucids had always regarded as rightfully theirs, in 200 B.C.E. The Seleucid conquest of Palestine seems to have made little internal difference at first, but it opened the way for some important changes because of its different form of administration. The Ptolemies were able to administer their empire by a highly centralized form of government. The size and diversity of the Seleucid Empire required a different approach, in which the Greek city played an important role (cf. Musti: 204–9; Davies: 304–20). Whereas the Ptolemies were not interested in founding new Greek cities, a steady procession of these cities emerged under Seleucid rule, often at the request of the native peoples.

Antiochus III was succeeded by his son Seleucus IV (187–175 B.C.E.). Seleucus had a reasonably quiet reign but was murdered by his minister Heliodorus. Although Seleucus had sons, his brother Antiochus, just returning from a period as hostage at Rome, seized the throne to become Antiochus IV (175–164 B.C.E.), one of the most able but enigmatic of the Seleucid rulers. His son Antiochus V Eupator (164–162 B.C.E.) was only nine years old on taking the throne and thus had little chance against his regents. He was plotted against by his cousin, the eldest son of Seleucus IV, who succeeded him as Demetrius I Soter (162–150 B.C.E.).

Rivalry for the throne by pretenders began in Demetrius's reign and continued for much of the rest of Seleucid rule. It started with Alexander Balas (150–145 B.C.E.), who claimed to be the son of Antiochus IV. For the next century until the end of the Seleucid kingdom, there were always at least two claimants to the throne, sometimes more. For example, in the period from about 95 to 83 B.C.E., no fewer than half a dozen persons fought over the throne. For a period of time (83–69 B.C.E.) Tigranes, king of Armenia, took over Syria and ruled it until he was defeated by the Romans. Antiochus XIII Asiaticus was placed briefly on the throne by the Romans but removed in 65 B.C.E. Asiaticus was the last ruler over the Seleucid kingdom, which then came to an end.

Rome, like Britain, acquired an empire in the East almost by accident. Rome realized that it had interests in that area and had already intervened at various times (e.g., against Antiochus III) to see that the balance of power was maintained, but this was not the same as acquiring possessions or taking over. For a century Rome was also occupied in its fight to the death with Carthage in the three Punic wars, which ended finally in 146 with the fall of Carthage and the conquest of Greece. The imperialistic stage in Roman history began in 133, when Rome was willed the kingdom of Pergamum on the death of its king, Attalus III. This was a mixed blessing, because Pergamum would require resources to defend it. It was the time of social reforms under the Gracchi brothers, however, and the issue became mixed up in the heated controversies between opposing social factions within Rome itself. Eventually, the bequest was accepted and made the Roman province of Asia, although portions of the original kingdom of Pergamum were given to other kingdoms or made independent.

After the transfer of Pergamum, Cilicia had become a stronghold of pirates, and the praetor Antonius was sent to rid the area of the problem. Part of his solution was to make Cilicia into a province in 102 B.C.E. As had already been recognized, such outposts were not necessarily easy to defend, especially with the troubles that affected Rome itself during this period. Mithridates VI, king of Pontus (120–63 B.C.E.), had already expanded his territory to the east and up the coast of the Black Sea. In 93 he attempted to move south into Cappadocia, and in 90, west into Bithynia, but he was stopped by Rome each time. The Italian War (91–87) provided the opportunity for Mithridates to try again. He took Bithynia and then Asia, where he was welcomed as a liberator. He even sent an army into Greece and, with the help of the Athenians, occupied most of the country. This began the First Mithridatic War (88–85). Despite troubles at home, the Roman general Sulla set out against Mithridates in 86, drove him out of the lands he had taken, and forced him to return to Pontus and pay a large indemnity for the trouble he had caused.

Mithridates was not beaten, however, and he had little trouble defeating the Roman commander during the so-called Second Mithridatic War (83–81 B.C.E.). It was also during this time that Tigranes I of Armenia (ca. 100–56 B.C.E.) began expanding, taking over the remaining Seleucid kingdom. The Third Mithridatic War (74–63 B.C.E.) was the decisive one. It was initiated by the Roman annexation of Bithynia, which had been willed to Rome on the death of its ruler. Mithridates captured Bithynia in the initial stages of the war but was worsted by the Roman consul Lucullus, who drove him into Armenia. Tigranes was continuing his drive down the Syrian coast and posing a major threat to Judea, which was then under the rule of Alexandra Salome (5.4.10). However, Tigranes turned back to Armenia when he heard of Mithridates' presence in his country. With Tigranes' help, Mithridates raised another army. Lucullus retaliated by taking Syria away from Tigranes and placing a Seleucid on the throne once again (Antiochus XIII Asiaticus). After Mithridates retook Pontus in 67, the new Roman commander sent to oppose him was the able and respected Pompey, who soon demonstrated why he bore the epithet "the Great."

Pompey was already in the eastern Mediterranean, where he had been commissioned in 67 to clear the area of pirates who had arisen again in the forty years since Antonius's campaign. Pompey took only about a year to defeat Mithridates decisively in 66. After fleeing to Colchis, the latter committed suicide a few years later when he was unable to gain support even from his own son for a further army. With this menace out of the way, Pompey proceeded to use the wide-ranging powers given him by the Senate and annex Asia Minor and Syria as far as the Euphrates. Among the casualties was Antiochus XIII, who, having been installed by the Romans, was now removed by them. One of the few areas to escape was Armenia, because Tigranes had the good sense to respect the Roman military power. However, Pompey was drawn into the internecine fighting of the Hasmonean rivals Hyrcanus II and Aristobulus II and put an end to the independence of that state.

5.4.1.3 Rise and Fall of the Jewish State

Bright, J. *A History of Israel* (1980).

Although the exact origin of the problems in Judah under Antiochus IV is still uncertain, they owe much to the rivalry over the high priesthood. Complicating matters was the request to Antiochus that Jerusalem become a Greek polis, although this did not immediately involve any significant breach of Jewish law. The fight over the priesthood was interpreted at one point as a revolt from Seleucid rule and brought armed intervention by Antiochus IV. This was followed by a decree forbidding the practice of traditional Judaism, although the precise reason for the decree is still debated.

The Maccabean revolt has rightly gone down in Jewish history as an important symbolic event. A small, persecuted group fighting for religious rights was able to face a giant, pagan empire and win. No doubt the initial success of the Maccabees and their supporters was unexpected, and the recapture and cleansing of the temple after only three years was a supreme achievement. Nevertheless, several points must be recognized: (1) the military victories of Judas were not "miraculous"; on the contrary, there were many defeats, and the victories could be explained by normal military factors (e.g., having a force the same size as or greater than the enemy's); (2) the success of the revolt was ultimately because of the rival pretenders to the Seleucid throne, who could be played against one another; and (3) what began as a religious crusade to restore Jewish worship soon turned into a war for an independent Jewish state, in which the Maccabean faction was only a minority movement for some of the time.

The Maccabean vision was eventually victorious. By political maneuvering and force of arms, the movement was able with time to establish its ascendancy over Judea and then to achieve independence from Seleucid control. For about eighty years Judea was an autonomous state, as in days of old, and its borders were extended probably as far as they had ever been, even at the height of the monarchy. This was a considerable achievement often overlooked in histories of Israel. It has long been the custom to locate the zenith of the Israelite nation during the pre-exilic period and to take it for granted that the end of the monarchy ended Israel's nationhood. Typical of this perspective is the statement by John Bright that with the fall of Jerusalem in 587/586, "The state of Judah had ended forever" (330). On the contrary, the state of Judah flourished under such leaders as John Hyrcanus, and seldom under the monarchy did Israelite power or territory rise to that under the Hasmoneans. Jewish descendants of later periods would look back on these days as a proud time.

They were indeed times for pride from one perspective; nevertheless, there was a price to be paid. It was not the age of unmixed blessings, oneness of purpose, or idyllic living that later generations would evoke. All the sons of Mattathias died "with their boots on," in actual warfare or as a result of ambush by opponents. Many Jews evidently regarded their claim on the high priestly office as usurpation. An internal opposition developed to a very strong level under Alexander Janneus, just as Judea reached its greatest area of territorial expansion, and the state quickly declined from this peak as a result of internal rivalry.

The ideology of an idyllic age does not just belong to a later time, for there was plenty of it in the literature from this period. One important concept was that of the land (5.4.12). How was Israel to relate itself to its gentile environment? Some saw it as Israel's duty not only to remain separate but to extend its borders into some sort of mythical "greater Israel." Others were more accommodating to the surrounding culture(s). An obvious example is the so-called Hellenists of the books of Maccabees although, as is shown elsewhere, these were not a monolithic group but represented a broad spectrum (*Tcherikover: 169–74; cf. 5.3.3; 5.4.3.2). Some may have been willing to adapt, to the point of syncretism and assimilation (cf. Artapanus [5.2.10.3]; Philo's "extreme allegorists" [7.2.2]; those who hid their circumcision [5.4.3.2]). Others, although quite happy with Greek culture, did not compromise on the religious essentials (Philo of Alexandria [7.2.2]; Jason the high priest; Ezekiel the Dramatist [5.2.10.5]; Aristobulus [5.2.10.4]). It was a time of quite varied views, once again belying the assumption of a "golden age," in which all adhered to some sort of "orthodox" model (8.3.1).

5.4.2 Antiochus III and the Seleucid Conquest

Taeubler, E. "Jerusalem 201 to 199 B.C.E.: On the History of a Messianic Movement." *JQR* 37 (1946–47) 1–30, 125–37, 249–63.

As noted in the previous chapter, Antiochus III finally—after an initial defeat—achieved what several of his ancestors had tried: gaining actual control over Coele-Syria, to which they had always had a legal claim. The differences in the Seleucid administration (compared with the Ptolemaic) were to have their effect over time, but there was little initially to show that the native peoples were under a different regime. The native customs, laws, and forms of administration were allowed to continue just as they had always done. Antiochus was a good administrator, as well as a capable and ambitious military leader, but the events of history intervened to frustrate him. Once he had taken Syria and Phoenicia from Egypt, he planned to reconquer areas in Asia Minor that had once been part of the Seleucid realm but had long since broken away. This brought him into conflict with Rome, however, which now had a major interest in the Greek East in the wake of the Second Punic War. Antiochus was defeated at Magnesia in 190 by the Romans; the terms of the treaty included not only a boundary of his kingdom at the Taurus Mountains and his son Antiochus being sent to Rome as hostage but also very stiff war reparations of 15,000 talents to the conqueror. To meet this expense,

Antiochus took to raiding and robbing temples; it was in the course of an attack on the temple at Elymais that he was killed in 187.

Several sources give some idea of the situation immediately following the conquest of Syro-Palestine by Antiochus III. There had been different factions among the Jews, some supporters of the Seleucids and some of Ptolemaic rule. For example, probably the best explanation for the rivalry within the Tobiad family is that part of the family took a pro-Seleucid stance and part a pro-Ptolemaic one (4.3.2). These internal divisions seem even to have led to some actual fighting among the Jews (cf. Taeubler). According to Josephus, Antiochus had come against Jerusalem in his advance south, and the city had opened its gates to him (*Ant.* 12.3.3 §§133, 138). There had also been military activity at Jerusalem—to take the Egyptian garrison left in the Akra—and the temple had to be repaired at the direction of Simon the high priest (Ben Sira 50:1-4).

From the preserved accounts it seems that pro-Seleucid sentiment was by far the stronger, as indicated by Antiochus's statement that "the Jews . . . gave us a splendid reception and met us with their senate" (*Ant.* 12.3.3 §§138; 5.3.1). Most of the Tobiad family had supported the Seleucids, with only Hyrcanus continuing on the side of the Ptolemies. After Antiochus's conquest, Hyrcanus withdrew to his fortress across the Jordan and maintained himself by raids on the neighboring Arabs (*Ant.* 12.4.11 §§228–34). Antiochus had received considerable aid, not merely free entry into Jerusalem, from those Jews who threw in their lot with his cause. He acknowledged this in a decree which expressed his gratitude for their supplying him with provisions for his soldiers and with war elephants, as well as for helping to take the citadel of the city from the Ptolemaic garrison (*Ant.* 12.3.3 §§138). The decree rewarded the Jews for this loyalty by granting certain tax concessions, an allowance of products for sacrifices, permission to restore the temple and city, and the right to live according to their ancestral laws (5.3.1).

Because the Jews were allowed to continue living as they had done, there is no indication of immediate change in the general circumstances of life in Judea. Antiochus III was occupied with persistent attempts to expand his empire into Asia Minor, until he was blocked by the Romans. He was succeeded by his son Seleucus IV Philopator (187–175 B.C.E.). Although Seleucus's rule seems a rather quiet one, this may be due to his administrative skills rather than a lack of ability or motivation. He also evidently maintained good relations with Jerusalem (2 Macc 3:2-3), with the exception of the incident involving his minister Heliodorus (5.4.3.2). Beyond this we hear nothing relating to Judea until the reign of Antiochus IV. Seleucus's reign came to an end in 175 when he was murdered by Heliodorus, the minister mentioned in 2 Maccabees.

5.4.3 Hellenistic Reform and Religious Suppression

5.4.3.1 Antiochus IV (175–164 B.C.E.)

Altheim, F., and R. Stiehl. "Antiochos IV. Epiphanes und der Osten." *Geschichte Mittelasiens im Altertum* (1970) 553–71.

Aymard, A. "Autour de l'avènement d'Antiochos IV." *Historia* 2 (1953–54) 49–73.

Bunge, J. G. "Münzen als Mittel politischer Propaganda: Antiochos IV. Epiphanes von Syrien." *Studii Clasice* 16 (1974a) 43–52.

———. " 'Theos Epiphanes': Zu den ersten fünf Regierungsjahren Antiochos' IV. Epiphanes." *Historia* 23 (1974b) 57–85.

———. " 'Antiochos-Helios': Methoden und Ergebnisse der Reichspolitik Antiochos' IV. Epiphanes von Syrien im Spiegel seiner Münzen." *Historia* 24 (1975) 164–88.

*Mørkholm.

Antiochus had been replaced as hostage in Rome by Seleucus IV's eldest son (later to become Demetrius I) and was on his way back to Syria when he heard of his brother's death, which gave him the opportunity to make his bid for the throne. He had little difficulty in taking the throne from his nephew (who may have already been proclaimed king), although the two apparently were joint rulers for a few years until Antiochus consolidated his power (then the younger Antiochus was evidently executed by his uncle). Thus began the reign of one of the most promising and perhaps one of the most able of the Seleucid rulers (*Mørkholm). However, like his father, he had history against him. Holding onto the ambitions of a proper Seleucid Empire, Antiochus spent the first five years of his reign accumulating the necessary resources to bring this empire about. During this time, he was quite happy to receive a large sum of money from Jason in order that Jason would become high priest in place of his brother and turn Jerusalem into a Greek foundation.

The exact chronology of the next few years is uncertain, though recent discoveries have made the picture clearer (5.3.7). Antiochus intended to gain control of Egypt: by becoming king, according to some, or as the power behind the throne, according to others. Whatever his intent, Ptolemy VI took the initiative by advancing into Syrian territory, most likely in late 170. Antiochus responded with a counterattack, which soon turned into an invasion of Egypt itself. Having defeated the Egyptians and succeeded in becoming the protector of his nephew Ptolemy VI, Antiochus returned in triumph about September 169.

His victory was followed by another invasion in 168, which seems to have been successful initially (it has even been argued that Antiochus was declared king of Egypt at one point in the campaign), but then the Romans intervened and Antiochus had no choice but to withdraw in the face of their ultimatum. At this point he intervened in the fighting between Jason's and Menelaus's forces in Jerusalem. The problems in Judea were undoubtedly important, but they were hardly the most important ones on his mind. More pressing concerns were the securing of funds for the treasury, depleted after his war expenses, and seeing to the rest of his empire. A year or two after the second invasion of Egypt, probably in the summer of 166, he organized an enormous celebration and military display at Daphne. Shortly after this, probably in the autumn of the same year, he began a series of campaigns toward the east, just about the time that Judea revolted. Antiochus's chief concern was probably to consolidate and expand his empire in an area where there were no constraints from the Romans, though he also took the occasion to replenish his coffers when he had a chance. It was on this campaign that he died, in late 164 B.C.E. For an assessment of his character, see 5.3.2.2.

5.4.3.2 A New Constitution for Jerusalem

Doran, R. "The Non-Dating of Jubilees: Jub 34–38; 23:14-32 in Narrative Context." *JSJ* 20 (1989) 1–11.

Hall, R. G. "Epispasm and the Dating of Ancient Jewish Writings." *JSP* 4 (1989) 71–86.

Zeitlin, S., and S. Tedesche, eds. *The First Book of Maccabees* (1950).

Sources: 1 Macc 1:10-15; 2 Maccabees 3–4; Josephus, *War* 1.1.1 §§31–33; *Ant.* 12.5.1 §§237–41.

The high priest at the beginning of Antiochus's reign was Onias III, who was evidently pro-Ptolemaic or at least open to that charge because he kept Hyrcanus Tobiad's money in the temple. Here another family becomes important for the story, three brothers from the "tribe of Benjamin." Although some have taken this to mean that they were literally Benjaminites (Schürer: 1.149; but cf. n.30), it is now generally agreed that they were actually priests. If they were not priests, then it seems strange that one was a temple warden (*prostatēs tou hierou* [2 Macc 3:4]) and another eventually high priest, without ever being accused of non-priestly activity in hostile sources. It has been suggested that they were of a priestly family named Benjamin (Zeitlin/Tedesche: 118). However, a variant reading, Balga, the name of a known priestly family (Neh 12:5, 18), is preferred by many scholars (*Tcherikover: 403–4). One brother was Simon, another was named Menelaus, and the third was Lysimachus.

Apparently, some sort of power play on Simon's part led to a dispute between him and Onias over the regulation of the city market. Unable to get his way, Simon reported to Seleucus IV's finance minister, Apollonius, that there was excess money in the temple treasury. If the daily sacrifices were financed from the Seleucid treasury, as some have suggested, it may have seemed that the temple had accumulated an unwonted surplus. There was also the fact that money of Hyrcanus Tobiad, who was regarded as an enemy of the state, was being kept there. Apollonius sent his prime minister, Heliodorus, to Jerusalem to confiscate the funds. When Onias somehow managed to prevent this (by means now obscure), Simon went on to accuse Onias of conspiracy. Onias journeyed to Antioch to protect himself, but before he got there Seleucus was assassinated and Antiochus IV came to the throne. When Onias's appeal eventually came to Antiochus, it was apparently unsuccessful, because Onias remained in Antioch.

Soon after Antiochus began to rule, Jason took advantage of his brother Onias's difficulties by applying to the new king to obtain the high priesthood for himself, promising to pay the large sum of 360 talents (probably the regular tribute) plus another 80 talents. In addition, he paid 150 talents to have Jerusalem made into a Greek foundation, with a gymnasium and *ephebeion* (institutes for Greek education) and a body of citizens known as Antiochenes (5.3.9). Although both 1 and 2 Maccabees castigate Jason's actions as impious in general terms, neither is able to bring any real evidence for the breaking of specific Jewish laws. Despite his intense passion against Jason, the most that the author of 2 Maccabees can say is that the priests "neglected" the sacrifices of the temple by going to watch games when the summons for the discus came (4:14). This hardly constitutes a major breach of religious rules. There is no reason to think the priests had to remain on duty twenty-four hours a day, and those not occupied were no doubt glad of a brief diversion. The temple service itself, however, was not impaired in any way.

It has often been stated that Jewish youths exercised naked, to the scandal of the more conservative, and that they may even have incorporated pagan ceremonies into the gymnasium routine. Again, there is no evidence for either claim. It was not a universal custom for exercise to be done in the nude (cf. Thucydides 1.6.5–6), and the Jews could have done their athletics in loincloths (*Goldstein 1983: 229–30). Although it was also normal for the Greek gymnasia to be dedicated to Hermes, we have no indication that this was the case in Jerusalem. We have to keep in mind that the author of 2 Maccabees is looking for any possible indication of scandal, and he is able to give none. His silence on both issues is a strong indication that neither nude exercise nor any pagan ceremonies were connected with Jason's gymnasium. (Appeal is frequently made to *Jub* 3:30-31 as evidence for nudity, but this passage is only a general comment and not clearly meant as a comment on a specific Jewish breach of custom; cf. also Doran: 10–11.)

There are only two hints of anything contrary to traditional Jewish practice in our literature. One is the statement that in honor of the quadrennial games at Tyre, Jason dispatched a sum of money to pay for sacrifices to "Hercules" (i.e., Melqart, the god of the city). Although Jason no doubt sent a sum of money in honor of the games, it is uncertain that it was intended for sacrifice. Second Maccabees 4:18-20 asserts that this was its intent but also goes on to note that the money was actually used to pay for war galleys. The claim is made that the messengers were the ones who changed the purpose, but this seems unlikely. More believable is that Jason meant the money to be so used from the beginning, and the author of 2 Maccabees only quotes a malicious rumor. A second hint is the statement in 1 Macc 1:15 that "they" removed the marks of circumcision, as if this were universal. Common sense dictates that this was done by a small minority because the operation would have been traumatic, requiring a high degree of motivation (to say the least), as is made clear by the following description of the operation in a classical medical treatise:

> And, if the glans is bare and the man wishes for the look of the thing to have it covered, that can be done; but more easily in a boy than in a man; in one in whom the defect is natural, than in one who after the custom of certain races has been circumcised. . . . Now the treatment for those in whom the defect is natural is as follows. . . . But in one who has been circumcised the prepuce is to be raised from the underlying penis around the circumference of the glans by means of a scalpel. This is not so very painful [!], for once the margin has been freed it can be stripped up by hand as far back as the pubes, nor in so doing is there any bleeding. The prepuce thus freed is again stretched forwards beyond the glans; next cold water affusions are freely used, and a plaster is applied. . . . And for the following days the patient is to fast until nearly overcome by hunger lest satiety excite that part. (Celsus 7.25.1)

Those who did this were probably part of a small, hard-core group who wanted to attend games in the wider Hellenistic world. This is the only charge of religious violation against the gymnasium that seems to stick, and we do not know that it was condoned by Jason himself. Interestingly, 2 Maccabees is silent on this, whereas Josephus ascribes it to the followers of Menelaus, although his account is somewhat confused (*Ant.* 12.5.1 §241).

Despite the question of legitimacy, Jason's move to take the high priesthood seems to have been successful, and he held the office for three years. At this time, however, Menelaus resorted to the same maneuver, promising Antiochus an even larger sum (300 talents in addition to what Jason was paying) if he could have the high priesthood. Jason fled Jerusalem to the trans-Jordanian area, presumably to Hyrcanus's fortress. Although it is often stated that Menelaus was an "extreme Hellenizer" (cf. *Tcherikover: 170–71), this designation does not appear very appropriate for several reasons. First, it seems that Jason's "Hellenistic reform" came to an end as such. That is, Jason's supporters are unlikely to have welcomed Menelaus, and the latter had no motivation to continue the gymnasium or other activities of the polis (*Bringmann: 93–94). Indeed, when opposition came to the surface, prominent in it were members of the gerousia (ruling council, or Sanhedrin) who had been Jason's supporters. Second, none of Menelaus's actions has anything particularly Hellenistic about it. Apart from his Greek name, we would not know that he differed from previous high priests who fought over the office; on the contrary, all that he did suggests a concern for power only. Third, the cult that became established at the temple, although "pagan," was not particularly Greek in character (see below). If the cult's establishment was partly or mainly the doing of Menelaus, as some think, then it would still not earn him the name "Hellenizer" (except as that term is sometimes used in a specialized sense as a synonym for "pagan").

Menelaus had promised an impossible sum for his office (perhaps as much as an annual fee of 890 talents), so it is hardly surprising that he failed to pay. While waiting for Antiochus, who was away, Menelaus tried to ingratiate himself with the governor, Andronicus, by giving him some of the golden temple vessels. When the former high priest, Onias III, objected strenuously to this, Menelaus is alleged to have instigated Onias's death at the hand of Andronicus (see below for the rather different story given by Josephus). Meanwhile, Menelaus's brother Lysimachus was temporarily in charge in Jerusalem. When it became known that he and others were engaged in plundering the temple by selling off various of the golden vessels, a riot broke out.

This is the first report of any reaction from the people of Jerusalem as a whole. The Hellenistic reform had been in effect for several years under Jason, yet there had been no indication of widespread dissatisfaction. No doubt there were grumbles among the more conservative members of the Jewish community, especially those living outside Jerusalem. In the eyes of some, Jason would have been considered a usurper, yet we have no hint of any overt reaction. Jason's reform was apparently accepted with scarcely a ripple, whatever the gossip in the wine houses and vegetable markets may have been. When the people did finally take to the streets, it was not because Jerusalem had been made into a Greek polis but because temple vessels were being stolen. Religious sensibilities had been offended but not by Hellenization as such. Therefore, when Antiochus returned to Antioch, a delegation from the Jerusalem gerousia appeared before him to present charges against Menelaus, but Menelaus got off through a bribe and the delegates of the gerousia were executed. It should be borne in mind that the gerousia was made up of citizens of the new Hellenistic aristocracy of Jerusalem set up by Jason, not of individuals who opposed the reform (of which we have so far heard nothing in our sources).

Up to this point 2 Maccabees has been the basic source followed; however, Josephus gives a somewhat different picture at specific points. In *War* (1.1.1 §31–33) he states that Onias (which?) gained the priesthood from rivals and expelled the Tobiads from Jerusalem. The Tobiads then went to Antiochus with charges against Onias. Onias was forced to flee to Egypt, where he presided over a temple at Leontopolis while Menelaus replaced him. *Antiquities* 12.5.1 §§237–41 states that Jason (Jesus) inherited the priesthood after the death of his brother Onias (III?). The office was taken from him by Antiochus and given to his brother [*sic*!], whose name was also Onias as well as Menelaus. This Onias/Menelaus then conspired with the Tobiads to have Jerusalem made into a Greek foundation. There is no doubt that much of Josephus's account is confused (e.g., Jason has two brothers with the name Onias); nevertheless, he seems to have information additional to his main source of 1 Maccabees and may give some useful information to help counter the prejudices of 1 and 2 Maccabees. Sorting out the usable data from the worthless is not easy, but two bits of data may be important: one is the statement that the Tobiads were involved in Menelaus's bid for power, and the other is that Onias III may not have been murdered but died naturally. Even the information that it was this Onias, replaced by Jason, rather than some mythical Onias IV who built the rival temple at Leontopolis may be important (on this temple, see 5.3.8). Pinning down this last point is difficult, if not impossible, but it suggests that there is still a lot we do not know.

5.4.3.3 The Practice of Judaism Prohibited

Sources: 1 Macc 1:16-63; 2 Maccabees 5–7; Josephus, *War* 1.1.2 §§34–35; *Ant.* 12.5.2–5 §§242–64.

Trying to sort out the precise sequence of events that led to the prohibition of Judaism and the Maccabean revolt is difficult. This is due not only to differences between the sources but also to complications within them that point to intrigues and intricate maneuverings by various interests and factions. Let us first rehearse each account separately, then try to construct a critical synthesis.

Second Maccabees 5–7 is our main source, because the others are generally quite skimpy on the events immediately preceding the suppression of Judaism. This means, however, that many of its points cannot be cross-checked. According to 2 Macc 5:1-27, Antiochus made a second expedition against Egypt at this time. While he was fighting there, a rumor arose that he had been killed. Jason took this opportunity to invade Jerusalem with a large force, in an attempt to regain the office of high priest. He was initially successful in entering the city, but Menelaus took refuge in the Akra. Eventually, Jason's forces were repulsed, and Jason himself was forced to flee. Antiochus, in the meantime, had heard that Jerusalem was in revolt and brought his army against the city, killing forty thousand inhabitants and enslaving another forty thousand. Antiochus himself entered the temple, with Menelaus, and took away a good deal of the gold. He left a viceroy (*epistatēs)* named Philip to keep the people in line. Later he sent Apollonius, who took Jerusalem with violence, killing and enslaving a large number of people. Finally, some time after this, Geron the Athenian (or "an elderly Athenian") was sent to compel the Jews to abandon their ancestral laws.

First Maccabees 1:16-63 states only that Antiochus invaded Egypt and conquered it. On his way back he took Jerusalem and despoiled the temple (this is similar to 2 Maccabees). Two years later he sent an officer of the tribute (apparently the same as Apollonius of 2 Maccabees) to take Jerusalem and to make the City of David into a fortress. After this, Antiochus issued a decree that all his subjects were to abandon their native laws and become one people. The "heathen" and "even many from Israel" obeyed this decree. It was at this point that the "abomination of desolation" was set up in the temple, and the revolt subsequently began.

According to Josephus (*Ant.* 12.5.2-4 §§242–56), Antiochus marched into Egypt and defeated Ptolemy VII, but the Romans intervened and forced him to abandon any designs on Egypt. On his way home he took Jerusalem and despoiled it. Two years later he took the city again and stopped the temple sacrifices.

It is important to be aware of the separate accounts and note the differences between them, because many modern reconstructions ignore them, especially those in the data of Josephus. There is a similarity in overall outline and even in many of the details, but the differences may be the key to a proper understanding of what actually took place. Each source is written from its own perspective with some unique data, and thus gives only part of the picture or even a false one.

None of our sources gives a coherent portrayal of the events leading up to the suppression of Jewish worship (the chronological scheme followed here is my own reconstruction; see 5.3.7 for the detailed arguments for it). For example, 2 Maccabees confuses two separate events, whereas 1 Maccabees records only the one invasion of Egypt (*Bickerman: 10, 45–46). From other sources we know that Antiochus invaded Egypt twice. The first time was about November 170, when he successfully defeated Ptolemy VI and then forced an alliance by marrying his daughter off to him (cf. Dan 11:28; 1 Macc 1:16-24). On his way back in September 169, he entered the Jerusalem temple and looted its treasures. Some think that he attacked the city at this time, but there is no reason why he should have engaged in any fighting. There is no evidence that any resistance was offered to his initial entry. Furthermore, when he took the temple money he apparently did not interfere with the temple cult. Thus no violence seems to have taken place at this time (cf. Dan 11:28). In the spring of 168 he invaded once again, but this time things were different (Dan 11:29-30; 2 Macc 5:1-17). Although he was victorious over the Egyptians, the Romans intervened and forced him to withdraw (July 168). It was probably then that news of Jason's siege of Menelaus came to his ears, and he sent a force to put down what he thought was a revolt (some want to connect this with his first invasion of Egypt).

The accounts at this point leave some major difficulties. If Antiochus took the city and put down the revolt, then why was there need to send Apollonius the Mysiarch (i.e., in charge of a contingent of Mysian soldiers) to take the city by subterfuge later (2 Macc 5:23-26; 1 Macc 1:29-36)? Moreover, Apollonius is said to have enslaved the inhabitants, a strange move after Antiochus had already slain or enslaved practically all of them! Furthermore, why did Antiochus feel it necessary even after that to send Geron the Athenian to set up pagan worship in the temple (2 Macc 6:1-11), when the supposed revolt of the Jews had long since been dealt with? We are simply not given sufficient data and can only make informed guesses at best.

There is no clear evidence that Antiochus himself took part in capturing the city (*Bringmann: 38; Schürer: 1.152 n.37; contra *Tcherikover: 186). Rather, the actions ascribed to him are probably those of Apollonius; that is, Apollonius was sent to put down a rebellion. When he got there, the city was already peaceful, but he took it by a ruse and carried out Antiochus's orders. After this, Philip the *epistatēs* was sent. It is often thought that his task was to settle a colony of soldiers in Jerusalem, that is, to establish a military cleruchy to be ready for any further trouble (*Tcherikover: 194–95; *Bringmann: 87–89, 127; however, Bar-Kochva argues no colony was founded, only a garrison [*438–44]). Philip remained there, with Menelaus continuing as high priest, until the actual Maccabean revolt began (cf. 2 Macc 6:11; 8:8).

The real puzzle is why a short time later Antiochus sent Geron to crush the Jewish religion. A number of suggestions have been made over the years, some of them to be rejected outright; others are better, but none is wholly satisfactory (5.3.2). This religious suppression was unique in antiquity. Religious intolerance has historically been a practice of monotheistic religions. Whereas Judaism itself was often seen by the Greeks and Romans as intolerant (7.3.8), polytheism is tolerant by its very nature. Antiochus was no religious zealot. He had no occasion to suppress Judaism for ideological reasons, and Jews outside Palestine itself and even in the capital of Antioch carried on their worship without hindrance (*Bickerman: 79–80; *Bringmann: 102 n.8). This has led some to see Menelaus as the instigator of the persecution. The problem with this is that Menelaus seems to have been not an ideologue but a power-seeker. It seems reasonable to assume that he was in some way involved in the prohibition, either as an active agent or simply as one who acquiesced to Antiochus's requirements. Whereas Bickerman's thesis of Menelaus as the creator of an "enlightened religion" does not stand up, Bringmann has argued that the imposed cult was the product of a power play by Menelaus himself.

To summarize, there is no doubt that suppression of Jewish worship was a watershed event, not only in Jewish history but also in the history of antiquity, because it had not been the custom to forbid local religious expression. None of the answers given by ancient sources or modern scholars has fully resolved the issue. One of the major difficulties is the strong partisanship of almost all the ancient sources. Not a single one attempts to give the side of the so-called Hellenists, and modern scholars have generally been equally biased in their presentation. Nevertheless, the data available indicate that even among the "Hellenists" there was a range of attitudes. Such hostile sources as 1 and 2 Maccabees cannot point to a single violation of Jewish law by Jason and his associates (with the possible exception of the money sent to Tyre). The case is different with Menelaus, who committed such acts as stealing temple vessels and accompanying Antiochus into the temple itself. Nevertheless, he appears more as an opportunist than a doctrinaire idealist trying to create some new, syncretistic religion. He wanted power and to line his own pockets, if his actions have been correctly reported, not to be the founder of an "enlightened Yahwistic cult." Nevertheless, even this interpretation, justified as it seems from data presently known, might well prove incorrect if we had further information. We must accept that there is a great deal that is still confusing about the situation, in no small measure due to the extreme prejudice and one-sidedness of all extant sources.

5.4.4 The Maccabean Revolt to the Death of Judas

Bar-Kochva, B. *The Seleucid Army: Organization and Tactics in the Great Campaigns* (1976a).

———. "Sēron and Cestius Gallus at Beith Ḥoron." *PEQ* 108 (1976b) 13–21.

Sources: 1 Macc 2:1—9:22; 2 Maccabees 8–15; Josephus, *War* 1.1.3–6 §§36–47; *Ant.* 12.6.1–11.2 §§265–434.

Because of the persecution, many people fled from Jerusalem into the countryside. Armed resistance allegedly began with the Hasmonean family. According to 1 Maccabees 2, the resistance was initially led by Mattathias, who was accompanied by his five sons, John, Simon, Judas (Maccabeus), Eleazar, and Jonathan. They had left Jerusalem to live in Modein, which was probably the ancestral home of the family. There soldiers of the king attempted to force a public pagan sacrifice. Mattathias killed both an apostate Jew who acceded to the order for sacrifice and the commander of the soldiers, and then fled with other Jews into the wilderness. He lived for only about a year after this and, on his deathbed, turned the military leadership over to Judas, who seems not to have been the eldest of the sons.

This story is widely repeated and may be true (cf. *Bar-Kochva: 196–99), but there are problems with it (*Sievers: 29–37). 2 Maccabees ignores Mattathias to focus on Judas. Although leadership may not have gone to the eldest son, chances are that it would have. So is it likely that Judas was only the third son? Scholars since Wellhausen have pointed out that 1 Maccabees seems to give the most prominence to Simon, suggesting that we may see an attempt here to downplay Judas's initiative to some extent (cf. *Tcherikover: 205, 384). The story as it stands has elements suggestive of romantic coloration (e.g., the Phineas-like act of Mattathias).

Whatever its precise origins, the Jewish resistance under Judas and his brothers took some time to get under way. Whether others joined them, as 1 Maccabees alleges, or whether it was they who joined others is a moot point (cf. *Sievers: 34). The first actions seem to have been against "apostate" Jews (1 Macc 2:44-48; 3:8). The village of Modein served as the center of operations (*Bar-Kochva: 194–99). Although close to the Seleucid garrisons at Jerusalem and Gezer and easily approachable by a hostile force, Modein was right next to the Gophna Hills, to which the Jewish fighters could easily retire if threatened. The resistance was conducted with guerrilla tactics initially and probably did not then worry the central Seleucid government; however, the local administration saw the need to do something about the harrassment.

The first attempt to crush the revolt came from Apollonius, probably the same person as the commander of the Mysians mentioned earlier (1 Macc 1:29). No real details are given except that Apollonius was killed. The next attempt was by Seron, defeated at the ascent of Beth Horon, a favorite spot for ambush (as the Romans found almost 250 years later [7.4.11.2; Bar-Kochva 1976b]). Despite the impression given by 1 Maccabees, both of these were local actions carried out by small contingents of Seleucid soldiers (*Bar-Kochva: 199–218). For example, Seron was not the "commander of the Syrian armies" (contra 1 Macc 3:13) but a low-ranking officer who apparently exceeded his authority (cf. v 14). Therefore, the statement that these defeats were enough to begin to make Judas's name known to the surrounding nations (1 Macc 3:25-26) is an exaggeration (*Bar-Kochva: 218).

Contrary to both 1 and 2 Maccabees, Antiochus had things far more important than the Jewish resistance demanding his attention. It is doubtful that news of the Jewish situation had even come to his ears, but if it had, then it was not likely to have seemed very significant to him. The problem with Judas's faction was brought to the administration's attention by Philip, the local governor in Jerusalem (cf. 2 Macc 5:22), who realized he needed help to gain the initiative against the resistance (2 Macc 8:8). Antiochus himself did not lead the fight to put down the Jewish revolt. Indeed, he was probably no longer at Antioch, because in late 166 he had put his companion Lysias in charge as vice-regent; made him guardian of his son (also Antiochus), who was only seven or eight years old; and led an expedition across the Euphrates to the eastern provinces. The response to Philip's appeal came from Ptolemy son of Dorymenes, the military commander (*stratēgos*) of Syria and Phoenicia, who appointed Nicanor and Gorgias to lead a larger force against the Jews (2 Macc 8:8-9). Although its precise size is uncertain (1 Macc 3:39 grossly exaggerates), it probably outnumbered the Jewish fighters. The total number was not the crucial factor, however, because Judas inflicted a decisive defeat on an advance unit of the Syrian army at Emmaus, which so demoralized the rest that they fled with little attempt to face the Jews. Even though Judas had only about six thousand men (2 Macc 8:16-25), his force was probably about the same strength as the Syrian unit that he attacked. This resulted not only in an enormous boost to Jewish morale and reputation but also in the capture of considerable funds, weapons, and other goods important to keep the resistance going. Included in this was a large sum of money left by slave dealers. Therefore, in one of those unusual happenings that history occasionally throws up, a spectacular victory was won, contrary to normal expectations.

The next year (ca. 165 B.C.E.) Lysias himself led an invasion force, this time coming from the south up through Idumea to Beth-Zur (1 Macc 4:28-35; also 2 Maccabees 11, though it misplaces the event chronologically). The number given for the Syrian force is the usual exaggeration, but interestingly the Jews are credited with ten thousand men. Although 1 and 2 Maccabees make the battle another Jewish victory, this seems doubtful (*Bar-Kochva: 134–35, 275–90). Lysias had superior numbers, and a major defeat of the Syrian forces as is described would have led to a panic-stricken rout, yet Lysias is said to have conducted an orderly retreat. If he was not defeated, however, then why did he withdraw to Antioch? Both 1 and 2 Maccabees ascribe it simply to divine favor and Jewish bravery. The actual reason is probably more prosaic and realistic: one possibility is that problems at Antioch may have required Lysias's presence there. There may be another reason, however, revealed in the letters of concession by Antiochus IV and Antiochus V. If these letters (2 Macc 11:16-33) are authentic, as is usually assumed (5.3.5), then they seem to show that Lysias withdrew because of attempts at negotiations. Representatives from some of the Jews (Judas's faction, or some other?) approached Lysias to ask for terms. About the same time, the high priest Menelaus went to Antiochus concerning the same issue:

> King Antiochus to the senate of the Jews. . . . Menelaus has informed us that you wish to return home to take care of your own affairs. Therefore those who return home up to the thirtieth day of Xanthicus will have our pledge free of all fear, that the Jews may use their own food and abide by their own laws, as they used to do. No one of them shall be molested in any way because of things that he might have done innocently. Then too I have sent Menelaus to stand by you. (2 Macc 11:27, 29-32)

Although Menelaus had not been mentioned for some time in the narrative, he was still the official high priest. This indicates that he at least had the wit to see the internal problems and attempt to persuade the Syrian government to make some concessions. The significance of the letters is discussed later in this section.

Because of Lysias's withdrawal and the general military situation, Judas felt sufficiently encouraged to march on Jerusalem and retake the temple area. There was apparently no resistance, but Judas appointed a guard to keep the Syrians holed up in the Akra while the temple was cleansed and rededicated. Interestingly, this was done not by Judas but by the priests, who evidently maintained a degree of independence vis-à-vis Judas (1 Macc 4:42-58; cf. *Sievers: 47–48). The description of the temple site in 1 Macc 4:38 ("weeds growing up in the courts as in a forest") indicates no activity had been going on there for some time. The rededication was accomplished on 25 Kislev, supposedly exactly three years after the temple was first polluted. One suspects that because they were near the third anniversary of the pollution, Judas specifically planned the rededication to fall on that exact day. Nevertheless, it was a memorable event of Jewish history, still commemorated in Judaism today by Hanukkah, or the Festival of Lights.

For the next year Judas seems to have operated free from bother by the Syrians. He turned his attention to the local neighbors in Idumea, Galilee, and Transjordan (1 Maccabees 5). As usual, the blame for starting the troubles is put on the Gentiles, although in some cases, at least, Judas's group seems to have taken the initiative. In any case, there seems to have been no official, state persecution of Jews (*Sievers: 57). Part of the campaign during these months involved rescue operations to help Jews attacked in areas outside Judea itself. Many Jews were brought back as refugees from Galilee and Transjordan.

As indicated by 1 Macc 6:18-27, Judas was also busy in Jerusalem itself. He had not only retaken the temple area but also was besieging the Seleucid garrison in the Akra; he had to be dealt with. Therefore, shortly after Antiochus IV's death, Lysias found it necessary to embark on a second expedition (summer 163). The course of the march was once again from the south through Idumea to Beth-Zur, to which Lysias laid siege. Judas left off his own siege of the Akra to meet the Syrians but was defeated in a battle near Beth-Zechariah. Lysias returned to Beth-Zur and took it, with the defenders agreeing to surrender the fort for a promise of safe conduct. Precisely what Judas did at this point is uncertain. According to the books of Maccabees, Judas took refuge in the temple, where he was besieged by Lysias (1 Macc 6:48-54; cf. 2 Macc 13:22-24); however, Josephus says that he fled to Gophna, which probably means the area around Modein, his original country of refuge (*War* 1.1.5 §45). Most likely, while some of his men were in the temple, Judas himself slipped off to his old base in the hills (*Bar-Kochva: 337–38).

Lysias did not press his siege of the temple but came to terms with the defenders. The reason was a problem in his own backyard: the general Philip, who had been given authority by Antiochus IV on his deathbed, attempted a coup in Antioch (1 Macc 6:55-63; 2 Macc 13:23-24). Lysias's basic concession was to confirm the freedom of the Jews to practice their traditional religion. Although this had already been done, it was important to provide further guarantees. At this time, probably on his way back from Judea, he ordered Menelaus executed. His reason is not made clear, but it was likely because he realized that no peace with the Jews would be possible as long as Menelaus continued to hold the office of high priest (*Ant*. 12.9.7 §§383–85). After the execution, Alcimus was appointed to take Menelaus's place (cf. 1 Macc 7:5; 2 Macc 14:3-13).

We are now in a position to summarize the course of events, making use of the additional information from original Seleucid documents, the letters of 2 Maccabees 11. These are very important for a reconstruction of what happened, but the dating of them is a problem (5.3.5). The order of events seems to be that Menelaus, realizing the situation, went to Antiochus IV and asked for an end to the religious measures. Antiochus conceded, with the understanding that hostilities by the Jews also cease (letter 3, Antiochus IV to the Jews: 11:27-33). About the same time, Lysias was negotiating with Jewish representatives. Because of these negotiations, he broke off his first engagement so that the Jews would have time to cease from hostilities and accept the new grant of religious freedom (letter 1: 11:16-21). The Romans, being apprised of this, indicated their opinion in a letter to the Jews (letter 4: 11:34-38). For over a year (autumn 165 to spring 163) the Syrians left Judea alone. Nevertheless, Judas's group had refused to cooperate, not only retaking the temple area but also besieging the Seleucid garrison in the Akra. Because the hostilities had not come to an end, Lysias found it necessary to invade once more (spring 163) and inflict a decisive defeat on Judas. Events in Antioch prevented Lysias's following up that victory, however, and he negotiated with those besieged in the temple. Finally, once Antiochus V was securely on the throne (but under Lysias's guardianship), he wrote confirming the concessions (letter 2, Antiochus V to Lysias: 11:22-26 [if it is genuine]).

About this time, Demetrius, the son of Seleucus IV, escaped from Rome. He had been sent as a hostage to replace his uncle Antiochus IV in 176. Despite repeated requests to the senate, he had not been allowed to return to Antioch. Once he finally did so, with the connivance of some of his Roman friends, he made his claim for the Seleucid throne as Demetrius I. In late 162 Lysias and the young Antiochus V were defeated and executed by Demetrius. Alcimus went to him for confirmation of his high priestly office and, at the same time, to ask for help against Judas's group, which was still offering military opposition to Alcimus and the new Seleucid administration, despite the declaration of religious freedom (1 Macc 10:37). Demetrius dispatched an army under his deputy Bacchides to install Alcimus in Jerusalem and deal with the problem of Judas.

This incident well illustrates the complexity of views and the divisions among the Jews at this time. First Maccabees 7:14 notes only that Alcimus was of the line of Aaron, suggesting that he was not of the Zadokite line (the traditional requirement for the high priest). However, a more careful look gives some reason to think that he was actually an Oniad (cf. *Sievers: 63 n.66). Regardless of whether this was so, many Jews were willing to accept him, including those who had opposed Menelaus. For example, the important (if enigmatic) group known as the Hasidim (8.2.1) gave up its part in the Jewish resistance and made peace with the Seleucids (1 Macc 7:12-14). Despite the impression given by the partisan account of 1 Maccabees, for many Jews the issue was simply one of religious freedom. These people were not interested in the broader nationalistic goals of Judas and his followers, which is why they took the opportunity to make peace when they were guaranteed freedom of worship under an acceptable high priest. The leadership of the Maccabean resistance by no means embodied the aspirations of the nation as a whole.

It is difficult to determine the size of the support for Judas, because the sources try to give the impression that most of the Jews were united under him. From the number of soldiers in his army, it seems likely that throughout most of the revolt he had considerable backing (*Bar-Kochva: 47–63, but note the criticisms of *Schwartz: 16 n.2). There are, however, a number of hints that this was not always the case. One of these is the action of the Hasidim; others are noted in the appropriate places below.

The author of 1 Maccabees ignores the implications of the move by the Hasidim to make peace; instead, he is quick to point out that they suffered for this: sixty of them were supposedly arrested and executed in one day by Bacchides (1 Macc 7:12-18). Because of the bias of our source at this point, it is difficult to evaluate precisely what happened and why. If those Hasidim were executed, as alleged, then it would no doubt have driven the group back into the arms of Judas. For exactly this reason, however, it was hardly in Bacchides' self-interest to provoke a section of the population which was willing to accept his orders; furthermore, we do not have any indication that the Hasidim as a group returned to Judas's camp. On the contrary, it appears that the Jews as a whole were willing to recognize Alcimus as high priest and accept Syrian domination, in return for freedom of worship (1 Macc 7:20-22).

Nevertheless, Judas continued his fight against Syrian rule, eventually making things so difficult that Alcimus once more had to appeal to Demetrius for help. This time Nicanor, the governor over Judea (2 Macc 14:12), was sent to deal with the situation. Initially, Nicanor followed a policy of attempting to negotiate with Judas, rather than meeting him in battle (1 Macc 7:27-28; 2 Macc 14:18-25). It is alleged that this policy was pursued with such patience that Judas even went so far as to marry and settle down for a period of time, at Nicanor's recommendation (2 Macc 14:25; though this is to be doubted: *Bar-Kochva: 354–56). There are, at least, suggestions that a truce was in place for some time, despite the attempt of 1 Maccabees to play it down (7:29-30). For whatever reason, the truce did not last (2 Macc 14:26-27 blames Alcimus), and the postponed showdown in battle came about. The description of the battle suggests that Judas actually had numerical superiority (*Bar-Kochva: 360), and Nicanor was defeated and killed. Judas had his head displayed in Jerusalem as a grisly token of victory and declared 13 Adar a public holiday, known as Nicanor's Day.

Second Maccabees breaks off at this point, seeing the defeat of Nicanor as the climax to Judas's career. Nevertheless, this was hardly the end of the story, which did not finish so gloriously. According to 1 Maccabees, Judas went on to send ambassadors to Rome to make a treaty of alliance with the senate (although the historicity of this has often been doubted [5.3.5]). If historical, then this treaty would no doubt have been a useful boost to the morale of Judas's party and would have further assisted the establishment of his rule over Judea, but it seems to have provided little practical help for the Jews against the Syrians. For shortly afterward, in the spring of 161 B.C.E., Bacchides invaded once more to avenge the humiliation of Nicanor's army. This time the battle went against the Jews; Judas was slain and his soldiers routed. The death of Judas marks the beginning of a period of several years during which we hear little or nothing further about his followers. The Maccabees were still a long way from gaining control of Judea and even further from independence of Syrian rule.

The successes achieved by Judas's force were extremely important for the course of Jewish history. There seems no doubt about the considerable tactical skill of its leaders and the fighting ability of the soldiers. The Maccabean resistance also deservedly goes down in history for one or two exceptional victories; nevertheless, most of its success is fully explicable by normal military factors.

First, the actual number of Seleucid troops is usually grossly exaggerated by the Jewish sources, whereas the Jewish numbers are often far too low (*Bar-Kochva: 29–68; 1976a: 7–19). For example, the expedition led by Nicanor is said to have included 40,000 foot soldiers and 7,000 cavalry (1 Macc 3:39), but even the alternative figure of 20,000 (2 Macc 8:9) is too large. The number of soldiers employed on each side, even in major military campaigns, was only about 50,000. At the important battle of Raphia, in which he confronted the entire Ptolemaic force (4.4.4), Antiochus III had 35,000 heavy infantry, 21,000 light, and 6,000 cavalry (Polybius 5.79; Bar-Kochva: *33; 1976a: 132). On the other hand, after retaking the temple, it appears that Judas could assemble a force of 20,000 at short notice (Bar-Kochva: *49–51; 1976a: 185–87).

Second, Judas's force was regarded only as a nuisance at the beginning, which is another reason why the initial forces sent against him would have been small. Despite the attempt by the Jewish sources to make the defeat of Jewish resistance the number one priority of Antiochus, he in fact had much larger things on his mind and left the quashing of this minor irritation to subordinates. As already noted, the initial campaigns were conducted locally, and the central government became involved only in response to a request for help from the governor of the Palestinian area (2 Macc 8:8).

Third, luck seems to have played an important part, as it has in many famous victories and defeats. No matter how carefully and brilliantly the strategy is planned, as all military historians are aware, much can go wrong in the actual battle. For example, it was more or less by chance that only a part of Nicanor's force at Emmaus first encountered Judas and thus was opposed by an enemy closer to its equal in strength than if the full Syrian army had been there (1 Macc 4:1-15; 2 Macc 8:16). The resulting defeat was sufficient to demoralize the rest of the Syrian forces and make possible a final Jewish victory against large odds. Therefore, although giving full credit to the Jews for their unusual successes, one should be careful not to regard them as unique in the annals of military history.

Finally, the Jewish sources sometimes ignore defeats and even make defeats appear as victories for the Jews. For example, although 2 Maccabees assures us that the Seleucid army was defeated in Lysias's second invasion (13:22), the rest of the data show that Judas had to go into hiding afterward. As the parallel account in 1 Macc 6:47-54 frankly admits, it was a Jewish defeat (which Josephus also confirms: *War* 1.1.5 §§41–46; cf. *Ant*. 12.9.4–5 §§367–78).

As Bar-Kochva notes, Judas's contribution lay not in miraculous victories against overwhelming odds but in a much more practical sphere, that of developing a regular army:

> The greatness of Judas Maccabaeus, however, lies not in local military-tactical achievements, but mainly in the construction and development of a great and powerful army which could not be destroyed by isolated failures. Even the defeats suffered by the Jewish commanders brought the independence they aspired to closer: to the enemy, unable to leave a large garrison in the country, they underlined the vast potential in the Jewish army, and the need to compromise with it. . . . The efforts of Judas Maccabaeus to modify his operational methods to conform to the

new circumstances after the purification of the Temple and organize his army accordingly, building an up-to-date large army, were much more demanding than the initial guerrilla war. (*407–9)

5.4.5 Jonathan Maccabee (161–143 B.C.E.)

Bar-Kochva, B. "Hellenistic Warfare in Jonathan's Campaign near Azotos." *Scripta Classica Israelica* 2 (1975) 83–96.

Burgmann, H. "Das umstrittene Intersacerdotium in Jerusalem 159–152 v. Chr." *JSJ* 11 (1980) 135–76.

Gera, D. "Tryphon's Sling Bullet from Dor." *IEJ* 35 (1985) 153–63.

Murphy-O'Connor, J. "Demetrius I and the Teacher of Righteousness (I Macc., x, 25–45)." *RB* 83 (1976) 400–420.

Sources: 1 Macc 9:23—12:53; Josephus, *War* 1.2.1 §§48–49; *Ant.* 13.1.1–6.6 §§1–212.

Jonathan was elected leader of the Maccabean resistance after Judas's death, but for a number of years they were very much on the run. The Jews as a whole seem to have accepted the continuance of Seleucid rule once they had an acceptable high priest in Alcimus and freedom to practice traditional Judaism. First Maccabees labels the ruling Jews and the supporters of Alcimus as "impious" (*asebeis*) men and says that "great tribulation" (*thlipsis megalē*) came upon Israel, but this is a partisan point of view (1 Macc 9:23-27). Those who were distressed were the Maccabean supporters, who seem very much a minority group at this time.

The Syrians were not content to let things stand as they were, however, and Bacchides pursued Jonathan. He probably recognized that this group would continue to be a thorn in the side unless destroyed once and for all. Jonathan's territory seems to have centered on the wilderness near Tekoa (1 Macc 9:33, 62), even though one fight with the Syrians took place on the Jordan. Despite several encounters, Jonathan managed to escape each time, but his brother John was killed by the Nabateans. Unsuccessful in taking Jonathan's group, Bacchides had to content himself with fortifying various sites with garrisons (Jericho, Emmaus, Beth Horon, Bethel, Timnath, Pharathon, Tephon, Beth-Zur, Gezer, the Jerusalem Akra [1 Macc 9:50-53]) and taking hostages from the leading Jews.

The high priest Alcimus died about 160 B.C.E. of something suggestive of a stroke. Because this happened during alterations to an inner wall of the temple, some Jews saw his death as divine punishment (cf. 1 Macc 9:54-56). There is no evidence of violation of the law, however, and the judgment probably only reflects different sectarian opinions about the arrangement of the temple courts (*Goldstein 1976: 391–92). His death was followed by several years of calm for Jonathan. Then, allegedly at the instigation of "lawless" (*anomoi* [v 58]) Jews, the fight was renewed with an attack by Bacchides on Jonathan's stronghold at Bethbasi, near Tekoa. Jonathan slipped away to get help from allies (cf. *Goldstein 1976: 395), leaving Simon in charge. In spite of an intense siege, Simon and his men managed to hold out, and eventually Bacchides had to withdraw, apparently angry at the Jews who had brought him in. On hearing of this, Jonathan took the opportunity to negotiate with the Syrian general, which led to a truce and the exchange of prisoners. Bacchides left the land, and Jonathan had free rein to begin establishing his dominance and get back at his Jewish opponents.

Jonathan's position was no doubt helped by the fact that no new high priest had been appointed in Alcimus's place, and a power vacuum now existed in the Jewish leadership. At least this is the impression left by our sources. It has been proposed (apparently first by H. Stegemann) that there was indeed another high priest during this time, one deliberately excised from the records by the pro-Hasmonean historians, the suggestion being that after he was ousted from his office, this individual became the Teacher of Righteousness, the leader of the Qumran group (Murphy-O'Connor). Although this is an ingenious proposal, it remains speculative, with little support from the preserved data (the Qumran documents being couched in allusive language). There is no reason to assume that a hiatus in the high priesthood would not have been allowed. The temple could function routinely on the cultic level without a serving high priest. (The one problem would be the ceremonies on the Day of Atonement [Leviticus 16].) For a further critique of the thesis, see Burgmann.

The real opportunity for the Maccabees came some years later, about 153 B.C.E., when Alexander Balas became the rival of Demetrius I for the Seleucid throne. Alexander claimed to be the son of Antiochus IV (and was so accepted by many in antiquity, although scholars generally doubt it today) and thus rightful heir to the throne. Having received permission from the senate, he set out to take the Seleucid throne (Polybius 33.18). Demetrius, knowing that he needed all the allies he could get, sent an offer of peace to Jonathan, with authority to assemble an army and to be given the Jewish hostages in the Akra. Jonathan had his headquarters at Michmash (1 Macc 9:73), but at this point he moved to Jerusalem and began fortifying it. It is important to note that, contrary to the impression given by 1 Maccabees, this seems to be the first time that Jonathan's authority was widely accepted by Jews, and the reason for their acquiescence was the official royal backing. Now Jonathan could establish his headquarters in Jerusalem with Seleucid authority. Having heard of the concessions made by Demetrius, Alexander Balas made his own promises to Jonathan. These included the title of high priest and the purple robe and gold crown that accompanied it, according to Seleucid tradition. Jonathan donned these at the Feast of Tabernacles (ca. 153 B.C.E.), thus formally beginning the tradition of the Hasmonean high priesthood. The Maccabees had established their leadership (although opposition continued, as noted below), but control was not completely in Jonathan's hands. At least two references from a slightly later time (1 Macc 12:6, 35) show that he was assisted—and constrained—by a council of elders, which was probably a continuation of the old *gerousia*.

Although Demetrius made further offers in a long letter "to the Jewish nation" (*tōi ethnei tōn Ioudaiōn* [1 Macc 10:25]), Jonathan did not believe his promises and continued to favor Alexander; indeed, the address of the letter implied that Jonathan's leadership would not have been recognized by Demetrius. In any case, the wisdom of this choice was demonstrated soon afterward, when Alexander defeated and killed Demetrius in battle in about 151 B.C.E. Afterward, when Alexander (150–145 B.C.E.) married Ptolemy VI Philometor's daughter, he invited Jonathan to Ptolemais and publicly honored him by making him "friend," general, and governor of the province of Judea. As this shows, despite the honors and concessions, Judea was still a province overseen from Antioch, and the Akra was still in the hands of a Syrian garrison. A delegation from the opposition to Jonathan's rule attempted to see Alexander but was refused a hearing. Judea was by no means united behind Jonathan even yet.

In 147 B.C.E. the son of Demetrius I, later to become Demetrius II (145–140, 129–126 B.C.E.), sailed from Crete in an attempt to take back his father's kingdom from Alexander. Among his actions was the appointment of a governor of Coele-Syria named Apollonius. Apollonius camped near Yavneh (Jamnia) and challenged Jonathan to fight him. Because Alexander was busy making secure his position in Antioch, Jonathan could not count on his help. Furthermore, Apollonius was superior in cavalry forces, which he could use against Jonathan in the Shephelah region. Nevertheless, Jonathan took him on and won a major victory, as well as receiving the submission of Joppa and Ascalon and taking Ashdod. In gratitude, Alexander also gave him Ekron, thus confirming Jewish control over the old area of Philistia.

At first Ptolemy VI supported his son-in-law Alexander, but then he turned against him and sided with Demetrius II. With the help of Ptolemy's forces, Demetrius was able to defeat Alexander and establish his rulership in 145 B.C.E. Taking advantage of the struggle over the Seleucid throne, Jonathan laid siege to the Akra, which was still in Syrian hands two decades after the rededication of the temple. When Demetrius heard of this after his own position was secure, he demanded an accounting from Jonathan. The latter not only had his troops continue the siege but also went boldly to Demetrius and came away with major concessions from the king, despite a delegation from "lawless" Jews with accusations against him (1 Macc 11:25). He was named "friend of Demetrius," had his high priesthood confirmed, and was allowed to govern Judea and the three provinces acquired from Samaria "free of tribute." This last concession may be less generous than it seems, because Jonathan actually promised three hundred talents to the king for it. The reason was most likely that Demetrius's coffers were empty, and a single payment on the spot was more attractive than the uncertain promise of future tribute (*Goldstein 1976: 430–31). The Akra, however, was evidently able to hold out against Jonathan's force.

Demetrius was soon glad of Jonathan as an ally, because troubles developed between Demetrius and his army. Jonathan requested that Demetrius turn the still-unconquered Akra over to him. The Syrian ruler was glad to make any promises necessary to gain loyal troops. A force of three thousand Jewish soldiers was dispatched to Antioch and arrived in time to help Demetrius put down a revolt of his own citizens in the city. Following this victory, Demetrius apparently reneged on any implied concessions, but the situation was quickly overtaken by events: Tryphon, a general of Alexander Balas, crowned Alexander's young son and proclaimed him king as a rival to Demetrius. In the resulting engagement Demetrius was defeated, and the new king, Antiochus VI, wrote to Jonathan to confirm him in his offices and to add one further district to his territory (although the exact identification of this district is not given in any of the sources). Simon was appointed general over the armies from the region of Tyre to the borders of Egypt (cf. *Ant.* 13.5.4 §146). Jonathan was probably commander over the whole of Coele-Syria (cf. 1 Macc 11:60).

Despite his initial defeat, Demetrius II was still alive and had not conceded the throne; therefore, it fell to Jonathan to make his area secure for Antiochus VI. As he marched through Philistia, Ascalon welcomed him, but Gaza submitted only after a siege. Jonathan left Simon to take care of Judah while he marched north to engage some of the generals loyal to Demetrius in Galilee and, later, in the area of Hamath. Simon laid siege to Beth-Zur and eventually expelled its Syrian garrison and replaced it with a Jewish one. He also took Joppa, which was about to go over to Demetrius.

With the military situation in hand, Jonathan proceeded to make the various strongholds in Judah more secure. Included in this process were plans to strengthen the defenses of Jerusalem and to press a more determined assault on the Akra. Simon had the responsibility of building and fortifying Adida (in Hebrew, Hadid). It was also about this time that Jonathan was alleged to have renewed the treaty with Rome and to have written a letter to the Spartans about the common kinship between them and the Jews (5.3.6). These activities all suggest that Jonathan was working hard for a situation in which Judea could be declared an independent state. That Roman goodwill would be very useful goes without saying, but the letter to Sparta was also important. The Spartans had Roman favor at this time, partly because of a claim to kinship with them (*Goldstein 1976: 447–48). A Jewish claim to common ancestry with the Spartans would not go amiss in the political maneuverings.

Jonathan's plans were cut short, however. Tryphon, although nominally still the guardian of Antiochus VI, was in fact planning to assassinate the king and take the crown himself. He first marched to Beth Shean in Judea, where he was met by Jonathan. He assured Jonathan of his peaceful intentions and suggested that the Jewish army be dismissed and the Jewish leader come to Ptolemais for a formal relinquishing of Syrian control over Judea. Jonathan accepted his word and came with only a bodyguard. Once in the city, the Jewish soldiers were slaughtered and Jonathan was taken captive. It now fell to Simon to oppose Tryphon's attack, which quickly followed. When Simon met the Syrian army at Adida, Tryphon attempted to negotiate by claiming that Jonathan was only a hostage for money owed to the Seleucid government. Simon paid the ransom demanded but to no avail, because Tryphon only pressed the attack without releasing Jonathan. Simon's army moved parallel to the Syrians without engaging them but forcing them to take an indirect route to avoid areas under Jewish control. It was apparently Tryphon's intent to relieve the garrison in the Akra, but he was prevented from doing this by a heavy snowfall. Instead, he executed Jonathan and retreated. Not long afterward, he carried out his plan of killing Antiochus VI and taking the throne for himself (ca. 142–138 B.C.E.).

5.4.6 Simon (143–135 B.C.E.)

Sources: 1 Macc 13:1—16:17; Josephus, *War* 1.2.3 §§50–54; *Ant.* 13.6.7–7.4 §§213–28.

Simon was now the last of the Maccabean brothers and the third to become leader of the Hasmonean movement. By now the majority of the Palestinian Jews seem to have accepted the Maccabees as leaders. With this popular backing and a temporary calm, Simon was in a position to continue his brothers' efforts to effect the independence of the state by building fortresses and preparing stores of food in case of protracted war (1 Macc 13:33). Tryphon had shown his true colors as far as the Jews were concerned, and Simon took the logical step of negotiating with Demetrius, who still sought to regain the throne. Once again, Demetrius made a variety of far-reaching concessions in a letter to Simon, even including permission to mint his own coinage (although to date no such coins have turned up [5.2.14.3]). This time Demetrius was not in a position to withdraw his offer, and the writer of 1 Maccabees could write that in the first year of Simon—the 170th year of the Seleucid era (143–142 B.C.E.)—"the yoke of the Gentiles was lifted from Israel" (13:41-42). Judea was now an independent state.

There is no doubt that this was a significant date and event, because Judah had been a vassal state of one sort or another since the time of Tiglath-pileser III (ca. 736 B.C.E.). Subsequent events were to show that this state of "liberation" was short-lived and that Simon himself died violently, as had his brothers. Nevertheless, as a psychological high point, the formal proclamation of liberty should be given its due. Indeed, for a time the Judeans dated their contracts and legal documents from Simon's first year. His reign is thus summarized:

> As long as Simon lived, Judaea was at peace. He promoted his people's welfare, and they lived happily all through the glorious days of his reign. . . . They farmed their land in peace, and the land produced its crops, and the trees in the plains their fruit. Old men sat in the streets, talking together of their blessings. . . . He restored peace to the land, and there were great rejoicings throughout Israel. Each man sat under his own vine and fig tree, and they had no one to fear. (1 Macc 14:4-15, NEB)

In Simon's third year a stela was erected that recounted his and his brothers' deeds and confirmed him in the office of high priest (1 Macc 14:27-47). Yet, when read carefully, this stela itself has an interesting message (*Sievers: 119–27). The fact that Simon's powers had to be officially granted, including his high priestly authority, indicates that many were not yet willing to accept these powers. Furthermore, his powers were apparently negotiated with various groups, which is why they were declared only in his third year.

A variety of accomplishments is credited to Simon. Perhaps the most important of these was finally taking the Akra and expelling the Syrian garrison from it in 142 B.C.E., thereby removing the last formal symbol of Seleucid rule over the country (1 Macc 13:49-52). He is said to have renewed the treaties with Rome and Sparta (1 Macc 14:16-24; 15:15-24), to have made Joppa into a Jewish port, and to have taken Gazara (Old

Testament, Gezer). According to Josephus's account, Simon also decided to level the citadel hill to prevent it from overlooking the temple area as it had always done (*Ant.* 13.6.7 §§215–17; *War* 1.2.2 §50 [cf. *War* 5.4.1 §139]). This is contradicted by 1 Macc 14:37, however, which states, "He settled Jews in it [the citadel] and fortified it for the security of the land of the city, and he raised the height of the walls of Jerusalem" (NEB). It seems unlikely that such a reduction in height ever took place (5.2.14.4).

After Demetrius II made concessions to Simon to enlist his friendship, he was too busy to be concerned with Judea. He marched east in the hope of gaining further assistance against Tryphon, but he was taken prisoner by the Parthians. Demetrius's wife Cleopatra sent for his brother Antiochus to marry her and take the throne as Antiochus VII Sidetes (138–129 B.C.E.). When besieging Tryphon in Dor, Antiochus applied to Simon for aid and received it. With Tryphon out of the way, however, Antiochus turned on Simon with demands which showed that he considered Judea still a Seleucid vassal; Simon's counteroffer was considered only an insult and an excuse to declare war on him. By this time Simon was too aged to take to the field, but his sons John and Judah assumed command and were able to defeat Antiochus's force.

After a rule of eight years, Simon was invited to a banquet in Jericho by his son-in-law, the Jewish general Ptolemy. Ptolemy used the occasion to assassinate Simon and imprison Simon's wife and two other sons, but the third son, John Hyrcanus, was forewarned and managed to escape. Thus the last of the Maccabean brothers met his end by violence, demonstrating that the promised peace of Simon's rule was more apparent than real. Nevertheless, Simon's achievement was considerable and his reign an important watershed in Jewish history.

5.4.7 John Hyrcanus (135–104 B.C.E.)

Rajak, T. "Roman Intervention in a Seleucid Siege of Jerusalem?" *GRBS* 22 (1981) 65–81.

Sources: 1 Macc 16:18-24; Josephus, *Ant.* 13.7.4–10.7 §§228–300; *War* 1.2.3–8 §§54–69.

After his escape, Hyrcanus acceded to the office of high priest and immediately turned the attack on Ptolemy but without success; Ptolemy murdered Hyrcanus's mother and brothers before escaping to Philadelphia. Soon afterward, Hyrcanus himself was besieged in Jerusalem by Antiochus VII, the reason apparently being the cities, such as Joppa, that

Simon had taken from the Syrians. Antiochus allowed a truce during the Feast of Tabernacles and even sent sacrifices to be offered on his behalf at the temple. Agreement was finally reached between Antiochus and Hyrcanus that tribute would be paid for Joppa and the other cities on Judea's border. It may have been more than merely Hyrcanus's skill as a negotiator that ended the fighting (Rajak); rather, the Romans intervened to provide the practical aid, which they had agreed to in theory in a treaty with Simon (but cf. *Sievers: 138–39). In any case, in addition to receiving payment for the cities, Antiochus tore down the defensive walls of Jerusalem. He wanted a Syrian garrison in the city as well, but Hyrcanus managed to substitute hostages and a further payment of silver instead. To obtain the necessary cash, Hyrcanus opened David's tomb and took out a large amount of silver. He used some of this to hire mercenaries, the first Jewish leader to do so.

For most of the rest of his reign Hyrcanus was free to conduct his own affairs, with little interference from the Syrians because of the rivalry between the two lines of contenders for the throne. Antiochus VII was killed fighting for the Parthians and succeeded by his brother Demetrius II, who had already been king once before (145–140, 129–126 B.C.E.). When Demetrius was defeated and killed, Antiochus VIII Grypus (126–113 B.C.E.) succeeded him. Set up as a rival was Alexander Zabinas (ca. 128–122 B.C.E.), alleged to be the son of Alexander Balas. Alexander showed himself to be a friend of Hyrcanus but soon died fighting Antiochus VIII. Antiochus did not go against Hyrcanus, however, out of fear of his half-brother Antiochus IX Cyzicenus (113–95 B.C.E.), who by this time had been placed on the throne as a rival. Upon the death of Antiochus IX, six claimants for the throne fought among themselves for the next twelve years.

This preoccupation of the Syrian rulers with securing their own thrones against rivals allowed Hyrcanus the freedom he needed. He gave no further tribute or help to them after the death of Antiochus VII (129 B.C.E. [*Ant.* 13.10.1 §273]); instead, he took the opportunity to expand his territory, which he did with considerable success. His most significant acts included the capture of Shechem (ca. 128 B.C.E.), at which time he allegedly destroyed the Samaritan temple, but the archeology does not support this (5.2.14.4). He next took some of the major cities of Idumea, extended his rule over the entire country, and is said to have forcibly converted the inhabitants to Judaism. Exactly how this is to be interpreted is difficult. Forced conversion is generally not very successful, yet Josephus states that the Idumeans continued to be Jews (*Ant.* 13.9.1 §258). See further at 6.3.6.

The next area to fall was the city of Samaria itself. After a lengthy siege, the citizens called on either Antiochus VIII (*War* 1.2.7 §65) or Antiochus IX (*Ant.* 13.10.2 §§276–78) for help that was readily given; however, Hyrcanus's sons defeated Antiochus's troops and resumed the siege. After a second request by the Samaritans, Antiochus sent a body of soldiers to invade Hyrcanus's territory and conduct guerrilla action without directly confronting the Jewish army. This did not work either, and Samaria fell after a year.

The Jews of Egypt and Cyprus were flourishing at this time (*Ant.* 13.10.4 §§284–87). Two of the sons of the Onias who built the temple at Leontopolis (5.3.8) were generals in the army of Cleopatra III (ca. 140–100 B.C.E.). The Jews in Palestine were also thriving. Nevertheless, opposition developed and Hyrcanus had to spend some time putting down rebels. Exactly what form this rebellion took or when it occurred is unclear. In the *War,* Josephus refers simply to some of Hyrcanus's "countrymen" (*epichōriōn* [1.2.8 §67]). In *Antiquities* he makes the opponents Pharisees, stating that Hyrcanus had been a Pharisee but, after falling out with them, became a Sadducee (13.10.5–7 §§288–99). In any event, Hyrcanus soon reduced the opposition and spent the rest of his reign peacefully, dying a natural death after a rule of thirty-one years. Coins have been preserved with the name "Johanan," identified with Hyrcanus by some; however, others argue that these should be dated to the reign of Hyrcanus II (5.2.14.3).

5.4.8 Aristobulus I (104–103 B.C.E.)

Sources: Josephus, *War* 1.3.1–6 §§70–84; *Ant.* 13.11.1–3 §§301–19.

Whereas Josephus's accounts of the previous Hasmonean rulers appeared in a much shorter version in the *War,* regarding Aristobulus the accounts in *War* and *Antiquities* are parallel and sometimes even in the same words. This suggests that Josephus used the same source in both cases. Only at the very end of the account does his later work have some additional information (*Ant.* 13.11.3 §§318–19). Was his source for the extra information the account given by Nicolaus of Damascus? If so, then why is the version in *War* so like the one in *Antiquities,* when normally the latter work represents a considerable elaboration? Was Josephus using another source for Aristobulus? Even though Aristobulus reigned for only one year, most of Josephus's description is taken up with how he was tricked into having his brother Antigonus killed, along with an anecdote about the remarkable prognostications of Judas the Essene. We therefore learn little about Aristobulus's reign, yet several points within the brief period are significant: (1) he was the first to actually take the diadem as king, previous Hasmonean high priests having acted as rulers but without using the actual title; (2) he had the title "Philhellene," which suggests that he contributed to particular building projects in Greek cities; and (3) he took the area of Iturea (in southern Lebanon) and required the inhabitants to adopt circumcision and live according to Jewish law (6.3.6). It has also been suggested that the coins bearing the name "Judah" were minted by Aristobulus I, but many argue these should be dated to Aristobulus II (5.2.14.3).

This all suggests that Aristobulus's reign was significant in various ways, despite its brevity. He is pictured as cruel, in that he supposedly starved his mother to death. This picture is contradicted, however, by Josephus's statement that the king was of a "kindly nature" and "wholly given to modesty," which is then backed up with a quotation from Strabo. There is no confirmation that he was a Philhellene, either in the *War* or the works of other historians, although one wonders why anyone would have invented such information. The statement that he conquered Iturea suggests that he continued with Hyrcanus's policy of expanding the borders of Judah. Again, the forced conversion is a point of interest (6.3.6).

5.4.9 Alexander Janneus (103–76 B.C.E.)

Rabin, C. "Alexander Jannaeus and the Pharisees." *JJS* 7 (1956) 3–11.
Schalit, A. "Die Eroberungen des Alexander Jannäus in Moab." *Theokratia* 1 (1967–69) 3–50.
Stern, M. "Judaea and Her Neighbors in the Days of Alexander Jannaeus." *Jerusalem Cathedra* 1 (1981) 22–46.

Sources: Josephus, *War* 1.4.1–8 §§85–106; *Ant.* 13.12.1–16.1 §§320–406.

Josephus gives more detail about Alexander Janneus than about any other Hasmonean ruler. Although *Antiquities* gives more information than the *War*, the overall picture is essentially the same, with one exception: the significance of the Pharisees. Most of what we learn about Alexander's reign is devoted to two issues: further expansion of territory and the internal Jewish opposition to his rule.

At the beginning of his rule, Alexander Janneus besieged the city of Ptolemais. The siege was maintained despite some slight aid sent to the city by Zoilus, ruler of Gaza. However, the city called on Ptolemy IX Lathyrus (116–96 B.C.E.) from Cyprus, who was rival to his mother, Cleopatra III Berenice of Egypt. After an initial attempt by Alexander to trick him into an alliance, Ptolemy invaded Galilee (taking Asochis) and defeated the Jewish army. At this point Cleopatra intervened and, after a period of maneuvering, forced Ptolemy to return to Cyprus. In concluding a treaty with Cleopatra, Alexander had the help of one of her generals who was Jewish (a son of Onias). The treaty left him free to pursue his conquests, which included the cities of Gadara, Amathus, Raphia, and Anthedon. He also took Gaza after a long siege.

At this point in Alexander's reign a revolt developed. It began at the Feast of Tabernacles, when he was pelted with citrons while sacrificing in his capacity as high priest. The exact reasons for this opposition are not clear. Josephus gives only the trivial charge that his mother had been a captive and that therefore he was unfit to hold the office (because she would most likely have been raped in captivity). This sounds more like a pretext than the true reason. Alexander contained the revolt, killing six thousand of his opponents, and continued his wars of conquest. This time he moved east, taking Moab and Galaaditis (Gilead). He also attacked the Arab king Obodas I but was decisively beaten and almost killed (6.3.6).

The defeat by the Arabs seems to have encouraged Alexander's opponents, because for the next six years he had a civil war on his hands. (During this time, the territory taken in Moab and Galaaditis was lost.) The climax came about 88 B.C.E. when his opponents called against him Demetrius III of Damascus (one of the Seleucid rivals at this time). Large numbers of Jews fought on both sides in the ensuing engagement. Demetrius seems to have got the better of the contest, and Alexander fled. However, when those who had asked Demetrius's aid abandoned him and a large number of Jews rallied to Alexander, Demetrius had little choice but to retire from the country. Alexander brought the revolt to a close by driving many of his opponents into the city of Bemeselis and taking it. He then had eight hundred of the men crucified and slaughtered their families before their eyes, while he and his concubines feasted and watched the spectacle. This unprecedented action had a great impact on his opponents, and eight thousand of them fled the country for as long as Alexander was alive. The incident also seems to be referred to in the Qumran *Commentary on Nahum* 2:12:

> Interpreted, this concerns the furious young lion [who executes revenge] on those who seek smooth things and hangs men alive, [a thing never done] formerly in Israel. (4QpNah 1.6–7, Vermes's translation)

Soon after the internal revolt was put down, Judah was invaded by the army of Antiochus XII Dionysus (ca. 86 B.C.E.), whose aim seems to have been only to march through to fight against Arabia. Alexander hastily constructed a defensive ditch and wooden wall, which Antiochus had no difficulty pushing through. What he would have done to Judah had his campaign been successful is not clear, but he was defeated and killed. Shortly afterward Aretas III, the Arab king, invaded Judah, but Alexander was able to come to terms with him (6.3.6).

His enemies now out of the way, Alexander Janneus was left to get on with his foreign military activities for the rest of his reign. He soon developed quartan fever but kept to the field until his death. His activities were mainly in the area northeast of the Sea of Galilee, where he took several cities. According to Josephus (*Ant.* 13.15.4 §§395–97), at the end of Alexander's reign Judah included most of the coastal cities as far north as Caesarea, Idumea, Samaria, Galilee, Moab, and northern Transjordan. If this is correct, then Alexander's territory was the largest extension of Israel since the time of Solomon and may well have rivaled that of the ancient Israelite king. Alexander Janneus died at the age of forty-nine, after reigning twenty-seven years.

At this point in the narrative, there is a significant difference between Josephus's two accounts. The *Antiquities* claims that before his death, Alexander advised his wife, Alexandra Salome, to make peace with the Pharisees, grant them a certain amount of power, and pretend to have disapproved of her husband's activities. The result was that they gave the king a magnificent funeral with many eulogies. This has led some scholars to infer that most of Alexander's opponents were Pharisees. Against this are two considerations: (1) the *War* is not only silent about this deathbed incident but makes no mention at all of the Pharisees during Alexander's reign; (2) despite this conclusion to his account in *Antiquities*, Josephus does not otherwise mention the Pharisees during Alexander's reign; indeed, he at no point specifically suggests that those who opposed, fought, and were killed by Alexander were Pharisees (cf. Rabin). Therefore, one can only conclude that Pharisaic opponents—which most probably existed—were only a part of the opposition to Alexander. One also suspects that the deathbed scene with regard to the Pharisees was an invention by Josephus to explain the influence of the Pharisees over Alexandra Salome during her rule.

5.4.10 Alexandra Salome (76–67 B.C.E.)

Sources: Josephus, *War* 1.5.1–4 §§107–19; *Ant.* 13.16.1–6 §§407–32.

The one feature that stands out in both of Josephus's accounts is the extent to which the Pharisees dominated the reign of Alexandra. In much later rabbinic literature there were still preserved traditions of the reign of Alexandra as a golden age (*b. Ta'an.* 23a). Although *Antiquities* says that Alexandra "restored" (*apokatestēsen*) the Pharisaic regulations which John Hyrcanus had abolished (13.16.2 §408), the *War* reveals nothing of this. As noted (5.4.9), there is reason to question the extent of Pharisaic influence in Alexander's time, and the ability of the Pharisees to impose their own regulations as law probably originated under Alexandra, as Josephus's earlier account seems to indicate (*War* 1.5.2 §110). The Pharisees possessed considerable political clout under Alexandra, however, including the ability to eliminate a number of their enemies. And finally the point was reached that some eminent citizens appealed directly to Alexandra (with the aid of her son Aristobulus) for a guarantee of safety. To appease them, she allowed some of the importunates to guard some of her fortresses.

Alexandra was evidently a good administrator, apart from the issue of the Pharisees. She doubled the size of the Jewish military forces, in addition to keeping a large mercenary contingent, and as a result was able to maintain peaceful relations with the surrounding rulers. She also concluded terms with Tigranes of Armenia when he was besieging Cleopatra in Ptolemais. Alexandra apparently supposed that Judea might be his next target. The treaty was never tested, however, because Tigranes returned quickly to Armenia when Mithridates of Pontus retreated there after his defeat by the Romans (5.4.1.2).

The one thorn in Alexandra's side was her son Aristobulus. The elder son, Hyrcanus, had been appointed high priest on Alexander Janneus's death and would have been the natural heir to his mother. But Aristobulus seems to have been the more dynamic of the two, and there were doubts about Hyrcanus's ability and desire to rule. When Alexandra became ill, Aristobulus took his chance. He occupied twenty-two fortresses in which a number of his supporters had been made guards, hired a mercenary army, and proclaimed himself king. He apparently used the pretext that if he did not, the Pharisees would seize power when his mother died. Alexandra quickly responded by imprisoning Aristobulus's wife and children, but her illness prevented her from taking further action. As Aristobulus was amassing a large army, she died at the age of seventy-three, after a reign of nine years.

The few evaluative statements made by Josephus up to this point indicate that Alexandra was a good administrator but was dominated by the Pharisees. At the end of the account in *Antiquities*, however, he gives a lengthy assessment, centering on the despotism of her rule and her lack of inhibitions one normally associates with a woman. Exactly what he has in mind is not clear, although he does refer to her siding with those "hostile to her family." Are these the Pharisees? Is his concluding verdict mainly hostility to her as a female ruler? Is he using a different source here? It is difficult to know, but these final comments seem somewhat at odds with the account of her reign he had given in the *War* and up to this point in *Antiquities.*

5.4.11 Aristobulus II and Hyrcanus II (67–63 B.C.E.)

Sources: Josephus, *War* 1.6.1–7.7 §§120–58; *Ant.* 14.1.2–4.5 §§4–79.

Hyrcanus became ruler of Judah as soon as his mother died, but lasted only for a short time. Aristobulus quickly attacked and defeated him; Hyrcanus took refuge in the temple citadel and, using Aristobulus's family as a bargaining chip, arranged a deal in which he was permitted to live unharmed as a private citizen while rule went to his brother. Although not made explicit at this point in the narrative, statements elsewhere indicate that Aristobulus also obtained the office of high priest (*Ant.* 14.6.1 §97; 20.10.4 §§243–44).

At this juncture Josephus introduces a character named Antipater, whom he identifies as an Idumean (but see 6.3.2), whose father had been appointed governor of Idumea by Alexander Janneus. Antipater after a time persuaded Hyrcanus that he had made a mistake in giving up the kingship and indeed was in danger of being executed by Aristobulus. Receiving a guarantee of safety from Aretas III of Petra, Hyrcanus fled to the Arab ruler. With the aid of an army (allegedly of fifty thousand) under Aretas, Hyrcanus attacked Aristobulus, defeated him, and besieged him in Jerusalem to which he had fled. The outcome of the siege was still in the balance when the Romans intervened.

The Roman general Pompey, who was fighting against the Armenians, had sent his lieutenant Scaurus to Syria. As soon as he arrived in Damascus, Scaurus heard of the Jewish civil war and marched south. Delegates from both sons of Alexandra met him with bribes, but Scaurus sided with Aristobulus and forced Aretas to raise the siege. Shortly afterward, Aristobulus defeated Hyrcanus in battle. This was how things stood until Pompey arrived in Syria, where he was entreated by both sides, as well as by a delegation from "the Jewish nation," that Judea be allowed to continue as a theocracy without the high priest also acting as a king. After hearing the different sides, Pompey delayed a decision. The delay was too much for Aristobulus, who set off for Judea. Pompey, taking this as an insult, followed with a large force and caught up with Aristobulus at the fortress of Alexandrium. At first the two leaders negotiated, then Pompey ordered Aristobulus to give up his fortresses. Aristobulus reluctantly sent instructions to the various commanders, as required by Pompey, but then withdrew to Jerusalem and prepared for war.

Pompey marched after him before the preparations had advanced very far. Aristobulus realized the folly of resistance and met Pompey on the last leg of his march, between Jericho and Jerusalem, promising money as well as entry into Jerusalem. Aristobulus's followers had a different idea, however, and closed off the city to the Romans. The people of the city were divided between the supporters of Aristobulus and those of Hyrcanus. The former withdrew into the temple, cutting the bridge to the upper city, while the latter opened the gates to Pompey. The siege of the temple lasted three months, until about midsummer. The Romans took advantage of the Sabbath to advance their siege, because the Jews would not fight on the Sabbath if not directly attacked. During this time, and even in the final assault when many were being killed, the priests continued their sacrificial duties. When the Romans finally broke into the temple, many of the defenders were slaughtered by fellow Jews who were adherents of Hyrcanus. Pompey and other Romans entered the temple area and even went inside the Holy of Holies, but the temple itself was respected. Neither the vessels nor the temple treasure was touched, and the temple itself was cleansed and the cult resumed the next day at Pompey's command.

Thus Judea as an independent kingdom came to an end. Although it was to be a vassal kingdom of Rome for many years under Herod the Great and Agrippa I, it was not to be a sovereign nation again for two millennia. The territory gained by successive Hasmonean rulers was taken away to leave only the area which roughly made up the province of Judah under the Babylonians and Persians. Although Hyrcanus was restored to the high priesthood, he did not have the title of king, and a heavy tribute was imposed on the country. Aristobulus and his sons were taken captive to Rome (although one son, Alexander, escaped en route).

5.4.12 Religious Developments

Davies, P. R. "Calendrical Change and Qumran Origins: An Assessment of VanderKam's Theory." *CBQ* 45 (1983) 80–89.

Davies, W. D. *The Gospel and the Land* (1974).

———. *The Territorial Dimensions of Judaism* (1982).

Mendels, D. *The Land of Israel as a Political Concept in Hasmonean Literature* (1987).

Talmon, S. "The Calendar Reckoning of the Sect from the Judaean Desert." *Aspects of the Dead Sea Scrolls* (1958) 162–99.

VanderKam, J. C. "The Origin, Character and Early History of the 364-day Calendar: A Reassessment of Jaubert's Hypotheses." *CBQ* 41 (1979) 390–411.

———. "2 Maccabees 6,7a and Calendrical Change in Jerusalem." *JSJ* 12 (1981) 52–74.

The most important religious issue during the Maccabean period was, naturally, the survival of Judaism itself. Antiochus made the first known attempt at suppressing the Jewish religion. However, the events surrounding the suppression are often misinterpreted. The issue was not Hellenization, as such. No doubt the Maccabean revolt included reactions against certain elements of Hellenization that were the most overt symbols of the Seleucid oppression, a common factor in anticolonial revolts. Many elements of Greek culture were already a part of the Jewish world, however, and were probably not even recognized as Greek in origin. More important is the fact that Hasmonean rule brought no change to the status of Hellenistic culture in Judea. Therefore, the claim often made that the Maccabean revolt was a revolt against Hellenization is misleading.

The "Hellenistic reform" of Jason does not appear to have infringed Jewish law in any way (5.4.3.2). The institution of a gymnasium and all that it implied did not make the citizens of Jerusalem any different from many Jews in the Diaspora. Many Jews in Egypt, Syria, and Asia Minor practiced their religion devoutly yet also entered the gymnasium and obtained a Greek education, witnessed Greek entertainments, spoke the Greek language, and otherwise participated in the Greek culture surrounding them. Why should this pass without question in the Diaspora but be condemned in Jerusalem? The issue in Jerusalem was not the new constitution as such but such questions as who was the legitimate high priest and, after 168, were the Jews to be allowed to worship according to the traditions of their ancestors.

Influence from Greek culture continued apace under the Hasmoneans. Most of the fragmentary Jewish-Greek writings (5.2.10) are probably the product of the Diaspora, but this is not certain for some. One or two have the definite appearance of having been written in Palestine. A prime example is the work of Eupolemus, who may have been the envoy of Judas to the Romans and also the son of the John who negotiated Jewish rights with Antiochus III (1 Macc 8:17; 2 Macc 4:11). Not only is his name Greek, but he wrote in Greek and followed Greek literary conventions (5.2.10.2).

An interesting development unique to Maccabean rule was the priest-king. In the early part of the Persian period a dyarchy of priest and civil leader arose (2.3.3). Through the period of Ptolemaic and Seleucid rule (and possibly also through part or much of the Persian period), the high priest was the major civil as well as religious leader (4.3.1). It is hardly surprising that, with independence, the priestly heads of state would eventually take the title of king, since they more or less functioned as kings. Although this continued trends that had begun in the period of the monarchy, the actual existence of priest-kings no doubt influenced messianic speculation, in which the civic and hierocratic functions were combined into one figure (8.3.5).

It is during the period of Hasmonean rule that we first hear about the major Jewish sects which tend to dominate religious discussions for this period. While the roots of some of these may be much earlier (cf. 2.3.11), Josephus does not mention them in his accounts until he discusses the Hasmoneans. Although the development of sects is a natural occurrence, they took the temple religion in new directions. Some, such as the Qumran group, regarded the temple at Jerusalem as polluted and the contemporary priesthood as illegitimate, which is hardly surprising since sects often arise from disagreements about control of the established cult. Others seem to have accepted the priestly establishment without being all that interested in it, at least as far as their major religious discussions were concerned (e.g., the Pharisees). Eventually some groups came to reject the temple altogether (cf. 9.2.3.2), although whether this is true of any in pre-Roman times uncertain. All in all, the sects served as agents of change and development in Judaism, with far-reaching consequences in one or two cases. (See chapter 8 for further information on the major sects.)

One subject which separated different groups was the calendar. The present Jewish calendar is a luni-solar one, which coordinates the lunar cycle with the solar year. (At times, the lunar year can be out of phase with the solar year by as much as several weeks, but over a complete nineteen-year cycle, they are harmonized.) It has been thought that some form of this calendar was used as the official liturgical calendar in Second Temple times. We know from Qumran and Jubilees, however, that some groups used a purely solar calendar of 364 days (Talmon). VanderKam has argued that in Maccabean times the luni-solar calendar was substituted for an original solar calendar in the temple, first during the persecutions of Antiochus, but then maintained by the Hasmonean priesthood. It was over this calendar change that groups such as Qumran split off (1979, 1981). There is a widespread view that the 364-day calendar is an old and perhaps even a priestly calendar. As Davies has pointed out, however, any change from the solar to the luni-solar calendar was likely to have been much earlier than Maccabean times. It would be surprising if such a significant event as a liturgical calendar change in the second century had left so few traces in the literature of the time.

The synagogue had become a well-established institution in the Diaspora from the mid-third century on (8.3.3). It was only a matter of time before it extended into Judea itself, but this did not happen quickly. The nearness of the temple in such a small state meant that most Jews could worship there regularly, especially at the annual festivals. At what time the need was felt for synagogues within Judea is not clear, because the archeological evidence is ambiguous.

Apocalypticism was quite important in this period, at least in some circles. A number of apocalypses and related genres of writing can be dated to around the time of the Maccabean revolt. The best known is Daniel 7–12, which, it is widely agreed, was written about 166 (5.2.3). Another is the *Apocalypse of Weeks* (*1 Enoch* 85–90 [4.2.5.7]). Although there is no proved connection between these two writings, both expected God to intervene in the near future to establish God's rule, punish the enemies, and reward the faithful Israelites. Whether such imminent expectations died away after the failure of the predictions and the success of the Maccabean military resistance is unknown (if they did, then they returned later). In Egypt a rather different sort of eschatology was manifested. In portions of the *Third Sibylline Oracle* that arise from the mid-second century, the hopes of the writer focus on one of the Ptolemaic rulers (9.2.3.2).

The Maccabean religious crisis also raised a number of issues about observance of the law. The Maccabees and their followers were quite willing to wage war to protect their religion, but others believed in passive resistance only. This seems to have been the attitude of the writer of Daniel 7–12 and is also illustrated by the later writing of 4 Maccabees, in which the blood of the martyrs—not military force—is what redeems the land. A similar attitude seems to be manifested in the *Testament of Moses* (5.2.11).

Another attitude involved the Sabbath. Some Jews who were not against taking up arms nevertheless refused to defend themselves on the Sabbath (1 Macc 2:31-38). This led to the decision to wage defensive war on the Sabbath if need be, but not to take offensive action (vv 40-41).

One interesting sidelight concerns the view that the Jerusalem temple was unique. This idea had begun at least as early as the time of Josiah (ca. 620 B.C.E.) but took time to catch on. Other cultic sites continued to operate even in the post-exilic period (e.g., the Jewish temple at Elephantine and the Samaritan cult on Gerizim), although most of the sites in Judea were eliminated. Nevertheless, Onias IV, the son of the deposed Onias III (or even the deposed Onias himself, according to one account [5.4.3.2]), apparently had no compunction about setting up his own temple in Leontopolis in Egypt, when it became clear that he was unlikely to receive his father's office after the religious suppression and the rise of the Maccabees.

The ideology of the land, which embraced several separate ideas, appears in a variety of sources (Mendels). The land was important to all Israelites, as it had been since the time of ancient Israel (Davies 1974; 1982). The one thing that is clear for the Second Temple period, however, is the variety of views. Perhaps with the expansion of actual territory more or less under Jewish independent sovereignty, the importance of land became more acute for some, although the subsequent loss of territory may have caused it to be viewed from a different perspective by others. There was also more than one view on how Israel should relate to its neighbors. Was Israel to be exclusivistic? Was it to tolerate Gentiles in its midst? A great many writers expressed their ideology in discussions about Old Testament Israel. Some were suspicious of foreigners and saw them only as a bad influence and a source of sin and evil (e.g., Jubilees). These writers often thought it Israel's duty not only to remain separate but also to extend its borders into some sort of mythical "greater Israel," which was ascribed to the time of David and Solomon (cf. the *Genesis Apocryphon*, although this probably belongs to a later time). Jason's new constitution, however, as well as other sources, shows that not all Jews felt the same way. There were those who did not believe an independent Judah should be antithetical to participation in the wider Hellenistic world.

INDEX OF PASSAGES

HEBREW BIBLE (OLD TESTAMENT)

Genesis
6:1-4 220

Leviticus
1–15 478
4:26 539
4:31 539
4:35 539
5:10 539
5:13 539
5:16 539
5:18 539
16 608
17–27 105
25:13-28 24

Numbers
18:21-32 416
24:17 580

1 Samuel
8:14 24

2 Kings
14:23-27 46
17 503
24:14 39

1 Chronicles
1–9 50
3:18 75, 76
3:19 69
9 40
24:10 39

2 Chronicles
35:1—36:21 53

Ezra
1–6 30, 43, 89, 128, 538
1–7 30
1 127
1:1—2:2 77
1:2-4 32, 34, 35, 127
1:8 75, 127
1:8-11 76
1:11 75
2 38, 127
2:1 39
2:1-2 38, 127
2:2 39
2:3-20 39
2:3-35 39
2:21 39
2:21-35 39
2:22-23 39
2:24-26 39
2:27-28 39
2:29-35 39
2:36-39 41
2:40-58 145
2:61 39
2:64 39
2:68 38
2:68-69 38
2:68-70 39
2:69 39
3–4 127
3–6 32
3 77
3:1 38
4–7 120
4 81, 132
4:4-24 32
4:6 94, 128
4:6-22 128
4:7-22 94, 129
4:8-23 132
4:11-16 32
4:12 90, 94
4:17-22 32
5:1—6:15 128
5:3-4 39
5:6-17 34
5:7-17 32
5:10 39
5:14 75, 127
5:14-16 76
5:16 75, 127
6 79, 131
6:3-5 32, 35
6:6-12 32, 34
6:9 34
6:14-22 79
6:15 43, 128, 131, 137
7–9 89
7–10 30, 31, 37, 97, 137
7 96, 131, 136
7:1-10 37
7:6 98
7:7-8 90, 131, 137
7:12-19 37
7:12-26 32, 34, 37, 95, 136
7:16 97
7:22 34, 98
7:24 145
7:25-26 95, 136
7:27-28 37
8:1-14 37
8:2 91
8:25-27 97
8:33 39
9–10 104, 144
9 90
9:1 137
9:1-2 90
9:9 92
10 97
10:2 524
10:6 62, 92, 141
10:15 144
10:18 137
10:23-24 145

Nehemiah
1:1-4 93
1:1—7:72a 36
2:1 89
2:10 88, 132, 133, 193
2:11-16 132
2:19 85, 88, 132, 133, 193
3 79, 80
3:1 41, 89
3:4 39
3:7 69
3:9 80
3:12 80
3:14 80
3:14-18 80
3:21 39
5 118
5:1-3 135
5:2-5 118
5:15 82
6 85
6:1 88
6:1-2 85
6:10-13 133
6:14 133
6:17-19 133, 134
7 31, 38, 127
7:5 134
7:6 39
7:6-7 38
7:7 39
7:8-24 39
7:8-42 39
7:25 39
7:25-38 39
7:26-33 39
7:34-42 39

7:39-42 41
7:43-60 145
7:63 39
7:66 39
7:69 (Eng. 7:70) 38
7:69-71 (Eng. 7:70-72) 39
7:70 (Eng. 7:71) 38
7:72 (Eng. 7:73) 38, 145
7:72 (Eng. 7:73)—8:12 53
8–9 37, 98
8–12 31
8 30
8:1 38, 98
8:9 92, 137
9–10 30
9:1-2 134
10 90
10:1 (Eng. 9:38) 134
10:2-28 (Eng. 10:1-27) 39
10:29 (Eng. 10:28) 145
10:29-32 (Eng. 10:28-31) 134
11 40, 41
11:1-2 36, 134, 145
11:1-24 40
11:25-30 40
12:1-7 41
12:1-26 41
12:5 278
12:6-7 41
12:10 114
12:10-11 41
12:11 41, 92
12:12 41
12:12-18 41
12:12-21 41
12:12-25 41
12:18 278
12:19-21 41
12:22 41
12:23 41
12:23-26 41
12:31-43 36
12:36 90, 92
13:1-3 134
13:4-9 134
13:4-31 36
13:6-7 89
13:23-25 134
13:23-27 144
13:25 90
13:28 63

Psalms
2 78
110 78

Ecclesiastes
1:1 175

Isaiah
13 47
19:18-22 266
24–27 103, 104, 108, 199
40–55 47
56–59 48
56–66 47, 103, 104, 107, 109, 119, 129
56 46
56:3-7 47
56:9—57:13 47
57:1-10 104
57:3-13 48
57:14-20 47
58 47
59 47, 111
59:1-21 48
59:2-8 47
60–62 47, 48
60:1-22 48
60:7 47
60:17 47
62:8-9 47
62:9 47
63–64 47
63:7—64:12 48
65:1-16 47, 48
65:13-16 104
65:16b-25 47
65:16—66:14 48
66:1-4 103, 104
66:1-6 48
66:5 104
66:6-16 47
66:15-23 48
66:17 104

Jeremiah
18 219
22:24-30 78
40:5 80
41:2 80
44:15-19 143
52:28-30 39

Ezekiel
11:15 144
18 219
27 118
33 219

Daniel
1–6 121, 226
3 226
4 226
5 226
6 (Eng. 5:30—6:28) 226
7–12 169, 226, 310, 467, 540
8:9 258
11 183, 227
11:3-4 210
11:28 283
11:29-30 283
11:30 250
11:31 258
11:39 253
11:45 226
12:2 219
12:11 258

Joel
3–4 108
4:4-8 (Eng. 3:4-8) 45

Jonah
2:3-10 (Eng. 2:2-9) 46

Haggai
1 127, 128, 144
1:1 44, 127
1:6 44
2:2 127
2:10 44
2:14 44
2:19 48
2:20 44
2:20-23 44, 78, 79
2:21 127
2:21-23 79

Zechariah
1–8 43, 44
1:1 43
1:7-17 44
2:1-4 (Eng. 1:18-21) 44
2:5-17 (Eng. 2:1-13) 44
3–4 44
3 78
3:1-5 44
3:2 107
4:1-6a 78
4:1-8 128
4:1-10 44, 127
4:6b-10a 78
4:10b-14 78
5:1-4 44
5:5-11 44
6:1-8 44
6:9-15 44, 78, 79, 107
6:12 78
7:1 43
9–11 44
9–14 42, 44, 45, 103, 104, 109
11:14 107
12–14 44, 107, 108
12:2-10 107

Malachi
1:2-5 45
1:6—2:9 45
1:11 46
3:13-21 104
2:10-16 42
2:14-16 45
2:17 45
3:6-12 45
3:13-18 45
3:23-24 (Eng. 4:5-6) 45

APOCRYPHA AND PSEUDEPIGRAPHA

Ben Sira
10:5 488
33:24-31 25
50:1-4 218, 275
50:1-21 145
50:1-24 176, 191
50:5-21 608
50:25-26 504

1 Enoch
1–36 180
6–11 180
12–36 151
37–71 181
72–82 609
83–84 180
83–90 180
85–90 180, 310
90:9-12 180
91:1-10 181
91:11-17 181
91:18-19 181
92:1-93 181
92:10 181

4 Ezra
3:1 562
5:34-35 586
11–12 562
13 552

Jubilees
3:30-31 279
50:6-13 235

1 Maccabees
1:10-15 277
1:15 279
1:16-24 283
1:16-63 281, 282
1:21 247
1:29 286
1:29-36 283
1:41-43 249
1:54 258
1:59 258
2 285
2:1—9:22 285
2:31-38 310
2:39-42 466
2:40-41 310
2:42 227
2:44-48 285
3:8 285
3:13 286
3:25-26 286
3:39 286, 291
4:1-15 292
4:28-35 287
4:42-58 288
4:43-47 258
5:3 329
5:25-26 332
5:42 488
5:65-68 329
6:18-27 288
6:20-53 266
6:47-54 292
6:48-54 288
6:55-63 288
6:57-59 262
7:5 289
7:12 488
7:12-14 290
7:12-16 466
7:12-18 290
7:13 488
7:14 290
7:20-21 290
7:27-28 290
7:29-30 291
8:17 237, 308
8:23-30 261
8:23-32 223, 260
9:23-27 293
9:23—12:53 293
9:33 293
9:35 332
9:36-42 332
9:50-53 293
9:54-56 293
9:58 294
9:62 293
9:73 294
10:18-20 260
10:18-45 267
10:21 265
10:25 295
10:25-45 260
10:37 289
11:25 296
11:27 390
11:30-37 260, 267
11:57 260
11:60 296
12:3 261
12:6 295
12:6-18 260
12:7-23 264
12:20-23 223, 260, 261
12:35 295
13:1—16:17 297
13:33 298
13:36-40 260, 267
13:41-42 298
13:43—16:24 228
13:49-52 298
14:4-15 298
14:8 269
14:12 269
14:16-24 298
14:17-18 261
14:20 390
14:20-23 260
14:24 261
14:27-47 298
14:28 390
14:37 299
15:2-9 260
15:6 242
15:15-24 298
15:16-24 260
16:18-24 299

2 Maccabees
1:1-9 224
1:1-10 (Eng. 1:1-9) 260, 261
1:10—2:18 260, 261
1:18-36 61
3–4 277
3:2-3 275
3:11 198
4:8 267
4:11 237
4:14 278
4:18-20 279
4:39-42 251
4:44 390
5–7 281, 282
5:1-17 283
5:1-27 282
5:14 25
5:17-20 247
5:22 286
5:23-26 283
6:1-2 504
6:1-11 283
6:2 259
6:7 258
6:8 258
6:11 284
6:12-16 247
6:18-31 488
7 224
8–15 285
8:8 284, 286, 292
8:8-9 286
8:9 291
8:16 292
8:16-25 286
9:19-27 261
9:19-29 261
11 224, 262, 287
11:16-21 261, 262, 289
11:16-33 287
11:22-26 261, 262, 263, 289
11:24 258
11:27 287
11:27-33 261, 263, 289
11:29-32 287
11:34-38 261, 263, 289
12:10-12 332
13:3-8 251
13:22 292
13:22-24 288
13:23-24 288
14:3-13 289
14:6 466, 467
14:12 290
14:18-25 290
14:25 291
14:26-27 291

3 Maccabees
1:1-7 177
1:3 536
1:8—2:24 177
2:25—6:22 177
6:23-29 177
6:30—7:23 177

4 Maccabees
5:4 488

Psalms of Solomon
2 552
17–18 552
17:7-18 316

Sibylline Oracles
3 310
3.1-96 563
3.97-349 563
3.193 563
3.318 563
3.350-488 563
3.489-829 563
3.608 563
3.652 563
4 540, 563
4.121 444
4.163-69 508
5 563

Testament of Moses
2.11 310
6:2-6 323
6:2-9 238

Tobit
1:4-6 177
1:6-8 177, 538
3:7-9 177
4:15 177
5:4-5 177
8:1-3 177
8:7 177
12:6-21 177
14:5 177

QUMRAN AND JUDEAN DESERT MANUSCRIPTS

(CD) Damascus Document
1.1—2:1 233
1.5–6 498
4.10—5.2 496
6.11–20 495
7.6 495
7.6–7 496
9.10–16 495
10.10–13 495
10.14—11.18 235, 495
11.18–21 495
12.1–2 495, 496
12.19—14.16 495
14.12–16 495
15.5 496
16.10–12 496
16.13 495
19.2 495
19.2–3 496

(1QGenApoc) Genesis Apocryphon 311

(1QH) Thanksgiving Hymns 232

(1QM) War Scroll 231
7.3 496

(1QpHab) Habakkuk Commentary 233, 498
7.1–5 544

(1QS) Community Rule 231
1.11–12 495
3.4–5 495
5.1–22 495
5.13–14 495
6.2 495
6.6–8 543
6.8–10 495
6.10–13 495
6.13–23 495
6.16–23 495
6.25 495
7.13 495
7.2–3 495
9.11 522

(1QSa) Rule of the Congregation
1.4 496
1.9–11 496

(4QMMT) *Miqsat Ma'aseh ha-Torah* 234

(4QpNah) Nahum Commentary 231
1.5 234
1.6–7 303
1.7–8 234
2.2 233

(4QpPs[a]) Commentary on Psalm 37 231, 233

(11QMelch) Melchizedek 552

(11QT) Temple Scroll 232

5/6Ḥev
42 576, 577

5/6ḤevEp gr
6 603

Murabba'at
18 380
19 380
21 380
30 576
32 380
72 380
74 380

PHILO

De animalibus 439

De vita contemplativa 499

Hypothetica
11.1-17 492–95

In Flaccum
1 395, 400

Legatio ad Gaium
13 429
115 402
133 397
157 396
159–60 395
184–338 402
190 400
199–202 402
203–6 402
207–19 402
212 393
248–49 404
254–60 403
256 402
260 404
261–75 403
276–330 403
317 396
331–33 403
334–36 403
334 404
337–38 403
357 404
367 403

Quod omnis probus liber sit
75–87 492–95

JOSEPHUS

Against Apion
1.1 §1 6
1.8 §41 522
1.9 §50 7
1.20 §§145–53 60
1.22 §§187–89 71, 192
1.22 §§209–11 174, 211
2.4 §§35–41 406
2.6 §77 396
2.16 §165 74

Antiquities
1.3.9 §108 315
1.8.2 §§166–68 8
2.6.8 §140 63
2.6.8 §155 63
6.4.3 §237 439
8.2.5 §§45–49 520
11.1.1–5.5 §§1–158 63
11.4.8 §111 321
11.5.6–8 §§159–83 63
11.6.1–13 §§184–296 63
11.7.1 §297 62
11.7.1 §§297–301 61, 62, 63
11.7.2 §302 41
11.7.2 §§302–3 63
11.7.2–8.7 §§302–47 504
11.8.1–6 §§304–45 174, 182
12.1.1 §§3–10 211
12.1.1 §6 174
12.1.1 §8 215, 405
12.2.1–15 §§11–118 174
12.3.3–4 §§129–53 246
12.3.3 §133 275
12.3.3 §§138 275
12.3.3–4 §§138–46 145, 241, 246
12.3.3 §142 488
12.3.4 §§148–53 201
12.4.1 §§157–59 191, 192, 197
12.4.1–11 §§157–236 174, 192
12.4.2 §160 196
12.4.7 §196 196
12.4.10 §§225–27 174, 196, 264
12.4.11 §§228–34 275
12.5.1 §§237–38 266, 277
12.5.1 §§237–41 281
12.5.1 §237—13.7.4 §229 228
12.5.1 §241 280
12.5.2 §§242–56 282
12.5.2–5 §§242–64 281
12.5.5 §§257–64 228
12.6.1–11.2 §§265–434 285
12.9.4–5 §§367–78 292
12.9.7 §§383–85 289
12.9.7 §385 251, 266
13.1.1–6.6 §§1–212 293
13.2.4–3.4 §§59–79 228
13.3.1–3 §§62–73 266
13.3.2 §70 266
13.3.3 §72 266
13.4.5–9 §§103–22 228
13.5.4 §146 296

13.5.9 §§171–72 485
13.5.9 §172 469
13.6.7–7.4 §§213–28 297
13.6.7 §§215–17 299
13.7.4–10.7 §§228–300 299
13.7.6 §214 228
13.9.1 §§257–58 323, 329
13.9.1 §258 300
13.10.1 §273 300
13.10.2 §§276–78 301
13.10.4 §§284–87 301
13.10.5 §288 470, 471, 472, 473
13.10.5–7 §§288–99 301
13.10.6 §§293–98 485
13.11.1–3 §§301–19 301
13.11.2 §311 497
13.11.3 §§318 331
13.11.3 §§318–19 301
13.12.1–16.1 §§320–406 302
13.12.6 §347 315, 317
13.13.3 §360 332, 357
13.15.4 §§395–97 304
13.15.4 §397 332
13.15.5 §§399–402 474
13.16.1 §407 324
13.16.1–6 §§407–32 305
13.16.2 §408 306
13.16.2 §§408–11 472, 473
14 323
14.1.2 §4 326
14.1.2–4.5 §§4–79 306
14.1.3 §8 322
14.1.3 §9 314, 323
14.1.4 §18 332
14.2.1 §§22–24 521
14.3.1 §35–36 315
14.4.3 §66 327
14.4.5 §77 338
14.5.1–9.1 §§80–157 340
14.5.4 §91 321
14.6.1 §97 306
14.6.2 §99 323
14.6.3 §101 323
14.6.4 §104 314, 315, 317, 322
14.7.2 §§111–18 315
14.7.3 §121 323
14.7.4 §126 343
14.8.1 §127 323
14.8.1 §§131–32 323
14.8.5 §144 324, 343
14.8.5 §151 343
14.9.1 §157 343
14.9.2 §158 324, 344
14.9.2–14.4 §§158–385 344
14.9.3 §165 343
14.9.4 §168 343
14.9.4 §172 343
14.9.4 §175 391
14.10.1–26 §§185–267 406
14.10.6 §202 355
14.10.6 §§202–3 335
14.10.8 §§213–16 398
14.11.2 §272 335
14.11.3 §277 346
14.11.4 §283 323
14.11.6 §290 346
14.14.5 §389 326, 349
14.15.2 §403 322, 364
14.15.6 §§432–33 350
14.15.10 §450 350
14.16.1 §468 350
14.16.2 §475 327
14.16.4 §487 327, 350
15–17 315
15.1.1 §§3–4 471
15.2.4 §22 388
15.3.1 §§39–41 388
15.3.1 §41 388
15.3.3 §§51–56 388
15.3.5–9 §§62–87 360
15.3.8 §79 351
15.4.1–2 §§94–96 325, 351
15.5.1 §110 352
15.6.2 §173 391
15.6.5 §§183–86 360
15.6.7 §195—17.8.3 §199 354
15.7.1–4 §§202–34 360
15.7.3 §217 325, 355
15.7.9 §§253–55 329
15.7.9 §254 325
15.8.1–2 §§267–79 356, 364
15.8.5 §292 356, 357
15.8.5 §§292–93 357
15.8.5 §§296–98 357
15.9.1–2 §§299–316 365
15.9.3 §318 356
15.9.3 §§320–22 388
15.9.3 §322 388
15.9.4 §§323–25 356
15.9.6 §§331–41 357
15.9.6 §341 357
15.10.1 §343 355
15.10.1 §§343–48 325
15.10.3 §360 325, 355
15.10.4 §§365–72 365
15.10.5 §373 497
15.11.1 §§380 365
15.11.1–7 §§380–425 357
15.11.4 §§403–9 425
15.11.5 §417 393
16.2.1 §13 357
16.2.3–5 §§27–65 366
16.2.5 §§64–65 365
16.5.1 §136 357
16.5.2 §145 336, 356, 357
16.6.1–7 §§160–73 406
16.7.1 §§183–86 314
16.7.6 §220 358
16.7.6 §§221–25 364
16.9.1–4 §§271–99 358
16.10.8–9 §§335–55 358
17.1.1 §10 358
17.2.1–2 §§23–27 336
17.2.4 §§41–44 361
17.2.4 §§42 546
17.4.2 §78 388
17.6.2–4 §§149–67 520, 547
17.6.3 §156 325
17.6.4 §164 388
17.6.4 §§164–67 388
17.6.4 §167 328
17.8.1 §189 425
17.8.1 §191 328
17.8.4–13.5 §§200–355 366
17.9.1–2 §§209–10 325
17.9.3 §213 328
17.10.2 §255 356
17.11.2 §§304–10 362
17.11.4 §§317–20 336
17.11.4 §319 425
17.13.1 §339 388
17.13.1 §341 388
17.13.2 §342 368
17.13.3 §§347–48 497
17.13.5 §355 385
18 479
18.1.1 §§1–10 384
18.1.1–4.4 §§1–100 422
18.1.1 §3 384, 388
18.1.1 §§4–10 500
18.1.2–4 §§11–15 470
18.1.3 §§12–15 469
18.1.3 §15 475
18.1.4 §§16–17 485
18.1.4 §17 470, 475
18.1.5 §§18–22 492–95
18.1.6 §23 500
18.2.1 §26 388
18.2.1 §27 426
18.2.2 §34 388
18.2.2 §35 388
18.2.3 §§36–38 426
18.2.4 §§39–52 371
18.3.1 §§55–59 396
18.3.1–2 §§55–62 423
18.3.5 §§81–84 398
18.4.1–2 §§85–89 423
18.4.2 §88 385
18.4.3 §§90–95 425
18.4.3 §95 388
18.4.4–5 §§96–105 371, 426
18.4.6 §106 425
18.4.6 §§106–7 426
18.5.1 §109 388
18.5.1–2 §§109–19 427

18.5.2 §§116–19 427
18.5.3 §123 388
18.5.3–8.9 §§126–309 430
18.6.5 §§170–78 423
18.6.8–10 §§205–27 371
18.7.1–2 §§240–56 428
18.7.2 §252 428
18.8.1 §§257–60 400, 402
18.8.2–9 §§261–309 402
18.8.2 §262 404
18.8.3 §272 404
18.9.1–9 §310–79 371
19.1.1–2.5 §§1–211 430
19.1.1–3.4 §§1–235 371
19.3.1–4.6 §§212–73 432
19.3.1–9.1 §§212–359 430
19.5.1 §§276–77 436
19.5.2 §§278–79 400, 407
19.5.2 §280–85 401
19.5.3 §§287–91 408
19.6.2 §297 388
19.6.4 §313 388, 389
19.7.2 §§326–27 432
19.8.1 §342 389
19.8.2 §§343–50 434
19.8.2 §352 336
19.9.1 §§354–55 436
19.9.1 §357 433
19.9.2 §§361–66 386, 436
19.9.2 §363—20.11.1 §258 437
20.1.1 §§6–14 436
20.1.3 §§15–16 391, 436
20.1.3 §16 389
20.2.1–4.3 §§17–96 371
20.2.3–4 §§34–48 535
20.2.5 §§49–53 439
20.5.1 §§97–99 550
20.5.2 §100 536
20.5.2 §§100–103 439
20.5.2 §103 389, 436
20.5.3 §112 440
20.6.1 §118 440
20.6.1 §121 441
20.6.2 §131 389
20.7.1 §§137–38 436
20.7.1 §138 371
20.7.3 §§145–47 436
20.8.1–3 §§148–57 371
20.8.4 §159 436
20.8.5 §161 441
20.8.5 §§162–63 388
20.8.6 §§167–72 520, 550
20.8.7 §§173 407
20.8.8 §179 389
20.8.8 §§179–81 416
20.8.8 §181 417
20.8.9 §§183–84 407
20.8.10 §188 443
20.8.11 §§194–95 389, 437
20.8.11 §196 389
20.9.1 §197 388
20.9.1 §§197–203 389, 443
20.9.1 §199 485
20.9.1 §§199–200 545
20.9.1 §§200–203 390, 393
20.9.1 §203 389
20.9.2–3 §§204–10 443
20.9.2–4 §§206–13 389
20.9.4 §213 389
20.9.5 §215 513
20.9.6 §§216–18 417
20.9.7 §§219–22 414
20.9.7 §§219–23 336
20.9.7 §222 336
20.9.7 §223 389
20.10.1 §227 389
20.10.4 §§243–44 306
20.10.5 §§247–48 388
20.10.5 §250 387
20.10.5 §251 385

Life
1 §5 5
2 §§8–12 470
2 §§10–11 492
2 §12 473, 479
4–5 §§17–23 446, 450
5 §21 472
6 §§24–27 448
7–74 §§28–411 371
7 §29 6
8 §§30–31 451
9 §§32–36 451
9 §41 371, 452
22 §104 451
22 §§104–11 451
25 §§123–24 451
38–39 §§189–98 452
38 §§190–91 472
38 §§190–94 482
38 §191 476
38–39 §§193–96 389
39 §§196–98 546
39 §197 472, 476
41 §204 389
44 §216 389
54 §277 541
60 §309 389
65 §§336–39 371
65 §§346–47 451
65 §§361–63 7
65 §§362–67 437
67 §§373–80 451
71 §§394–97 451
74–76 §§407–23 454
74 §411 451
76 §422 583

War
1.Pref.1 §3 7
1.1.1 §§31–33 277, 281
1.1.1–2.2 §§31–53 227
1.1.2 §§34–35 281
1.1.3–6 §§36–47 285
1.1.5 §§41–46 292
1.1.5 §45 288
1.2.1 §§48–49 293
1.2.2 §50 299
1.2.3 §§50–54 297
1.2.3–8 §§54–69 299
1.2.7 §65 301
1.2.8 §67 301
1.3.1–6 §§70–84 301
1.4.1–8 §§85–106 302
1.5.1–4 §§107–19 305
1.5.1 §109 324
1.5.2 §110 306
1.5.2–3 §§110–14 470
1.6.1–7.7 §§120–58 306
1.6.2 §123 322
1.8.1–10.4 §§159–202 340
1.8.5 §§170 321
1.8.7 §175 323
1.8.7 §178 322
1.8.9 §181 323
1.9.2 §§185–86 343
1.9.3 §§187–88 323
1.9.4 §190 324
1.10.3 §199 324
1.10.4 §§202–3 324, 343
1.10.4–14.4 §§203–85 344
1.10.9 §214 343
1.11.2 §220 335
1.11.3 §223 346
1.11.7 §232 346
1.15.1–20.3 §§286–393 349
1.16.6 §319 502
1.18.2 §351 327, 350
1.18.5 §§361–62 325
1.20.3–33.9 §§393–673 354
1.20.3 §396 325
1.20.3–4 §§396–400 355
1.20.4 §398 325
1.20.4 §400 325
1.21.1 §401 356, 357
1.21.1 §402 356
1.21.2 §403 357
1.21.5–7 §§408–14 357
1.21.8 §415 356
1.21.8 §416 357
1.21.9 §417 356, 357
1.21.9 §418 356, 357
1.21.10 §§419–21 356
1.21.12 §426 315
1.22.2–4 §§436–44 359
1.23.1–27.6 §§445–551 360
1.24.3 §479 488
1.26.3 §529 488
1.29.2 §571 471
1.29.3 §§574–77 358
1.33.2–4 §§648–55 520, 547

1.33.3 §652 325
1.33.8 §665 328
2.1.1–7.4 §§1–116 366
2.1.3 §8 325
2.1.3 §10 328
2.5.2–3 §§72–79 329
2.6.2 §§84–86 362
2.6.3 §§94–95 426
2.6.3 §95 425
2.7.3 §111 368
2.8.1 §§117 384, 392
2.8.1–9.4 §§117–77 422
2.8.2–13 §§120–61 492–95
2.8.14 §162 469
2.8.14 §§162–63 469
2.8.14 §166 469, 484
2.9.1 §168 426
2.9.2–3 §§169–74 396
2.9.2–4 §§169–77 423
2.9.5–11.6 §§178–219 430
2.9.6 §183 428
2.10.1–5 §§184–203 402
2.10.4 §197 396
2.10.5 §200 404
2.10.5 §203 404, 439, 451
2.11.1–5 §§204–17 432
2.11.6 §§218–19 432
2.11.6 §220 436, 438, 439
2.11.6–14.3 §§220–83 437
2.12.1 §223 436
2.12.1 §227 440
2.12.3 §232 440
2.12.4 §235 441
2.12.5–6 §§240–43 388
2.12.6 §243 389
2.12.8 §247 436
2.13.2 §252 371, 436
2.13.2 §253 441
2.13.3 §256 388
2.13.4–6 §§258–65 520, 550
2.13.5 §262 441
2.13.6 §§264–65 442
2.14.1 §§272–76 443
2.14.4–15.6 §§284–332 447
2.14.4–17.5 §§284–424 446
2.14.4 §285 541
2.15.1 §309 439
2.16.4 §§345–401 7, 448
2.17.1 §405 447
2.17.2–3 §§410–11 471
2.17.6–19.9 §§425–555 448
2.17.6 §427 416
2.17.6 §429 389
2.17.8 §§433–34 501
2.17.9 §§441–42 389
2.17.9 §§443–46 501
2.18.7 §§487–88 405
2.18.7–8 §§487–98 439
2.20.1 §§556–57 450
2.20.1–4 §§556–68 450
2.20.3 §§562–63 450
2.20.3–4 §§562–68 6
2.20.3 §562—3.2.4 §34 371
2.20.3 §563 389
2.20.4 §566 387
2.20.4 §567 497
2.20.5–21.10 §§569–646 451
2.21.7 §§626–28 452
2.21.10 §§645–46 451
2.21.10 §646 451
2.22.1 §647—7.11.5 §455 454
2.22.1–2 §§648–53 389
3.2.1 §11 497
3.2.4 §§30–34 451
3.3.5 §§54–56 386
3.4.1 §§59–63 451, 455
3.4.2 §68 333
3.5.1–8 §§70–109 7
3.6.1 §§110–14 455
3.7.3 §143 455
3.8.9 §§399–407 522
4.3.4–9 §§138–61 457
4.3.7–5.2 §§151–325 389
4.3.8 §155 389
4.3.9 §160 389
4.4.1 §225 459
4.4.3–5.2 §238–325 389
4.5.5 §§345–52 458
4.8.1 §445 386
4.9.11 §§566–70 458
4.9.11 §574 387
5.1.1–4 §§1–26 459
5.1.6 §§45–46 439
5.4.1 §139 299
5.12.4 §523 581
5.13.1 §527 387
5.13.1 §532 488
5.13.1 §533 460
6.2.2 §114 389
6.2.4 §124–28 393
6.2.4 §126 393
6.5.2 §282 416
6.5.2 §§283–85 413
6.5.2 §§283–87 550
7.6.2 §§171–77 357
7.6.6 §216–17 583
7.6.6 §217 581
7.8.3–4 §§280–303 357
7.10.2 §423 266
7.10.2–4 §§423–36 266
7.10.3 §427 266

NEW TESTAMENT

Matthew
2:16-18 362
3:7-10 476
9:10-13 476
12:1-8 477
12:9-14 477
12:38 476
15:1-20 476
16:1 476
19:3-12 477
21:45 476
22:15-22 477
22:16 501
22:41-46 477
23:2 476
26:3 388
26:57 388

Mark
1–13 489
2:6 476
2:15-17 476
2:16 489
2:23-28 477
3:1-6 476, 477
3:6 501
6:14-28 427
7:1-23 476
7:5 476
8:11 476
8:15 502
10:2-12 477
12:13 476, 501
12:13-17 414, 477
12:35-37 477
12:38 476

Luke
2:1-5 384
2:23 539
2:41 539
2:41-47 5
3:2 388
3:7-9 476
5:1 539
5:21 476
5:29-32 476
6:1-5 477
6:6-11 477
7:1-5 541
7:2-11 539
7:30 490
10:22 539
11:37-41 476
16:18 477
20:20-26 477
20:41-44 477
23:6-12 428

John
5:2-7 530
7:2-9 529
7:53—8:11 394
9 546
9:13-34 542
11:49 388
18:13 388
18:13-24 388
18:14 388
18:24 388
18:28 388
18:31 394

Acts
2:1 586
4:1 485
4:1-21 395
4:5-8 390
4:6 388
4:23 390
5 487
5:17 485
5:21-34 390
5:33-40 394, 395
5:34 482
5:36 438, 550
5:37 423
6:12 394
6:12—7:1 395
7 540
7:44-50 586
7:54-58 394, 395
8:9-24 518
9:1-2 546
10:1 386
12:1 430
12:1-19 433
12:20-23 433
18:2 398, 399, 560
18:18 539
21:17-26 586
21:23 539
21:37-38 520
21:38 441, 550
22:30—23:7 390
23:2 389
23:6-10 485
23:9 489
24:1 389
24:22-27 441
24:24—26:32 436
25:1-6 442
25:24 436

EARLY CHRISTIAN LITERATURE

Apostolic Constitutions 6.6 508

Barnabas 16:4 570

Epiphanius
Panarion 17 508

Eusebius
Chron. 99, 559, 576
Hist. eccl.
2.5.7 395
4.2.1–5 559
4.6.1–4 560
4.6.4 572
4.22.5 508
4.22.7 508
Praep. evang.
8 492

Hippolytus
Philosophumena
9.18.2–9.29.4 492

Jerome
Comm. in Dan.
to 8:9 258

Julius Africanus
in Eusebius, *Hist. eccl.*
1.7.11 322

Justin
Apologia
1.31.6 580
Dial. Trypho
52 322
80.4 508

Origen
Contra Celsum 10

Orosius
3.7.6 99
7.6.15–16 398, 560
7.12.6–8 560–61
7.13.4–5 561

Syncellus
1.486.10–14 99

RABBINIC LITERATURE

Babylonian Talmud
Avod. Zara 8b 393
B. Batra
134a 478
Qid. 76a 503
Sanh. 41a 393
Suk. 28a 478
Ta'an. 23a 306
Yeb. 46a 535
Yoma 69a 182

Jerusalem Talmud
Ned. 5.6 478
Sanh.
1.1, 18a 393
7.2, 24b 393
Ta'an.
4.5, 69a 569
4.8, 68a 579

Mishnah
Avot 2.8 482
Mig. 4.5 478
Rosh ha-Shan. 1.7 545
Shab. 1.4 478
Suk. 2.7 478
Ta'an. 3.8 521

Tosefta
Hag. 2.3 517
Shab. 15[16]:9 571, 573

Other Rabbinic Literature
Eccl. Rabba
on Eccl
3:17 568
Gen. Rab.
64.10 570
Josippon 10 182
Meg. Ta'an.
6 394
12 568
Seder Olam Rabbah
(Ratner ed., p. 145) 367

GREEK AND ROMAN WRITINGS

Appian
Bell. civ.
2.90.380 598
5.75.319 326, 355
13–18 318
Syr.
11 240
50.253 414

Aristotle
Athen. Polit.
5–9 119

Cassius Dio
2.1.1 575
37–54 317, 327
49.22.4 327
55 317, 320
55–60 379
57.18.5 398
60.6.6 398
61–69 379
68.32.1–3 556
69.12 571
69.12.1–14.3 556

Celsus
7.25.1 279

Demotic Chronicle 164

Diodorus
3.43.5 331
11–16 66
17 183
17.5.3–6 141
18–20 184
19.94–100 331
20 184
40.3.1–7 216

Herodotus
3.4–9 85
3.61–79 125
3.89–97 125
3.97 85

Historia Augusta
Hadr.
5.2 558, 568
14.2 558, 570

Justinian
Digesta
48.8.11 571

Livy
1–10 317
21–45 317

Nabonidus Chronicle
2.16 123
3.15–16 123
3.21 35
3.22 123

Oracle of Bocchoris or the Lamb
164

Pliny the Elder
5.14.70 386
5.73 492

Pliny the Younger
Epistles 10.96 558

Plutarch
Crassus 33 157

Polybius
1–5 184
5.79 292
26.1 248
28.18 248
33.18 294

Potter's Oracle
164

Quintus Curtius
4.8–10 55
4.8.9–11 504

Solinus
Collect. 35.4 99

Strabo
15.2.34 330
16 317
16.2.28–46
§§759–65 239
16.2.30 240
16.4.8 331

Suetonius
Claud.
25.4 398
28 441
Tib.
36 398
41 423

Tacitus
Ann.
1–6 378, 421
1.80 423
2.42.5 385, 414
2.85.4 398
15.44.3 423
Hist.
1–4 378
2.78.4 386
5.8 248

Thucydides
1.6.5–6 278
1.128–29 34

Valerius Maximus
1.3.3 397

INSCRIPTIONS

Behistun Inscription
§6:1.14–17 125
§§10–13:1.26–61 125

Cowley
21 54, 90
30.29 135
30–31 62
30–32 54, 97, 135, 138
31.28 135
32 32
81 184

CPJ
1.21–23 178
1.88 598
1.90–91 599
1.92–93 598
1.115–30 172
1.126 193
2.25–107 399
2.36–55 407
2.188–97 438
2.189 439
2.195 439
2.225–60 565
2.226 597
2.228–33 598
2.236–40 598
2.257 598

Hefzibah Inscription
241, 246

Jerusalem Inscription = SEG 1695
241

***PSI* 406**
203

***P. Zen.* 59012**
202

SB 8008 = Rainer papyrus (Lenger 21–22)
186, 191, 203

Tel Dan Inscription
187

XPh §46b:35–41 = Kent: 150–51
130

INDEX OF NAMES AND SUBJECTS

Aaron, 290, 466, 586
Abdera, 99, 173, 174, 191, 212, 216, 264, 410
Abila, 321, 371, 436
abomination of desolation, 247, 258, 259, 266, 282
Abraham, 8, 114, 237, 264, 528
Acco. *See* Ptolemais
Acheus, 214
Achzib, 84
Acra, 245, 282
Acrabet(t)a, 386, 451
Acta Alexandrinorum, 399, 401
Actium, 325, 338, 349, 351, 352, 563, 614
Adam, 505, 528
Adar, 291
Adaros, 84
Adiabene, 371, 439, 535, 536, 596
Adida, 297
Adonis, 46
Adora, 321
Aegean, 120, 149, 155, 212
Aelia Capitolina, 556, 560, 561, 570–72, 574, 576, 578, 600–602, 605
Aelius Gallus, 333, 560
Aemilius, 234
Africa, 339, 340, 344, 523, 587, 600
Africanus, 322, 374, 375
afterlife, 487, 526, 531
Agatharchides of Cnidus, 174, 211
Agesilaus, 139
Agricola, 591
Agrippa, Marcus, 327, 348, 354, 356–58, 365, 406
Agrippa I, 7, 74, 307, 336, 363, 364, 369, 378, 381–83, 386, 388, 389, 391, 396, 400–405, 412, 418–20, 425, 426, 428–30, 431–37, 502, 549, 614
Agrippa II, 336, 363, 371, 374, 382, 389, 391, 393, 417, 418, 430, 434–38, 440, 441, 443, 447–50, 454, 456, 457, 564, 589, 615
Agrippeum, 356
Agrippias, 357
Agrippina, 435
Agrippium, 357
Aher, 514
Ahiqar, 181, 226
Ahura Mazda, 130, 159
Ai, 162, 165
Aineias, 193
Akiba. *See* Aqiva
Akko. *See* Ptolemais
alabarch, 373, 431, 436, 438
Alcimus, 289–91, 293, 294, 466, 467, 482, 488, 497
Alexander the Great, xxv, xxvi, 2, 3, 8, 9, 16, 23, 32, 41, 45, 55, 61, 63, 71, 73, 88, 100, 113, 125, 130, 141, 142, 147–50, 159–62, 165, 166, 168, 171, 174, 181–84, 188, 189, 204–11, 218, 256, 399, 405, 406, 504
Alexander b. Aristobulus II, 307, 340, 341, 343
Alexander b. Herod, 360, 361, 368
Alexander, brother of Philo, 373, 431, 436, 438
Alexander Balas. *See* Balas, Alexander
Alexander Janneus. *See* Janneus, Alexander
Alexander Zabinus, 300
Alexandra Salome, 234, 272, 304–6, 470–72, 475, 480, 481, 483, 485
Alexandra, daughter of Hyrcanus II, 351
Alexandria, xxviii, 3, 10, 170, 179, 189–91, 200, 207, 215, 236, 274, 340, 348, 349, 372–74, 393, 399, 400, 405–9, 411, 431, 438, 439, 447, 449, 454, 559, 561, 598
Alexandrians, 399, 407, 408, 569
Alexandrium, 245, 306, 341, 357
allegorists, 274, 372, 374
allegory, 238
Allogenes, 517
almsgiving, 178
altar, 145, 162, 189, 258, 259, 402, 403, 405, 480, 529, 539, 541, 586, 608
Amathus, 303, 321
Ambivulus, Marcus, 423
Amicitia, 320
am/ammei ha-aretz, 523
Ammianus, 317, 378
Ammon, 85, 88, 182, 193, 207
Ammonite, 88, 133, 193
amphitheater, 356, 432
Ananel, 351, 388
Ananias, 387
Ananias b. Nedebaeus, 389, 440, 443
Ananus b. Ananus, 392, 393, 443, 451, 458, 473, 485
Ananus b. Seth, 388
Ancyra, 206, 213
Andreas, 556
Andreius, 598
Andromachus, 208
Andronicus, 280
angel, angelology, 102, 177, 486, 509, 514, 517, 518
Angra Mainyu, 102
Annius Rufus, 423
Anthedon, 303, 321, 325, 355, 357
Antigonus Gonatas, 211
Antigonus Monophthalmus, 209, 210, 331
Antigonus, brother of Aristobulus I, 301
Antigonus, son of Aristobulus II, 314, 319, 340, 341, 343, 344, 346–51, 418
Antioch, 213, 262, 263, 278, 281, 284,

INDEX OF NAMES AND SUBJECTS

286–89, 295, 296, 343, 351, 402, 406, 407, 449, 454, 576, 595, 596, 600, 611
Antiochenes, 278, 406
Antiochus I, 212, 213, 249
Antiochus I of Commagene, 159
Antiochus II, 213
Antiochus III, 174, 176, 177, 191, 192, 196, 198, 201, 212, 214, 218, 240, 241, 246, 249, 267, 270, 271, 274, 275, 291, 308, 390, 611
Antiochus IV, 8, 148, 154, 160, 197, 198, 214, ch. 5 passim, 330, 331, 401, 403, 410, 504, 563, 575, 611, 612
Antiochus V Eupator, 261–63, 270, 287, 289
Antiochus VI, 260, 296, 297
Antiochus VII Sidetes, 243, 299, 300
Antiochus VIII Grypus, 243, 300, 301
Antiochus IX Cyzicenus, 300, 301
Antiochus XII Dionysus, 303
Antiochus XIII, 271, 272
Antiochus Hierax, 213, 214
Antipas, Herod, 333, 366, 367, 382, 386, 419, 423, 425, 426–28, 431, 434
Antipater, 205, 209, 243, 306, 314, 322–24, 330, 338, 340, 341, 343, 345, 346, 357, 360, 361, 400, 411
Antipatris, 357
Antonia, 356, 425, 447
Antoninus Pius, 570, 571, 577
Antonius, 271, 272, 441, 453
Antony, Mark, 326, 327, 335, 338, 340, 343, 344, 346–52, 355, 356, 360, 589
Apamea, 449
Apelles, 402
Aphrodisias, 534, 536
Aphrodite, 534
Apion, 10, 406
apocalypse, 4, 100, 108, 145, 180, 181, 198–200, 218, 226, 310, 531, 532, 541, 551, 561, 562, 574, 585, 586
apocalyptic, apocalypticism, 44, 100, 102, 104, 108, 109, 111, 145, 180, 198–200, 217–19, 225, 238, 310, 413, 465, 514, 516, 517, 533, 537, 542, 551, 574, 580, 586, 602
Apocrypha, 3, 4, 100, 198, 231, 562
Apollinopolis, 597
Apollo, 59, 250, 322
Apollonia, 321, 597
Apollonius, Egyptian finance minister, 172, 193
Apollonius the Mysiarch, 251, 278, 282, 283, 286
Apollonius, governor of Coele-Syria, 295
Apollonius, Egyptian strategos, 597
Appian, 240, 318, 326, 355, 414, 598
Aqiva, 579–81, 603
aqueduct, 23, 424, 566
Aquila, 398
Arab, 18, 79, 83–85, 94, 121, 124, 132, 133, 167, 198, 218, 275, 303, 304, 306, 313, 324, 325, 328, 329, 331–33, 352, 357, 358, 425
Arabia, 84, 85, 149, 202, 215, 303, 328, 329, 332, 333, 351, 357–59, 425, 427, 512, 575, 595
Aramaic, 7, 30, 32, 34, 35, 53–55, 58, 68, 71, 72, 76, 81, 85, 88, 96, 120, 129, 150, 153, 157, 158, 170, 180, 185, 187, 193, 319, 379, 380, 394, 496, 509, 565, 603
Arameans, 54
Araq el-Emir, 188, 193
Archelaus, 228, 320, 338, 361, 366–68, 370, 384–86, 388, 394, 422, 425, 497, 549
Areios, 264
Aretas I, 331
Aretas II, 331, 332
Aretas III, 304, 306, 331, 332, 340
Aretas IV, 333, 358, 359, 427
Arethusa, 321
Areus, 260, 261, 264
Aristeas, Letter of Aristeas, 170, 173, 179, 200, 218, 239, 540
Aristobulus of Cassandria, 183
Aristobulus, writer, 237
Aristobulus b. Alexander, high priest, 388
Aristobulus I, 242–44, 301, 331, 497, 550
Aristobulus II, 242–44, 272, 302, 306, 307, 321, 322, 332, 335, 338, 340, 341, 343, 346, 348, 473, 613
Aristobulus b. Herod, 360, 361, 430
Ariston, 560
Aristotle, 119
Armenia, 210, 248, 271, 272, 306, 348, 429, 444, 445, 595, 596
Armenian, 157, 306, 426, 465, 559, 595
Aroandas, 140
Arpaksad, 178
Arsaces, 139
Arsacid, 160, 212
Arsames, 131, 138
Arses, 55, 141
Artabanus, time of Xerxes, 130
Artabanus III, 426, 427, 510
Artabanus V, 510
Artapanus, 237
Artavasdes, 157
Artaxerxes I, 32, 62, 89, 90, 94, 95, 97–99, 128, 130, 131, 136–38
Artaxerxes II, 56, 65, 67, 88, 89, 91, 97, 139
Artaxerxes III, 55, 57, 62, 63, 88, 113, 140, 141, 178
Artaxerxes IV, 141
Artemion, 556, 598
Artemis, 497
Artoxares, 138
Asael, 180
Ascalon, Ashkelon, 70, 84, 295, 296, 321, 322, 325, 449, 454
ascetic, asceticism, 5, 177, 255, 508, 530, 608
Ashdod, 73, 84, 295
Asia, 16, 17, 22, 59, 74, 116, 122, 126, 138–40, 161, 164, 168, 202, 204, 205, 209, 210, 212–15, 254, 271, 272, 274, 275, 308, 320, 340, 344, 357, 406, 409, 576, 600, 614
Asiatic, 16, 17, 21, 22, 115
Asinius, 326
Asochis, 302
Asoka, 156, 157
assassins, 460, 500
Assyria, 81, 83, 338, 412, 596, 597
Assyrian, 64, 80, 82, 83, 84, 115, 122, 157, 167, 177, 504
astrology, 8, 237, 519, 520, 526, 530, 531
Astyages, 122
Atargatis, 158
Athens, Athenians, 23, 65, 119, 131, 138, 139, 147, 161, 166, 184, 205, 210, 236, 271, 282, 283, 436, 562, 575, 576, 600
Atossa, 129
Attalid, 161, 162
Attalus, 161, 214, 271
Atticus, 566
Augustus, 3, 8, 177, 228, 315, 318, 325, 352–63, 366–68, 379, 382, 384, 385, 392, 397, 399, 406–8, 419–21, 425, 426, 434, 435, 587, 588, 595, 600, 614
Auranitis, 325, 355, 367, 386, 425
Avesta, 101
Axidares, 595
Azekah, 80
Azotus, 293, 321, 325

Baal, Baalshamem, 42, 254, 259
Baba Rabba, 505

Babata, Babatha, 20, 576, 577
Babylon, 35, 38, 39, 44, 47, 56, 57, 76, 81, 84, 88, 89, 116, 117, 120, 123, 124, 126, 129, 130, 132, 137, 159, 160, 165, 207–10, 213, 225, 226, 323, 336, 351, 388, 412, 498, 538, 596
Babylonia, 16, 56, 59, 60, 101, 144, 156, 159, 201, 519, 537, 596
Babylonians, 8, 80, 99, 117, 121, 123, 160, 307
Bacchides, 289–91, 293, 294, 466
Bacchus, 252
Bactria, 130, 209
Bagoas, 62, 63, 140, 141
Bagohi, 62, 63, 72, 138, 140, 141
Bagoses, 61–63, 88, 99, 113
Balagrae, 597
Balas, Alexander, 260, 270, 294–96, 300
banditry, bandits, 345, 350, 391, 398, 419, 438, 441, 499, 512, 513, 549, 552, 560. *See also* brigand
baptism, 508, 509, 535
Baptist, John the, 426, 427, 508, 510, 511, 517, 550
Baptists, 507
Bar Kokhba, xxiii, 2, 380, 555, 556, 559, 561, 563–65, 569, 570, 572–75, 577–81, 583, 585, 601–5
Bardya, 124, 125
Baruch, Apocalypse of (2 Baruch), 541, 561, 562, 574, 586
Barzaphranes, 347
Bassus, 345, 460, 583
Batanea, 325, 355, 367, 386, 425, 436
Beer-sheba, 85
Behistun inscription, 54, 58, 64, 125
Beirut, 432, 460
Belshazzar, 226
Beluchistan, 208
Bemeselis, 303
Ben Sira. *See* Sira, Joshua b.
Benjamin, 73, 80, 117, 129, 130, 132, 277
Benjaminites, 277
Berenice, 213, 302, 436, 437, 447, 589, 597
Berossus, 10, 56, 59, 60, 159, 165
Berytus, 432, 460
Bessus, 207
Beth Shean, 297
Bethar, Betar, 569, 604, 605
Betharamphtha, 423, 426
Bethbasi, 294
Bethel, 293
Beth-haccerem, 80
Beth-haram, 426
Bethlehem, 362
Bethleptenpha, 386
Bethsaida, 423, 425, 426
Beththera, 560
Beth-Zechariah, 288
Bezetha, 432
Bigvai, 39
Bisitun. *See* Behistun
Bithynia, 271, 272, 558
Bocchoris, Oracle of, 164
Boethus, 387, 388, 486, 487
Boethusians, 484, 486, 487
Boetia, 67
Bostra, 333
Boudicca, 444
boule. *See* Sanhedrin
brigand(s), brigandage, 349, 358, 372, 438, 441, 442, 444, 452, 457
Britain, 15, 167, 271, 429, 435, 444, 557, 587, 588, 590, 600
Britannia, 435
Britannicus, 435
Brundisium, 326, 344
Brutus, 343, 344
bulla, bullae, 55, 156, 242
Byblos, 160, 161
Byzantine, 120, 184, 240, 384

Cabi, 389
Cadmus, 264
Cadousii, 141
Caecina, 589
Caesar, 8, 245, 316, 320, 322, 335, 338–40, 343–45, 348, 352, 355, 367, 368, 382–84, 392, 406–8, 411, 440, 442, 448, 502, 583. *See also* Augustus, Claudius, Hadrian, Julius, Nero, Sextus, Titus
Caesarea, 202, 304, 355–57, 386, 405, 407, 413, 423–25, 434, 442, 443, 446, 449, 450, 454, 455, 457, 460, 541, 566
Caesareum, 356
Caesarion, 348
Caiaphas, 388
Calchis, 391
calendar, 103, 234, 235, 262, 307–9, 482, 486, 507, 529, 545, 608, 609
Caligula, 370, 371, 373, 378, 382, 395, 400–405, 407, 420, 422, 426, 428–32, 434, 435, 444
Callias, peace of, 131
Callisthenes, 182, 207
Calvinus, 326
Cambyses, 61, 64, 77, 85, 95, 123–25, 127
Camei, 389
Camithus, 388
Camoedi, 389
Camudus, 389
Canaanite, 48, 158, 161, 257, 259
Caninius Gallus, 327
canonization, 103
Cantheras, 388, 389
Capitolina. *See* Aelia
Cappadocia, 212, 271, 357, 361
Capri, 421, 422, 429, 431
Caria, 205, 210
Carmel, 347
Carpentras, 405
Carpocrates, 517
Carthage, 271, 600
Cassander, 209, 210
Cassandria, 183
Cassius, assassin of Caesar, 335, 338, 341, 343–47
Cassius Dio, 240, 317, 320, 327, 328, 378, 379, 398, 432, 556, 571, 575, 601
castration, 570, 571
Cataonia, 139
Caucasus, 124, 596
Celer, 440
celibacy, 496, 608
Celsus, anti-Christian writer, 10
Celsus, encyclopedist, 279
Celtic, 205, 213
Celts, 162
census, 19, 39, 370, 378, 383–85, 414, 423
Cestius Gallus, 6, 8, 285, 444, 446–50, 454, 455
Chaeronea, 67
Chalcis, Herod of, 382, 389, 430, 432, 436, 438
Chaldean, 58, 122, 123
Chosroes, 595
Chremonidean War, 213
Chrestus, 398
Christ, xxvii, 172, 362, 392, 502, 574, 586
Christianity, 4, 100, 187, 362, 370, 372, 374, 376, 377, 381, 401, 430, 463, 465, 468, 502, 514, 515, 517, 519, 526, 527, 574, 602
Chronicle, Demotic. *See Demotic Chronicle*
Chronicles, 27, 31, 32, 40, 49–51, 53, 57, 91, 99, 108, 145
chronicles, Babylonian, 57
chronicles, Samaritan, 502, 505, 506
Cicero, 339, 343, 344, 531
Cilicia, 206, 210, 271, 436
circumcision, 250, 254, 255, 259, 274, 279, 302, 329, 330, 331, 373, 410, 528, 529, 534–36, 570, 571, 573, 601, 602
Cisalpine, 344
citizenship, 165, 166, 343, 400, 401, 405–8, 411, 442, 446
Claudius Caesar, 382, 398, 407, 431, 432, 434–36, 438, 440, 441, 587

INDEX OF NAMES AND SUBJECTS

Clement of Alexandria, 236
Cleopatra, wife of Demetrius II, 299
Cleopatra III Berenice, 301–3
Cleopatra Selene, 305
Cleopatra VII, 324, 325, 335, 340, 348, 349, 351, 352, 355, 563, 589
cleruchies, 215, 325
cleruchy, 22, 193, 215, 252, 255, 284
client-king, 324, 325, 358, 513
Cnidus, 174, 211
Codommanus, 141
Coele-Syria, 84, 139, 177, 191, 196, 204, 212, 214, 215, 217, 274, 295, 296, 345, 351, 358, 609, 610, 611
Colchis, 272
Colosseum, 589
Commagene, 159
consul(s), 260, 272, 327, 339, 340, 343, 344, 353, 354, 408, 430, 575
Coponius, 370, 384, 392, 394, 423
Corbulo, 445
Corinth, 543
Corinthian, 205, 543
Corinthios, 262
Cornelius, 67, 378
Cos, 320
Costobarus, 329
Crassus, 335, 338, 339, 341
Crete, 295
Crocodilopolis, 84
Croesus, 122
Ctesias, 65–67, 120, 131, 138
Ctesiphon, 596
Cumanus, 437, 440, 441
Curtius, 55, 183, 504
Cuspius, 438
Cypros, 323, 356
Cyprus, 99, 202, 204, 210, 212, 301–3, 439, 556, 561, 587, 596, 598, 599, 601
Cyren, 405, 567, 596
Cyrenaica, 212, 213, 392, 597
Cyrenaica, Roman legion, 568
Cyrene, 190, 224, 228, 389, 392, 406, 407, 461, 501, 556, 559, 561, 567, 568, 587, 596, 597–99, 601
Cyropaedia, 65
Cyrus the Great, 1, 32, 34, 35, 39, 56, 57, 60, 61, 64, 66, 76, 77, 79, 81, 108, 120–24, 126, 127, 129, 142, 143, 226, 607
Cyrus the Younger, 65, 66, 138, 139
Cyrus, battle of, 211
Cyzicenus, 300

Dacians, 591, 595
Daliyeh, Wadi, 55, 69, 112, 135, 208, 504
Damascene, 315
Damascus, 9, 206, 228, 229, 235, 301, 303, 306, 314–16, 322, 330, 332, 333, 345, 351, 359, 360, 363, 366, 367, 370, 472, 491, 494–96, 498, 546, 576, 600
Damnaeus, 389
Dan, 158, 187, 188, 210, 219, 225, 250, 253, 258, 283
Daniel, 34, 51, 53, 108, 109, 121, 169, 183, 184, 225–27, 238, 239, 253, 258, 270, 310, 410, 465–67, 486, 501, 502, 540
Danube, 453, 454, 457, 590, 591
Daphne, 264, 277
Dardanelles, 205
"Darius the Mede," 122, 123
Darius I, 32, 41, 43, 44, 54, 56, 58, 59–61, 64, 70, 79, 81, 82, 95, 97, 115, 116, 123–29, 131, 138, 139, 159, 178, 182, 206, 207, 225, 226, 608
Darius II Ochus, 41, 59, 138, 139, 140
Darius III Codommanus, 41, 56, 141
Datames, 139
David, 52, 145, 245, 246, 282, 300, 311, 317, 355, 412, 526, 552, 574
Davidic, 69, 79, 107, 128, 143
Davidide, 78
Decapolis, 321, 568
Decebalus, 591, 595
Decimus, 344
Deiotariana, Roman legion, 577
Delaiah, Delayah, 135, 138
Delphi, 67
Demetrius, minister of Ptolemy II, 179
Demetrius Poliorcetes, 210, 211
Demetrius the Chronographer, 181, 236
Demetrius I Soter, 270, 276, 289, 290, 293–95, 466, 467
Demetrius II, 260, 295, 296, 298–300
Demetrius III, 234, 303
demiurge, 516
demon, 530
demonology, 102, 177
Demotic language/texts, 60, 61, 157, 163, 176
Demotic Chronicle, 60, 61, 163, 164
Deutero-Isaiah, 47, 96, 108
Deuteronomy, 105, 480
Deutero-Zechariah, 44
Diadochi, 73, 171, 174, 180, 184, 185, 188, 199, 204, 209–11, 217, 331, 610
Diocletian, xxvii
Diodorus Siculus, 66, 67, 99, 120, 141, 173, 183, 216, 239, 331
Diodotos, 158
Dionysus, 252, 253, 258, 259, 303
Dios, 262
Dium, 321
Diyllus, 184
Domitia, 591
Domitian, 7, 318, 378, 379, 382, 383, 453, 558, 562, 571, 581, 584, 588, 590, 591, 595
Domitius Calvinus, 326
Dor, 83, 84, 188, 293, 299
Dora, 321, 432
Doris, 360
Dorymenes, 286
Dosa, 519–21
Dositheans, 503
Dositheus, 536
dreams, 180, 182, 211, 368, 497, 531, 552
Drusilla, 441
Drusus, 421
dyarchy, 74, 75, 77, 308, 607
Dystros, 186, 262

earthquake, 232, 352, 499, 596
Ebir-nari, 81, 82, 84, 123, 127, 130, 131, 136, 139
Ecbatana, 207
eclipse, 328, 361
Edessa, 596
Edom, 45, 84, 85, 185
Edomite(s), 80, 84, 85, 121, 185, 329, 330. *See also* Idumea(ns)
Egypt, 8, 19, 54, 55, 61, 62, 72, 73, 84, 85, 97, 124, 126, 129–31, 138–41, 143, 148, 149, 154, 156, 163–66, 168, 171–73, 177, 182, 189, 190, 192, 193, 196, 197, 202–4, 206–15, 217, 235, 237, 248, 251, 253, 254, 261, 265, 266, 274, 276, 277, 281–83, 296, 301, 302, 308, 310, 338, 340, 343, 348, 349, 353, 355, 373, 386, 397, 399, 400, 403, 405, 406, 408, 411, 412, 439, 453, 457, 460, 499, 501, 531, 533, 540, 548, 556, 557, 559, 561, 563, 565, 569, 575–77, 587, 596–601, 610, 613
Ekron, 295
Elamite, 56, 58, 510
Elchasai, 507, 508, 509
Elchesaites, 509
Elcheseans, 509
Eleazar, high priest, 179
Eleazar Maccabee, 285

Eleazar, brother of Joazar, 388
Eleazar, bandit chief, 441
Eleazar, temple official, 443
Eleazar, martyr, 448
Eleazar, the Pharisee, 470
Eleazar, priest under Bar Kokhba, 601, 603
Eleazar b. Ananias, 448
Eleazar b. Ananus, 388
Eleazar b. Hyrcanus, 579, 592, 593
Eleazar b. Jairus, 448
Eleazar b. Neus, 451
Eleazar b. Simon, 459, 501
Elephantine, 34, 54, 60, 62, 71, 83, 88, 97, 99, 135, 138, 141, 184, 253, 310
el-Ghuweir, 229
Eliashib, 41, 62, 89, 92, 113, 114, 134
Elijah, 105, 522
Elionaeus, 389
Elisha, 105, 517
Elisha b. Abuya, 517
Ellemus, 388
Elnathan, 69
Elul, 394
Elxai, 508
Elymais, 275
Emmaus, 286, 292, 293, 386, 451, 581, 583
Engedi, 73, 386, 492, 576–78, 604
Enoch, 150, 151, 180, 199, 211, 217–20, 234, 542
ephah, 44
ephebate, 166, 406
ephebeion, 278
Ephesus, 213, 406
Ephorus, 66, 67
Ephraim, 233
Epiphanes, 196, 214, 248, 264, 265, 276, 575
Epiphanius, 508, 577
epispasm, 277, 536, 571, 573
equites, 587
Esagila, 130
eschatology, 45, 49, 100, 102, 108, 110, 218, 219, 229, 310, 481, 491, 527, 551–54, 562, 563
Esdras, 9, 32, 50, 53, 61, 63, 92, 561, 562
Essenes, 5, 151, 229, 368, 466, 467, 469, 471, 473, 481, 491–99, 502, 509, 522, 528, 540, 546, 548, 550, 587, 615
Esther, 9, 27, 51, 52, 61, 63, 82, 121, 225, 226, 231
Ethiopians, 237
ethnarch, 243, 245, 320, 338, 343, 366, 367, 368, 370, 423
Euergetes, 176, 178, 196, 214
Eumenes, 162
Eupator, 270
Euphrates, 84, 204, 207, 208, 213, 263, 272, 286, 348, 350, 427
Eupolemus, 237, 308
Eutropius, 67
Exagoge, 238
exodus, 35, 96
exorcism, 520, 523
Ezekias, 71, 192, 212, 345
Ezekiel, 46, 109, 118, 219, 238, 274, 498
Ezekiel the Dramatist, 238, 274
Ezra, 4, ch. 2 passim, 152, 171, 173, 504, 524, 538, 541, 552, 561, 562, 574, 585, 586, 608–10
Ezra, Apocalypse of (4 Ezra), 541, 552, 561, 562, 574, 585, 586

Fadus, Cuspius, 436, 438, 550
Failaka, 164, 165
Falasha, 169
Fayum, 172
Felix, 5, 437, 441, 442
Ferrata, Roman legion, 566, 575
Festus, 392, 436, 437, 442, 443
Fiscus Judaicus, 581
Flaccus, 400, 409, 431
Flavians, 558, 564
Florus, Gessius, 9, 444, 446–49
Fourth Philosophy, 500, 501, 549
Fretensis, Roman legion, 566
Gabara, 451, 455
Gabinius, 320–22, 338, 340, 341
Gadara, 161, 303, 321, 325, 355, 449, 456
Gadatas, 34, 59
Gaius. *See* Caligula
Galaaditis, 303
Galatians, 162
Galba, 445, 453, 457
Galilee, 4, 6–9, 72, 84, 147, 151, 157, 227, 242, 288, 296, 302, 304, 321, 331, 334, 336, 341, 344–46, 349, 350, 355, 367, 369, 386, 420, 425, 426, 446, 449–52, 454–56, 463, 482, 500, 529, 566, 567, 583, 604, 609
Gallus, 285, 327, 333, 444, 446
Gamala, Gamla, 451, 456, 471, 541
Gamaliel I, 378, 478, 482, 483, 547
Gamaliel II, 478, 592, 593
Gaugamela, 207
Gaul, 339, 344, 353, 354, 368, 428, 600
Gaulanitis, 325, 425, 436
Gautama, 125
Gaza, 70, 73, 84, 85, 182, 202, 203, 206, 208, 210, 212, 215, 296, 302, 303, 321, 325, 332, 355, 576
Gazara, 298
Gemellus, 422
Gera, 293
Gerasa, 568, 576
Gerizim, 113, 188, 189, 244, 310, 424, 455, 506, 507, 540, 541
Germanicus, 382, 407, 408, 421, 422, 429
Germany, 15, 404, 429, 588, 592
Geron, 282–84
gerousia. *See* Sanhedrin
Geshem, 85, 132, 133
Gessius, 444
Gezer, 73, 245, 285, 299
Gibeon, 69, 80
Gilboa, 345
Gilead, 303, 332
Gioras. *See* Simon b. Gioras
Gischala, John of (John b. Levi), 420, 451, 452, 456–60
Givat ha-Mivtar, 318, 319
Gnostic(s), 509, 511, 514–18, 551
Gnosticism, 464, 511, 514–19, 551
Gobryas, 123
Godfearers, 534
Golan, 2, 570, 574
Gonatas, 211
Gophna, 286, 288, 386, 451
Gorgias, 286
Gorion, Joseph b., 451
Gospel(s), 376, 377, 384, 394, 426, 428, 476, 481, 485, 488–90, 501, 502, 508, 521, 522, 539, 549, 550
Gracchi, 271, 313, 369
Grypus, 300
Gubaru, 123, 226
gymnasium, 165, 278, 279, 280, 308, 373, 400, 612

Hadad, 158
Hadid, 297
Hadrian, 16, 318, 556–58, 560, 561, 563, 566, 568–76, 587, 591, 596, 599–602, 605, 607
Haggai, 31, 43, 44, 48, 78, 79, 127, 128, 144, 538
Halafta, Yose b., 514
Halicarnassus, 205
Hamath, 296
Hanina b. Dosa, 519, 520, 521
Hanukkah, 260, 288
haoma, 55
Haran-Gawait, 510
Hasideans, 465, 466
Hasidim, 108, 110, 169, 226, 227, 251, 252, 290, 465–67, 483, 488, 496, 519
Hasmonean(s), xxvii, 14, 25, 74, 80, 150, 154, 164, 178–81, 188, 221, 222, 223, 228, 229, 233, 234, 237, 238, 240, 242–46, 256, 267–69, 272, 273, 285, 295,

297, 301, 302, 307–9, 316, 325, 329, 330, 332, 334, 335, 337, 338, 340, 351, 355, 362, 365, 370, 386, 390, 411, 412, 417, 418, 465, 476, 481, 487, 497, 532, 538, 613, 614
Hattush, 91
Hauran, 332
haverim, 523
havurot, 524
Hazor, 73
heber. See hever
Hebron, 329, 578
Hecateus, 99, 173, 174, 191, 192, 212, 216, 218, 264, 410
Hefzibah, 240
Hegra, 333
Helena, 439
Helicon, 402
Heliodorus, 241, 270, 275, 276, 278
Heliopolis, 266
Helix, 346
Hercules, 182, 206, 279
Hermes, 279
Hermon, 432
Hermopoli, 53
Herod the Great, 2, 8, 9, 19, 25, 74, 151, 154, 178, 228, 229, 238, 245, 307, ch. 6 passim, 370, 378, 381, 384, 385, 387, 388, 391, 394, 396, 407, 412, 414, 417–20, 425, 430, 432–34, 442, 471–73, 476, 481, 483, 484, 486, 488, 497, 502, 512, 520, 544–50, 555, 607, 614, 615
"Herod Agrippa," 430
Herod Antipas. *See* Antipas, Herod
Herod of Chalcis. *See* Chalcis, Herod of
Herodes, 313, 322
Herodians, 476, 501, 502, 549
Herodias, 426–28, 431
Herodium, 356, 364, 386, 457, 460, 537, 541, 578, 604
Herodotus, 34, 64, 65, 84, 85, 124, 125
Heshbon, 325
hever, 242, 578
Hezekiah, 71, 105, 192, 212, 345
Hierax, 213, 214
Hieronymus. *See* Jerome
Hillel, 15, 468, 478, 479, 481, 483, 484, 547, 594
Hippicus, 355
Hippo, 355
hippodrome, 356
Hippolytus, 491, 492, 518, 569
Hippos, Hippus, 321, 325, 449
Historia Augusta, 557, 558, 568, 572
Holophernes, 178
Homer, 238
Honi the Circler, 520, 521, 550
horoscopes, 520
Horvat Eqed, 604
Huleh, 355
hyparchy, 186, 190, 191
Hyrcania, 99, 245
Hyrcanus I, John, 223, 234, 242–44, 273, 299–302, 329, 330, 470–72, 475, 482, 483, 485, 497, 507
Hyrcanus II, 242–45, 272, 301, 306, 307, 321–24, 332, 335, 338, 340, 341, 343, 345–48, 350, 351, 359, 387, 391, 400, 411, 417, 473
Hyrcanus Tobiad, 165, 174, 188, 189, 193, 197, 198, 217, 218, 275, 277, 278, 280. *See also* Eleazar b. Hyrcanus
Hystaspes, 59, 100, 163, 164

Icarus, 165
Idumea, Idumeans, 85, 158, 188, 287, 288, 300, 304, 306, 321, 322, 323, 325, 326, 328–33, 347, 349, 350, 355, 364, 367, 386, 411, 451, 457, 458. *See also* Edom(ites)
Illyrian, 337
Illyricum, 339
imperator, 335
imperium, 354
Inarus, 65, 131
India, 167, 204, 207, 208
Ionia(n), 126, 139, 162, 205, 358, 406
Ipsus, Ipsos, 3, 147, 210
Ir Nahash, 578
Iran, 16, 27, 56, 100, 212, 509
Iranian, 34, 56, 100–102, 219
Iraq el-Emir. *See* Araq el-Emir
Isaiah, 46–49, 93, 103, 104, 107–9, 111, 119, 129, 145, 199, 266
Ishmael, 387–89, 437, 592, 593
Isidorus, 400, 401
Isis, 159, 371, 397, 398, 533, 534
Issus, 206, 207, 212
Isthmian, 445
Italy, Italian, 20, 23, 24, 271, 339, 344, 348, 349, 384, 385, 386, 431, 453, 457
Iturea, Itureans, 302, 331, 332, 343, 360, 411, 425
Iyyar, 576
Izates, 439, 535

Jaddua, 41, 62, 70, 71, 113, 114
Jaddus, 181
Jaffa, 73, 84, 202, 242, 568
Jairus, 448
James, brother of Jesus, 392, 443, 473, 485, 545
James, brother of John, 433
James, son of Judas the Galilean, 439
Jamnia. *See* Yavneh, Jamnia
Janneus, Alexander, 234, 240, 242–44, 273, 302–4, 306, 325, 332, 365, 470–72, 482, 483, 485, 497
Janus, 353
Japha, 455
Jason, high priest, 170, 227, 250, 251, 253, 254, 256, 257, 266, 267, 274, 276, 277–84, 308, 311, 379, 466, 573, 611, 612, 613
Jason of Cyrene, 224, 228
Jeconiah, 76
Jehohanah, 318
Jehoshaphat, 105
Jeremiah, 46, 51, 219, 225
Jericho, 80, 100, 245, 293, 299, 307, 321, 324, 349, 350, 351, 355–57, 381, 386, 451, 457
Jeroboam, 46
Jerome, 225, 227, 258, 259, 559
Jeshua, 77, 113
Jesus (Joshua), brother of high priest, 62, 114
Jesus of Nazareth, xxvii, 5, 15, 221, 313, 369, 376, 384, 392, 428, 443, 467, 473, 476, 477, 485, 512, 519–22, 530, 539, 545, 549, 555
Jesus b. Damnaeus, 389
Jesus b. Gamaliel, 389
Jesus b. Phiabi, 388
Jesus b. Saphat, 455
Jesus b. Sapphas (Sapphias, 387), 451
Joannes, 240
Joazar, 388
Joel, 42, 45, 103, 104, 108
Joezer, 380
Johanan, 41, 62, 63, 70, 71, 88, 113, 114, 141, 242–44, 301, 592
John b. Ananias, 451
John the Baptist. *See* Baptist, John the
John the Essene, 451, 454, 497, 548
John of Gischala. *See* Gischala, John of
John Hyrcanus. *See* Hyrcanus I, John
Joiada, 41, 113, 114
Joiakim, 41, 113, 114
Jonah, 42, 46
Jonathan, high priest in Nehemiah, 41
Jonathan Maccabee, 233, 234, 242, 260, 261, 264, 285, 293, 294, 295, 296, 297, 497
Jonathan b. Ananus, 388, 389, 440, 441

Joppa, 295, 296, 298–300, 321, 325, 335, 349, 355, 357, 440, 449, 451, 456
Jordan, 188, 193, 197, 208, 218, 275, 293, 425, 438, 457, 509, 550, 566
Joseph, in Genesis, 63, 506
Joseph, brother of Herod, 349, 350, 359, 360
Joseph Cabi, 389
Joseph Caiaphas, 388
Joseph b. Camei, 389
Joseph b. Ellemus, 388
Joseph b. Gorion, 450
Joseph b. Simon, 451
Joseph Tobiad, 165, 174, 191, 192, 196–98, 216–18
Joshua, Old Testament, 438, 505, 506, 542
Joshua, high priest, 31, 39–41, 44, 62, 76–78, 107, 113, 127–29, 141
Josiah, 105, 310
Josippon, 182
Jotapata, 6, 8, 454, 455, 583
Jozadak, 113
Jubilees, Book of, 235, 279, 311
Judaea Capta, 383, 564
Judas the Essene, 497, 548, 550
Judas the Galilean, 423, 439, 471, 500, 501, 549
Judas Maccabeus, 180, 222, 223, 260, 261–63, 266, 269, 273, 285–93, 308, 329, 466, 467
Judas the "scribe," 361, 520, 547, 550
Judith, 178, 217, 239
Julia, 423, 426
Julias, 423, 426, 436
Julius Caesar, 8, 245, 316, 318, 320, 322, 335, 338–40, 343–45, 348, 355, 373–75, 406, 411, 430, 436, 438, 536, 557
Jupiter, 453, 461, 556, 572, 573
Justin, 67, 322, 508, 517, 518, 580
Justinian, 570, 571
Justus of Tiberias, 5, 9, 371, 372, 374, 375, 451, 452

Kandahar, 157
Kallinikos, 158
Karaite(s), 169, 486, 487
Kedron, 459
Keilah, 80
Keraunos, 211
Khanum, 162, 164, 165
Khirbet el-Kom, 158, 166, 185, 217, 230
Kislev, 288
Kitos, 567
Kittim, 231, 234
komarchs, 186

Laberius, 583
Lacedemonians, 264
Lachish, 73, 84
Lagides, 163
Lagus, 211
Lamb. See Bocchoris, Oracle of
Lamnian, 209
Lampo, 400, 401
Laodice, 213
Laodicea, 611
Lathyrus, 302
Latrun, 578
Lebanon, 302, 325, 425, 432
Leontopolis, 261, 266, 267, 281, 301, 310, 461, 540
Lepidus, 344, 348
Levi, 452, 456, 506, 586
Levites, 41, 145, 416, 417
Libya, 126, 560, 568
Livia, 382, 420, 426
Livias, 426
Livy, 240, 317, 378
Lucceius, 443
Lucian, 158
Lucilius, 460
Lucuas, Lukuas, 559, 598
Lucullus, 272
Lukas, 377
Lulianus, 568
Lupus, 559
Lusitania, 453
Lusius, 556, 559, 596
Lycia, 55, 435
Lydda, 386, 451, 457
Lydia, 122, 201
Lysanias, 241, 436
Lysias, 261, 262, 286–89, 292
Lysimachus, 209–11, 254, 256, 268, 278, 280

Macedon, 140, 141, 181, 209, 211
Macedonia, 204, 205, 207, 209–11, 213, 321
Macedonian(s), 55, 166, 207, 208, 213, 262, 317, 337, 405, 406
Machaeras, 350
Macherus, 245, 357, 457, 460
Macrobius, 363
Magas, 213
Magharians, 514
magi, 101, 124, 362
magic, 519, 520, 523
Magnesia, 59, 274
Malachi, 42, 45, 107
Malalas, John, 258
Malichus, Jewish leader, 346
Malichus I, 332, 348, 352
Malichus II, 331, 333
Mamre, 526
Manaemus the Essene, 497, 550
Manasseh, 113, 233
Manasses, 451
Mandaic, 507, 509–11
Mandean(s), 508–11, 550
Manetho, 10, 165
Mani, 507, 508
mantic, 199
Marathon, 126
Marcellinus, 317, 378
Marcellus, 424, 589
Marcion, 516
Marcius, 559
Marcus Agrippa, consul, 327, 348, 354, 357, 420
Marcus Ambivulus. *See* Ambivulus, Marcus
Marcus Julius Alexander, 436
Marduk, 123, 126, 130
Maretania, 429
Mariamme, 315, 350, 359–61
Marion, 346
Marisa, 188, 321, 329
Maritima, 356
Mark Antony. *See* Antony, Mark
Marsus, 432, 433
Marsyas, 241
martyrdom, 224, 227, 238, 395, 467, 488, 532, 553
Marxist, 18, 21, 22, 546
Masada, 8, 233, 245, 347, 349, 357, 364, 370, 372, 379, 380, 420, 448, 457, 458, 460, 492, 501, 537, 541, 578, 587, 605
Mattathias, 242, 273, 285, 351, 466
Matthias b. Ananus, 389
Matthias b. Boethus, 387
Matthias b. Theophilus, 388
Matthias the "scribe," 361, 520, 547, 550
Mauretania, 435, 600
Mausolus, 162
Mede, 122, 225, 226
Medes, 120, 122, 138
Median, 27, 122
Medism, 122
Megabyzus, 94, 120, 131
Megiddo, 73, 83, 84
Megillat Ta'anit, 380, 394, 568
Melchireša', 100
Meleager, 161
Melqart, 206, 279
Memar Marqa, 503, 506, 517
Memnon, 139, 205
Menahem, 448, 500, 501, 549
Menander, 517
Mendes, 202
Menelaus, 169, 227, 250–52, 254–57, 259, 263, 277, 278, 280–84, 287, 289, 290, 466, 612, 613
merkavah, 514, 515, 551
Mesopotamia, Mesopotamian, 7, 16, 36, 55, 56, 116, 120, 143, 159, 168, 201, 202, 211, 213, 338, 371, 511, 559, 561, 569, 587, 596, 597, 600, 613
Messalina, 435
Messiah, 111, 477, 481, 512, 519, 552, 554, 579, 580, 581, 587, 603
messiahs, 514, 552
messiahship, 579, 580

messianic, 77, 78, 79, 107, 128, 274, 309, 317, 413, 500, 501, 512, 513, 523, 549, 552, 553, 562, 563, 574, 580, 598, 599, 602, 603, 605
messianism, 143, 500, 514, 527, 553
Michmash, 294
Miletus, 205
Mishnah, xxviii, 13, 14, 389, 390, 463, 467, 468, 477, 478, 479, 481, 527, 530, 543, 592, 593, 616
Mithraism, 534
Mithridates I, 159
Mithridates VI, 271, 272
Mithridates of Pergamus, 343
Mizpah, 80
Mnesimachus, 16
Moab, 85, 302, 303, 304, 332
Modein, 285, 288, 603
Moesia, 591
Molon, 214
Mordecai, 51
Mucianus, 454, 457
Murabba'at, 379, 380, 565
Murasu, 58, 116, 120
Murcus, 345
Mycale, 130
Mysia, 140
Mysian, 283
Mysians, 282, 286
mysiarch, 283
mysteries, 544, 551

Nabatea, 333, 576, 577
Nabatean(s), 85, 293, 319, 331–33, 340, 352, 357, 364
Nablus, 506
Nabonidus, 35, 57, 122, 123, 126, 127, 225, 226
Nabonidus Chronicle, 57
Nabopolassar, 122
Nag Hammadi, 515, 519
Naḥal Ḥever, 578
Nahal Michmas, 379
Nahal Mishmar, 565
Nahal Seelim, 565
Nahum, 231, 234, 303
Nanâ-Iddin, 156
Neapolis, 457
Nebuchadnezzar, 80, 93, 130, 132, 136, 166, 178, 226
Nectanebo, 139, 140
Nedebaeus, 389, 443
Negev, 73, 80, 141, 325, 329, 333, 566
Nehemiah, 24, 152, 173, 193, 245, 246, 504, 609, 610, 611
Nekhtenebef, 139
Neoplatonist, 227
Neoptolemos, 158
Nepo, Cornelius, 67
Nero, 3, 5, 8, 313, 369, 371, 378, 383, 391, 407, 429, 435, 436, 437, 439, 442–48, 453, 454, 457, 587, 588, 591
Neronias, 443
Nerva, 558, 581, 584, 591, 592
Netinim, 145
Nicanor, 286, 290–92
Nicaso, 113
Nicator, 250
Nicolaus of Damascus, 9, 228, 229, 301, 314–17, 323, 324, 330, 351, 359–61, 363, 366–68, 370, 468, 472
Niger the Perean, 451, 454
Nikeratos, 185
Nile, 126, 202
Nippur, 59, 126
Nisan, 265, 328
Nisibus, 596
Noadiah, 133
Noah, 180
nomarch, 189, 190
Norbanus, 327

Obadiah, 85
Obodas I, 303, 331, 332
Obodas II, 331–33, 358
Ochus, 138, 140
Octavia, 348, 445
Octavian, 325, 326, 335, 338, 343, 344, 347–49, 351–53, 355, 614
Olivet, 459
Olympias, 209, 257
Olympios, 575
Olympius, 249, 250, 258, 259
Oniad, 198, 247, 290, 418
Oniads, 196
Onias I, 113, 114, 260, 264
Onias II, 191, 196–98, 217
Onias III, 169, 198, 227, 247, 251, 254, 257, 266, 277, 278, 280, 310, 611
Onias IV, 175, 266, 267, 281, 301, 303, 310, 343, 461. *See also* Honi the Circler
Ophla, 459
Opis, 123
oracles, 43, 44, 77, 78, 110, 164, 207, 235, 310, 508, 523, 540, 562, 563
Origen, 10
Orontes, 140
Orosius, 99, 398, 560, 569, 597
Osiris, 46
ossuaries, 152, 380, 525, 526, 531
Oxus, 164

Pacorus, 347, 595
Pakistan, 207
Pallas, 435, 442
Palmyra, 600
Paneas, 325, 355, 425
Pannonia, 591
papponymy, 88, 113, 114
Pappus, 568
Parthamasiris, 595
Parthia, 321, 327, 335, 341, 348, 353, 426, 429, 444
Parthian(s), 121, 299, 300, 332, 338, 339, 341, 344, 347, 348, 351, 371, 426, 428, 435, 445, 595–97, 599, 600
Parysatis, 138
Passover, 54, 55, 90, 91, 138, 328, 362, 366, 423, 427, 440, 459, 507, 529, 538, 539, 577
Patmos, 100, 163
Paul, 5, 333, 377, 441, 442, 485, 543
Peitholaus, 341, 343
Pella, 321, 386, 560
Peloponnesian, 65, 138
Pelusium, 124, 340, 600
Pentateuch, 29, 95, 98, 136, 145, 179, 200, 216, 217, 236, 373, 416, 486, 503, 506, 528, 529, 542
Pentecost, 347, 366, 486, 487, 529, 549
Perdiccas, 209
Perea, 367, 386, 426, 436, 438, 451, 454
Perean(s), 438, 451, 456
Pergamum, 161, 162, 212, 214, 271
Persepolis, 53, 55, 56, 58, 124, 130, 162, 207
Persia, 21, 22, 56, 57, 101, 126, 131, 140, 141, 164, 205
Persian(s), xxiii, xxv, xxvi, xxviii, 2, 9, 18, 20, 21–24, ch. 2 passim, 173, 174, 178, 188, 191–93, 199, 204–9, 212, 216, 218, 219, 242, 267, 307, 308, 309, 321, 324, 329, 331, 386, 410, 419, 498, 596, 597, 607, 609, 610, 612
pesharim, 231, 543
Petra, 306, 333, 347, 600
Petronius, 402–5, 432, 445
Phanasus, 389
Phanni, 389
pharaoh, 97, 124, 190
pharaohs, 166
Pharathon, 293
Pharisees, 5, 14, 15, 112, 154, 178, 233, 242, 244, 301, 302, 304–6, 309, 361, 375, 423, 433, 463–86, 488–92, 497, 500, 502, 524, 528, 530, 541, 542, 546–48, 551, 567, 586, 587, 594–95, 615–16
Pharnabazus, 138, 139
Pharsalus, 340
Phasael, 345–48, 355–56
Phasaelis, 336, 357
Pheroras, 361, 471
Phiabi, 387–89
Philadelphus, 186, 212
Philetaerus, 161
philhellene, 302
Philip II of Macedonia, 140, 141, 205

Philip III, 209
Philip, Syrian *epistatēs*, 282–84, 286
Philip, general of Antiochus IV, 288
Philip the tetrarch, 361, 367, 382, 386, 419, 423, 425–27, 431, 434, 436
Philippi, 344, 355, 423, 425, 443, 460
Philippica, 67
Philistia, 144, 160, 295, 296
Philistines, 504
Philo, xxviii, 3, 151, 160, 161, 170, 200, 274, 372–74, 393, 395–97, 399–406, 408–9, 422, 429, 431, 438, 492–96, 498, 499, 516, 531, 536, 542, 544, 548, 551
Philometor, 295, 563
Philopator, 275
Phineas, 285
Phoenicia, 73, 84, 99, 140, 158, 160, 161, 186, 187, 190, 202, 206, 274, 286, 351
Phoenician(s), 70, 73, 84, 99, 149, 160, 161, 182, 190, 206, 249, 259, 264, 332
Photius, 437
Phrygia, 140, 201, 209
Pilate, 370, 394–96, 412, 421, 422–25
Pistus, 451
Pius, 570, 571, 577
Placidus, 454
Plato, 238
Platonism, 373, 517
Platonist, 227, 372, 544
Pliny, 386, 492, 494, 558
Plutarch, 67, 157, 183, 184, 239, 379, 531
politeuma, 405, 407
Pollio, 326, 400
Pollion, 471
Polybius, 184, 239, 248, 294, 317
Polyhistor, 236
Polyperchon, 209
Pompeii, 590
Pompeius, 67, 239, 348
Pompey, xxiii, 272, 306, 307, 316, 320, 321, 324, 327, 332, 335, 338–41, 343, 345, 348, 350, 387, 397, 438, 575, 600, 602
Pontius, 422, 423
Pontus, 212, 271, 272, 306, 357, 421, 558
Poppea, 5, 437, 445
Porcius, 442
Porphyry, 184, 227, 258
Praetorian, 421, 429, 445, 453, 589, 591
prefect(s), 386, 400, 407, 421, 439, 445, 589, 591
Primus, Antonius, 453
Priscilla, 398
procurator, 343, 373, 384, 438, 583
prophet(s), 4, 30, 42, 46, 47, 79, 96, 104, 105, 128, 129, 133, 144, 217, 379, 380, 438, 441, 486, 508, 512, 519, 520, 522, 542, 544, 550
prophetess, 133
proselytes, 151, 534–36, 584
proselytizing, 398, 423, 534
Pseudo-Callisthenes, 182, 183
Pseudo-Clementines, 518
pseudo-Skylax, 84
Ptolemais, Acco, Akko, 158, 202, 295, 297, 302, 306, 402, 404, 406, 449, 454, 455, 598
Ptolemy I, 71, 72, 174, 183, 185, 192, 204, 209–12, 215, 217, 399, 405
Ptolemy II Philadelphus, 72, 172, 179, 185, 186, 193, 200, 212, 213, 217
Ptolemy III, 196, 197, 213, 217
Ptolemy IV Euergetes, 177, 190, 200, 214, 236
Ptolemy V Epiphanes, 196, 214, 217
Ptolemy VI Philometor, 237, 276, 277, 283, 295, 563
Ptolemy VII, 178, 282, 563
Ptolemy VIII Euergetes, 176, 563
Ptolemy IX Lathyrus, 302
Ptolemy XII, 340
Ptolemy XIII, 340
Ptolemy XIV, 348
Ptolemy, son of Dorymenes, 286
Ptolemy, son-in-law of Simon Maccabee, 299
Ptolemy the Iturean, 343
Punic, 184, 271, 274, 317, 339
Pythagorean, 219

Qedar, 84, 85
Qedarites, 85
Qohelet, 152, 153, 175, 176, 216, 220, 609
Quadratus, 440
Quietus, 559, 568, 569, 596, 599
Quintus Curtius, 55, 183, 504
Quirinius, 370, 378, 383–85, 388, 423
Qumran, xxvi, 3, 12, 100, 102, 150, 153, 180, 201, 229–35, 266, 267, 294, 303, 307, 309, 379, 486, 491, 492, 494–99, 508, 520, 522, 542, 544, 548, 587, 615
Qumranites, 151

Rabel I, 331
Rabel II, 331, 333
Ramath-Rahel, 80
Raphia, 177, 178, 190, 212, 214, 291, 303, 321
recircumcision, 571–74
resurrection, 102, 219, 485, 486, 552
Rhodes, 213, 352
Rhoxane, 209
Rubicon, 339
Rufus, 423, 559, 580
Ruth, 46, 51, 52, 534

Sabbath, 211, 235, 307, 310, 327, 328, 406, 456, 466, 477, 486, 493, 495, 508, 529, 541, 571, 605
sabbatical year, 327, 404
Sabina Augusta, 572
Sabinus, 366, 367
Sadducees, 5, 112, 154, 233, 301, 433, 463, 464, 469, 470, 473, 475, 476, 479, 484–87, 489, 546, 548, 549, 586, 587, 615
Salamis, 130, 561
Salome, Alexandra. *See* Alexandra Salome
Salome, daughter of Herodias, 426–28
Salome, sister of Herod, 358, 360, 364, 366, 367
Samaias, 471
Samaria, 53, 54, 72, 73, 81, 83, 84, 113, 122, 129, 130, 132, 133, 135, 138, 188, 207, 208, 211, 217, 241, 243, 244, 296, 300, 301, 304, 321, 325, 326, 345, 349, 350, 355, 357, 367, 386, 432, 504
Samaritan, 69, 73, 84, 88, 112, 174, 188, 189, 257, 259, 300, 310, 424, 440, 486, 502–7, 517, 518
Samaritans, 44, 96, 107, 111, 208, 212, 235, 258, 301, 325, 326, 368, 423, 424, 440, 441, 455, 486, 487, 502–4, 506, 541, 542
Samosata, 350
Samuel, 49, 50, 51, 103, 147, 148, 156, 163, 389, 552
Sanchuniathon, 161
Sanhedrin, 74, 191, 281, 325, 337, 345, 365, 375, 385–87, 389–95, 417–19, 443, 447, 471, 473, 482, 483, 485, 487, 488, 545, 546, 567, 607, 610, 613, 614
Sapphas, 451
Sapphia, 387
Sarah, 177
Sardinia, 348, 398
Sardis, 16, 122, 214, 406, 407
Sassanian, 96, 102
Satan, 102, 220, 517

satrap, 72, 82, 94, 123, 130, 131, 138–40, 162, 207, 347
satrapies, 84, 115, 116, 124, 125, 191, 214
satraps, 83, 116, 126, 139, 140, 207
satrapy, 81, 83–85, 126, 136, 139, 207
Saturninus, 358
Saul, 154
Scaurus, 234, 306, 332, 338, 340
Scipio, 214
Scopus, 380, 459
Scythopolis, 321, 449
Sebaste, 357
Seder Olam Rabbah, 567, 569
Seir, 504
Sejanus, 395, 396, 421–23, 429
Seleucia, 213
Seleucia-on-the-Tigris, 159, 596
Seleucus I, 209–12, 249, 250
Seleucus II, 213–14
Seleucus III, 214
Seleucus IV Philopator, 196, 198, 270, 275, 276, 278, 298, 611
semi-proselyte, 535
Senaah, 80
Sepphoris, 6, 321, 349, 367, 423, 426, 451, 454
Septuagint, 200, 201
Seron, 286, 446
Seth, 388
Severus, 460, 557
Sextus Caesar, 344, 345
Sextus Pompeius, 348
Shalshalah, 505
Shammai, 478, 479, 481, 483, 484, 547, 594
Shammaite, 478
Sharon, 357
Shechem, 70, 208, 245, 257, 300, 457, 504, 506
Shelomith, 68, 69
Shemaiah, Shemayah, 133
Shemihazah, 180
Shenazzar, 76
Shephelah, 73, 84, 121, 141, 295, 601, 604
Sheshbazzar, 30–32, 39, 75–77, 81, 83, 95, 96, 127, 128
Shiloh, 2, 506
Shiqmona, 84
Shir ha-Shirim Rabbah, 52
Sibyl, 507, 562
Sibyllina, 507, 562
Sibylline, 164, 235, 310, 508, 540, 562, 563
Sicarii, 441–43, 448, 458, 460, 461, 499–501, 513, 549
Sicarius, 448
Sicily, 348
Siculus, 66, 173, 183, 216, 239
Sidetes, 299
Sidon, 73, 84, 140, 335, 434, 449
Sidonian, 100, 142
Silva, 460
Simon I, high priest, 113
Simon II, 191, 196, 198, 218
Simon b. Boethus, 388
Simon b. Camithus, 388
Simon b. Cantheras, 388, 389
Simon the Essene, 497, 550
Simon b. Gamaliel, 452, 458, 472–76, 478, 482, 483, 547
Simon b. Gioras, 458–60, 500
Simon, brother of Menelaus 278
Simon Maccabee, 229, 233, 234, 242, 246, 260, 261, 269, 275, 285, 294, 296–300
Simon Magus, 514, 517, 518
Simon Tobiad, 254
Simon, son of Judas the Galilean, 439
Sinai, 235
Sippor, 73
Sira, Joshua b., 25, 46, 145, 175, 176, 191, 196, 217–20, 239, 275, 379, 380, 488, 504, 608
Siwa, 207
Sobbathos, 185
Soemus, 360
Solinus, 99
Solomon, 52, 304, 311, 316, 325, 338, 412, 520, 551, 557, 614
Solomon, Testament of, 520
Solon, 119
Sossius, 350
Soter, 270
Spain, 339, 340, 353, 354, 428, 445, 600
Sparta, 65, 139, 205, 223, 260, 264, 297, 298
Spartans, 138, 139, 174, 260, 261, 263, 264, 297
Spitamenes, 207
Stephen, 395, 540
Strabo, 9, 228, 239, 302, 315, 317, 328, 330, 331
Strato, 202, 321, 325, 355, 357
Suetonius, 318, 378, 379, 398, 399, 423, 441, 558
Sukkot, 383, 487, 538
Sullo, 596
Sulpicius, 383
Susa, 52, 60
Suweinit, 379
Syene, 54
Syllaeus, 333, 358, 359
synagogue, xxvii, 310, 364, 396, 398, 400, 410, 432, 446, 520, 526, 529, 531, 534, 536, 537, 539, 541, 542, 546, 568, 598, 608
Syncellus, 99
Syria, 16, 17, 139, 150, 156, 158, 160, 172, 186, 187, 190, 197, 202–4, 207–8, 210–11, 213, 215, 221, 270–72, 274, 276, 286, 306, 308, 320, 332, 334, 341, 344, 346–48, 353, 358, 361, 384–86, 402, 408, 414, 421, 424, 431, 432, 445, 449, 457, 557, 589, 600
Syrians, 248, 254, 259, 287–89, 291, 293, 297, 300, 325, 345, 442

Tachos, 139, 140
Tacitus, 240, 248, 317, 318, 378, 385, 386, 398, 414, 421, 422, 423, 437, 591
Talmud, 13, 15, 182, 521, 569
Talmuds, 13, 478
Tarfon, 592
Taricheae, 341, 343, 455
Tarsus, 206
Tattenai, 39, 77, 81, 82, 126, 127
Taurus, 274
Tekoa(h), 80, 293, 294, 578
Tell el-Maskhuta, 84
Tell el-Yehudieh, 266
Tennes, 99, 140, 142
Tephon, 293
tetrarchs, 347, 382, 423, 425
tetrarchy, 382, 419, 431, 436
Teucheira, 597
Thamna, 386, 451, 454, 457
Thebes, 205
theocracy, 1, 73–75, 96, 122, 136, 154, 192, 216, 267, 306, 321, 338, 385, 607, 613
Theodotus, 541
Theophilus, 318, 388, 389
Theophrastus, 173
Therapeutae, 496, 499, 548
Thessaly, 205
Theudas, 438, 550
Tholomeus, 438
Thrace, 205, 209, 210, 435
Thucydides, 19, 34, 64–66, 184, 278, 317
Tiberias, 5, 6, 9, 157, 370, 371, 374, 382, 402, 423, 426, 431, 432, 436, 451, 452, 455, 456
Tiberius, 369, 371, 373, 378, 382, 395–98, 407, 408, 414, 420–22, 424–29, 431, 434, 555
Tiberius Alexander, 438–40, 449, 453, 457, 536, 589
Tiburtinus, 384, 386, 422
Tiglath-pileser III, 298
Tigranes, 271, 272, 306

Tigris, 207, 596, 597
Timagenes, 331
Timnath, 293
Timothy, 533
Tineius, 580
Tishri, 265, 328, 529, 576
Tissaphernes, 138, 139
tithes, 416, 417, 612
Titulus, 384, 422
Titus, 1, 6–8, 143, 333, 382, 383, 393, 420, 435, 436, 439, 454–57, 459, 460, 558, 564, 569, 588–90
Tobiads, 133, 151, 165, 174, 175, 188, 189, 191–93, 196–98, 204, 216, 217, 228, 247, 250, 252, 254, 275, 277, 278, 288, 609, 610
Tobiah, 88, 132–35, 188, 193
Tobias, 165, 174, 177, 188, 189, 193, 196–98, 215, 217
Tobit, 176, 217, 226, 538
Tolidah, 502, 505
Tosefta, 13, 572, 593
Toubias, 193
Trachonitis, 325, 336, 355, 358, 367, 386, 425, 436
Traianus Quintus, 569
Trajan, 240, 333, 401, 556, 558, 559, 563, 566–69, 571, 587, 591, 592, 595–97, 599, 600
Trajana, Roman legion, 577
Transjordan, 72, 84, 85, 196–98, 288, 304, 321, 325, 334
Tripolis, 212
Trito-Isaiah, 47, 48, 103, 109, 110, 129, 145
Trito-Zechariah, 44, 108, 110
triumvir(s), 339, 341, 348
triumvirate, 339, 344, 348
Trogus, 67, 239
Tryphon, 293, 296–99
Tyre, 182, 206, 208, 279, 284, 296, 320, 346, 347, 434, 449
Tyrian, 84, 319, 320, 383

Udjahorresnet, 60, 61, 94, 95, 97, 124
Uruk, 156, 159, 160
Ushan, 390

Valentinius, 519
Valerius Gratus, 388, 397, 423
Varus, 329, 367, 436
Vashti, 52
Ventidius, 349, 440
Vespasian, 6–8, 382, 383, 387, 420, 439, 451, 453–57, 461, 500, 558, 564, 569, 581, 583, 585, 587–92, 595
Vesuvius, 558
Vitellius, 388, 424–28, 453, 457, 561, 590

Wadi Daliyeh. *See* Daliyeh
wavesheaf, 486

Xandikos, 193
Xanthicus, Xanthikos, 263, 287
Xanthos, 32, 34, 54, 97
Xenophon, 65, 66, 139
Xerxes, 32, 56, 61, 64, 93, 94, 128–30, 138, 207

Yahweh, 32, 42, 45, 72, 105–7, 134, 135, 254, 507, 516, 517, 607
Yahwism, 46, 47, 143, 170, 250, 504
Yahwist, 134, 135
Yahwistic, 134, 284, 506
Yahwists, 135
Yavnean, 484, 530, 567, 593, 595
Yavneans, 482
Yavneh, Jamnia, 14, 84, 208, 295, 321, 402–5, 457, 463, 464, 467, 468, 482, 484, 517, 530, 547, 564, 592, 593, 594, 616
Yehud, 68, 70–72, 79, 116
Yehuda b. Menasheh, 601
Yohanan b. Zakkai, 14, 478, 482, 592, 593
Yom Kippur, 328

Zabinas, 300
Zadok, 471, 487
Zadok the Pharisee, 423, 500
Zadokite, 290, 484, 491
Zamaris, 334
Zanoah, 80
Zealots, 446, 456, 457–59, 499, 501, 511, 513, 549
Zebedee, 433
Zechariah, 30, 31, 42–45, 74, 77–79, 82, 103, 104, 108–10, 119, 127–29, 145, 199
Zenon, 165, 171, 172, 188, 189, 193, 196, 202–4, 215, 218
Zerubbabel, 30–32, 38, 39, 41, 44, 69, 74–79, 81–83, 93–96, 98, 107, 126–29, 136
Zeus, 159, 249, 250, 254, 257–59, 504, 572, 575
Zeuxis, 201
Zipporah, 238
Zoilus, 302
Zonaras, 240
Zoroaster, 101, 102
Zoroastrian, 98, 100–102, 220
Zoroastrianism, 27, 29, 100, 102
Zoroastrians, 101

INDEX OF MODERN AUTHORS

Abel, F.-M., 222, 224, 225
Aberbach, M., 437
Ackroyd, P. R., xxviii, 28, 36, 42, 50, 51, 77, 78, 79, 83, 91, 94, 117, 137, 143
Adler, E. N., 502, 505
Aharoni, Y., 79, 80
Ahlström, G. W., 42
Albrektson, B., 107, 110
Albright, W. F., 39, 114, 116
Aleksandrov, G. S., 579, 580
Alexander, P. S., 514
Allison, D. C., 362, 376, 467
Allrick, H. L., 36
Alon, G., 459, 460
Alt, A., 79
Altheim, F., 276
Andrewes, A., 66
Applebaum, S., 241, 334, 336, 337, 355, 357, 405, 406, 413, 416, 499, 511–13, 555, 567, 568, 574, 581, 583, 596–98, 601
Arav, R., 1, 2, 188, 189, 245
Archer, G. L., 227
Archer, L. J., 16, 19
Atkinson, K. T. M., 16, 124
Attridge, H. W., 4, 13
Aune, D. E., 519–22, 526, 527
Austen, M. M., 3
Avery-Peck, A. J., 468
Avi-Yonah, M., 1, 2, 79–81, 83, 84, 147, 148, 158, 159, 313, 318, 319, 324, 381, 445, 566, 567
Avigad, N., 1, 2, 68, 69, 245, 246
Aymard, A., 276

Bagatti, B., 380
Bagnall, R. S., 3, 185, 186, 189–91
Bailey, H. H., 100, 101
Balcer, J. M., 64
Balsdon, J.P.V.D., 420, 428
Bammel, E., 392
Bar-Adon, P., 229
Bar-Kochva, B., 189, 190, 221–24, 227, 246, 252, 255, 259, 262, 263, 284–87, 288, 290–93, 446, 450
Barag, D., 70, 71, 99, 100, 244, 318, 564
Barber, G. L., 66
Barker, M., 77
Barnes, T. D., 326, 557, 559, 596–99
Barnett, P. W., 519
Barr, J., 100–102, 107, 110, 160, 161
Barrett, A. A., 428, 430
Bartlett, J. R., 84, 85
Batten, L. W., 27, 28, 34
Bauer, T., 56
Bauer, W., 526
Baumgarten, A. I., 467, 475, 483, 491, 492
Beall, T. S., 491
Beckwith, R., 537, 542
Ben-Arieh, S., 381
Ben-David, A., 16, 18
Ben-Dor, N., 355
Bengtson, H., 189, 190
Benoit, P., 379, 380, 565
Berg, S. B., 51, 52
Berger, P.-R., 57, 58, 75, 76
Berman, D., 519, 522
Bernard, P., 164, 165
Bernegger, P. M., 326, 328
Betz, H. D., 519, 522
Beyse, K. M., 77, 78
Bickerman, E. J., 34, 35, 59, 124, 125, 148, 150, 171, 172, 201, 202, 221, 223, 246, 247, 249, 250–55, 258, 259, 261, 263–67, 283, 284, 326, 327, 391, 393, 501, 502, 537
Bigwood, J. M., 65–67
Bilde, P., 4, 9, 13, 401, 403–5, 412
Biran, A., 187
Bivar, A. D. H., 70
Black, M., 180, 500
Blenkinsopp, J., 27, 28, 32, 34, 35, 37–43, 48, 50, 60, 73, 75, 78, 89, 94, 95–97, 103, 104, 112, 114, 117, 118, 537
Blinzler, J., 391, 392
Boer, W. den, 569
Boffo, L., 59
Bogaert, P., 561, 562
Bokser, B. M., 519, 521
Borg, M., 499, 500
Borger, R., 77
Bousset, W., 463, 464
Bowersock, G. W., 328, 333, 425, 427, 570, 572
Bowker, J., 13
Bowman, J., 502, 503, 505
Bowman, R. A., 53, 55
Box, G. H., 372
Boyce, M., 29, 100–102, 123, 130
Brandstein, W., 59
Braun, R., 175, 176
Braun, R. L., 49, 50, 51, 153
Braund, D. C., 3, 320, 322, 324, 334, 337, 391, 392
Braverman, J., 225
Brawley, R. L., 377
Breitenbach, W., 66
Brenner, A., 51, 52
Bresciani, E., 53, 55
Briant, P., 16, 18, 21, 22
Bright, J., 88, 272, 273, 419, 538
Bringmann, K., 221, 222, 247, 249, 250, 251, 253, 255, 257, 258, 259, 262–65, 267, 280, 283, 284
Briscoe, J., 240
Brock, S. P., 200, 201
Brooke, G. J., 229, 231
Broshi, M., 16, 19, 25, 334, 336
Broughton, T. R. S., 16, 74, 75
Brown, R. E., 376, 377, 526, 530, 542, 545, 546
Brown, T. S., 64, 124
Brownlee, W. H., 229, 233, 491

Bruce, I. A. F., 581, 584
Bruggen, J. van, 326, 328
Brunt, P. A., 413, 416, 587
Büchler, A., 181, 192
Bultmann, R., 425, 428, 516
Bunge, J. G., 225, 264, 276
Burchard, C., 491, 492
Burgmann, H., 293, 294
Burrows, M., 42, 46
Burstein, S. M., 3, 60, 147, 159, 162
Byatt, A., 16, 19, 24

Callaway, P. R., 229
Cameron, G. G., 57, 58, 124, 125
Cameron, R., 507
Campbell, E. F., 51
Cardascia, G., 59
Cardauns, B., 263
Cargill, J., 122, 123
Carlebach, A., 581
Carlo, Z., 16, 22
Carratelli. *See* Pugliese Carratelli, G.
Carroll, R. P., 108–10
Cary, M., 171, 221, 222, 313, 314, 369, 370, 555
Catchpole, D. R., 391, 393
Cavallin, H.C.C., 552, 553
Cazelles, H., 50, 54, 94
Charles, R. H., 3, 180, 225, 561
Charlesworth, J. H., xxviii, 3, 199, 519
Chiat, M.J.S., 537, 541
Childs, B. S., 29
Clements, R. E., 42, 46
Clines, D.J.A., xxviii, 27–29, 32, 36–41, 50–52, 89, 90, 137
Cody, A., 142, 145
Coggins, R. J., 42, 502–4, 507
Cohen, G. M., 201, 202
Cohen, S.J.D., 4, 7, 9, 10, 11, 181, 201, 202, 227, 228, 369, 370, 372, 452, 463–65, 467, 479, 482, 523, 524, 533–35
Colella, P., 68
Colledge, M., 162
Collins, J. J., 100, 102, 163, 164, 198, 199, 225–27, 229, 236, 239, 465–67, 507, 508, 562, 563. *See also* Yarbro Collins, A.
Coogan, M. D., 59
Cook, J. M., 27, 29, 126
Cook, M. J., 467, 468, 476, 477, 488–90
Cousin, G., 59
Cowley, A., 27, 33, 54, 62, 90, 97, 135, 138, 184
Coxon, P. W., 507, 510
Craven, T., 178
Crawford, M. H., 221, 222, 313, 314
Crenshaw, J., 175, 176, 218, 220
Cross, F. M., 61, 68, 88, 112–14, 187, 229, 230, 233, 282
Crown, A. D., 502

Dalman, G., 16, 18
Dandamaev, M. A., 16, 18, 22, 27, 29, 55, 115, 116, 123, 124, 125, 130
Daniel, C., 501
Daniel, J. L., 409
Daube, D., 484, 485, 486, 487
Davies, J. K., 16, 18, 19, 22, 202, 270
Davies, P. R., xxviii, 225, 229–34, 307, 309, 311, 465–67, 491, 494, 496–98, 537, 542
Davies, P. S., 396, 397
Davies, W. D., 307, 362, 376
Davis, N., 70, 72
Day, P. L., 100
Deferrari, R. J., 560
Delavault, B., 68
Delcor, M., 266, 267
Demsky, A., 79, 80
Dentzer, J. M., 188, 189
Dequeker, L., 245, 246
Derow, P., 3, 185, 186
Deschamps, G., 59
Deselaers, P., 176
Dessau, H., 383
Dewey, A. J., 507
Diakonov, I. M., 16, 18
Diamond, F. H., 173
DiLella, A. A., 176, 225
Dillon, J., 372, 373
Dimant, D., 229, 230, 491, 498
Dion, P. E., 75, 76
Dittenberger, W., 435, 436
Doran, R., 224, 234–36, 277, 279
Doty, L. T., 156
Douglas, M., 537, 540
Downey, G., 420
Drews, R., 64–67
Driver, G. R., 53, 55
Dubberstein, W. H., 124
Due, B., 65
Dumbrell, W. J., 84, 85
Dunn, S. P., 16
Dyson, S. L., 511

Eddy, S. K., 163, 164
Edwards, O., 326, 328
Efron, J., 221
Eilers, W., 57
Eissfeldt, O., 29
Ellenson, D., 467, 488, 489
Emerton, J. A., 88, 90, 91
Endres, J. C., 234
Eph'al, I., 84, 85
Epp, E. J., 375, 376
Eskenazi, T. C., 27, 28, 53

Fehling, D., 64
Feldman, L. H., 4, 8, 12, 13, 150, 151, 152, 264, 362, 363, 409, 410, 533, 535, 536
Filmer, W. E., 326–28
Finkelstein, L., 579
Finley, M. I., 16–19, 22, 114, 116
Fischel, H. A., 154, 155
Fischer, T., 221, 226, 240, 241, 242, 260–62
Fischer, U., 552
Fitzmyer, J. A., 229, 230, 376, 379, 380, 383, 384, 425, 428, 555, 565, 605
Flesher, P.V.M., 537, 541
Flusser, D., 100, 163, 164, 181, 318
Fohrer, G., 29, 30, 52
Follet, S., 575
Forrer, E., 83
Forster, G., 537, 541
Fossum, J. E., 514, 517, 518
Fox, M., 51
France, R. T., 362
Frank, F., 16, 18
Frerichs, E. S., 409, 524, 552
Freyne, S., 16, 24, 519, 521, 522
Frye, R. N., 27, 29, 100, 102, 116
Fuks, A., 153, 565, 596
Fuks, G., 396, 397
Funk, R. W., 245

Gager, J. G., 409, 410, 534, 536
Galili, E., 212, 214
Galling, K., 27, 28, 32, 35, 38, 83, 84, 96
Garbini, G., 156, 157
Garnsey, P., 16, 18, 20, 23, 24, 369, 370
Garzetti, A., 369, 370, 555
Gauger, J.-D., 173, 201, 202, 260, 261
Gelston, A., 75, 76
Gelzer, H., 375
Geraty, L. T., 185
Gereboff, J., 592
Gerhardsson, B., 519, 521
Gershenzon, R., 514
Gese, H., 142, 145
Geva, H., 355, 566
Gichon, M., 355, 357, 446, 601, 604
Gilboa, A., 344
Glasson, T. F., 100, 218
Glazier-McDonald, B., 42, 45
Golan, D., 570, 574
Goldingay, J., 225
Goldschmidt-Lehmann, R. P., 355
Goldstein, J. A., 174, 175, 221–25, 228, 235, 241, 248, 251–53, 255, 259, 261, 264, 278, 293, 294, 296, 297
Goldwasser, O., 68

Gomme, A. W., 64
Goodblatt, D., 467, 474, 480, 592, 593, 601
Goodenough, E. R., 372, 374, 524, 525, 531
Goodhart, H. L., 372
Goodman, M., xxviii, 147, 148, 157, 369, 370, 405, 411, 413, 416–18, 463, 491, 524, 542, 543, 547, 548, 552, 566, 567, 581, 584
Grabbe, L. L., 1, 4, 13, 28, 32, 34, 61–63, 94, 97, 108, 110, 112, 114, 122, 123, 181, 183, 198–200, 218–20, 225, 226, 265, 326, 327, 372, 491, 498, 502, 504, 526, 527, 537, 541, 542, 561, 562
Graf, D. F., 122
Grayson, A. K., 57
Green, W. S., 519, 553, 592
Greenfield, J. C., 54, 55, 58
Grelot, P., 54, 55
Gressmann, H., 192, 463, 464
Griffin, M. T., 444
Griffith, G. T., 147, 148, 164
Griffiths, J. G., 158
Grimal, P., 171, 221, 222
Groag, E., 435
Gruber, M. I., 467, 480
Gruen, E. S., 221, 222, 263
Gruenwald, I., 514–16
Guelich, R. A., 376
Gunneweg, A.H.J., 27, 28, 32, 34, 37–40, 97, 142, 145
Guterman, S. L., 409

Habicht, C., 224, 225, 248, 260, 262
Hachlili, R., 381
Hadas, M., 179
Haenchen, E., 377, 397, 399
Hall, R. G., 277
Hallock, R. T., 58
Halpern, B., 77, 78
Halpern-Zylberstein, M. C., 188
Hamel, G., 16, 18, 19, 22, 24, 25, 414, 416
Hann, R. R., 316
Hansen, E. V., 161
Hansen, O., 59
Hanson, J. S., 512, 519
Hanson, P. D., 48, 104, 107–10, 198, 219
Hanson, R. S., 242
Har-El, M., 446
Harmatta, J., 184, 185
Harper, C. M., 16, 172
Harrelson, W., 77
Harrington, D. J., 221, 222, 379, 380, 488, 565
Hartman, L. F., 225
Hasel, G. F., 142, 143
Hata, G., 4, 13
Hausmann, J., 142, 143
Hay, D. M., 372, 374
Hayes, J. H., xxvi
Hayward, R., 266
Heichelheim, F. M., 17, 334, 335
Heinemann, I., 250, 251
Hellholm, D., 198
Helm, R., 99, 559, 575, 576
Hemer, C. J., 377
Hengel, M., 147–55, 157, 158, 160, 161, 169, 171, 190, 221, 222, 250–52, 257, 267, 377, 499, 500, 512, 596, 599
Henricks, A., 507, 508
Henry, K. H., 17, 24
Hensley, L. V., 32, 35
Henten, J. W. van, 525, 526
Hilgert, E., 372, 374
Hill, A. E., 42
Hill, D., 519
Hinnells, J., 100
Hirsch, S. W., 65, 66
Hoehner, H. W., 425, 428
Holbert, J. C., 42, 46
Holladay, C. R., 236, 374, 375, 519, 522
Hölscher, G., 387
Hopkins, K., 17, 18
Horgan, M. P., 230, 231
Hornblower, S., 28, 29, 162, 171, 183
Horowitz, G., 188
Horsley, G.H.R., 187
Horsley, R. A., 17, 23, 499–501, 512–14, 519, 522, 523
Hout, M. van den, 59
Houtman, C., 95, 98
Hughes, G. R., 60
Hultgård, A., 100
Humphries, W. L., 51, 52, 225, 226
Hurvitz, A., 29
Hüttenmeister, F., 537, 541

In der Smitten, W. T., 28, 32, 36, 37, 97
Isaac, B., 1, 318, 512, 566, 567, 581, 583, 601, 602, 604
Isser, S. J., 503
Iwry, S., 51, 103

Jacobson, H., 238
Jacoby, F., 59, 60, 65, 228, 229
Jagersma, H., xxvi
Japhet, S., 31, 32, 49–51, 75, 76
Jellicoe, S., 200, 201
Jeremias, J., 267, 268, 369, 387, 488, 489
Jeselsohn, D., 70, 72, 242, 244
Johnson, J. H., 60, 163, 164
Jones, A.H.M., 320, 414
Jones, B. W., 435, 588

Kamil, M., 53, 55
Kampen, J., 465–67, 491, 497
Kanael, B., 2, 3, 70, 320–22, 575
Kanter, S., 592
Karst, J., 559
Kasher, A., 84, 85, 313, 328, 330–32, 352, 357, 399, 401, 405, 408, 409, 412, 413, 425, 427, 448, 449, 596, 598, 599
Katzoff, R., 264
Kazis, I. J., 181, 182
Kellermann, D., 142
Kellermann, U., 28, 36, 37, 38, 40, 108, 142, 145
Kennedy, D. L., 575, 577
Kent, R. G., 56, 58, 130
Keppie, L.J.F., 566
Keresztes, P., 590
Kervran, M., 56
Kindler, A., 70, 242
Kippenberg, H. G., 17, 114, 118, 119, 267, 268, 334, 336
Klijn, A.F.J., 561
Kloner, A., 318, 601, 604
Knibb, M. A., 142, 143, 180, 198, 199, 230, 235
Knight, D. A., 29, 30
Kobelski, P. J., 100, 102
Koch, K., 42, 44, 46, 48, 95, 96, 97
Koenen, L., 507
Koester, C., 230
Koester, H., 519, 522
Koffmahn, E., 379
König, F. W., 65, 158, 225
Koopmans, J. J., 54
Kraabel, A. T., 2, 319, 381, 534, 535, 536
Kraay, C. M., 70, 72
Krader, L., 17, 21
Kraeling, E. G., 54
Kraft, R. A., xxvii, 313, 319, 369, 526, 527
Krauss, S., 17, 18
Kreissig, H., 17, 18, 21, 22, 114, 117, 118, 202, 267, 268, 414
Krueger, P., 570, 571
Kuhn, H.-W., 318
Kuhnen, H.-P., 2, 188, 245, 318, 319, 329, 381, 564
Kuhrt, A., 28, 56, 57, 60, 64, 129, 130, 147, 148, 156, 159, 160, 161, 165
Kümmel, W. G., 375, 376
Kvanig, H. S., 198, 199

La Barre, W., 163, 164
Ladiray, D., 56
Ladouceur, D. J., 359, 361, 370, 372
Lambert, W. G., 198, 199
Landau, Y. H., 240, 241
Landsberger, B., 56
Laperrousaz, E. M., 74, 75, 245, 246, 381, 601, 604

INDEX OF MODERN AUTHORS

Lapp, N. L., 54, 55, 112, 188, 189
Lapp, P. W., 54, 55, 112, 188, 189
Laqueur, R., 314, 315, 323, 324
Larché, R., 188
Lease, G., 525
Lebram, J.C.H., 28, 34, 36, 97, 225
Lecoq, P., 125
Lemaire, A., 68, 79, 84, 85
Lémonon, J.-P., 391, 392, 395, 397
LeMoyne, J., 484, 486
Lenger, M.-T., 185, 186
Lesky, A. H., 64, 183, 239, 317, 378
Leszynsky, R., 484
Leuze, O., 83
Levick, B., 395, 420, 434
Levine, B. A., 230, 232
Levine, L. I., 2, 318, 319, 355, 381
Lewis, D. M., 59, 64
Lewis, N., 565
Lichtenstein, H., 379, 380, 391, 394
Lichtheim, M., 60
Lieberman, S., 154, 155
Liebesny, H., 186
Lifshitz, B., 381, 565, 566, 570, 572, 603
Lightstone, J. N., 131, 134, 463, 465, 466, 484, 487, 544
Lipinski, E., 68
Lloyd, A. B., 60, 163
Loretz, O., 153, 175, 176
Lüdemann, G., 377, 430, 514
Lührmann, D., 488
Lukonin, V. G., 16, 18, 22, 27, 29, 115, 116
Lundquist, J. M., 537
Lust, J., 75, 126, 127
Luttikhuizen, G. P., 507, 509

Maccoby, H., 463, 464
McConville, J. G., 30
McCown, C. C., 188
Macdonald, J., 503, 505, 506
McEleney, N. J., 526, 527, 534, 536
McEvenue, S. E., 79, 81, 82, 83
McKenzie, S. L., 49, 50
MacLennan, R. S., 534, 536
Macmullen, R., 512, 519, 520
McNamara, M., 225, 226
McNulty, I. B., 381
Macrae, G. W., 375
Macuch, R., 507, 509, 510
Magie, D., 320
Maier, J., xxviii
Maier, P. L., 396, 397
Mallau, H. H., 30, 32, 34
Mantel, H., 389, 390, 570, 577
Marcus, R., 181, 246, 315, 323, 327, 348, 354, 357
Margalith, O., 95
Marshall, A. J., 409
Marshall, I. H., 383, 384, 409
Mason, R., 42–45
Mason, S. N., 468, 471, 473, 474, 476
Mattill, A. J., 377
May, H. G., 42, 44
Mayer, G., 17, 19, 372, 374
Mayrhofer, M., 56, 59
Mazar, B., 192, 193, 355, 370, 372, 381
Meeks, W. A., 514, 518, 519, 522
Meiggs, R., 59
Mendels, D., 173, 307, 311
Mendelson, A., 372, 373, 374
Meshorer, Y., 2, 3, 70–72, 242–45, 318–20, 329, 381, 382, 555, 564, 580, 603
Metzger, H., 54, 55
Meyer, E., 28, 32, 34, 35, 37, 98
Meyers, C. L., 2, 42, 43, 78
Meyers, E. M., 2, 42, 43, 68, 69, 78, 319, 381, 525, 526
Meyshan, J., 381
Michel, O., 500
Mielziner, M., 13
Mildenberg, L., 70–72, 555, 564, 570, 572, 573, 575, 576, 578–81, 583, 600, 601, 603
Milik, J. T., 180, 230, 234, 379, 380
Millar, F., xxvii, 150, 152, 156, 158, 160, 161, 352, 556
Miller, J. M., xxvi
Mills, W. E., 377
Mitchell, H. G., 28, 45
Mittwoch, A., 267, 268
Moehring, H. R., 4, 10, 11, 383, 397, 398, 405, 406
Momigliano, A., 17, 18, 65, 147, 148, 150, 153, 181, 192, 201, 202, 224, 260–62, 314, 320, 322, 334, 336, 337, 434, 557
Mommsen, T., 570, 571
Montgomery, J. A., 225, 503
Moore, C. A., 51, 52, 178, 225
Moore, G. F., 463, 464
Mor, M., 601, 605
Morgenstern, J., 93
Mørkholm, O., 221, 222, 248–50, 276
Mosshammer, A. A., 559
Mowinckel, S., 28, 37, 40, 41, 96, 143
Mueller, J. R., 198
Müller, H.-P., 199
Murphy, F. J., 561, 562
Murphy, R., 51
Murphy-O'Connor, J., 230, 231, 234, 293, 294, 491, 494, 496, 497, 498
Murray, O., 173
Musti, D., 270
Musurillo, H. A., 399, 401
Myers, J. M., 561

Naveh, J., 54, 55, 68, 85, 242, 319, 507, 510
Neill, S., 375, 376
Neirynck, F., 376
Nestle, E., 258, 259
Netzer, E., 355, 356, 381
Neubauer, A., 503
Neuhaus, G. O., 222, 223
Neusner, J., xxviii, 13–16, 389, 390, 409, 463, 464, 468, 474–82, 488, 519, 521, 523, 524–27, 537, 539, 540, 541, 543, 544, 547, 552, 553, 567, 570, 573, 579, 584, 586, 592, 593, 594
Nicholson, E. W., 523, 524
Nickelsburg, G.W.E., xxvii, xxviii, 180, 235, 238, 313, 319, 369, 552
Nicols, J., 587
Nikiprowetzky, V., 499
Nolland, J., 534–36

Oden, R. A., 158, 258, 259
Ogilvie, R. M., 240
O'Leary, L., 17, 22
Olmstead, A. T., 28, 29, 77, 116, 120, 124, 126, 127, 131
Oppenheim, A. L., 56, 57, 123
Oppenheimer, A., 523, 524, 601, 602, 604
Otto, E., 60
Otto, W., 313, 315, 337

Pardee, D., 230, 233, 565
Parente, F., 177, 178
Parker, H.M.D., 575
Patai, R., 537, 539
Pauritsch, J., 46, 48
Pearson, B., 514, 515
Pearson, L., 183
Peli, P. H., 524
Pelletier, A., 179
Peremans, W., 163
Perowne, S., 570, 575
Perrot, C., xxvi
Perrot, J., 56
Petersen, D. L., 42, 77, 78
Petersen, H., 6
Petit, T., 122, 123
Pfister, F., 181, 182
Pflaum, H.-G., 566, 567
Pietersma, A., 104, 106
Plöger, O., 108, 192, 219
Plümacher, E., 377
Pohlmann, K.-F., 53
Polotsky, H. J., 565

Pope, M., 29
Porten, B., 54, 55
Porter, J. R., 88
Porton, G. G., 463, 592
Posener, G., 60
Prandi, L., 422
Pucci, M., 596, 597
Puech, E., 379, 380
Pugliese Carratelli, G., 156, 157
Pummer, R., 503, 506, 507
Purvis, J. D., 503, 506, 507

Qimron, E., 230, 234
Quispel, G., 514

Raban, A., 356
Rabello, A. M., 409
Rabin, C., 242, 244, 304
Rabinowitz, I., 85, 491, 498
Radice, R., 372, 374
Rainey, A. F., 83, 85
Rajak, T., 4, 10, 11, 147, 148, 300, 369, 370, 374, 452
Rappaport, U., 70, 71, 72, 242, 243, 329, 412, 413, 451
Ratner, B., 367
Ray, J. D., 265
Redditt, P. L., 42, 44, 45, 103, 104
Reeg, G., 537
Reggiani, C. K., 401
Reich, R., 245
Reif, S., 175
Reinhardt, K., 64
Reinhold, M., 17, 18
Reinmuth, O. W., 438, 439
Reitzenstein, R., 516
Rendtorff, R., 95, 98
Rengstorf, K. H., 4, 12, 512
Reynolds, J., 534, 536
Rhoads, D. M., 500, 545–47
Riaud, J., 499
Richardson, P., 356, 362, 364
Rigsby, K. J., 248, 250, 258, 259
Rivkin, E., 390, 467, 468, 479, 482, 488, 489
Roaf, M., 56
Roberts, J.J.M., 108, 110, 537, 538
Rofé, A., 103
Rokeah, D., 567, 568
Roll, I., 1, 566, 567, 601
Rosenthal, E. S., 319
Rostovtzeff, M., 17, 18, 74, 75, 156, 164, 171, 172, 186, 190
Roueché, C., 165
Roux, G., 405
Roux, J., 405
Rowley, H. H., 88, 91, 225, 226, 501, 502
Rudolph, K., 507–11, 514
Rudolph, W., 28, 32, 38, 40
Ruhl, F., 374
Runia, D. T., 372, 374
Ruppel, W., 405

Sachs, A. J., 265
Safrai, S., 392, 566, 567
Safrai, Z., 384
Saldarini, A. J., 14, 15, 463, 464, 466, 474, 476, 477, 479, 481–84, 486–90, 524, 592
Saley, R. J., 88, 89
Saller, R., 16, 18, 20, 23, 24, 369, 370
Sancisi-Weerdenburg, H., 28
Sanders, E. P., 199
Sanders, J. T., 176
Sandmel, S., 363, 372–74
Sarkisian, G. K., 159, 160
Sasson, J. M., 51, 52
Sauer, G., 77
Saulnier, C., xxvi
Schaeder, H. H., 32, 35, 95, 96
Schäfer, P., xxvi, 555, 570, 572–80
Schalit, A., 171, 201, 202, 221, 222, 238, 302, 313, 321, 322, 324, 334–37, 352, 362, 363, 374
Scharbert, J., 115, 117
Schein, B. E., 381
Schiffman, L. H., 230, 234, 503, 507, 552, 553
Schnabel, P., 60
Scholem, G. G., 514, 515
Schottroff, W., 115
Schreckenberg, H., 4, 13, 377
Schüller, S., 264
Schunck, E., 222, 223, 265, 266
Schürer, E., xxvi, xxvii, 173, 176–81, 200, 248, 261, 266, 269, 277, 283, 313, 315, 316, 319, 337, 369, 372, 375, 384, 386, 387, 390, 392, 414, 425, 426, 433, 496, 499, 535, 536, 553, 555, 562, 563, 567, 570, 572, 578, 597
Schwartz, D. R., 369, 370, 373, 387, 389, 398, 399, 401, 404, 408, 422, 428, 430, 432, 433, 434, 468, 471, 472, 474, 480
Schwartz, E., 66
Schwartz, S., 4, 6, 7, 221–23, 290, 369, 370, 433, 437, 448, 450, 468, 480, 584, 586
Scott, S. P., 570
Scramuzza, V. M., 434
Scullard, H. H., 221, 222, 313, 314, 369, 370, 555
Seel, O., 67
Segal, A., 2, 352
Segal, A. F., 463, 464, 514, 516, 517, 519, 520
Segal, J. B., 54
Segelberg, E., 507, 509
Sekeles, E., 319
Seligsohn, M., 502
Sellers, O. R., 70, 245
Sevenster, J. N., 409, 410
Seybold, K., 77
Shaked, S., 54, 55, 100–102
Shanks, H., 381
Shaw, B. D., 512
Shedl, C., 178
Sherk, R. K., 3
Sherwin-White, A. N., 320, 392, 558
Sherwin-White, S. M., 129, 130, 147, 148, 156, 159, 160, 161, 164, 165
Shutt, R.J.H., 228, 314
Sievers, J., 221–24, 227, 244, 261, 285, 288, 290, 298, 300, 465
Skaist, A., 185
Skeat, T. C., 265
Skehan, P. W., 176
Slomovic, E., 514
Smallwood, E. M., xxiii, xxvii, 320, 369, 373, 384, 392, 398, 399, 401, 403, 422, 441, 444, 445, 555, 566–68, 570, 572, 573, 578, 581, 590, 591, 597
Smith, J.M.P., 45
Smith, J. Z., 158, 199, 200, 526, 533, 534, 537, 539, 543
Smith, M., 79, 81–83, 93, 94, 104–7, 110, 135, 137, 155, 159, 463, 468, 474–77, 480, 488, 491, 492, 499, 500, 502, 507, 519, 520, 521, 530, 552
Smith, R. L., 42, 44, 45
Smith, S., 56
Soden, W. von, 225, 226
Soggin, J. A., 29, 30, 52
Sokoloff, M., 319
Spaer, A., 70, 71
Sparks, H., 4
Speidel, M. P., 384, 386
Spek, R. J. van der, 159, 160
Sperber, D., 242, 244
Spiegelberg, W., 60
Stadelmann, H., 176
Starr, C. G., 147, 148, 162
Steckoll, S. H., 266, 267
Ste. Croix, G.E.M. de, 17, 22
Stegemann, H., 230, 232, 294
Stein, A., 435
Stemberger, G., 13
Stern, M., 1, 2, 3, 28, 67–70, 72, 73, 79–81, 84, 100, 153, 173, 188, 228, 302, 313, 314, 326, 327, 384, 386, 441, 589
Stiehl, R., 276
Stinespring, W. F., 575
Stolper, M. W., 129, 130, 138, 139
Stone, M. E., xxvi, 199, 218, 241, 456, 541, 562, 585, 586

Strack, H. L., 13
Strange, J. F., 319, 520, 525, 526
Stronach, D., 56
Stroumsa, G.A.G., 514, 516, 517
Strugnell, J., 230, 234
Sullivan, R. D., 425, 430, 436
Sundberg, A. C., 537, 542
Svencickaja, I. S., 17
Swete, H., 200, 201
Syme, R., 378, 384, 386, 422, 423, 558

Tadmor, H., 124, 125
Taeubler, E., 274, 275
Talmon, S., 103, 307, 309
Talshir, D., 49, 51
Tannenbaum, R., 534, 536
Tarn, W. W., 147, 148, 164
Tcherikover, V. A., 153, 154, 171, 172, 177–79, 182, 190, 202, 203, 216, 221, 222, 247, 249–53, 255, 257, 259, 262, 263, 274, 278, 280, 283–85, 390, 399, 405, 408, 565, 599
Tedesche, S., 277
Teeple, H. M., 520, 522
Teixidor, J., 158
Telford, W. R., 468
Terian, A., 373, 374
Thackeray, H. St. J., 4, 12
Thomas, J., 508
Thompson, L. A., 581, 584
Throntveit, M. A., 49, 51
Tiede, D. L., 520
Timpe, D., 260
Torrey, C. C., 28, 32, 34, 97
Tov, E., 200, 379, 380
Townsend, J. T., 13
Troeltsch, E., 110
Trump, S., 552
Tsafrir, Y., 245, 356, 357
Tucker, G. M., 29
Tuland, C. G., 126
Tuplin, C., 115
Turner, E. G., 438
Tushingham, A. D., 245, 246
Tzori, N., 566

Urman, D., 2

Vallat, F., 56
VanderKam, J. C., 180, 199, 235, 307–9
Vaux, R. de, 32, 48, 126, 230, 232, 267, 491, 496
Vermes, G., xxvii, 3, 230, 233, 303, 491, 496, 499, 520, 521, 544
Vermeylen, J., 46
Vidal-Naquet, P., 370, 372
Villalba i Varneda, P., 4
Vincent, L. H., 172
Vogel, E. K., 2
Voigtlander, E. N. von, 58

Wacher, J., 369, 370
Wacholder, B. Z., 173, 228, 237, 260, 261
Walbank, F. W., 147, 148
Waldmann, H., 158, 159
Walter, N., 236, 237, 527
Waltke, B. K., 503
Warmington, B. H., 444
Waterman, L., 77, 79
Watson, A., 570, 571
Watson, J. S., 67
Weber, M., 110
Weinberg, J. P., 75, 83, 115, 117, 118
Weippert, H., 2, 67, 68, 72
Weissbach, F. H., 56, 58
Welles, C. B., 3
Wellesley, K., 453
Wellhausen, J., 29, 285
Wells, C. M., 313, 314, 369, 370
Welwei, K. W., 17, 22
Wenning, R., 329
Westermann, C., 47, 48
Whitley, C. F., 175
Whittaker, C. R., 16–18, 22
Whybray, R. N., xxviii, 29, 47, 48, 175, 176
Widengren, G., 28, 29, 81, 91, 92, 99, 114
Wiesehöfer, J., 59
Wikgren, A., 12
Wild, R. A., 468
Wilkinson, J., 2, 356, 381
Will, E., 17, 18, 23, 202, 313
Willi, T., 49
Williams, R. S., 320
Williamson, H.G.M., xxviii, 28, 30–32, 35–41, 49–51, 53, 61–63, 79, 82, 89–92, 137, 245, 246
Wilson, B. R., 463, 465
Winston, D., 100
Winter, P., 392
Wirgin, W., 260, 261, 264, 430
Wiseman, D. J., 265
Wiseman, T. P., 384, 385
Wolff, H., 42, 44–46, 78
Worsley, P., 163, 164
Woude, A. D. van der, 42, 45, 221
Wright, J. S., 51, 52
Wright, T., 375, 376

Yadin, Y., 2, 230–32, 319, 356, 379–81, 460, 565, 576
Yamauchi, E. M., 27, 28, 508, 510, 511, 514–16
Yarbro Collins, A., 199
Yardeni, A., 54, 55

Zahavy, T., 592
Zangemeister, C., 560
Zeitlin, S., 277, 401, 404
Zias, J., 319
Zimmermann, F., 177